C000077008

HAITIAN HIS'

Despite Haiti's proximity to the United States, and its considerable import-ance to our own history, Haiti barely registered in the historic conscious-ness of most Americans until recently. Those who struggled to understand Haiti's suffering in the earthquake of 2010 often spoke of it as the poorest country in the Western hemisphere, but could not explain how it came to be so.

In recent years, the amount of scholarship about the island has increased dramatically. Whereas once this scholarship was focused on Haiti's polit-ical or military leaders, now the historiography of Haiti features lively debates and different schools of thought. Even as this body of knowledge has developed, it has been hard for students to grasp its various strands. *Haitian History* presents the best of the recent studies on Haitian history, by both Haitian and foreign scholars, moving from colonial Saint Domingue to the aftermath of the 2010 earthquake. It will be the go-to one-volume introduction to the field of Haitian history, helping to explain how the promise of the Haitian Revolution dissipated, and presenting the major debates and questions in the field today.

Alyssa Goldstein Sepinwall is Professor of History at California State University-San Marcos.

Rewriting Histories focuses on historical themes where standard conclusions are facing a major challenge. Each book presents papers (edited and annotated when necessary) at the forefront of current research and interpretation, offering students an accessible way to engage with contemporary debates.

Series editor **Jack R. Censer** is Professor of History at George Mason University.

REWRITING HISTORIES

Edited by Jack R. Censer

HAITIAN HISTORY

New Perspectives

Edited by
Alyssa Goldstein Sepinwall

Routledge
Taylor & Francis Group

NEW YORK AND LONDON

First published 2013
by Routledge
711 Third Avenue, New York, NY 10017

Simultaneously published in the UK
by Routledge
2 Park Square, Milton Park, Abingdon, Oxon OX14 4RN

Routledge is an imprint of the Taylor & Francis Group, an informa business

© 2013 Taylor & Francis

The right of the editor to be identified as the author of the editorial material, and of the authors for their individual chapters, has been asserted in accordance with sections 77 and 78 of the Copyright, Designs and Patents Act 1988.

Trademark notice: Product or corporate names may be trademarks or registered trademarks, and are used only for identification and explanation without intent to infringe.

Library of Congress Cataloging in Publication Data
Sepinwall, Alyssa Goldstein, 1970–
Haitian history : new perspectives / by Alyssa Goldstein Sepinwall.
p. cm. – (Rewriting histories)
Includes index.
1. Haiti–History.   I. Title.
F1921.S45 2012
972.94–dc23
2012023195

ISBN: 978-0-415-80867-5 (hbk)
ISBN: 978-0-415-80868-2 (pbk)

Typeset in Palatino
by RefineCatch Limited, Bungay, Suffolk, UK

SFI Certified Sourcing
www.sfiprogram.org
SFI-00453

Printed and bound in the United States of America
by Edwards Brothers, Inc.

CONTENTS

ACKNOWLEDGMENTS

The collection grows out of a graduate seminar on the historiography of Haiti, which I first taught at California State University, San Marcos in Fall 2010. I am very grateful to my students (Herbert Alarcon, Sarah Wolk, Jake Lewis, Lezlie Lee-French, Alex Duran and Timothy Engstrom) for the insights and energy that they brought to our discussions. I am also immensely grateful to Jack Censer for sharing my enthusiasm about the value of such a reader, and to Kimberly Guinta, Rebecca Novack and Sioned Jones for their expert help with preparing it.

I would also like to thank all of those who helped me transform this collection from idea into print. Jack Censer and the four anonymous reviewers of my initial book proposal offered excellent suggestions, as did numerous colleagues at Cal State San Marcos (especially Cynthia Chavez Metoyer, Peter Arnade, Jill Watts, Jeff Charles, Sheryl Lutjens, Janet McDaniel, Katherine Hijar and Marion Geiger). At Arizona State University, where I gave an early talk about this project, Andrew Barnes, Joni Adamson, Alex Bontemps, Kent Wright and Rachel Fuchs offered invaluable suggestions and encouragement. I also owe heartfelt thanks to the authors who granted me permission to reproduce their work here and who supported the idea of such a collection.

Once I developed the manuscript, I had a dream team of readers, inside and outside of Haitian history, who offered sage guidance about how to make my historiographical survey as thorough and accessible as possible. Though all errors remain my own, I am deeply indebted to Matthew Smith, Gusti-Klara Gaillard-Pourchet, Laurent Dubois, Claudy Delné, Dominique Rogers, Sue Peabody, Madison Smartt Bell, Matthew Casey, Harriet Sepinwall, Joellyn Zollman, Ashli White, Grace Sanders, Sarah Wolk, Allan Arkush and Erica Peters for their careful reading of drafts and their extremely helpful counsel. I owe a special debt to the late Yves Benot, who first urged me to study the impact of the Haitian Revolution in the United States, and to many other colleagues, especially Marcel Dorigny, David Geggus, John Garrigus, Jeremy Popkin, Elizabeth Colwill, Carolyn Fick, Malick Ghachem, Stewart King and André Elizée, for years of collegial discussions on the historiography of colonial Saint-Domingue and the

Haitian Revolution. Gary Kates offered expert practical tips on developing such a reader; Jennifer Heuer helped me think through numerous aspects of the book's conception and development. Sarah Sussman, Patricia Goldsworthy and Richard Keller offered some precious bibliographical suggestions.

At a time when Haiti's own libraries are in disarray, I am acutely conscious of how fortunate I have been to gain access to so many works on Haitian history. My research would have been impossible without the efforts of countless North American acquisitions librarians who purchase important Haitian and French books and without the interlibrary loan networks that librarians have so carefully constructed to share those books. Teresa Roudenbush, Debbie Blair and the entire Circulation staff at CSUSM (and in the San Diego Circuit) fed my near-endless appetite for Haiti-related books; they drew on the generosity of institutions across North America and the Caribbean. This book also benefited from faculty development funding at CSUSM, including a University Professional Development Grant and a CHABSS Faculty Development Grant.

My deepest gratitude goes to my family, particularly my kind and supportive husband Steven Goldstein, my loving and beautiful mother Harriet Lipman Sepinwall, and my sweet and funny son Jacob Goldstein. Their patience and love – as well as that of my extended family and dear friends – did much to sustain me throughout my work on this study.

PREFACE

Rewriting history, or revisionism, has always followed closely in the wake of history writing. In their efforts to re-evaluate the past, professional as well as amateur scholars have followed many approaches, most commonly as empiricists, uncovering new information to challenge earlier accounts. Historians have also revised previous versions by adopting new perspectives, usually fortified by new research, which overturn received views.

Even though rewriting is constantly taking place, historians' attitudes towards using new interpretations have been anything but settled. For most, the validity of revisionism lies in providing a stronger, more convincing account that better captures the objective truth of the matter. Although such historians might agree that we never finally arrive at the "truth," they believe it exists and over time may be better approximated. At the other extreme stand scholars who believe that each generation or even each cultural group or subgroup necessarily regards the past differently, each creating for itself a more usable history. Although these latter scholars do not reject the possibility of demonstrating empirically that some contentions are better than others, they focus upon generating new views based upon different life experiences. Different truths exist for different groups. Surely such an understanding, by emphasizing subjectivity, further encourages rewriting history. Between these two groups are those historians who wish to borrow from both sides. This third group, while accepting that every congeries of individuals sees matters differently, still wishes somewhat contradictorily to fashion a broader history that incorporates both of these particular visions. Revisionists who stress empiricism fall into the first of the three camps, while others spread out across the board.

Today the rewriting of history seems to have accelerated to a blinding speed as a consequence of the evolution of revisionism. A variety of approaches has emerged. A major factor in this process has been the enormous increase in the number of researchers. This explosion has reinforced and enabled the retesting of many assertions. Significant ideological shifts have also played a major part in the growth of revisionism. First, the crisis of Marxism, culminating in the events in Eastern Europe in 1989, has given rise to doubts about explicitly Marxist accounts. Such doubts have spilled over into the entire field of social history, which has been a dominant subfield of the discipline for several decades. Focusing on society and its class divisions implied that these are the most important elements in historical analysis. Because Marxism was built on the same claim, the whole basis of social history has been questioned, despite the very many studies that had little to do with Marxism directly. Disillusionment with social history simultaneously opened the door to cultural and linguistic approaches largely developed in anthropology and literature. Multiculturalism and feminism further generated revisionism. By claiming that scholars had, wittingly or not, operated from a white European/American male point of view, newer researchers argued that other approaches had been neglected or misunderstood. Not surprisingly, these last historians are the most likely to envision each subgroup rewriting its own usable history, while other scholars incline towards revisionism as part of the search for some stable truth.

Rewriting Histories will make these new approaches available to the student population. Often new scholarly debates take place in the scattered issues of journals, which are sometimes difficult to find. Furthermore, in these first interactions, historians tend to address one another, leaving out the evidence that would make their arguments more accessible to the uninitiated. This series of books will collect in one place a strong group of the major articles in selected fields, adding notes and introductions conducive to improved understanding. Editors will select articles containing substantial historical data, so that students – at least those who approach the subject as an objective phenomenon – can advance not only their comprehension of debated points but also their grasp of substantive aspects of the subject.

Although Haiti has been in and out of the news for centuries, interest among historians has been strangely absent. Only recently with a heightened interest in subaltern groups and global connections, have courses and work on Haiti begun to proliferate. In fact, for the revolutionary period, scholars have embraced the subject, and syntheses as well as articles and books have been pouring out. But for subsequent eras, scholarly attention has still been limited.

Alyssa Sepinwall's collection seeks to remedy these lacuna, including a selection of first rate pieces on the eighteenth century. This book follows with enough articles to provide an interesting and nuanced picture of life and developments in Haiti. The studies focus on external interventions as well as domestic problems, all of which contributed to Haiti's turbulent past. Beyond painting a picture of the last three centuries, the book provides information and insights into the combination of greed, authoritarian governments, and self-seeking foreign powers that influenced Haiti's history. To be sure, some of these forces issued from good intentions, but the results were often deleterious.

In sum, Alyssa Sepinwall's work has created an up-to-date collection of highly readable and accessible articles that flesh out our understanding and reveal the forces at play in the making of the island country.

INTRODUCTION

Alyssa Goldstein Sepinwall

After the earthquake that ravaged Port-au-Prince in January 2010, foreign media poured into Haiti to record the devastation. Before 2010, Haiti had often been ignored by foreigners (including Americans, despite Haiti's proximity to Florida and the two countries' long and entangled history of relations). Once the earthquake struck, however, Haiti became the subject of 24-hour worldwide news coverage, including a telethon featuring Hollywood stars and pop music icons. Nevertheless, the nonstop attention to Haiti only underscored foreigners' scant knowledge of the country's past. Those who struggled to understand Haiti's suffering often referred to it as the poorest country in the Western hemisphere, but could not explain how it came to be so.

Certainly, most commentators did not echo televangelist Pat Robertson's declaration that Haiti's plight stemmed from having made a pact with the devil in 1791 (the beginning of a slave revolt that would ultimately lead to Haitian independence). But other comments (for example, that Haiti is poor because its leaders have always been corrupt) were almost as simplistic. In a paradigmatic example of innocents abroad, the American actress Demi Moore visited Haiti in April 2010, and declared to CNN anchor Anderson Cooper that "Americans have to carry out . . . [Abraham] Lincoln's promise, and . . . bring about freedom [in Haiti]." Moore's comments ignored the fact that Haitian slaves had won their freedom almost seventy years before Lincoln's Emancipation Proclamation (the first African slaves in the Western hemisphere to do so), and that slave-owners in the United States and other countries had isolated Haiti for decades after its independence as punishment. Denunciations by Moore, Cooper and others of the *restavek* system in Haiti (in which poor children are entrusted to wealthier families by parents desperate to give them a better life, but often end up reduced to servile conditions) lacked historical context; the origins of the poverty that fed the *restavek* system remained unaddressed.[1] Even these misguided analyses of Haiti soon disappeared from view, however. Within months after the earthquake, Haiti was forgotten again, displaced from the headlines by newer tragedies.

1

Why has there been so little knowledge about the history of Haiti, a country that the United States occupied from 1915 to 1934 and in which it intervened militarily in 1994 and 2004? For one thing, American and other foreign scholars are only beginning to acknowledge the importance of Haitian history. The birth of Haiti, the Haitian Revolution of 1791–1804, was part of the same process of Atlantic Revolutions (1770s–1820s) as its more famous American, French and Latin American counterparts. Yet for too long, most foreign scholars wrote the Haitian Revolution out of history. Aside from a few works that attracted attention outside Haitian history (such as C. L. R. James' 1938 *The Black Jacobins: Toussaint Louverture and the San Domingo Revolution* and Aimé Césaire's 1960 *Toussaint Louverture, la Révolution Française et le problème colonial*), the Haitian Revolution went unmentioned in historical surveys. Even works specifically on the Atlantic Revolutions (such as R. R. Palmer's *Age of the Democratic Revolution: A Political History of Europe and America, 1760–1800* [1959] and Jacques Godechot's *France and the Atlantic Revolution of the Eighteenth Century, 1770–1799* [1965]) said little about Haiti.

In the last fifteen years, this situation has changed, as scholars have paid increasing attention to the Haitian Revolution and to its global historical significance.[2] In a 2000 essay in the *American Historical Review*, Franklin Knight called the Haitian Revolution "the most thorough case study of revolutionary change anywhere in the history of the modern world"; he added that, unlike other revolutions of its time, it had rendered all citizens "legally equal, regardless of color, race or condition." Similarly, in his 2004 book *Avengers of the New World: The Story of the Haitian Revolution*, Laurent Dubois argued that the Haitian Revolution was more radically egalitarian than either the American or French Revolution:

> By creating a society in which all people, of all colors, were granted freedom and citizenship, the Haitian Revolution forever trans- formed the world. It was a central part of the destruction of slavery in the Americas, and therefore a crucial moment in the history of democracy, one that laid the foundation for the contin- uing struggles for human rights everywhere. In this sense we are all descendants of the Haitian Revolution, and responsible to these ancestors.[3]

Whereas historians of the French Revolution once treated the Haitian Revolution as a footnote, if at all, university courses on the French Revolution in Anglophone countries now regularly discuss French colo- nial Saint-Domingue (the prerevolutionary name for Haiti) and the uprising of its slaves.[4] This growing attention to the Haitian Revolution in the United States has not been confined to academic history, but has filtered down to the K-12 school system, as World and Western Civilization textbooks increasingly mention the Revolution and the man who became its leader, General Toussaint Louverture.

Nevertheless, even to many who now acknowledge the importance of the Haitian Revolution, the rest of Haitian history – what happened between 1804 and the Duvalier regime (1957–1986), or even until the 2010 earthquake – remains a mystery. Haiti completely disappears in most world history textbooks after its revolution, except for occasional references to the 1915–1934 U.S. occupation of the island in chapters on imperialism. Moreover, even when the Revolution is invoked in these texts, it is often discussed in a superficial or outdated way, presented as a kind of imitation of the French Revolution without discussion of ongoing slave resistance or of the ideas that slaves brought with them from Africa.

One might surmise that the limited knowledge about Haitian history results from a dearth of scholarship. Haiti has not traditionally received the same attention in North American universities as have countries such as Britain, France or even Cuba. Nevertheless, there is a long tradition of historical writing on Haiti, produced both by Haitian scholars and by foreigners. The last two decades have witnessed an explosion of Anglophone scholarship on Haiti, sparked by the rise of Atlantic history and the new World History, as well as by interest in the histories of race, colonialism and migration. Within Haiti, there has also been a renaissance of historical scholarship, occasioned by the fall of the Duvalier regime and the end of its persecution of intellectuals.

Still, for many outside the field, this work remains a well-kept secret. Whereas many studies provide introductions to scholarly debates on American or other areas of world history, there has not been a convenient entry point for learning about the major questions and debates in Haiti's history. In fact, the surge of new scholarship has itself made it more challenging to understand the field. Studies relating to Haiti are being produced in so many fields (whether in Haitian history, Atlantic history, African-American history, French history, Caribbean history, or allied disciplines such as political science, literary criticism, sociology and anthropology), and published in so many venues, that it is challenging even for specialists to keep abreast of new works.[5] While a few English-language narratives on Haiti's history exist,[6] there are few systematic analyses of Haitian historiography.[7]

This volume attempts to remedy these gaps by introducing readers to a sample of the new scholarship on Haiti; I aim to present an accessible snapshot of the field that can be used by anyone seeking an introduction to the history and historiography of Haiti. Fifteen of the best recent articles on the country's history are gathered here; they range chronologically from French colonial Saint-Domingue to the 2010 earthquake. The topics include not only Haiti's first independence in 1804, but also, following exciting new work by scholars such as Matthew J. Smith, Haiti's lesser-known second independence in 1934 after U.S. forces withdrew.

3

The volume is organized into three sections: Section I (*From Saint-Domingue to Haiti*); Section II (*Independent Haiti in a Hostile World: Haiti in the Nineteenth Century*); and Section III (*From the Occupation to the Earthquake: Haiti in the Twentieth and Twenty-First Centuries*). Each section begins with an introduction that offers historical background, previews each essay, and surveys other important historiography on the period. These introductions also explore new directions in research on each era and suggest other areas meriting further study. Following each section's introduction is a substantial For Further Reading list.

Though all of the works reprinted here originally appeared in English, each section introduction also references important works by Haitian scholars (as well as scholars in France and Latin America). Haitians have a long tradition of chronicling their own past; as Patrick Bellegarde-Smith has noted, until the 1950s, Haiti had a higher per capita rate of historians and other writers than most countries.[8] Thomas Madiou's and Beaubrun Ardouin's detailed histories of Haiti, written in the nineteenth century, are still essential references for scholars today. In general, however, much of the historiography produced by Haitians, written in French and published in small runs in Port-au-Prince, has been difficult for foreign scholars to access. Many important works by Haitian scholars such as Horace Pauléus Sannon, Hénock Trouillot, Ghislain Gouraige, Leslie Manigat, Jean Fouchard, Roger Gaillard, Alain Turnier, Michel Hector, Suzy Castor, Gusti-Klara Gaillard-Pourchet and Vertus Saint-Louis remain untranslated. They are therefore invoked in foreign scholarship far less frequently than North American or French historians of Haiti. Meanwhile, Haitian scholars do not always know about new Anglophone studies, not only because of language issues but also because Haitian libraries do not have the funds to order them. It is my hope that, by integrating both Haitian and foreign contributions to Haitian history, this volume can help bridge this gap and help scholars obtain a more complete understanding of Haiti's past.

Even as this volume focuses on newer scholarship, I also hope to show how historical writing on Haiti has evolved. Research on Haiti's history by nineteenth and early twentieth-century Haitian, American, Caribbean and French historians (such as Madiou, Ardouin, C. L. R. James, James Leyburn, Rayford Logan and Gabriel Debien) remains foundational in many respects. However, whereas histories of Haiti once focused on the island's political, diplomatic or military leaders, the historiography of Haiti has moved in new directions. It now features lively debates and different schools of thought; it draws on multiple methodologies, from social history to postcolonial theory, to construct a broader picture of Haitian history.

One of the guiding principles of this volume is that Haitian history should not be studied in isolation; instead, I approach its history from a world historical perspective. Certainly, no nation is an island in its historical developments – not even an island nation like Haiti. Nevertheless, Haiti has been subject to more than its fair share of foreign interference.

From the time of Columbus' arrival, the inhabitants of Hispaniola (the island that is home today to both Haiti and the Dominican Republic) have faced the consequences of foreign actions. The original Taino inhabitants were virtually wiped out within a few decades of contact with the Spanish; colonialism and the slave trade brought new populations to the island. The Haitian Revolution resulted from these successive waves of migration, and it grew out of processes in Caribbean, French and African history. Rather than being passively acted upon by foreigners, Haitians have also had a profound influence elsewhere. The Haitian Revolution deeply affected slave societies in the United States, Cuba and Latin America; it frightened slaveowners and provided inspiration to slaves and free blacks.

Haiti's history, like all national histories but perhaps to an even greater degree, has thus been a complex interaction of internal and external forces. The essays gathered here treat both kinds of factors; they underscore that Haiti's successes or failures since independence cannot be explained simply by the policies of individual leaders. Whether through embargoes, occupations, indemnities or more subtle forms of international pressure, Haiti has never been left alone to determine her destiny. While this perspective on Haitian history corresponds to the new wave of world history in Anglophone scholarship, it is also a part of the conceptual framework that Haitian historians apply to their own history (see Section II introduction).

The first section of the book covers the late French colonial period and the Haitian Revolution. Though there is comparatively little published on the island's history before European contact or on Spanish colonial rule, the periods of French colonialism and the Haitian Revolution are among the most fertile areas of recent scholarship. Section I presents a sample of four essays from this literature (by Michel-Rolph Trouillot, Carolyn Fick, David Geggus and John Thornton). It also introduces other major works on this period as well as areas of dispute. I discuss how new scholarship on the Revolution builds on James's *The Black Jacobins*, while departing from it in some respects. Some of the questions addressed are: *To what extent has the Haitian Revolution been forgotten, and why? What were conditions like for slaves, and what prompted the Revolution?* I also survey other areas of recent research, such as the status of free men of color in Saint-Domingue and that of enslaved and free women of color. The section also considers debates about the Revolution's historical significance.

Section II looks at Haiti from its independence in 1804 through to the end of the nineteenth century. The section includes a sample of works on this era (by Ashli White, Ada Ferrer, Mimi Sheller, David Nicholls and Leslie Alexander), and moves from the 1790s through the 1860s. Since most English-language studies of the nineteenth century have focused on this period, I also survey the mostly French-language scholarship on the last third of the century. The section considers questions such as: *How did foreigners (both white and black) respond to Haitian independence?* The essays also touch upon issues such as how foreign reactions affected Haitian policy-making and how Haitian peasants responded to their leaders' policies. Other questions include: *What role did ideas about gender play in constructing the Haitian nation-state? How did foreign debt affect Haitian history?* The section also considers larger questions such as: *Why wasn't Haiti able to become the egalitarian society that the Revolution seemed to promise?* and *Can the roots of authoritarianism in modern Haiti be traced to the nation's earliest decades?*

Section III covers one of Haiti's most turbulent periods, the twentieth and early twenty-first centuries. The essays (by Brenda Plummer, Matthew Smith, Patrick Bellegarde-Smith, Robert Fatton Jr., Paul Farmer and Évelyne Trouillot) span from the U.S. occupation of Haiti to the 2010 earthquake. They help answer questions such as: *Why did the United States occupy Haiti, and what was its legacy there? Why didn't Haiti achieve prosperity after its second independence? How did the Duvalier regime rise, and what role did foreign governments play in keeping it in power?* The section also looks at the so-called "interminable democratic transition" in Haiti since 1986, as well as at Jean-Bertrand Aristide's presidency and the two coups that toppled him. In addition, the section considers foreign "development" aid in Haiti and how it has perversely increased poverty when not designed with the interests of Haiti's poor in mind. The section closes with a May 2010 essay by Évelyne Trouillot as a sample of work grappling with the earthquake in its immediate aftermath.

Because space constraints prevent every aspect of Haitian life from being treated here, I also include works on other areas of Haitian history and culture in the For Further Reading lists. These include Haitian art and music, both of which are key repositories of the viewpoints and historical perspectives of ordinary Haitians.[9] While the centrality to Haitian history of the Vodou religion (called voodoo in foreign distortions) is invoked in many excerpts in this volume (see Fick, Geggus, Thornton, Sheller and Bellegarde-Smith), it is also the subject of a sizable literature in its own right.[10] The same is true for the topics of women and gender. Although Mimi Sheller's essay has gender analysis at its core, and brief mentions of women's roles in resistance movements appear in the excerpts by Fick and by Nicholls, readers can find further information on the history of Haitian women referenced in each section introduction.

* * *

For too long Haiti has received what Robert Lawless has termed "a bad press," with its people distorted into caricatures when they are discussed at all. These include seeing Haitians as "savage cannibals," "mud-eaters," transmitters of AIDS, bloodthirsty and unfixable.[11] By highlighting here some of the best new writing on Haitian history, I hope to make available more complex understandings of Haitian history and people and to help stimulate further research. I also aim to highlight the relevance of Haitian history to other historical fields. The historiography of Haiti interrogates issues that are widely applicable in world history: *Are events shaped prima-rily by local or global processes? Whose history is recorded in the archives? How can historians try to uncover the ideas and experiences of non-elites?* Other questions include: *Does the end of colonialism leave a nation free to chart its own course? How do ideas about gender and race influence the course of history? What kinds of agency do non-elites have when they are oppressed?* These are but a few of the many questions raised in recent scholarship on Haiti.

In 1990, Michel-Rolph Trouillot argued in his famous essay "The Odd and the Ordinary: Haiti, the Caribbean and the World" that foreigners have long treated Haiti as an "unexplainable" country, set apart from history's normal workings.[12] The new historiography on Haiti demon-strates that Haiti is not an exception outside history but rather has a history deeply intertwined with other national histories, a history that is an exemplar of many modern historical processes. May the present volume help this rich and complex new scholarship gain a wider audience, at a time when Haiti itself deserves greater understanding.

A Note on Editorial Practice

Almost all of the essays in this volume have been reduced from their orig-inal length, whether minimally or more extensively, excepting only those essays that were already very brief (Geggus, Ferrer, Smith and Évelyne Trouillot). I have nevertheless endeavored to preserve the core framework of each author's argument. A few essays (those of Fick, Geggus, Ferrer and Smith) include corrections from their original versions made in consulta-tion with the author; they range from the rectification of typographical errors to updated tables (1.2 and 1.3) supplied by Geggus for his article. All cuts in the body of the essays are marked with bracketed ellipses; numbering of the notes has been adjusted accordingly. All endnotes are original author's notes, unless marked as editor's notes.

NOTES

1 Demi Moore, interview with Anderson Cooper, April 2010, at http://ac360. blogs.cnn.com/2010/04/15/video-demi-moores-quest-to-end-child-slavery/ (accessed December 18, 2011); see also reference in P. Bellegarde-Smith, "A Man-Made Disaster: The Haitian Earthquake of January 12, 2010 – A Haitian Perspective," *Journal of Black Studies* 42 (2011), p. 269. See also Bellegarde-Smith's discussion of how reporters hounded him to discuss Haitian "blood rituals" and "animal sacrifice" and the website for Moore's foundation (http:// demiandashton.org/action/demi-travels-haiti-address-child-slavery), which calls on "U.S. political leaders to make Haitian redevelopment funds conditional on the end of this terrible [*restavek*] system" without any recogni-tion that ill-conceived development funds have often excerbated Haitian poverty (see Section III) and fostered this system's growth.
2 For a fuller analysis of this turn toward Haiti, which has been greater in the U.S. than in France, see Sepinwall (2009).

3 Knight (2000), pp. 103–105 and Dubois (2004), p. 7.
4 The same is not yet true in France; see Sepinwall (2006).
5 In addition to journals dedicated to Haitian history (*Journal of Haitian Studies*, *Revue de la société haïtienne d'histoire et de géographie*, and *Conjunction: revue franco-haïtienne*), articles on Haitian history have appeared in myriad other journals, from *Slavery and Abolition* to *The History of the Family*.
6 The best Anglophone surveys of Haitian history are Dubois (2012) and Bellegarde-Smith (2004). See also Dash (2001), pp. 1–28 and Arthur and Dash (1999), which offers an excellent series of short excerpts on Haitian history but has not been updated since publication. Leyburn (1941) is outdated in many respects but remains a classic; Coupeau (2008) has a helpful bibliography but includes numerous errors and lacks footnotes; Heinl and Heinl (1978) and Girard (2005) offer much useful information, but see Dash (2008) on their limits. Monographs with a narrower focus that span multiple periods of Haitian history include M.-R. Trouillot (1989), Dupuy (1989), Lundahl (1992), Laguerre (1993) and Nicholls (1996).
7 For analyses of particular periods, see the survey of Haitian Revolution historiography in Geggus (2002), pp. 33–42 and the bibliographic essays by Geggus, Smith and Dubois in De Barros, Diptee and Trotman (2006). M.-R. Trouillot (1997) is a fascinating history of history-writing and history-teaching within Haiti since colonial times, but does not cover scholarship by foreigners. In French, Pressoir, E. Trouillot and H. Trouillot (1953) survey writings on Haiti from 1492 to 1937, while Laurent (1996) offers biographical sketches of historians in late twentieth-century Haiti. See also Nicholls (1974). Older but still useful bibliographies include those by D. Nicholls and F. Moya Pons in Bethell (1995); Laguerre (1982); Hector (1993) and Schutt-Ainé (1994), pp. 257–281. More recent works are included in Bellegarde-Smith (2004), pp. 281–297; see also the list of classic works in the *Journal of Haitian Studies* 10, no. 1 (2004), pp. 188–192.
8 See Bellegarde-Smith (2004), p. 8, citing Edmund Wilson. Though Haitian historians typically write in French, some recent works have been published in Kreyòl for a more general readership. See M.-R. Trouillot (1977), Hector (1992) and Casimir (2004).
9 On Haitian art, see Rodman (1988), Brown (1995), Cosentino (1995), Grandjean (2002), Célius (2007) and Butcher (2010); on music, see Averill (1997), McAlister (2002), Largey (2006), Braziel (2008); and the liner notes and music in *Rhythms of Rapture* (1995) and *Angels in the Mirror* (1997).
10 For English-language treatments of Vodou, see Métraux (1972); Laguerre (1989); Desmangles (1992); Hurbon (1993, 2001, 2008); Dayan (1995); Brown (2001); McAlister (2002); Bellegarde-Smith (2004), pp. 21–36; Bellegarde-Smith and Michel (2006); Largey (2006); Michel and Bellegarde-Smith (2006); Ramsey (2011), as well as the articles by Mintz and M.-R. Trouillot and by Hurbon in Cosentino (1995); and the liner notes in *Rhythms of Rapture* (1995) and *Angels in the Mirror* (1997). See also the brief survey of scholarship on Vodou in colonial Saint-Domingue by Geggus in De Barros, Diptee and Trotman (2006), pp. 6–7; the excerpts on Vodou in Arthur and Dash (1999), pp. 255–288 and Beaubrun (2010), including an introduction by Madison Smartt Bell.
11 Lawless (1992) and also Potter (2009).
12 M.-R. Trouillot (1990).

FOR FURTHER READING

Angels in the Mirror: Vodou Music of Haiti. New York: Ellipsis Arts, 1997. Produced by J. Charno, H. Nicholas, D. Yih and E. McAlister. With helpful guide introducing Vodou music, edited by E. McAlister and written by E. McAlister and D. Yih. Music by Premye Nimewo, Rara La Bel Fraicheur de l'Anglade and others. Compact disc.

Anglade, Georges. *Atlas critique d'Haïti*. Montreal: Groupe d'études et de recherches critiques d'espace/UQAM, 1982.

Ardouin, Beaubrun. *Etudes sur l'histoire d'Haïti suivies de la vie du général J.-M. Borgella*. Paris, 1853; reprint, Port-au-Prince: F. Dalencour, 1958.

Arthur, Charles. *Haiti: A Guide to the People, Politics and Culture*. New York: Interlink Books, 2002.

Arthur, Charles, and J. Michael Dash, eds. *Libète: A Haiti Anthology*. Princeton: Markus Wiener Publishers, 1999.

Averill, Gage. *A Day for the Hunter, a Day for the Prey: Popular Music and Power in Haiti*. Chicago: University of Chicago Press, 1997.

Beaubrun, Mimerose P. *Nan dòmi, le récit d'une initiation vodou*. Introduction by Madison Smartt Bell. La Roque d'Anthéron: Vents d'ailleurs, 2010.

Bellegarde-Smith, Patrick. *Haiti: The Breached Citadel*. 2nd ed. Toronto: Canadian Scholars' Press, 2004.

Bellegarde-Smith, Patrick, and Claudine Michel, eds. *Haitian Vodou: Spirit, Myth, and Reality*. Bloomington: Indiana University Press, 2006.

Bethell, Leslie. *The Cambridge History of Latin America: Vol. XI, Bibliographic Essays*. Cambridge: Cambridge University Press, 1995 [includes essays by Frank Moya Pons, "The Independence of Haiti and the Dominican Republic," 234–238, and "Haiti and the Dominican Republic [c. 1820–1870]," 270–72; and by David Nicholls, "Haiti [c. 1870–1930]," 426–471, and "Haiti [1930–c. 1990]," 741–44].

Braziel, Jana Evans. *Artists, Performers, and Black Masculinity in the Haitian Diaspora*. Bloomington: Indiana University Press, 2008.

Brown, Karen McCarthy, ed. *Tracing the Spirit: Ethnographic Essays on Haitian Art, from the Collection of the Davenport Museum of Art*. Seattle: University of Washington Press, 1995.

Brown, Karen McCarthy. *Mama Lola: A Vodou Priestess in Brooklyn*. 2nd ed. Berkeley: University of California Press, 2001.

Butcher, Pablo. *Urban Vodou: Politics and Popular Street Art in Haiti*. Introduction by Carl-Hermann Middelanis. Oxford: Signal Books, 2010.

Casimir, Jean. *Pa Bliye 1804, Souviens-toi de 1804*. N.p.: Jean Casimir, 2004.

Célius, Carlo A. *Langage plastique et énonciation identitaire: l'invention de l'art haïtien*. Québec: Presses de l'Université Laval, 2007 [includes an extensive bibliography on Haitian art].

Corbett, Bob. Haitian History Website. http://www.webster.edu/~corbetre/haiti/history/history.htm [includes primary sources and commentary from all periods of Haitian history].

Cosentino, Donald, ed. *Sacred Arts of Haitian Vodou*. Los Angeles: UCLA Fowler Museum of Cultural History, 1995 [esp. S. Mintz and M.-R. Trouillot, "Social History of Haitian Vodou," 123–147, and L. Hurbon, "American Fantasy and Haitian Vodou," 181–197].

Coupeau, Steeve. *The History of Haiti*. Westport, CT: Greenwood Press, 2008.

Dash, J. Michael. *Culture and Customs of Haiti*. Westport, CT: Greenwood Press, 2001.

Dash, J. Michael. "The (Un)kindness of Strangers: Writing Haiti in the 21st Century." *Caribbean Studies* 36, no. 2 (2008): 171–178.

Dayan, Joan. *Haiti, History, and the Gods*. Berkeley: University of California Press, 1995.

De Barros, Juanita, Audra Diptee, and David Vincent Trotman, eds. *Beyond Fragmentation: Perspectives on Caribbean History*. Princeton: Markus Wiener Publishers, 2006 [includes D. Geggus, "Slavery and Emancipation in the French Caribbean," 3–34; M. J. Smith, "Two-Hundred-Year-Old Mountains: Issues and Themes in the Historiography of the Modern Francophone Caribbean," 113–140; and L. Dubois, "History's Quarrel: The Future of the Past in the French Caribbean," 213–230].

Desmangles, Leslie Gérald. *The Faces of the Gods: Vodou and Roman Catholicism in Haiti*. Chapel Hill: The University of North Carolina Press, 1992.

Dubois, Laurent. *Avengers of the New World: The Story of the Haitian Revolution*. Cambridge, MA: Belknap Press of Harvard University Press, 2004.

Dubois, Laurent. *Haiti: The Aftershocks of History*. New York: Metropolitan Books, 2012.

Dupuy, Alex. *Haiti in the World Economy: Class, Race, and Underdevelopment Since 1700*. Boulder: Westview Press, 1989.

Geggus, David. *Haitian Revolutionary Studies*. Bloomington: Indiana University Press, 2002.

Girard, Philippe R. *Paradise Lost: Haiti's Tumultuous Journey from Pearl of the Caribbean to Third World Hot Spot*. New York: Palgrave Macmillan, 2005 [revised paperback edition published 2010].

Grandjean, Michèle, and Association pour la promotion des arts du monde. *Artistes haïtiens = Haitian Artists* [bilingual edition]. Translation by Michèle Paris and Les Cook. Nîmes: APAM, 2002.

Hector, Michel. "L'historiographie haïtienne après 1946 sur la Révolution de Saint-Domingue." In *Révolutions aux colonies* [reprint of *Annales historiques de la Révolution française*, nos. 293–4], 209–217. Paris: Société des Etudes Robespierristes, 1993.

Hector, Michel. *Sou travayè agrikòl yo nan peyi a: yon ti rale sou istwa ak sou kèk pwoblèm òganizasyon-yo*. N.p.: Kiskeya Pres, 1992.

Heinl, Robert Debs and Nancy Gordon Heinl. *Written in Blood: The Story of the Haitian People, 1492–1971*. Boston: Houghton Mifflin, 1978.

Hurbon, Laënnec. "Current Evolution of Relations Between Religion and Politics in Haiti." In *Nation Dance: Religion, Identity, and Cultural Difference in the Caribbean*, edited by Patrick Taylor, 118–125. Bloomington: Indiana University Press, 2001.

Hurbon, Laënnec. "Globalization and the Evolution of Haitian Vodou." In *Òrìsà Devotion as World Religion: The Globalization of Yorùbá Religious Culture*, edited by Jacob K. Olupona and Terry Rey, 263–277. Madison: University of Wisconsin Press, 2008.

Hurbon, Laënnec. *Voodoo: Search for the Spirit*. Translated by Lory Frankel. New York: H.N. Abrams, 1993 [illustrated introduction to Vodou].

Knight, Franklin. "The Haitian Revolution." *American Historical Review* 105, no. 1 (2000): 103–115.

Laguerre, Michel S. *The Complete Haitiana: A Bibliographic Guide to the Scholarly Literature, 1900–1980*. 2 vols. Millwood, NY: Kraus International Publications, 1982.

Laguerre, Michel S. *Voodoo and Politics in Haiti*. New York: St. Martin's Press, 1989.

Laguerre, Michel S. *The Military and Society in Haiti*. Knoxville: University of Tennessee Press, 1993.

Largey, Michael D. *Vodou Nation: Haitian Art Music and Cultural Nationalism*. Chicago: University of Chicago Press, 2006.

Laurent, Gérard M. *Les historiens haïtiens de la fin du XXème siècle: réflexions historiques*. Port-au-Prince: Imprimeur II, 1996.

Lawless, Robert. *Haiti's Bad Press*. Rochester, VT: Schenkman Books, 1992.

Léger, J. N. *Haiti, Her History and Her Detractors*. New York: Neale Pub., 1907.

Leyburn, James Graham. *The Haitian People*. New Haven: Yale University Press, 1941.

Lundahl, Mats. *Politics or Markets? Essays on Haitian Underdevelopment*. New York: Routledge, 1992.

Madiou, Thomas. *Histoire d'Haïti*. Port-au-Prince, 1848; reprint, Port-au-Prince: Impr. E. Chenet, 1922–3.

McAlister, Elizabeth A. *Rara! Vodou, Power, and Performance in Haiti and its Diaspora*. Berkeley: University of California Press, 2002.

Métraux, Alfred. *Voodoo in Haiti*. Translated by Hugo Charteris, introduction by Sidney W. Mintz. New York: Schocken Books, 1972.

Michel, Claudine, and Patrick Bellegarde-Smith, eds. *Vodou in Haitian Life and Culture: Invisible Powers*. New York: Palgrave Macmillan, 2006.

Nicholls, David. *From Dessalines to Duvalier: Race, Colour and National Independence in Haiti*. 2nd edition. New Brunswick, NJ: Rutgers University Press, 1996.

Nicholls, David. "A Work of Combat: Mulatto Historians and the Haitian Past, 1847–1867." *Journal of Interamerican Studies and World Affairs* 16, no. 1 (1974): 15–38.

Paquin, Lyonel. *The Haitians: Class and Color Politics*. Brooklyn: Multi-Type, 1983.

Potter, Amy E. "Voodoo, Zombies, and Mermaids: U.S. Newspaper Coverage of Haiti." *Geographical Review* 99, no. 2 (2009): 208–230.

Pressoir, Catts, Ernst Trouillot, and Hénock Trouillot. *Historiographie d'Haïti*. Mexico: Instituto Panamericano de Geografía e Historia, 1953.

Ramsey, Kate. *The Spirits and the Law: Vodou and Power in Haiti*. Chicago: University of Chicago Press, 2011.

Rhythms of Rapture: Sacred Musics of Haitian Vodou. Washington, DC: Smithsonian/Folkways, 1995. Compiled and produced by E. McAlister. With lengthy liner notes introducing Vodou and Vodou music, by E. McAlister, G. Averill, G. Fleurant, D. Yih and others. Music by Boukman Eksperyans, Cité Soleil Rara, and others. Compact disc. Liner notes online at http://media.smithsonianfolkways.org/liner_notes/smithsonian_folkways/SFW40464.pdf.

Schutt-Ainé, Patricia. *Haiti, A Basic Reference Book*. Miami, FL: Librairie Au Service de la Culture, 1994.

Sepinwall, Alyssa Goldstein. "Atlantic Amnesia: French Historians, the Haitian Revolution and the 2004–6 CAPES Exam." In *Proceedings of the Western Society for French History* 34 (2006): 300–314 [available at http://quod.lib.umich.edu/w/wsfh/volumes.html (Long Beach)].

Sepinwall, Alyssa Goldstein. "The Specter of Saint-Domingue: American and French Reactions to the Haitian Revolution." In *The World of the Haitian Revolution*, edited by Norman Fiering and David Geggus, 317–338. Bloomington: Indiana University Press, 2009.

Trouillot, Michel-Rolph. *Ti difé boulé sou Istoua Ayiti*. Brooklyn: Koléksion Lakansièl, 1977.

Trouillot, Michel-Rolph. *Haiti, State Against Nation: The Origins and Legacy of Duvalierism*. New York: Monthly Review Press, 1989.

Trouillot, Michel-Rolph. "The Odd and the Ordinary: Haiti, the Caribbean and the World." *Cimarrón* 2, no. 3 (1990): 3–12.

Trouillot, Michel-Rolph. "Historiography of Haiti." In *General History of the Caribbean*, vol. 6: *Methodology and Historiography of the Caribbean*, edited by B. W. Higman, 451–477. London: Unesco Publishing, 1997.

When the Drum is Beating. Directed by Whitney Dow. 88 min. First Run Features/ Two Tone Productions, 2005. DVD [featuring Haiti's Orchestre Septentrional]. Bonus features available at http://www.pbs.org/independentlens/ when-the-drum-is-beting/.

DIGITAL REPOSITORIES WITH MATERIAL ON HAITI

Digital Library of the Caribbean (dLOC). http://www.dloc.com/; search under Haiti.

Haiti Digital Library/Bibliyotèk Dijital Ayisyen/Bibliothèque Digitale sur Haïti. Project of the Duke Haiti Lab, directed by Deborah Jenson and Laurent Dubois. http://sites.duke.edu/haitilab/english/.

Internet Archive, Ebooks and Texts Archive. http://www.archive.org/details/ texts; search under Haiti.

Remember Haiti Project, John Carter Brown Library http://www.brown.edu/ Facilities/John_Carter_Brown_Library/remember_haiti/index.php. Also direct link to JCB Haiti materials at Internet Archive, http://www.archive.org/ details/jcbhaiti.

University of Florida Digital Collections on Saint-Domingue http://ufdc.ufl.edu/ results/?t=saint-domingue [on Saint-Dominque] and http://ufdc.ufl.edu/ results/?t=haiti.

Section I

FROM SAINT-DOMINGUE TO HAITI

Spanish colonization of what is now Haiti began soon after Christopher Columbus' arrival in Hispaniola in 1492. The Spanish imposed forced labor on the indigenous Tainos, gradually exterminating them through both violence and via smallpox microbes they unwittingly carried to the New World. The Spanish continued to occupy Hispaniola for the next two centuries, but by the early seventeenth century had shifted their attentions to establishing silver-mining colonies in Central and South America. By 1629, French and English pirates had settled clandestinely in north-western Hispaniola; by the end of the seventeenth century, England and Spain began to recognize a French presence in Western Saint-Domingue, which was ratified formally by the Treaty of Aranjuez in 1777. This treaty established a split between a French colony called Saint-Domingue on the western third of the island and Spanish San Domingo to the east.[1]

The French worked to exploit Western Saint-Domingue to a greater extent than the Spanish had. They set up sugar, coffee and indigo planta-tions and imported massive numbers of enslaved Africans to work on them (by one estimate, 800,000 Africans were forcibly brought to the colony from 1680 to 1786; because harsh conditions killed many new arrivals, an ever-increasing supply of new captives was required).[2] In contrast to Haiti's poverty today, Saint-Domingue brought untold riches to French merchants, as it became one of the world's wealthiest colonies. Called the "pearl of the Caribbean," Saint-Domingue was the world's leading exporter of coffee and sugar in the eighteenth century and the major trading partner of the British colonies in North America (the future United States). One estimate places Haiti's worth in 1791 at $300 million, with exports to France that year alone reaching $41 million.[3] While amassing this wealth, the French set in motion the environmental devasta-tion that still plagues Haiti; they deforested enormous tracts of land to grow sugar, loosening the soil and heightening vulnerability to natural disasters.

13

The French colonial period is one of the most studied eras in Haitian historiography; its chroniclers include scholars trained in French history, Haitian historians interested in their country's origins and specialists in Caribbean and Atlantic history. For much of the nineteenth and twentieth centuries, histories of Saint-Domingue focused on the colony's whites. Though whites comprised fewer than 10 percent of the colony's population (40,000 versus approximately 500,000 slaves and 30,000 free people of color), their views predominate in French colonial records and other contemporary sources. Whether by reading these sources creatively or by finding documents produced by people of color, recent scholarship has sought to illuminate the lives of all portions of society in colonial Saint-Domingue. Greater attention is now directed toward the history of slaves and of free people of color (whether born free or emancipated). Consequently the history of whites in Saint-Domingue attracts less attention than in the past. Still, a number of recent studies have deepened our knowledge of colonial white society, on topics such as the colony's cities, its intellectual life and its legal system.[4]

Free people of color in eighteenth-century Saint-Domingue (sometimes called *gens de couleur* or *libres de couleur*) have attracted the interest of a growing number of scholars.[5] Past work had noted the existence of exceptional individuals such as Julien Raimond, a wealthy plantation-owner who became the leading spokesperson for Saint-Domingue's people of color during the French Revolution.[6] Still, the overwhelming emphasis of earlier scholarship on *gens de couleur* had been on institutionalized racism in colonial Saint-Domingue and on the discrimination that people of color faced even if they were free. Recent work (notably by John Garrigus, Stewart King and Dominique Rogers) has challenged the idea of rigid racial boundaries in Saint-Domingue. Garrigus has argued that discriminatory legislation against the *gens de couleur* dates chiefly from the 1760s. Whereas before the 1760s, wealthy *gens de couleur* were "used to being treated as 'whites,' " after this period a wave of discriminatory legislation created a "new color line" in Saint-Domingue.[7]

New scholarship has also looked beyond formal legislation for evidence of everyday practices. Garrigus, King and Rogers have studied not only the wealthy and educated "great men" of color such as Raimond, but also *libres de couleur* of more modest means. They have used a previously neglected source: the archives of the notaries who recorded everyday business transactions and family ties. Each has examined notarial archives from different parts of the colony (the South, for Garrigus; the urban centers of the North and West, for Rogers; and a mix of northern and western parishes for King). Each has arrived at a slightly different conclusion about the condition of free people of color on the eve of the Revolution. Where Garrigus finds their legal status declining after the 1760s, Rogers has concluded that (at least in Cap-Français and Port-au-Prince) free people of color were becoming more integrated in practice. Although

14

Julien Raimond had complained that people of color could never receive justice if they were harmed by whites, Rogers has found in one court that *gens de couleur* won almost 60 percent of civil suits they brought against whites. King has chronicled the growth of a free colored military elite who had fought in the American Revolution (as part of French military support of the American colonists, particularly in the Battle of Savannah in 1779).[8]

Another active area of research on Saint-Domingue concerns women and gender. The classic depiction of women of color in Saint-Domingue comes from a work published in the 1790s by the French colonist Moreau de Saint-Méry. While classifying the different populations on the island, Moreau portrayed mixed-race women as sexually obsessed and female slaves as having a mania for underwear. Moreau's generalizations about women of color have permeated literary and even some historical works on Saint-Domingue. In the last fifteen years, a slew of new studies have reacted against Moreau's stereotypes and sought to offer more nuanced accounts of the lives of women of color. While noting that sexual relations with whites were one of the few means by which women of color could advance their status (if it would lead whites to grant their freedom or that of their children), several recent studies offer a broader picture of the economic activities of free women of color, focusing on women merchants and property-owners.[9] Other work has critically examined colonists' discourse about mixed-race women's sexuality and economic activities; Garrigus and King have considered how ideas about the inordinate sexual and economic power of women of color were used to feminize men of color.[10] Still other scholarship has centered on women slaves and their resistance efforts.[11]

New research also has been done on slaves in Saint-Domingue more generally, even though they are the most challenging portion of colonial society to study since they left the fewest written records. Even when slaves were able to produce letters and other documents, little was preserved long-term. In the 1970s, the French scholar Gabriel Debien did landmark work on the lives of slaves using colonists' plantation records. More recently, Gérard Barthélemy focused on the tensions between the different slave populations in the colony, those born on the island ("creoles") and those born in Africa ("bossales").[12]

Because of the difficulty of finding colonial-era sources from slave perspectives, scholarship on slaves has often worked backwards from the Haitian Revolution, reconstructing colonial life from revolution-era documents. The essays in this section (by Michel-Rolph Trouillot, Carolyn Fick, David Geggus and John Thornton) all focus to some extent both on the revolution led by slaves from 1791 to 1804 and on the eighteenth-century background to the revolution. The Haitian Revolution had many twists and turns, and scholarship on it has grown exponentially in the last two decades. It was actually less a single revolution than three different but simultaneous movements sparked soon after the revolution in France in

1789: one by colonial whites against metropolitan authorities, one by free people of color against colonial whites and another by slaves seeking freedom. The latter movement would ultimately triumph, leading to the abolition of slavery in 1793–1794 and the establishment of Haitian independence in 1804. Although contemporaries referred to the turmoil of this period as the Revolution of Saint-Domingue (or as a colonial branch of the French Revolution), recent scholarship tends to refer to the uprising by slaves as the Haitian Revolution and to treat it as an autonomous revolution, even while acknowledging how events in France influenced the timing of events in the colony.

Detailed chronologies of the Haitian Revolution can be found in several excellent works in French and English.[13] Rather than offering a complete narrative of the Revolution, the essays in this section offer a glimpse into some of the major debates in Haitian revolutionary historiography. These include: *Why was the Revolution ignored by non-Haitian historians for many years?* and *Why did the Revolution happen?*

Before introducing the essays individually, it is useful to note what new scholarship has sought to correct. As David Geggus wrote in 2002, "For sixty years a single work has dominated study of the Haitian Revolution in the English-speaking world": C. L. R. James's 1938 *The Black Jacobins*.[14] New scholarship on the Revolution builds on James' work while also departing from it in some respects. *The Black Jacobins* introduced generations of readers to the Haitian Revolution, and it is still celebrated for having taken the Revolution seriously as an anticolonial movement and for having established its international significance. Yet where James suggested that the Revolution "was almost entirely the work of a single man – Toussaint Louverture," recent work has looked at the Revolution more from below, tracing the efforts of multiple kinds of actors. Moreover, where James suggested that slaves were "sleeping" before 1791 and that it was only "the quarrel between the whites and Mulattoes that woke" them, Jean Fouchard and Carolyn Fick have contended that slave resistance had begun long before 1791. Finally, where James described the rebel masses as "lacking civic discipline," "running wild" and being without culture, recent work has offered a more complex view of Saint-Domingue's slaves, half of whom in 1791 had been born on the African continent and had survived the dehumanizing horrors of the Middle Passage.[15]

Beyond James, scholars have reacted to a more pernicious target: a Western academic tradition that has minimized – or ignored – the significance of the Haitian Revolution, as part of undervaluing the historical contributions of non-Europeans more generally. The first article in this section focuses on this issue, as it asks: *Why was the Haitian Revolution ignored or forgotten for so long outside of Haiti?* This essay, "An Unthinkable History: The Haitian Revolution as a Non-Event," comes from Michel-Rolph Trouillot, an anthropologist who hails from one of Haiti's most distinguished intellectual families. Trouillot's article discusses how the

Haitian Revolution shocked whites across the Atlantic; he argues that they could not conceive of slaves as thinking persons capable of organized revolt. They deemed every act of resistance to be the result of a single individual's pathology rather than a sign of Africans' determination to end slavery. As revolution progressed and such beliefs became harder to maintain, white observers decided that slaves could not be directing the rebellion but must be the puppets of others.

Rather than ending his analysis in 1804, Trouillot argues that these older ways of thinking about Haiti persist, even among scholars. He identifies two tropes in modern historical writing about Haiti by foreigners: "formulas of erasure" and "formulas of banalization." Where the former omits the Haitian Revolution from history books, the second acknowledges the Revolution but dismisses its significance.[16] Trouillot's article has become a classic of historical theory for the larger issues it raises: *Who controls how the past is told? How do the histories of colonized peoples get suppressed by more powerful peoples?*

Carolyn Fick's essay "Slave Resistance" examines the Revolution from a different angle. Like Trouillot, Fick contests the notion that the Revolution was produced by outsiders; she emphasizes the actions and agency of slaves themselves. Where Trouillot's argument concentrates on the history of Euro-American ideas about Haiti, Fick's work is rooted in the tradition of "history from below." Just as in other fields where "great men" approaches long dominated, the history of the Haitian Revolution has often been told (by James and others) as the history of Toussaint Louverture and other military leaders. By contrast, Fick follows in the tradition of her mentor George Rudé, a pioneer in studying the French Revolution from the perspective of ordinary people; she also builds on the work of Jean Fouchard, a Haitian historian who did pioneering research on maroons (runaway slaves) in Saint-Domingue.[17] Fick has aimed to uncover: *What were the actions and motivations of the ordinary Haitian men and women who made the Revolution?*

Fick looks back at eighteenth-century Saint-Domingue to identify the many ways that slaves resisted, even without erupting into open revolt. Although it is always a challenge for historians to discern the motives of people who for the most part did not write, Fick aims to overcome this problem through careful attention to evidence in French archives and in contemporary publications by whites. She explores the multiple ways that slaves resisted their condition, from poisoning masters to *marronage* (running away) to participation in Vodou. Fick suggests that the idea for the Haitian Revolution did not come from the French Revolution and its ideals of liberty. Instead, the latter revolution merely offered an opportune moment for Saint-Domingue's slaves to seize the freedom they had long desired.

David Geggus, who is widely viewed as the dean of Haitian revolutionary studies in English, takes a more skeptical view of the extent of slave resistance in his essay "Saint-Domingue on the Eve of the Haitian Revolution." On the one hand, Geggus disputes Trouillot's position that the Haitian Revolution was unthinkable to whites; he argues that "widespread fears" about an impending revolt indicate that it was all too imaginable.[18] On the other hand, Geggus disagrees with Fick about the amount of resistance by slaves in the colony. Geggus maintains that *marronage* was not a nascent form of revolution and that Vodou often served as an alternative to violent revolt rather than as a clandestine cover for resistance. Overall, Geggus argues that it is unclear that slaves in Saint-Domingue were waiting to erupt in revolution; instead, he suggests, they might not have done so without the changes wrought by the French Revolution.[19]

Trouillot's, Fick's and Geggus' work all seek to answer a crucial question on the Haitian Revolution: *To what extent was it sparked by French revolutionary ideals as opposed to being a continuation of prerevolutionary slave resistance?* John Thornton's article, " 'I am the Subject of the King of Congo': African Political Ideology and the Haitian Revolution," also deals with this question, but from a fresh angle. Thornton's work is one of the most exciting pieces to emerge from the new "world history." Thornton applies his training as an Africanist to understand Saint-Domingue's slaves. In the case of those born in Africa and only recently arrived in the colony, he asks how their ideals and practices had been shaped by their experiences in Africa before being captured and sold. Western scholars have often pointed to Haitian rebels' declarations of royalism as evidence that they were either not revolutionary in the French sense or were political simpletons. Thornton notes that scholars from Eugene Genovese to C. L. R. James saw the slaves' royalist views as backwards compared to the republican ideals being developed in "forward-looking Europe." Against this older view, Thornton argues that "Kongo might be seen as a fount of revolutionary ideas as much as France was," because Kongo also had absolutist and republican conceptions of government. Thornton further contends that other scholars have misinterpreted slave utterances because of a lack of familiarity with the slaves' African background.

Thornton thus adds a new twist to debates about what sparked the Haitian Revolution. Instead of assuming that slaves' political ideals came from the Enlightenment, his work suggests that African influences may have turned Saint-Domingue slaves into Haitian revolutionaries. In other work, Thornton has examined the military experience of Haiti's African-born slaves. Where other scholars have been puzzled by the success of Saint-Domingue's slaves against the French army, Thornton notes that newly arrived slaves often had a great deal of military experience from African wars. "Looking at the rebel slaves of Haiti as African veterans rather than as Haitian plantation workers," he has argued, may solve "the mystery of the success of the largest slave revolt in history."[20]

At stake in arguments such as Thornton's is not only the precise origins of the Haitian Revolution, but also the larger issue of non-Europeans' role as agents of change in world history. *Have Africans and other non-Westerners been capable of formulating complex ideologies and effecting dynamic historical change, as recent postcolonial historians have suggested, or have they been mere imitators of Western ideas?* Thornton's essay typifies how the Haitian Revolution – and the question of what drove slaves to revolt – looms as an important symbol in such debates.

Debates over the Revolution have also concerned its larger significance: *Was Haiti the most radically universalist of all of the Atlantic Revolutions or was it essentially repressive?* Similarly, as the Haitian scholar Michèle Oriol has recently asked, "Was it a victorious slave revolt or an aristocratic conspiracy to ruin Saint-Domingue and spark a counter-revolution in France? Was it the political and military genius of a glorious army of downtrodden soldiers, or the retreat of troops worn down by yellow fever and cut off from their rearguard by an English blockade? Was it the starting point of a free and independent nation or the birth of the earliest form of a deadly neo-colonialism?"[21] Debates over the Revolution's significance have drawn not only historians, but also literary critics, political scientists and philosophers. Much recent scholarship has followed the interpretation of scholars such as Franklin Knight and Laurent Dubois, who have seen the Revolution as a "a crucial moment in the history of democracy" (see Introduction). Nick Nesbitt, for instance, called the Haitian Revolution "the culminating, most progressive event of the Age of the Enlightenment." Reflecting long-held views by Haitian scholars about the Revolution's singularity, Michel Hector has recently argued that "the Haitian Revolution represents the sole liberating movement of the era which created a total rupture with existing economic, political and social structures."[22]

Such views of the Haitian Revolution have not been uncontested, however. As Trouillot indicates, an older tradition viewed the revolutionaries as authoritarian and bloodthirsty rather than as radically universalist. Some newer work continues to reflect this view. Wim Klooster has called the Haitian Revolution the least radical of the Atlantic revolutions, arguing that its leaders "had an aversion to *any* form of democracy" and that "authoritarianism was the rule there." Philippe Girard has contended that the ex-slaves' struggles against white colonists as they fought for independence constituted "genocide," though other scholars such as David Geggus have maintained that it was the French military that "veered toward a strategy of genocide."[23] French scholars have also tended not to view the Haitian Revolution as more radical than the French Revolution. With some exceptions such as Yves Benot, Marcel Dorigny, Bernard Gainot and Anne Jollet, French scholars have tended to see the Haitian Revolution as a branch or imitation of the French Revolution, rather than as an autonomous revolution.[24]

Other debates concerning the Revolution continue. One centers on the 1791 Vodou ceremony in a forest called Bois Caïman, which has long been viewed as the catalyst for the Revolution. Whereas the event is as central to Haiti's national identity as Lexington and Concord are for Americans, Léon-François Hoffmann (a Princeton University specialist in French and Haitian literature) famously argued at an international conference in 1991 that the ceremony never happened, angering many Haitian attendees. More recently, Geggus has concluded that the ceremony "did indeed take place . . . but that much of what has been written about it is unreliable," such as where and when it occurred.[25]

Another ongoing debate concerns who actually abolished slavery in Saint-Domingue: the French revolutionaries in Paris, the commissioners sent by the revolutionaries to the island, or the slaves themselves. Textbooks referencing the French colonies and slavery have long said that the National Convention abolished slavery in a February 1794 decree as an extension of ideals of *liberté* and *egalité*. More recently, scholars such as Fick and Dubois have joined Haitian historians in maintaining that freedom was won by the slave insurrection even before the National Convention ratified it as a fait accompli. Other work has emphasized the actions of Sonthonax and Polverel, the commissioners sent from Paris to Saint-Domingue in 1792 to re-establish order. Amid a series of revolts against French revolutionary authorities (by slaves, free people of color and white counter-revolutionaries), Sonthonax and Polverel proclaimed the freedom in June 1793 of any slave willing to fight for the French republican army. In Fall 1793, in an effort to quell continued fighting, Sonthonax issued a decree freeing all of Saint-Domingue's slaves. Focusing on events in June 1793 in Cap Français, Jeremy Popkin has recently emphasized the contingency of Sonthonax and Polverel's actions as well as of the Convention's ratification of them. He argues that without "disastrous miscalculation" by the outgoing French governor-general Galbaud as he led a group of men against Sonthonax and Polverel, "there would have been no emancipation decree of June 21 and very likely no abolition decree" by the Convention.[26] As with the question of the Revolution's origins, this debate has been so animated because of the larger issues it raises about historical causality.

Gender and the Revolution is another important area of new research. Adding to findings in the 1950s by the Haitian scholar Madeleine Bouchereau, a growing body of new scholarship, by Carolyn Fick, Elizabeth Colwill, Sue Peabody, Laurent Dubois, Judith Kafka, Sabine Manigat and others, has considered how women's experiences in the Revolution paralleled or diverged from men's. This scholarship has shown that women slaves were not emancipated in the same way as men were. The decrees issued in June 1793 by Sonthonax and Polverel only freed men who were willing to enlist in the French revolutionary army. Women did not have this option, and could be freed only if they were chosen in marriage by one of the newly free soldiers. Even when Sonthonax issued his more general emancipation decree, women were not treated equally.

The new labor regimes proposed by Sonthonax and Polverel to compel former slaves to return to plantations compensated women less than men for the same work. Recent scholarship has emphasized that women vigorously protested against this policy. New work has also examined women's active roles in the Revolution. Following Bouchereau, recent scholarship has noted that women served in combat and as spies. Dubois has found that women insurgents were said to have treated white prisoners more harshly than male soldiers, but he adds that "they had their reasons" given the prevalence of rape under colonialism.[27]

While much scholarship has focused on the Revolution's earliest phase (1791–1794), new scholarship has also examined its later years. Recent research has looked past the emancipation of 1793–1794 to the compulsory labor systems of Sonthonax and Polverel, the invasion of Saint-Domingue by the British and Spanish and the rise of Toussaint Louverture as the Revolution's leader. New work has also treated the expedition sent in 1801 by Napoleon (following lobbying by exiled white colonists) to regain control of the colony from Louverture; though Toussaint still proclaimed loyalty to France, Napoleon viewed him as too independent. This expedition, led by Napoleon's brother-in-law General Leclerc, arrived in 1802 to try to capture Toussaint and to reinstate the old colonial order. Although Leclerc's forces successfully kidnapped Louverture and sent him to die in an isolated mountain prison in France, many of Leclerc's men (including the General himself) died of yellow fever. Under the leadership of Louverture's successor Jean-Jacques Dessalines, the island's former slaves fought to the death to maintain their freedom. After a decisive victory in December 1803 expelled the last French troops from the island, Dessalines proclaimed an independent Haiti on January 1, 1804.[28] Despite Louverture's death, he has remained an important symbol of the Revolution – even more so than Dessalines – and the number of studies on him continues to grow.[29] Another flourishing area of scholarship concerns the Revolution's impact abroad, in other parts of the Caribbean as well as in North and South America and in Europe.[30] A final area of research, particularly strong among Haitians who study these years, has focused on the Revolution's effect on Haiti's long-term development.[31]

Even with a mounting number of works on colonial Saint-Domingue and the Revolution, there is still room for innovative new scholarship. For one thing, as Jeremy Popkin has recently argued, echoing Geggus, "historians have only begun to exploit the documents available" on the Revolution.[32] In addition, Anglophone scholars could do more to eliminate the chasm between colonial and revolutionary studies on one hand, and post-independence historiography on the other; many Anglophone specialists in the former periods (especially if they are coming from French or Atlantic history) have limited knowledge of the latter. Finally, as Yvonne Fabella has lamented, despite the increased Anglophone attention to the Haitian Revolution, "one is still left with a nagging discomfort provoked by the knowledge that so few Haitian voices are involved in this international conversation, and that the attention tends not to benefit the Haitian people directly."[33] One of the ironies of scholarship on colonial and revolutionary Saint-Domingue is that foreigners often have greater access to archives than do Haitians, since many sources are conserved in France and the United States. Haitian historians, however, have their own perspectives on their country's history, shaped by experiences over the long term. Even when foreign scholars have better access to archives, greater integration of foreign and Haitian perspectives can only advance the field. One thing is certain: as historians become increasingly convinced of the Haitian Revolution's historical significance, the field will continue to expand. There will therefore be many opportunities for archival discoveries to be combined with new perspectives.

NOTES

1 For more on French colonization of Saint-Domingue before 1700, see Madiou (1848, reprint 1922–1923), Hector and Moïse (1990), Moreau (1992), Adélaïde-Merlande (1994) and Boucher (2008). Although nearly all histories of Saint-Domingue refer to the Treaty of Ryswick (1697) as dividing Hispaniola, Blancpain (2008) has found that the Spanish did not approve this division until 1777.
2 See Fick (1990), p. 26. Other detailed overviews of colonial Saint-Domingue include Stein (1988); Fick (1990), ch.1; Hector and Moïse (1990); Geggus (2002), ch. 1; Dubois and Garrigus (2006), introduction; and Saint-Louis (2008).
3 Heinl and Heinl (1978), p. 32.
4 McClellan (1992), Regourd (2001), Ogle (2003), Garraway (2005), Navarro-Andraud (2007), Popkin (2007), Boucher (2008), Frostin (2008), Donnadieu (2009) and Ghachem (2012). Many of these works build on the classic description of white Saint-Domingue society by Moreau de Saint-Méry (1797–1798; translation 1985).
5 Although whites often referred to people of mixed-race as "mulattoes," members of the latter group in late eighteenth-century Saint-Domingue preferred the label *gens de couleur*, since *mulattoes* was a derogatory term meaning "mule people." Recent scholarship generally avoids using *mulatto*, preferring instead the French terms *gens de couleur* or *libres de couleur*, or the English expressions *people of mixed-race* or *free coloreds*. Even though many people of mixed-race were enslaved, and the "free people of color" included free blacks, scholarship sometimes uses the terms *free people of color* and *people of mixed-race* interchangeably.
6 See for instance Cook (1941), L. Nemours (1951) and Garrigus (2007a).
7 Garrigus (2007a), p. 4; Garrigus (2006), p. 8; King (2001); Rogers (1999, 2003); see also Auguste (1996).
8 Garrigus has also begun blending great man history with social history to prepare social biographies of Julien Raimond and Vincent Ogé (another *libre de couleur* active in the Revolution); see Garrigus (2007a, 2010). On the participation of free men of color from Saint-Domingue in the American Revolution, see also A. Nemours (1952).
9 See Moreau (1797–1798; trans. 1985), Socolow in Gaspar and Hine (1996), Geggus in Gaspar and Hine (1996), Rogers (1999, 2003) and Rogers and King (forth-

coming, 2012). See also Garraway (2005) and Peabody (2005) on how French colonial laws and mentalities treated women of color in Saint-Domingue.

10 Garrigus (1997), King (2001); and also Dayan (1995) and Fabella (2007).

11 Gautier (1985), Fick (1990), Moitt in Gaspar and Hine (1996), Boisvert (2001) Moitt (2001) and also E. Trouillot (2003, 2004).

12 Debien (1974) and Barthélemy (2000); see also L. Manigat (2001–2003), Weaver (2006) and overview of recent work on slaves in Geggus (2002), pp. 33–42. See also the forthcoming work by Deborah Jenson and Laurent Dubois on slaves' ethnic self-conceptions, based upon data mining of ads for runaway slaves in the Marronnage in Saint-Domingue database coordinated by Jean-Pierre Le Glaunec (http://marronnage.info/en/index.html).

13 See esp. James (1963); Benot (1987, 1991); Fick (1990); Forster (1994); Hector (1995); Geggus (2002), chs. 1 and 10; Oriol (2002), Moïse (2003), Dubois (2004a), Dorigny (2004), Saint-Louis (2006), Popkin (2010, 2012) and Geggus (2011). A fictionalized but well-researched account of the Revolution can also be found in Bell (1995–2004).

14 Geggus (2002), p. 33.

15 See James (1963 [orig. published 1938]), pp. ix, 73, 152; cf. Fouchard (1981) and Fick (1990).

16 Trouillot's analysis of the silencing of the Haitian Revolution by scholars updates earlier work by Yves Benot ("Dans le miroir trunqué des historiens" in Benot [1987], pp. 205–217). For a more recent discussion of French minimization of the Haitian Revolution, see Sepinwall (2006) and the works discussed in the Section II Introduction.

17 See Fouchard (1981). For a survey of recent work on *marronage*, see Franklin Midy, "Marrons de la liberté, révoltés de la libération: *Le Marron inconnu* revisité," in Hector and Hurbon (2009), pp. 119–147.

18 For other critiques of Trouillot, see Fischer (2006) and Ferrer in Section II.

19 Geggus is widely acknowledged as the master of the archives on Saint-Domingue and the Revolution; see however Trouillot's critique of Geggus on this point (and his critique of Fick on different grounds) in n47 of his essay (ch. 1 here).

20 Thornton (1991), p. 75.

21 Oriol (2002), p. 9.

22 Knight (2000); Dubois (2004a); Nesbitt (2008), p. 2; Hector, "Réflexion sur les particularités de la Révolution haïtienne," in Casimir, Hector, and Bégot (2006), p. 12; see also Buck-Morss (2009). For an overview of recent work on the Revolution's significance, see Hurbon, "La Révolution haïtienne: une avancée postcoloniale," in Hector and Hurbon (2009), pp. 65–75.

23 Klooster (2009), p. 166; Girard (2005); Geggus (2011), p. 544. For a position akin to Geggus's, see Dubois (2012), pp. 42–43.

24 See Sepinwall (2006).

25 Hoffmann, "Un mythe national: la cérémonie du Bois-Caïman," in Barthélemy and Girault (1993), pp. 434–448, with a summary of the debate at pp. 445–448; and Geggus, "The Bois Caïman Ceremony," in Geggus (2002), pp. 81–92.

26 Popkin (2010), p. 385. On Sonthonax, see Laurent (1965), Stein (1985), and Dorigny (1997); on Polverel, see Jacques Cauna, "Polverel ou la Révolution Tranquille," in Hector (1995), I: pp. 384–399. For a fuller discussion of this debate, see Bongie (2011).

27 Bouchereau (1957), pp. 61–64; Fick (1990); Kafka (1997); Peabody (2005); Colwill (2009, 2010); Colwill in Geggus and Fiering (2009), pp. 125–155; Girard (2009b); Manigat in Hector and Hurbon (2009), pp. 313–319; and Dubois (2010), p. 63.

28 See works on Sonthonax listed in note 26 above, along with Auguste and Auguste (1985), Benot (1991), Fick (2000, 2009), Oriol (2002), Benot and Dorigny

(2003), Section II of Hector and Hurbon (2009), Colwill (2010) and Popkin (2012). Scholarship has long suggested that Napoleon sent the expedition in order to reinstate slavery; for a critique of this position, see Girard (2009a and 2011).

29 In addition to James (1963) and Césaire (1962), see Pluchon (1989); Moïse (2001); S. Manigat, "La résistance populaire au corps expéditionnaire du général Leclerc et au rétablissement de l'esclavage à Saint-Domingue," in Benot and Dorigny (2003), pp. 109–126; Cauna (2004); Bell (2007); Jenson (2011), ch. 1; Desormeaux (2011); Girard (2011) and the forthcoming new edition of Toussaint's letters by Deborah Jenson.

30 See Geggus (1982), Gaspar and Geggus (1997), Dubois (2004b), Geggus and Fiering (2009) and the other works cited in the Section II introduction on this topic.

31 See for example the classic works of Madiou (1848; reprint 1922–1923) and Ardouin (1853; reprint 1958), along with newer works such as L. Manigat (2001–2003) and Hector and Hurbon (2009).

32 Popkin (2010), p. 5; and Geggus, "Underexploited Sources," in Geggus (2002), pp. 43–51.

33 See comment by Smith (2006), p. 127n3, on the omission of post-1804 specialists' perspectives on Haiti from the bicentennial conferences on the Revolution; and Fabella (2011).

FOR FURTHER READING

Accilien, Cécile, Jessica Adams, and Elmide Méléance, eds. *Revolutionary Freedoms: A History of Survival, Strength and Imagination in Haiti*. Coconut Creek, FL: Caribbean Studies Press, 2006.

Adélaïde-Merlande, Jacques. *Histoire Générale des Antilles et des Guyanes: Des Précolombiens à nos Jours*. Paris: Éditions Caribéennes/L'Harmattan, 1994.

Ardouin, Beaubrun. *Etudes sur l'Histoire d'Haïti Suivies de la vie du Général J.-M. Borgella*. Port-au-Prince: F. Dalencour, 1958 [first edition published 1853].

Auguste, Claude B. "André Rigaud, Leader des Anciens Libres." *Revue de la Société Haïtienne d'Histoire de Géographie* 52, no. 187 (1996): 15–39.

Auguste, Claude B. "Les congos dans la Révolution haïtienne." *Revue de la société haïtienne d'histoire de géographie* 46, no. 168 (1990): 11–42.

Auguste, Claude Bonaparte, and Marcel Bonaparte Auguste. *L'expédition Leclerc, 1801–1803*. Port-au-Prince: H. Deschamps, 1985.

Barthélemy, Gérard. *Créoles – bossales: conflit en Haïti*. Petit-Bourg, Guadeloupe: Ibis rouge éditions, 2000.

Barthélemy, Gérard, and Christian A. Girault, eds. *La République haïtienne: état des lieux et perspectives*. Paris: Karthala, 1993.

Bell, Madison Smartt. *All Souls' Rising*. New York: Pantheon Books, 1995 [and its sequels *Master of the Crossroads* (2000) and *The Stone That the Builder Refused* (2004)].

Bell, Madison Smartt. *Toussaint Louverture: A Biography*. New York: Pantheon Books, 2007.

Bellegarde-Smith, Patrick and Robert Fatton Jr., eds. Special bicentennial issue. *Journal of Haitian Studies* 10, no.1 (2004).

Benot, Yves. *La révolution française et la fin des colonies*. Paris: La Découverte, 1987.

Benot, Yves. *La démence coloniale sous Napoléon*. Paris: La Découverte, 1991.

Benot, Yves, and Marcel Dorigny, eds. *Grégoire et la cause des noirs (1789–1831), combats et projets*. Paris: Société française d'histoire d'outre-mer/APECE, 2000.

Benot, Yves, and Marcel Dorigny, eds. *Rétablissement de l'esclavage dans les colonies françaises: Aux origines de Haïti*. Paris: Maisonneuve et Larose, 2003.

Benot, Yves. *Les lumières, l'esclavage, la colonisation*. Edited by Roland Desné and Marcel Dorigny. Paris: La Découverte, 2005 [esp. parts II and III].

Blackburn, Robin. "Haiti, Slavery, and the Age of the Democratic Revolution." *The William and Mary Quarterly* 63, no. 4 (2006): 643–674.

Blancpain, François. *La colonie française de Saint-Domingue: de l'esclavage à l'indépendance*. Paris: Karthala, 2004.

Blancpain, François. *Haïti et la République dominicaine: une question de frontières*. Matoury, Guyane: Ibis Rouge Editions, 2008.

Boisvert, Jayne. "Colonial Hell and Female Resistance in Saint-Domingue." *Journal of Haitian Studies* 7, no. 1 (2001), 61–76.

Bonacci, Giulia, ed. *La révolution haïtienne au-delà de ses frontières*. Paris: Karthala, 2006.

Bongie, Chris. "Jeremy D. Popkin and Haitian Revolutionary Studies." H-LatAm, May 2011. Available at http://www.h-net.org/reviews/showrev.php?id=31431.

Boucher, Philip P. *France and the American Tropics to 1700: Tropics of Discontent?* Baltimore: Johns Hopkins University Press, 2008 [the book's extensive bibliography is posted at http://www.philipboucher.com/references.html].

Bouchereau, Madeleine G. *Haiti et ses femmes: une étude d'évolution culturelle*. Port-au-Prince: Les Presses Libres, 1957.

Boulle, Pierre H. *Race et esclavage dans la France de l'Ancien Régime*. [Paris]: Perrin, 2007.

Buck-Morss, Susan. *Hegel, Haiti and Universal History*. Pittsburgh, PA: University of Pittsburgh Press, 2009.

Casimir, Jean, Michel Hector, and Danielle Bégot, eds. *La révolution et l'indépendance haïtiennes: autour du bicentenaire de 1804, histoire et mémoire [actes du 36e colloque de l'Association des historiens de la Caraïbe, Barbade, mai 2004]*. Gourbeyre: Archives départementales, 2006.

Cauna, Jacques de, ed. *Toussaint Louverture et l'indépendance d'Haïti*. Paris: Karthala, 2004.

Césaire, Aimé. *Toussaint Louverture, la Révolution française et le problème colonial*. Revised ed. Paris: Présence africaine, 1962.

Colwill, Elizabeth. "Gendering the June Days: Race, Masculinity, and Slave Emancipation in Saint Domingue." *Journal of Haitian Studies* 15, no. 1 and 2 (2009): 103–124.

Colwill, Elizabeth. "Freedwomen's Familial Politics: Marriage, War and Rites of Registry in Post-Emancipation Saint-Domingue." In *Gender, War, and Politics: The Wars of Revolution and Liberation – Transatlantic Comparisons, 1775–1820*, edited by Karen Hagemann, Gisela Mettele, and Jane Rendall, 71–92. New York: Palgrave Macmillan, 2010.

Cook, Mercer. "Julien Raimond." *Journal of Negro History* 26, no. 2 (1941): 139–170.

Corvington, Georges. *Port-au-Prince au cours des ans*. 3rd ed. 7 vols. Port-au-Prince: Impr. Henri Deschamps, 1992–1994 [vol I: *La Ville coloniale, 1743–1789*, vol II: *Sous les assauts de la Révolution 1789–1804*].

Dayan, Joan. *Haiti, History, and the Gods*. Berkeley: University of California Press, 1995.

Debbasch, Yvan. *Couleur et liberté. Le jeu de critère ethnique dans un ordre juridique esclavagiste. Vol. 1: L'Affranchi dans les possessions françaises de la Caraïbe, 1635–1833*. Paris: Dalloz, 1967.

Debien, Gabriel. *Les colons de Saint-Domingue et la Révolution: essai sur le club Massiac (août 1789-août 1792)*. Paris: A. Colin, 1953.

Debien, Gabriel. *Les esclaves aux Antilles françaises, XVIIe – XVIIIe siècles*. Basse-Terre: Société d'histoire de la Guadeloupe, 1974.

Desormeaux, Daniel, ed. *Mémoires du général Toussaint Louverture*. Paris: Classiques Garnier, 2011.

Donnadieu, Jean-Louis. *Un grand seigneur et ses esclaves: le comte de Noé entre Antilles et Gascogne, 1728–1816*. Toulouse: Presses universitaires du Mirail, 2009.

Dorigny, Marcel, ed. *Léger-Félicité Sonthonax: La première abolition de l'esclavage. La Révolution française et la Révolution de Saint-Domingue*. Paris: Société française d'histoire d'outre-mer, 1997 [originally published as vol. 84, no. 316, of the *Revue française d'histoire d'outre-mer*].

Dorigny, Marcel, ed. *Esclavage, résistances et abolitions. 123e Congrès des sociétés historiques et scientifiques (Fort-de-France-Schoelcher, 6–10 avril 1998)*. Paris: CTHS, 1999.

Dorigny, Marcel, ed. *The Abolitions of Slavery: From Léger Félcité Sonthonax to Victor Schoelcher, 1793, 1794, 1848*. New York: Berghahn Books/UNESCO Publishing, 2003 [translation of *Les abolitions de l'esclavage de Léger Félcité Sonthonax à Victor Schoelcher 1793–1794–1848*].

Dorigny, Marcel. *Révoltes et révolutions en Europe et aux Amériques (1773–1802). Historiographie – Bibliographie – Enjeux*. Paris: Belin, 2004 [esp. 18–21, 78–86, 134–152].

Dorigny, Marcel, and Bernard Gainot. *La société des amis des noirs 1788–1799: contribution à l'histoire de l'abolition de l'esclavage*. Paris: Éditions UNESCO, 1998.

Dubois, Laurent. *Avengers of the New World: The Story of the Haitian Revolution*. Cambridge, MA: Belknap Press of Harvard University Press, 2004a.

Dubois, Laurent. *A Colony of Citizens: Revolution and Slave Emancipation in the French Caribbean, 1787–1804*. Chapel Hill: Omohundro Institute/University of North Carolina Press, 2004b.

Dubois, Laurent. "Gendered Freedom: *Citoyennes* and War in the Revolutionary French Caribbean." In *Gender, War, and Politics: The Wars of Revolution and Liberation – Transatlantic Comparisons, 1775–1820*, edited by Karen Hagemann, Gisela Mettele, and Jane Rendall, 58–70. New York: Palgrave Macmillan, 2010.

Dubois, Laurent, and John D. Garrigus, eds. *Slave Revolution in the Caribbean, 1789–1804: A Brief History with Documents*. New York: Bedford/St. Martins, 2006.

Duchet, Michèle. *Anthropologie et Histoire au siècle des lumières: Buffon, Voltaire, Rousseau, Helvétius, Diderot*. Paris: François Maspero, 1971.

Égalité for All: Toussaint Louverture and the Haitian Revolution. Directed by Nolan Walker. 60 min. PBS Home Video, 2009. DVD [including interviews with Laurent Dubois, Jean Casimir, Madison Smartt Bell and narration by Edwidge Danticat].

Fabella, Yvonne. "An Empire Founded on Libertinage? The Mulâtresse and Colonial Anxiety in Saint Domingue." In *Gender, Race and Religion in the Colonization of the Americas*, edited by Nora Jaffary, 109–124. Burlington, VT: Ashgate, 2007.

Fabella, Yvonne. Review of Geggus and Fiering, *The World of the Haitian Revolution*. In *New West Indian Guide* 85, no. 1–2 (2011): 130–2.

Fick, Carolyn E. *The Making of Haiti: The Saint Domingue Revolution from Below*. Knoxville: University of Tennessee Press, 1990.

Fick, Carolyn. "Emancipation in Haiti: From Plantation Labour to Peasant Proprietorship." *Slavery and Abolition* 21, no. 2 (2000): 11–73.

Fick, Carolyn. "The Saint-Domingue Slave Revolution and the Unfolding of Independence, 1791–1804." In *The World of the Haitian Revolution*, edited by Norman Fiering and David Geggus, 177–195. Bloomington: Indiana University Press, 2009.

Fischer, Sibylle. "Unthinkable History? The Haitian Revolution, Historiography, and Modernity on the Periphery." In *A Companion to African-American Studies*, edited by Lewis R. Gordon and Jane Anna Gordon, 360–376. Malden, MA: Blackwell, 2006.

Forster, Robert. "The French Revolution, People of Color, and Slavery." In *The Global Ramifications of the French Revolution*, edited by Joseph Klaits and Michael H. Haltzel, 89–104. New York: Woodrow Wilson Center/Cambridge University Press, 1994.

Fouchard, Jean. *The Haitian Maroons: Liberty or Death*. New York: E.W. Blyden Press, 1981 [translation of *Les marrons de la liberté*, 1972].

Fouchard, Jean. *Langue et littérature des aborigènes d'Ayti*. Paris: Éditions de l'École, 1972.

Frostin, Charles. *Les révoltes blanches à Saint-Domingue aux XVIIe et XVIIIe siècles (Haïti avant 1789)*. 2nd edition. Rennes: Presses universitaires de Rennes, 2008.

Gainot, Bernard. *Les officiers de couleur dans les armées de la République et de l'Empire (1792–1815): De l'esclavage à la condition militaire dans les Antilles françaises*. Paris: Karthala, 2007.

Garraway, Doris Lorraine. *The Libertine Colony: Creolization in the Early French Caribbean*. Durham, NC: Duke University Press, 2005.

Garraway, Doris Lorraine. *Tree of Liberty: Cultural Legacies of the Haitian Revolution in the Atlantic World*. Charlottesville: University of Virginia Press, 2008.

Garrigus, John D. " 'Sons of the Same Father': Gender, Race and Citizenship in French Saint-Domingue, 1760–1792." In *Visions and Revisions of Eighteenth-Century France*, edited by Christine Adams, Jack R. Censer, and Lisa Jane Graham, 137–153. University Park: Pennsylvania State University Press, 1997.

Garrigus, John D. *Before Haiti: Race and Citizenship in French Saint-Domingue*. New York: Palgrave Macmillan, 2006.

Garrigus, John D. "Opportunist or Patriot? Julien Raimond (1744–1801) and the Haitian Revolution." *Slavery and Abolition* 28, no. 1 (2007a): 1–21.

Garrigus, John D. " 'To Establish a Community of Property': Marriage and Race Before and During the Haitian Revolution." *The History of the Family* 12, no. 2 (2007b): 142–152.

Garrigus, John D. " 'Thy Coming Fame, Ogé! Is Sure: New Evidence on Ogé's 1790 Revolt and the Beginnings of the Haitian Revolution." In *Assumed Identities: The Meanings of Race in the Atlantic World*, edited by John D. Garrigus and Christopher Morris, 19–45. College Station: Texas A&M University Press, 2010.

Gaspar, David Barry, and Darlene Clark Hine, eds. *More Than Chattel: Black Women and Slavery in the Americas*. Bloomington: Indiana University Press, 1996 [includes articles on enslaved and free women of color in Saint-Domingue by S. Socolow, D. Geggus, and B. Moitt].

Gaspar, David Barry, and David Patrick Geggus, eds. *A Turbulent Time: The French Revolution and the Greater Caribbean*. Bloomington: Indiana University Press, 1997 [esp. articles by D. Geggus, C. Fick, K. Hanger and R. Paquette].

Gauthier, Florence. *Périssent les colonies plutôt qu'un principe!: contributions à l'histoire de l'abolition de l'esclavage, 1789–1804*. Paris: Société des études robespierristes, 2002.

Gautier, Arlette. *Les soeurs de solitude: la condition féminine dans l'esclave aux Antilles du XVIIe au XIXe siècle*. Paris: Éditions Caribéennes, 1985.

Geggus, David. *Slavery, War, and Revolution: The British Occupation of Saint Domingue, 1793–1798*. New York: Oxford University Press, 1982.

Geggus, David. *Haitian Revolutionary Studies*. Bloomington: Indiana University Press, 2002.

Geggus, David. "The Caribbean in the Age of Revolution." In *The Age of Revolutions in Global Context, c. 1760–1840*, edited by David Armitage and Sanjay Subrahmanyam, 83–100. New York: Palgrave Macmillan, 2009.

Geggus, David. "Resistance and Emancipation: The Case of Saint Domingue." In *Who Abolished Slavery? Slave Revolts and Abolitionism*, edited by Seymour Drescher and Pieter C. Emmer, 112–119. New York: Berghahn Books, 2009.

Geggus, David. "The Haitian Revolution in Atlantic Perspective." In *The Oxford Handbook of the Atlantic World, c.1450–c.1850*, edited by Nicholas P. Canny and Philip D. Morgan, 533–549. New York: Oxford University Press, 2011.

Geggus, David, and Norman Fiering, eds. *The World of the Haitian Revolution*. Bloomington: Indiana University Press, 2009 [esp. sections I and II on colonial Saint-Domingue and the Revolution].

Ghachem, Malick W. *The Old Regime and the Haitian Revolution*. Cambridge: Cambridge University Press, 2012.

Ghachem, Malick W. "Prosecuting Torture: The Strategic Ethics of Slavery in Pre-Revolutionary Saint-Domingue (Haiti)." *Law and History Review* 29, no. 4 (2011): 985–1029.

Girard, Philippe R. "Caribbean Genocide: Racial War in Haiti, 1802–4," *Patterns of Prejudice* 39, no. 2 (2005): 138–161.

Girard, Philippe R. "Napoléon Bonaparte and the Emancipation Issue in Saint-Domingue, 1799–1803." *French Historical Studies* 32, no. 4 (2009a): 587–618.

Girard, Philippe R. "Rebelles with a Cause: Women in the Haitian War of Independence, 1802–04." *Gender & History* 21, no. 1 (2009b): 60–85.

Girard, Philippe R. *The Slaves Who Defeated Napoleon: Toussaint Louverture and the Haitian War of Independence, 1801–1804*. Tuscaloosa: University of Alabama Press, 2011.

Hector, Michel, ed. *La Révolution française et Haïti: filiations, ruptures, nouvelles dimensions*. Port-au-Prince: Société haïtienne d'histoire et de géographie/H. Deschamps, 1995.

Hector, Michel, and Laënnec Hurbon, eds. *Genèse de l'état haïtien (1804–1859)*. Paris: Maison des sciences de l'homme, 2009.

Hector, Michel, and Claude Moïse, eds. *Colonisation et esclavage en Haïti: le régime colonial français à Saint-Domingue (1625–1789)*. Port-au-Prince: H. Deschamps, 1990.

Heinl, Robert Debs and Nancy Gordon Heinl. *Written in Blood: The Story of the Haitian People, 1492–1971*. Boston: Houghton Mifflin, 1978.

Hoffmann, Léon-François, Frauke Gewecke, and Ulrich Fleischmann, eds. *Haïti 1804 – lumières et ténèbres: impact et résonances d'une révolution*. Madrid: Iberoamericana, 2008.

Hurbon, Laënnec, ed. *L'insurrection des esclaves de Saint-Domingue, 22–23 août 1791: actes de la table ronde internationale de Port-au-Prince, 8 au 10 décembre 1997*. Paris: Karthala, 2000.

James, C. L. R. *The Black Jacobins: Toussaint L'Ouverture and the San Domingo Revolution*, 2nd ed. New York: Vintage Books, 1963 [first edition published 1938].

Jenson, Deborah. *Beyond the Slave Narrative: Politics, Sex, and Manuscripts in the Haitian Revolution*. Liverpool: Liverpool University Press, 2011.

Kadish, Doris Y., ed. *Slavery in the Caribbean Francophone World: Distant Voices, Forgotten Acts, Forged Identities*. Athens: University of Georgia Press, 2000.

Kafka, Judith. "Action, Reaction and Interaction: Slave Women in Resistance in the South of Saint-Domingue, 1793–94." *Slavery and Abolition* 18, no. 2 (1997): 48–72.

King, Stewart R. *Blue Coat or Powdered Wig: Free People of Color in Pre-Revolutionary Saint Domingue*. Athens: University of Georgia Press, 2001.

Klooster, Wim. *Revolutions in the Atlantic World: A Comparative History*. New York: New York University Press, 2009.

Knight, Franklin. "The Haitian Revolution." *American Historical Review* 105, no. 1 (2000): 103–115.

Laurent, Gérard M. *Le Commissaire Sonthonax à Saint Domingue*. Port-au-Prince: La Phalange, 1965.

Liu, Tessie P. "The Secret beyond White Patriarchal Power: Race, Gender, and Freedom in the Last Days of Colonial Saint-Domingue." *French Historical Studies* 33, no. 1 (2010): 387–416.

Madiou, Thomas. *Histoire d'Haïti*. Port-au-Prince, 1848; reprint, Port-au-Prince: Impr. E. Chenet, 1922–3.

Manigat, Leslie F. *Eventail d'histoire vivante d'Haïti: des préludes à la Révolution de Saint Domingue jusqu'à nos jours, 1789–1999*. 3 vols. [vol. I: *La Période Fondatrice (1789–1838)*]. Port-au-Prince: CHUDAC, 2001–2003.

Martin, Michel Louis, and Alain Yacou, eds. *De la Révolution française aux révolutions créoles et nègres*. Paris: Éditions Caribéenes, 1989.

McClellan, James. *Colonialism and Science: Saint-Domingue in the Old Regime*. Baltimore: Johns Hopkins University Press, 1992.

McNeill, John Robert. *Mosquito Empires: Ecology and War in the Greater Caribbean, 1620–1914*. New York: Cambridge University Press, 2010.

Meadows, R. Darrell. "The Planters of Saint-Domingue, 1750–1804: Migration and Exile in the French Revolutionary Atlantic." Ph.D. diss, Carnegie Mellon University, 2004.

Moïse, Claude. *Le projet national de Toussaint Louverture et la Constitution de 1801*. Montreal: CIDIHCA, 2001.

Moïse, Claude, ed. *Dictionnaire Historique de la Révolution Haïtienne (1789–1804)*. Montreal: Éditions Images/CIDIHCA, 2003 [contributions by C. B. Auguste, M. B. Auguste, C. Fick, D. Geggus, M. Hector, G. Jean-Charles, S. Manigat, F. Midy, K. Millet, and P. Simon].

Moitt, Bernard. *Women and Slavery in the French Antilles, 1635–1848*. Bloomington: Indiana University Press, 2001.

Moreau de Saint-Méry, Médéric-Louis-Elie. *A Civilization that Perished: The Last Years of White Colonial Rule in Haiti*. Translated, edited and abridged by Ivor D. Spencer. Lanham, MD: University Press of America, 1985.

Moreau, Jean-Pierre. *Les Petites Antilles de Christophe Colomb à Richelieu: 1493–1635*. Paris: Karthala, 1992.

Munro, Martin, and Elizabeth Walcott-Hackshaw, eds. *Echoes of the Haitian Revolution, 1804–2004*. Kingston, Jamaica: University of the West Indies Press, 2008.

Munro, Martin, and Elizabeth Walcott-Hackshaw, eds. *Reinterpreting the Haitian Revolution and Its Cultural Aftershocks*. Kingston, Jamaica: University of the West Indies Press, 2006.

Navarro-Andraud, Zélie. "Les élites urbaines de Saint-Domingue dans la seconde moitié du XVIIIe siècle: la place des administrateurs coloniaux (1763–1792)." Doctoral thesis, Université de Toulouse II-Le Mirail, 2007.

Nemours, Alfred. *Haïti et la Guerre de l'indépendance américaine*. Port-au-Prince: H. Deschamps, 1952.

Nemours, Luc. "Julien Raymond, le chef des gens de couleur." *Annales historiques de la révolution française* 23 (1951): 257–262.

Nesbitt, Nick. "Turning the Tide: The Problem of Popular Insurgency in Haitian Revolutionary Historiography." *Small Axe* 12.3 (2008): 14–31.

Nesbitt, Nick. *Universal Emancipation: The Haitian Revolution and the Radical Enlightenment*. Charlottesville: University of Virginia Press, 2008.

Ogle, Gene Edwin. "Policing Saint Domingue: Race, Violence, and Honor in an Old Regime Colony." Ph.D. diss., University of Pennsylvania, 2003.

Oriol, Michèle. *Images de la révolution à St.-Domingue*. Port-au-Prince: H. Deschamps, 1992.

Oriol, Michèle. *Histoire et dictionnaire de la révolution et de l'indépendance d'Haïti, 1789–1804*. Port-au-Prince: Fondation pour la recherche iconographique et documentaire, 2002.

Ott, Thomas O. *Haitian Revolution, 1789–1804*. Knoxville: University of Tennessee Press, 1973.

Peabody, Sue. *'There Are No Slaves in France': The Political Culture of Race and Slavery in the Ancien Régime*. Oxford: Oxford University Press, 1996.

Peabody, Sue. "Négresse, Mulâtresse, Citoyenne: Gender and Emancipation in the French Caribbean, 1650–1848." In *Gender and Slave Emancipation in the Atlantic World*, edited by Pamela Scully and Diana Paton, 56–78. Durham, NC: Duke University Press, 2005.

Peabody, Sue. "Taking Haiti to the People: History and Fiction of the Haitian Revolution." *Slavery and Abolition* 27, no. 1 (2006): 125–132.

Peabody, Sue, and Tyler Edward Stovall, eds. *The Color of Liberty: Histories of Race in France*. Durham, NC: Duke University Press, 2003 [esp. essays by P. Boulle, A. Sepinwall, C. Blanckaert, J. Garrigus and L. Dubois].

Pluchon, Pierre. *Toussaint Louverture: un révolutionnaire noir d'Ancien Régime*. Paris: Fayard, 1989.

Popkin, Jeremy D. *Facing Racial Revolution: Eyewitness Accounts of the Haitian Insurrection*. Chicago: University of Chicago Press, 2007.

Popkin, Jeremy D. *You are All Free: The Haitian Revolution and the Abolition of Slavery*. Cambridge: Cambridge University Press, 2010.

Popkin, Jeremy D. *A Concise History of the Haitian Revolution*. Malden, MA: Wiley-Blackwell, 2012.

Pritchard, James S. *In Search of Empire: The French in the Americas, 1670–1730*. Cambridge: Cambridge University Press, 2004.

Régent, Frédéric. *La France et ses esclaves: de la colonisation aux abolitions, 1620–1848*. Paris: Grasset, 2007.

Regourd, François. "Lumières coloniales. Les Antilles françaises dans la république des lettres." *Dix-huitième siècle*, no. 33 (2001): 183–200.

Révolutions aux colonies. Reprint of *Annales historiques de la Révolution française*, nos. 293–4. Paris: Société des Études Robespierristes, 1993.

Roberts, Kevin D. "The Influential Yoruba Past in Haiti." In *The Yoruba Diaspora in the Atlantic World*, edited by Toyin Falola and Matt D. Childs, 177–182. Bloomington: Indiana University Press, 2004.

Rogers, Dominique. "Les libres de couleur dans les capitales de Saint-Domingue: Fortune, mentalités, et intégration à la fin de l'ancien régime (1776–1789)." Doctoral thesis, Université Michel de Montaigne, Bordeaux III, 1999.

Rogers, Dominique. "Réussir dans un Monde d'Hommes: les Strategies des Femmes de Couleur du Cap-Francais, " *Journal of Haitian Studies* 9, no. 1 (2003): 40–51.

Rogers, Dominique, and Stewart King. "Housekeepers, Merchants, Rentières: Free Women of Color in the Port Cities of Colonial Saint-Domingue, 1750–1790." In *Women in Port: Gendering Communities, Economies, and Social Networks in Atlantic Port Cities, 1500–1800*, edited by Douglas Catterall and Jodi Campbell. Leiden: Brill Academic Publishers, forthcoming 2012.

Saint-Louis, Vertus. *Système colonial et problèmes d'alimentation: Saint-Domingue au XVIIIe siècle (1700–1789)*. Montreal: CIDIHCA, 2003.

Saint-Louis, Vertus. *Aux origines du drame d'Haïti: droit et commerce maritime (1794–1806)*. [Port-au-Prince]: Bibliothèque nationale d'Haïti, 2006.

Saint-Louis, Vertus. *Mer et liberté Haïti (1492–1794)*. [Port-au-Prince]: Bibliothèque nationale d'Haïti, 2008.

Sala-Molins, Louis. *Dark Side of the Light: Slavery and the French Enlightenment*. Minneapolis: University of Minnesota Press, 2006.

Sepinwall, Alyssa Goldstein. "Atlantic Amnesia: French Historians, the Haitian Revolution and the 2004–6 CAPES Exam." In *Proceedings of the Western Society for French History* 34 (2006): 300–314 [available at http://quod.lib.umich.edu/w/wsfh/volumes.html (Long Beach)].

Smith, Matthew J. "Two-Hundred-Year-Old Mountains: Issues and Themes in the Historiography of the Modern Francophone Caribbean." In *Beyond Fragmentation: Perspectives on Caribbean History*, edited by Juanita De Barros, Audra Diptee and David Vincent Trotman, 113–140. Princeton: Markus Wiener Publishers, 2006.

Stein, Robert Louis. *The French Slave Trade in the Eighteenth Century: An Old Regime Business*. Madison: University of Wisconsin Press, 1979.

Stein, Robert Louis. *Léger Félicité Sonthonax: The Lost Sentinel of the Republic*. Rutherford, NJ: Fairleigh Dickinson University Press, 1985.

Stein, Robert Louis. *The French Sugar Business in the Eighteenth Century*. Baton Rouge: Louisiana University Press, 1988.

Thornton, John. *Africa and Africans in the Making of the Atlantic World*. Cambridge: Cambridge University Press, 1992.

Thornton, John K. "African Soldiers in the Haitian Revolution." *Journal of Caribbean History* 25, nos. 1 and 2 (1991): 59–80.

Trouillot, Évelyne. *Rosalie l'infâme*. Paris: Dapper, 2003.

Trouillot, Évelyne. "Infamy Revisited." *Africultures*, no. 58 (2004); available at www.africultures.com/php.index.php?nav=article&no=5717.

Trouillot, Michel-Rolph. *Silencing the Past: Power and the Production of History*. Boston, MA: Beacon Press, 1995.

Tyson, George F. *Toussaint L'Ouverture*. Englewood Cliffs, NJ: Prentice-Hall, 1973 [includes translations of primary source materials by Toussaint].

Weaver, Karol K. *Medical Revolutionaries: The Enslaved Healers of Eighteenth-Century Saint Domingue*. Urbana: University of Illinois Press, 2006.

Yacou, Alain, ed. *Saint-Domingue espagnol et la révolution nègre d'Haïti (1790–1822): commémoration du bicentenaire de la naissance de l'état d'Haïti (1804–2004)*. Paris: Karthala, 2007.

1

AN UNTHINKABLE HISTORY

The Haitian Revolution as a Non-Event

(*excerpts*)

Michel-Rolph Trouillot

The young woman stood up in the middle of my lecture. "Mr. Trouillot, you make us read all those white scholars. What can they know about slavery? Where were they when we were jumping off the boats? When we chose death over misery and killed our own children to spare them from a life of rape?"

I was scared and she was wrong. She was not reading white authors only and she never jumped from a slave ship. I was dumbfounded and she was angry; but how does one reason with anger? I was on my way to a Ph.D., and my teaching this course was barely a stopover, a way of paying the dues of guilt in this lily-white institution. She had taken my class as a mental break on her way to med school, or Harvard law, or some lily-white corporation.

I had entitled the course "The Black Experience in the Americas." I should have known better: it attracted the few black students around—plus a few courageous whites—and they were all expecting too much, much more than I could deliver. They wanted a life that no narrative could provide, even the best fiction. They wanted a life that only they could build right now, right here in the United States—except that they did not know this: they were too close to the unfolding story. Yet already I could see in their eyes that part of my lesson registered. I wanted them to know that slavery did not happen only in Georgia and Mississippi. I wanted them to learn that the African connection was more complex and tortuous than they had ever imagined, that the U.S. monopoly on both blackness and racism was itself a racist plot. And she had broken the spell on her way to Harvard law. I was a novice and so was she, each of us struggling with the history we chose, each of us also fighting an imposed oblivion.

Ten years later, I was visiting another institution with a less prestigious clientele and more modest dreams when another young black woman, the same age but much more timid, caught me again by surprise. "I am tired," she said, "to hear about this slavery stuff. Can we hear the story of the black millionaires?" Had times changed so fast, or were their different takes on slavery reflections of class differences?

I flashed back to the first woman clinging so tightly to that slave boat. I understood better why she wanted to jump, even once, on her way to Harvard law, med school, or wherever. Custodian of the future for an imprisoned race whose young males do not live long enough to have a past, she needed this narrative of resistance. Nietzsche was wrong: this was no extra baggage, but a necessity for the journey, and who was I to say that it was no better a past than a bunch of fake millionaires, or a medal of St. Henry and the crumbling walls of a decrepit palace?

I wish I could shuffle the years and put both young women in the same room. We would have shared stories not yet in the archives. We would have read Ntozake Shange's tale of a colored girl dreaming of Toussaint Louverture and the revolution that the world forgot. Then we would have returned to the planters' journals, to econometric history and its industry of statistics, and none of us would be afraid of the numbers. Hard facts are no more frightening than darkness. You can play with them if you are with friends. They are scary only if you read them alone.

We all need histories that no history book can tell, but they are not in the classroom—not the history classrooms, anyway. They are in the lessons we learn at home, in poetry and childhood games, in what is left of history when we close the history books with their verifiable facts. [. . .]

Unthinking a Chimera

In 1790, just a few months before the beginning of the insurrection that shook Saint-Domingue and brought about the revolutionary birth of independent Haiti, French colonist La Barre reassured his metropolitan wife of the peaceful state of life in the tropics. He wrote: "There is no movement among our Negroes . . . They don't even think of it. They are very tranquil and obedient. A revolt among them is impossible." And again: "We have nothing to fear on the part of the Negroes; they are tranquil and obedient."[1] [. . .]

La Barre's views were by no means unique. Witness this manager who constantly reassured his patrons in almost similar words: "I live tranquilly in the midst of them without a single thought of their uprising unless that was fomented by the whites themselves."[2] There were doubts at times. But the planters' practical precautions aimed at stemming individual actions or, at worst, a sudden riot. No one in Saint-Domingue or elsewhere worked out a plan of response to a general insurrection.

Indeed, the contention that enslaved Africans and their descendants could not envision freedom—let alone formulate strategies for gaining and securing such freedom—was based not so much on empirical evidence as on an ontology, an implicit organization of the world and its inhabitants. Although by no means monolithic, this worldview was widely shared by whites in Europe and the Americas and by many non-white plantation owners as well. Although it left room for variations, none of these variations included the possibility of a revolutionary uprising in the slave plantations, let alone a successful one leading to the creation of an independent state.

The Haitian Revolution thus entered history with the peculiar characteristic of being unthinkable even as it happened. Official debates and publications of the times, including the long list of pamphlets on Saint-Domingue published in France from 1790 to 1804, reveal the incapacity of most contemporaries to understand the ongoing revolution on its own terms.[3] They could read the news only with their ready-made categories, and these categories were incompatible with the idea of a slave revolution.

The discursive context within which news from Saint-Domingue was discussed as it happened has important consequences for the historiography of Saint-Domingue/Haiti. If some events cannot be accepted even as they occur, how can they be assessed later? In other words, can historical narratives convey plots that are unthinkable in the world within which these narratives take place? How does one write a history of the impossible?

The key issue is not ideological. Ideological treatments are now more current in Haiti itself (in the epic or bluntly political interpretations of the revolution favored by some Haitian writers) than in the more rigorous handling of the evidence by professionals in Europe or in North America. The international scholarship on the Haitian Revolution has been rather sound by modern standards of evidence since at least the 1940s. The issue is rather epistemological and, by inference, methodological in the broadest sense. Standards of evidence notwithstanding, to what extent has modern historiography of the Haitian Revolution—as part of a continuous Western discourse on slavery, race, and colonization—broken the iron bonds of the philosophical milieu in which it was born?

A Certain Idea of Man

The West was created somewhere at the beginning of the sixteenth century in the midst of a global wave of material and symbolic transformations.[4] [. . .] What we call the Renaissance, much more an invention in its own right than a rebirth, ushered in a number of philosophical questions to which politicians, theologians, artists, and soldiers provided both concrete and abstract answers. What is Beauty? What is Order? What is the State? But also and above all: What is Man?

Philosophers who discussed that last issue could not escape the fact that colonization was going on as they spoke. Men (Europeans) were conquering, killing, dominating, and enslaving other beings thought to be equally human, if only by some. [. . .]

The seventeenth century saw the increased involvement of England, France, and the Netherlands in the Americas and in the slave trade. The eighteenth century followed the same path with a touch of perversity: the more European merchants and mercenaries bought and conquered other men and women, the more European philosophers wrote and talked about Man. [. . .] All assumed and reasserted that, ultimately, some humans were more so than others.

35

For indeed, in the horizon of the West at the end of the century, Man (with a capital M) was primarily European and male. [. . .]

Negative connotations linked to skin colors increasingly regrouped as "black" had first spread in Christendom in the late Middle Ages. They were reinforced by the fanciful descriptions of medieval geographers and travellers. Thus, the word "nègre" entered French dictionaries and glossaries with negative undertones increasingly precise from its first appearances in the 1670s to the universal dictionaries that augured the Encyclopedia.[5] By the middle of the eighteenth century, "black" was almost universally bad. What had happened in the meantime, was the expansion of African-American slavery.

[. . .]

Colonization provided the most potent impetus for the transformation of European ethnocentrism into scientific racism. [. . .]

With the place of blacks now guaranteed at the bottom of the Western nomenclature, anti-black racism soon became the central element of planter ideology in the Caribbean. By the middle of the eighteenth century, the arguments justifying slavery in the Antilles and North America relocated in Europe where they blended with the racist strain inherent in eighteenth-century rationalist thought. The literature in French is telling, though by no means unique. Buffon fervently supported a monogenist viewpoint: blacks were not, in his view, of a different species. Still, they were different enough to be destined to slavery. Voltaire disagreed, but only in part. Negroes belonged to a different species, one culturally destined to be slaves. That the material well-being of many of these thinkers was often indirectly and, sometimes, quite directly linked to the exploitation of African slave labor may not have been irrelevant to their learned opinions. By the time of the American Revolution, scientific racism, whose rise many historians wrongly attribute to the nineteenth century, was already a feature of the ideological landscape of the Enlightenment on both sides of the Atlantic.[6]

[. . .]

In the name of freedom and democracy also, in July 1789, just a few days before the storming of the Bastille, a few planters from Saint-Domingue met in Paris to petition the newly formed French Assembly to accept in its midst twenty representatives from the Caribbean. The planters had derived this number from the population of the islands, using roughly the mathematics used in France to proportion metropolitan representatives in the Assembly. But they had quite advertently counted the black slaves and the *gens de couleur* as part of the population of the islands whereas, of course, they were claiming no rights of suffrage for these non-whites. Honoré Gabriel Riquetti, Count of Mirabeau, took the stand to denounce the planters' skewed mathematics. Mirabeau told the Assembly:

Are the colonies placing their Negroes and their *gens de couleur* in the class of men or in that of the beasts of burden?

If the Colonists want the Negroes and *gens de couleur* to count as men, let them enfranchise the first; that all may be electors, that all may be elected. If not, we beg them to observe that in proportioning the number of deputies to the population of France, we have taken into consideration neither the number of our horses nor that of our mules.[7]

Mirabeau wanted the French Assembly to reconcile the philosophical positions explicit in the Declaration of Rights of Man and its political stance on the colonies. [. . .] The National Assembly granted only six deputies to the sugar colonies of the Caribbean, a few more than they deserved if only the whites had been counted but many less than if the Assembly had recognized the full political rights of the blacks and the *gens de couleur*. In the mathematics of realpolitik, the half-million slaves of Saint-Domingue-Haiti and the few hundred thousands of the other colonies were apparently worth three deputies—white ones at that.

The ease with which the Assembly bypassed its own contradictions, an echo of the mechanisms by which black slaves came to account for three-fifths of a person in the United States, permeated the practices of the Enlightenment. [. . .]

The Enlightenment, nevertheless, brought a change of perspective. The idea of progress, now confirmed, suggested that men were perfectible. Therefore, subhumans could be, theoretically at least, perfectible. More important, the slave trade was running its course, and the economics of slavery would be questioned increasingly as the century neared its end. Perfectibility became an argument in the practical debate: the westernized other looked increasingly more profitable to the West, especially if he could become a free laborer. A French memoir of 1790 summarized the issue: "It is perhaps not impossible to civilize the Negro, to bring him to principles and *make a man out of him:* there would be more to gain than to buy and sell him." Finally, we should not underestimate the loud anti-colonialist stance of a small, elitist but vocal group of philosophers and politicians.[8]

The reservations expressed in the metropolis had little impact within the Caribbean or in Africa. Indeed, the slave trade increased in the years 1789–1791 while French politicians and philosophers were debating more vehemently than ever on the rights of humanity. Further, few politicians or philosophers attacked racism, colonialism, and slavery in a single blow and with equal vehemence. In France as in England colonialism, pro-slavery rhetoric, and racism intermingled and supported one another without ever becoming totally confused. So did their opposites. That allowed much room for multiple positions.[9]

Such multiplicity notwithstanding, there was no doubt about Western superiority, only about its proper use and effect. *L'Histoire des deux Indes,* signed by Abbé Raynal with philosopher and encyclopedist Denis Diderot acting as ghost—and, some would say, premier—contributor to the anti-colonialist passages, was perhaps the most radical critique of colonialism from the France of the Enlightenment.[10] Yet the book never fully questioned the ontological principles behind the colonialist enterprise, namely that the differences between forms of humanity were not only of degree but of kind.[11] [. . .]

Behind the radicalism of Diderot and Raynal stood, ultimately, a project of colonial management. It did indeed include the abolition of slavery, but only in the long term, and as part of a process that aimed at the better control of the colonies.[12] Access to human status did not lead *ipso facto* to self-determination. In short, here again, as in Condorcet, as in Mirabeau, as in Jefferson, when all is said and done, there are degrees of humanity.

The vocabulary of the times reveals that gradation. When one talked of the biological product of black and of white intercourse, one spoke of "man of color" as if the two terms do not necessarily go together: unmarked humanity is white. The captain of a slave boat bluntly emphasized this implicit opposition between white "Men" and the rest of humankind. After French supporters of the free coloreds in Paris created the *Société des Amis des Noirs*, the pro-slavery captain proudly labelled himself "l'Ami des Hommes." The Friends of the Blacks were not necessarily Friends of Man.[13] The lexical opposition Man-versus-Native (or Man-versus-Negro) tinted the European literature on the Americas from 1492 to the Haitian Revolution and beyond. Even the radical duo Diderot-Raynal did not escape it. Recounting an early Spanish exploration, they write: "Was not this handful of *men* surrounded by an innumerable multitude of *natives* . . . seized with alarm and terror, well or ill founded?"[14]

One will not castigate long-dead writers for using the words of their time or for not sharing ideological views that we now take for granted. Lest accusations of political correctness trivialize the issue, let me emphasize that I am not suggesting that eighteenth-century men and women *should* have thought about the fundamental equality of humankind in the same way some of us do today. On the contrary, I am arguing that they *could not have* done so. But I am also drawing a lesson from the understanding of this historical impossibility. The Haitian Revolution did challenge the ontological and political assumptions of the most radical writers of the Enlightenment. *The events that shook up Saint-Domingue from 1791 to 1804 constituted a sequence for which not even the extreme political left in France or in England had a conceptual frame of reference.* They were "unthinkable" facts in the framework of Western thought.

Pierre Bourdieu defines the unthinkable as that for which one has no adequate instruments to conceptualize.[15] [. . .] In that sense, the Haitian Revolution was unthinkable in its time: it challenged the very framework within which proponents and opponents had examined race, colonialism, and slavery in the Americas.

Prelude to the News: The Failure of Categories

Between the first slave shipments of the early 1500s and the 1791 insurrection of northern Saint-Domingue, most Western observers had treated manifestations of slave resistance and defiance with the ambivalence characteristic of their overall treatment of colonization and slavery. On the one hand, resistance and defiance did not exist, since to acknowledge them was to acknowledge the humanity of the enslaved.[16] On the other hand, since resistance occurred, it was dealt with quite severely, within or around the plantations. Thus, next to a discourse that claimed the contentment of slaves, a plethora of laws, advice, and measures, both legal and illegal, were set up to curb the very resistance denied in theory.

Publications by and for planters, as well as plantation journals and correspondence, often mixed both attitudes. Close as some were to the real world, planters and managers could not fully deny resistance, but they tried to provide reassuring certitudes by trivializing all its manifestations. Resistance did not exist as a global phenomenon. Rather, each case of unmistakable defiance, each possible instance of resistance was treated separately and drained of its political content. Slave A ran away because he was particularly mistreated by his master. Slave B was missing because he was not properly fed. Slave X killed herself in a fatal tantrum. Slave Y poisoned her mistress because she was jealous. The run-away emerges from this literature—which still has its disciples—as an animal driven by biological constraints, at best as a pathological case. The rebellious slave in turn is a maladjusted Negro, a mutinous adolescent who eats dirt until he dies, an infanticidal mother, a deviant. To the extent that sins of humanity are acknowledged they are acknowledged only as evidence of a pathology.

[. . .]

In fact, this argument didn't convince the planters themselves. They held on to it because it was the only scheme that allowed them not to deal with the issue as a mass phenomenon. [. . .] To acknowledge resistance as a mass phenomenon is to acknowledge the possibility that something is wrong with the system. [. . .]

Yet, as time went on, the succession of plantation revolts, and especially the consolidation—in Jamaica, and in the Guianas—of large colonies of runaways with whom colonial governments had to negotiate, gradually undermined the image of submission and the complementary argument of pathological misadaptation. However much some observers wanted to see in these massive departures a sign of the force that nature exerted on the animal-slave, the possibility of mass resistance penetrated Western discourse.

The penetration was nevertheless circumspect. When Louis-Sébastien Mercier announced an avenger of the New World in 1771, it was in a novel of anticipation, a utopia.[17] The goal was to warn Europeans of the fatalities that awaited them if they did not change their ways. Similarly, when the

duo Raynal-Diderot spoke of a black Spartacus, it was not a clear predic-
tion of a Louverture-type character, as some would want with hindsight.[18]
In the pages of the *Histoire des deux Indes* where the passage appears, the
threat of a black Spartacus is couched as a warning. The reference is not to
Saint-Domingue but to Jamaica and to Guyana where "there are two
established colonies of fugitive negroes [. . .], and the negroes lack only a
chief courageous enough to drive them to *revenge and to carnage*. Where is
he, this great man whom nature owes *perhaps* to the honor of the human
species? Where is this new Spartacus? . . ."[19]

In this version of the famous passage, modified in successive editions of
the *Histoire*, the most radical stance is in the unmistakable reference to a
single human species. But just as with Las Casas, just as with Buffon or the
left of the French Assembly, the practical conclusions from what looks like
a revolutionary philosophy are ambiguous. In Diderot-Raynal, as in the
few other times it appears in writing, the evocation of a slave rebellion
was primarily a rhetorical device. The concrete possibility of such a rebellion flourishing into a revolution and a modern black state was still part of
the unthinkable.

[. . .]

More important, "slavery" was at that time an easy metaphor, accessible to a large public who knew that the word stood for a number of evils
except perhaps the evil of itself. Slavery in the parlance of the philosophers could be whatever was wrong with European rule in Europe and
elsewhere. To wit, the same Diderot applauded U.S. revolutionaries for
having "burned their chains," for having "refused slavery." Never mind
that some of them owned slaves. The *Marseillaise* was also a cry against
"slavery."[20] Mulatto *slave owners* from the Caribbean told the French
Assembly that their status as second-class free men was equivalent to
slavery.[21] [. . .] References to slave resistance must thus be regarded in light
of these rhetorical clichés. For if today we can read the successive
"Declarations of the Rights of Man" or the U.S. Bill of Rights as naturally
including every single human being, it is far from certain that this
revisionist reading was the favored interpretation of the "men" of 1789
and 1791.[22]

[. . .]

To sum up, in spite of the philosophical debates, in spite of the rise of
abolitionism, the Haitian Revolution was unthinkable in the West not only
because it challenged slavery and racism but because of the way it did so.
When the insurrection first broke in northern Saint-Domingue, a number
of radical writers in Europe and very few in the Americas had been willing
to acknowledge, with varying reservations—both practical and philosophical—the humanity of the enslaved. Almost none drew from this
acknowledgment the necessity to abolish slavery immediately. Similarly, a
handful of writers had evoked intermittently and, most often, metaphorically the possibility of mass resistance among the slaves. Almost none

had actually conceded that the slaves could—let alone should—indeed revolt.[23] Louis Sala-Molins claims that slavery was the ultimate test of the Enlightenment. We can go one step further: The Haitian Revolution was the ultimate test to the universalist pretensions of both the French and the American revolutions. And they both failed. *In 1791, there is no public debate on the record, in France, in England, or in the United States on the right of black slaves to achieve self-determination, and the right to do so by way of armed resistance.*

Not only was the Revolution unthinkable and, therefore, unannounced in the West, it was also—to a large extent—unspoken among the slaves themselves. By this I mean that the Revolution was not preceded or even accompanied by an explicit intellectual discourse.[24] One reason is that most slaves were illiterate and the printed word was not a realistic means of propaganda in the context of a slave colony. But another reason is that the claims of the revolution were indeed too radical to be formulated in advance of its deeds. Victorious practice could assert them only after the fact. In that sense, the revolution was indeed at the limits of the thinkable, even in Saint-Domingue, even among the slaves, even among its own leaders.

We need to recall that the key tenets of the political philosophy that became explicit in Saint-Domingue/Haiti between 1791 and 1804 were not accepted by world public opinion until after World War II. [. . .] Claims about the fundamental uniqueness of humankind, claims about the ethical irrelevance of racial categories or of geographical situation to matters of governance and, certainly, claims about the right of *all* peoples to self-determination went against received wisdom in the Atlantic world and beyond. [. . .] By necessity, the Haitian Revolution thought itself out politically and philosophically as it was taking place. [. . .]

The Haitian Revolution expressed itself mainly through its deeds, and it is through political practice that it challenged Western philosophy and colonialism. It did produce a few texts whose philosophical import is explicit, from Louverture's declaration of Camp Turel to the Haitian Act of Independence and the Constitution of 1805. But its intellectual and ideological newness appeared most clearly with each and every political threshold crossed, from the mass insurrection (1791) to the crumbling of the colonial apparatus (1793), from general liberty (1794) to the conquest of the state machinery (1797–98), from Louverture's taming of that machinery (1801) to the proclamation of Haitian independence with Dessalines (1804). Each and every one of these steps—leading up to and culminating in the emergence of a modern "black state," still largely part of the unthinkable until the twentieth century—challenged further the ontological order of the West and the global order of colonialism.

This also meant that the Haitian revolutionaries were not overly restricted by previous ideological limits set by professional intellectuals in the colony or elsewhere, that they could break new ground—and, indeed, they did so repeatedly. But it further meant that philosophical and political debate in the West, when it occurred, could only be reactive. It dealt with the impossible only after that impossible had become fact; and even then, the facts were not always accepted as such.

Dealing with the Unthinkable: The Failures of Narration

When the news of the massive uprising of August 1791 first hit France, the most common reaction among interested parties was disbelief: the facts were too unlikely; the news had to be false. Only the most vocal representatives of the planter party took them seriously, in part because they were the first to be informed via their British contacts, in part because they had the most to lose if indeed the news was verified. Others, including colored plantation owners then in France and most of the left wing of the French assembly, just could not reconcile their perception of blacks with the idea of a large-scale black rebellion.[25] In an impassioned speech delivered to the French assembly on 30 October 1791, delegate Jean-Pierre Brissot, a founding member of the *Amis des Noirs* and moderate anti-colonialist, outlined the reasons why the news had to be false: a) anyone who knew the blacks had to realize that it was simply impossible for fifty thousand of them to get together so fast and act in concert; b) slaves could not conceive of rebellion on their own, and mulattoes and whites were not so insane as to incite them to full-scale violence; c) even if the slaves had rebelled in such huge numbers, the superior French troops would have defeated them. Brissot went on:

> What are 50,000 men, badly armed, undisciplined and used to fear when faced with 1,800 Frenchmen used to fearlessness? What! In 1751, Dupleix and a few hundred Frenchmen could break the siege of Pondichéri and beat a well-equipped army of 100,000 Indians, and M. de Blanchelande with French troops and cannons would fear a much inferior troop of blacks barely armed?[26]

With such statements from a "Friend," the revolution did not need enemies. Yet so went majority opinion from left to center-right within the Assembly until the news was confirmed beyond doubt. Confirmation did not change the dominant views. When detailed news reached France, many observers were frightened not by the revolt itself but by the fact that the colonists had appealed to the English.[27] A serious long-term danger coming from the blacks was still unthinkable. Slowly though, the size of the uprising sank in. Yet even then, in France as in Saint-Domingue, as indeed in Jamaica, Cuba, and the United States before, planters, administrators, politicians, or ideologues found explanations that forced the rebellion back within their worldview, shoving the facts into the proper order of discourse. Since blacks could not have generated such a massive endeavor, the insurrection became an unfortunate repercussion of planters' miscalculations. It did not aim at revolutionary change, given its royalist influences. It was not supported by a majority of the slave population. It was due to outside agitators. It was the unforeseen consequence of various conspiracies connived by non-slaves. Every party chose its favorite enemy as the most likely conspirator behind the slave uprising. [. . .]

For thirteen years at least, Western public opinion pursued this game of hide-and-seek with the news coming out of Saint-Domingue. [. . .] By the spring of 1792, for instance, even the most distant observer could no longer deny the extent of the rebellion, the extraordinary number of slaves and plantations involved, the magnitude of the colonists' material losses. But then, many even in Saint-Domingue argued that the disaster was temporary, that everything would return to order. Thus, an eyewitness commented: "If the whites and the free mulattoes knew what was good for them, and kept tightly together, it is quite possible that things would return to normal, *considering the ascendancy that the white has always had over the negroes.*"[28] Note the doubt (the witness is tempted to believe his eyes); but note also that the nomenclature has not moved. Worldview wins over the facts: white hegemony is natural and taken for granted; any alternative is still in the domain of the unthinkable. Yet this passage was written in December 1792. At that time, behind the political chaos and the many battles between various armed factions, Toussaint Louverture and his closest followers were building up the avant-garde that would push the revolution to the point of no return. Indeed, six months later, civil commissar Léger Félicité Sonthonax was forced to declare free all slaves willing to fight under the French republican flag. A few weeks after Sonthonax's proclamation, in August 1793, Toussaint Louverture raised the stakes with his proclamation from Camp Turel: immediate unconditional freedom and equality for all.

By then, the old conspiracy theories should have become irrelevant. Clearly, the Louverture party was not willing to take orders from colonists, French Jacobins, or agents of foreign powers. What was going on in Saint-Domingue was, by all definitions, the most important slave rebellion ever witnessed and it had developed its own dynamics. Surprisingly, conspiracy theories survived long enough to justify the trials of a few Frenchmen accused to have fomented or helped the rebellion, from Blanchelande, the old royalist governor of 1791, to republican governor Lavaux, to Félicité Sonthonax, the Jacobin.[29]

As the power of Louverture grew, every other party struggled to convince itself and its counterparts that the achievements of the black leadership would ultimately benefit someone else. The new black elite had to be, willingly or not, the pawn of a "major" international power. Or else, the colony would fall apart and a legitimate international state would pick up the pieces. Theories assuming chaos under black leadership continued even after Louverture and his closest lieutenants fully secured the military, political, and civil apparatus of the colony. If some foreign governments—notably the United States—were willing to maintain a guarded collaboration with the Louverture regime, it was in part because they "knew" that an independent state led by former slaves was an impossibility. Toussaint himself may have not believed in the possibility of independence whereas, for all practical purposes, he was ruling Saint-Domingue as if it were independent.

Opinion in Saint-Domingue, in North America, and in Europe constantly dragged after the facts. Predictions, when they were made, revealed themselves useless. Once the French expedition of reconquest was launched in 1802, pundits were easily convinced that France would win the war. In England, the *Cobbett Political Register* doubted that Toussaint would even oppose a resistance: he was likely to flee the country.[30] Leclerc himself, the commander of the French forces, predicted in early February that the war would be over in two weeks. He was wrong by two years, give or take two months. Yet planters in Saint-Domingue apparently shared his optimism. [. . .]

By mid-1802, the debacle of Louverture's army seemed to verify that prophecy. The rejection of the truce by a significant minority of armed rebels—among whom was Sans Souci—and the full-scale resumption of military operations when the war within the war forced the colonial high brass to rejoin the revolution in the fall of 1802 did little to change the dominant views. Despite the alliance between the forces of Dessalines, Pétion, and Christophe and the repeated victories of the new revolutionary army, few outside of Saint-Domingue could foresee the outcome of this Negro rebellion. As late as the fall of 1803, a complete victory by the former slaves and the creation of an independent state was still unthinkable in Europe and North America. Only long after the 1804 declaration of independence would the fait accompli be ungraciously accepted.

Ungraciously, indeed. The international recognition of Haitian independence was even more difficult to gain than military victory over the forces of Napoleon. It took more time and more resources, more than a half century of diplomatic struggles. France imposed a heavy indemnity on the Haitian state in order to formally acknowledge its own defeat. The United States and the Vatican, notably, recognized Haitian independence only in the second half of the nineteenth century.

Diplomatic rejection was only one symptom of an underlying denial. [. . .] Between the Haitian independence and World War I, in spite of the successive abolitions of slavery, little changed within the various ladders that ranked humankind in the minds of the majorities in Europe and the Americas. In fact, some views deteriorated.[31] The nineteenth century was, in many respects, a century of retreat from some of the debates of the Enlightenment. Scientific racism, a growing but debated strain of Enlightenment thought, gained a much wider audience, further legitimizing the ontological nomenclature inherited from the Renaissance. The carving up of Asia and above all of Africa reinforced both colonial practice and ideology. Thus in most places outside of Haiti, more than a century after it happened, the revolution was still largely unthinkable history.

Erasure and Trivialization: Silences in World History

I have fleshed out two major points so far. First, the chain of events that constitute the Haitian Revolution was unthinkable before these events happened. Second, as they happened, the successive events within that chain were systematically recast by many participants and observers to fit a world of possibilities. That is, they were made to enter into narratives that made sense to a majority of Western observers and readers. I will now show how the revolution that was thought impossible by its contemporaries has also been silenced by historians. Amazing in this story is the extent to which historians have treated the events of Saint-Domingue in ways quite similar to the reactions of its Western contemporaries. That is, the narratives they build around these facts are strikingly similar to the narratives produced by individuals who thought that such a revolution was impossible.

The treatment of the Haitian Revolution in written history outside of Haiti reveals two families of tropes that are identical, in formal (rhetorical) terms, to figures of discourse of the late eighteenth century. The first kind of tropes are formulas that tend to erase directly the fact of a revolution. I call them, for short, formulas of erasure. The second kind tends to empty a number of singular events of their revolutionary content so that the entire string of facts, gnawed from all sides, becomes trivialized. I call them formulas of banalization. The first kind of tropes characterizes mainly the generalists and the popularizers—textbook authors, for example. The second are the favorite tropes of the specialists. The first type recalls the general silence on resistance in eighteenth-century Europe and North America. The second recalls the explanations of the specialists of the times, overseers and administrators in Saint-Domingue, or politicians in Paris. Both are formulas of silence.

The literature on slavery in the Americas and on the Holocaust suggests that there may be structural similarities in global silences or, at the very least, that erasure and banalization are not unique to the Haitian Revolution. At the level of generalities, some narratives cancel what happened through direct erasure of facts or their relevance. "It" did not *really* happen; it was not that bad, or that important. Frontal challenges to the fact of the Holocaust or to the relevance of Afro-American slavery belong to this type: The Germans did not really build gas chambers; slavery also happened to non-blacks. On a seemingly different plane, other narratives sweeten the horror or banalize the uniqueness of a situation by focusing on details: each convoy to Auschwitz can be explained on its own terms; some U.S. slaves were better fed than British workers; some Jews did survive. The joint effect of these two types of formulas is a powerful silencing: whatever has not been cancelled out in the generalities dies in the cumulative irrelevance of a heap of details. This is certainly the case for the Haitian Revolution.[32]

The general silence that Western historiography has produced around the Haitian Revolution originally stemmed from the incapacity to express the unthinkable, but it was ironically reinforced by the significance of the revolution for its contemporaries and for the generation immediately following. From 1791–1804 to the middle of the century, many Europeans and North Americans came to see that revolution as a litmus test for the black race, certainly for the capacities of all Afro-Americans. As Vastey's pronouncements on Sans Souci clearly show, Haitians did likewise.[33] Christophe's forts and palaces, the military efficiency of the former slaves, the impact of yellow fever on the French troops, and the relative weight of external factors on revolutionary dynamics figured highly in these debates. But if the revolution was significant for Haitians—and especially for the emerging Haitian elites as its self-proclaimed inheritors—to most foreigners it was primarily a lucky argument in a larger issue. Thus apologists and detractors alike, abolitionists and avowed racists, liberal intellectuals, economists, and slave owners used the events of Saint-Domingue to make their case, without regard to Haitian history as such. Haiti mattered to all of them, but only as pretext to talk about something else.[34]

With time, the silencing of the revolution was strengthened by the fate of Haiti itself. Ostracized for the better part of the nineteenth century, the country deteriorated both economically and politically—in part as a result of this ostracism.[35] As Haiti declined, the reality of revolution seemed increasingly distant, an improbability which took place in an awkward past and for which no one had a rational explanation. The revolution that was unthinkable became a non-event.

Finally, the silencing of the Haitian Revolution also fit the relegation to an historical backburner of the three themes to which it was linked: racism, slavery, and colonialism. In spite of their importance in the formation of what we now call the West, in spite of sudden outbursts of interest as in the United States in the early 1970s, none of these themes has ever become a central concern of the historiographic tradition in a Western country. [. . .] The less colonialism and racism seem important in world history, the less important also the Haitian Revolution.

Thus not surprisingly, as Western historiographies remain heavily guided by national—if not always nationalist—interests, the silencing of Saint-Domingue/Haiti continues in historical writings otherwise considered as models of the genre. The silence is also reproduced in the textbooks and popular writings that are the prime sources on global history for the literate masses in Europe, in the Americas, and in large chunks of the Third World. This corpus has taught generations of readers that the period from 1776 to 1843 should properly be called "The Age of Revolutions." At the very same time, this corpus has remained silent on the most radical political revolution of that age.

In the United States, for example, with the notable exceptions of Henry Adams and W. E. B. Du Bois, few major writers conceded any significance to the Haitian Revolution in their historical writings up to the 1970s. Very few textbooks even mentioned it. When they did, they made of it a "revolt," a "rebellion." The ongoing silence of most Latin-American textbooks is still more tragic. Likewise, historians of Poland have paid little attention to the five thousand Poles involved in the Saint-Domingue campaigns. The silence also persists in England in spite of the fact that the British lost upward of sixty thousand men in eight years in an anti-French Caribbean campaign of which Saint-Domingue was the most coveted prize. The Haitian Revolution appears obliquely as part of *medical* history. The victor is disease, not the Haitians. The Penguin *Dictionary of Modern History*, a mass circulation pocket encyclopedia that covers the period from 1789 to 1945, has neither Saint-Domingue nor Haiti in its entries. Likewise, historian Eric Hobsbawm, one of the best analysts of this era, managed to write a book entitled *The Age of Revolutions, 1789–1843*, in which the Haitian Revolution scarcely appears. [. . .][36]

The secondary role of conscious ideology and the power of the historical guild to decide relevance become obvious when we consider the case of France. France was the Western country most directly involved in the Haitian Revolution. France fought hard to keep Saint-Domingue and paid a heavy price for it. Napoleon lost nineteen French generals in Saint-Domingue, including his brother-in-law. France lost more men in Saint-Domingue than at Waterloo—as did England.[37] And although France recovered economically from the loss of Saint-Domingue, it had indeed surrendered the control of its most valuable colony to a black army and that loss had ended the dream of a French empire on the American mainland. The Haitian Revolution prompted the Louisiana Purchase. One would expect such "facts," none of which is controversial, to generate a chain of mentions, even if negative. Yet a perusal of French historical writings reveals multiple layers of silences. [. . .]

In fact, French historians continue to neglect the colonial question, slavery, resistance, and racism more than the revolutionary assemblies ever did. Most historians ignored or simply skipped whatever record there was. A few took the time for short and often derogatory passages on the Haitian revolutionaries before moving, as it were, to more important subjects.

The list of writers guilty of this silencing includes names attached to various eras, historical schools, and ideological positions, from Mme. de Staël, Alexis de Tocqueville, Adolphe Thiers, Alphonse de Lamartine, Jules Michelet, Albert Mathiez, and André Guérin, to Albert Soboul.[38] [. . .]

The public celebrations and the flood of publications that accompanied the Bicentennial of the French Revolution in 1989–1991 actively renewed the silence. Massive compilations of five hundred to a thousand pages on revolutionary France, published in the 1980s and directed by France's most prominent historians, show near total neglect both for colonial issues and the colonial revolution that forcibly brought them to the French estates. Sala-Molins describes and decries the near total erasure of Haiti, slavery, and colonization by French officials and the general public during ceremonies surrounding the Bicentennial.[39]

As this general silencing goes on, increased specialization within the historical guild leads to a second trend. Saint-Domingue/Haiti emerges at the intersection of various interests: colonial history, Caribbean or Afro-American history, the history of slavery, the history of New World peasantries. In any one of these sub-fields, it has now become impossible to silence the fact that a revolution took place. Indeed, the revolution itself, or even series of facts within it, have become legitimate topics for serious research within any of these subfields.

How interesting then, that many of the rhetorical figures used to interpret the mass of evidence accumulated by modern historians recall tropes honed by planters, politicians, and administrators both before and during the revolutionary struggle. Examples are plentiful, and I will only cite a few. Many analyses of marronage ("desertion" some still would say) come quite close to the biophysiological explanations preferred by plantation managers.[40] I have already sketched the pattern: slave A escaped because she was hungry, slave B because she was mistreated. . . . Similarly, conspiracy theories still provide many historians with a *deus ex machina* for the events of 1791 and beyond, just as in the rhetoric of the assemblymen of the times. The uprising must have been "prompted," "provoked," or "suggested" by some higher being than the slaves themselves: royalists, mulattoes, or other external agents.[41]

The search for external influences on the Haitian Revolution provides a fascinating example of archival power at work, not because such influences are impossible but because of the way the same historians treat contrary evidence that displays the internal dynamics of the revolution. Thus, many historians are more willing to accept the idea that slaves could have been influenced by whites or free mulattoes, with whom we know they had limited contacts, than they are willing to accept the idea that slaves could have convinced other slaves that they had the right to revolt. The existence of extended communication networks among slaves, of which we have only a glimpse, has not been a "serious" subject of historical research.[42]

Similarly, historians otherwise eager to find evidence of "external" participation in the 1791 uprising skip the unmistakable evidence that the rebellious slaves had their own program. In one of their earliest negotiations with representatives of the French government, the leaders of the rebellion did not ask for an abstractly couched "freedom." Rather, their most sweeping demands included three days a week to work on their own gardens and the elimination of the whip. These were not Jacobinist demands adapted to the tropics, nor royalist claims twice creolized. These were slave demands with the strong peasant touch that would characterize independent Haiti. But such evidence of an internal drive, although known to most historians, is not debated—not even to be rejected or interpreted otherwise. It is simply ignored, and this ignorance produces a silence of trivialization.

In that same vein, historian Robert Stein places most of the credit for the 1793 liberation of the slaves on Sonthonax. The commissar was a zealous Jacobin, a revolutionary in his own right, indeed perhaps the only white man to have evoked concretely and with sympathy the possibility of an armed insurrection among Caribbean slaves both *before the fact* and in a public forum.[43] We have no way to estimate the probable course of the Revolution without his invaluable contribution to the cause of freedom. But the point is not empirical. The point is that Stein's rhetoric echoes the very rhetoric first laid out in Sonthonax's trial. Implicit in that rhetoric is the assumption that the French connection is both sufficient and necessary to the Haitian Revolution. That assumption trivializes the slaves' independent sense of their right to freedom and the right to achieve this freedom by force of arms. Other writers tend to stay prudently away from the word "revolution," more often using such words as "insurgents," "rebels," "bands," and "insurrection." Behind this terminological fuzziness, these empirical blanks and these preferences in interpretation is the lingering impossibility, which goes back to the eighteenth century, of considering the former slaves as the main actors in the chain of events described.[44]

Yet since at least the first publication of C. L. R. James's classic, *The Black Jacobins* (but note the title), the demonstration has been well made to the guild that the Haitian Revolution is indeed a "revolution" in its own right by any definition of the word, and not an appendix of Bastille Day. But only with the popular reedition of James's book in 1962 and the civil rights movement in the United States did an international counter-discourse emerge, which fed on the historiography produced in Haiti since the nineteenth century. That counter-discourse was revitalized in the 1980s with the contributions of historians whose specialty was neither Haiti nor the Caribbean. Then, Eugene Genovese and—later—Robin Blackburn, echoing Henry Adams and W. E. B. Du Bois, insisted on the central role of the Haitian Revolution in the collapse of the entire system of slavery.[45] The impact of this counter-discourse remains limited, however, especially since Haitian researchers are increasingly distant from these international debates.

Thus, the historiography of the Haitian Revolution now finds itself marred by two unfortunate tendencies. On the one hand, most of the literature produced in Haiti remains respectful—too respectful, I would say—of the revolutionary leaders who led the masses of former slaves to freedom and independence. Since the early nineteenth century, the Haitian elites have chosen to respond to racist denigration with an epic discourse lauding *their* revolution. The epic of 1791–1804 nurtures among them a positive image of blackness quite useful in a white-dominated world. But the epic is equally useful on the home front. It is one of the rare historical alibis of these elites, an indispensable reference to their claims to power.

The empirical value of this epic tradition has steadily declined after its spectacular launching by such nineteenth-century giants as Thomas Madiou and Beaubrun Ardouin, and in spite of individual achievements of the early twentieth century. Unequal access to archives—products and symbols of neo-colonial domination—and the secondary role of empirical precision in this epic discourse continue to handicap Haitian researchers. They excel at putting facts into perspective, but their facts are weak, sometimes wrong, especially since the Duvalier regime explicitly politicized historical discourse.[46]

On the other hand, the history produced outside of Haiti is increasingly sophisticated and rich empirically. Yet its vocabulary and often its entire discursive framework recall frighteningly those of the eighteenth century. Papers and monographs take the tone of plantation records. Analyses of the revolution recall the letters of a La Barre, the pamphlets of French politicians, the messages of Leclerc to Bonaparte or, at best, the speech of Blangilly. I am quite willing to concede that the conscious political motives are not the same. Indeed again, that is part of my point. Effective silencing does not require a conspiracy, not even a political consensus. Its roots are structural. Beyond a stated—and most often sincere—political generosity, best described in U.S. parlance within a liberal continuum, the narrative structures of Western historiography have not broken with the ontological order of the Renaissance. This exercise of power is much more important than the alleged conservative or liberal adherence of the historians involved.

The solution may be for the two historiographic traditions—that of Haiti and that of the "foreign" specialists—to merge or to generate a new perspective that encompasses the best of each. There are indications of a move in this direction and some recent works suggest that it may become possible, sometime in the future, to write the history of the revolution that was, for long, unthinkable.[47]

But [. . .] neither a single great book nor even a substantial increase in slave resistance studies will fully uncover the silence that surrounds the Haitian Revolution. For the silencing of that revolution has less to do with Haiti or slavery than it has to do with the West.

Here again, what is at stake is the interplay between historicity 1 and historicity 2, between what happened and that which is said to have happened. What happened in Haiti between 1791 and 1804 contradicted much of what happened elsewhere in the world before and since. That fact itself is not surprising: the historical process is always messy, often enough contradictory. But what happened in Haiti also contradicted most of what the West has told both itself and others about itself. The world of the West basks in what François Furet calls the second illusion of truth: what happened is what must have happened. How many of us can think of any non-European population without the background of a global domination that now looks preordained? And how can Haiti, or slavery, or racism be more than distracting footnotes within that narrative order?

The silencing of the Haitian Revolution is only a chapter within a narrative of global domination. It is part of the history of the West and it is likely to persist, even in attenuated form, as long as the history of the West is not retold in ways that bring forward the perspective of the world. Unfortunately, we are not even close to such fundamental rewriting of world history, in spite of a few spectacular achievements.[48] [. . .]

NOTES

1 Quoted by Roger Dorsinville in *Toussaint Louverture; ou, La vocation de la Liberté* (Paris: Julliard, 1965).
2 Cited by Jacques Cauna in *Au temps des isles à sucre* (Paris: Karthala, 1987), 204.
3 Most of these pamphlets, including those cited here, are included in the Lk12 series at the Bibliothèque Nationale, in Paris. Others were reproduced by the French government (e.g., French National Assembly, *Pièces imprimées par ordre de l'Assemblée Nationale, Colonies* (Paris: Imprimerie Nationale, 1791–92).
4 Michel-Rolph Trouillot, "Anthropology and the Savage Slot: The Poetics and Politics of Otherness," in *Recapturing Anthropology: Working in the Present*, ed. Richard G. Fox (Santa Fe: School of American Research Press, 1991), 17–44.
5 *Notre Librairie* (October–December 1987) no. 90, Images du noir dans la littérature occidentale; vol. I: Du Moyen-Age à la conquête coloniale. Simone Delesalle and Lucette Valensi, "Le mot 'nègre' dans les dictionnaires français d'ancien régime: histoire et lexicographie," *Langues françaises*, no. 15.
6 Gordon Lewis, *Main Currents in Caribbean Thoughts, The Historical Evolution of Caribbean Society in its Ideological Aspects, 1492–1900*, chap. 3 (Baltimore: The Johns Hopkins University Press, 1983); William B. Cohen, *The French Encounter with Africans: White Response to Blacks, 1530–1880* (Bloomington: Indiana University Press, 1980); Winthrop D. Jordan, *White over Black: American Attitudes toward the Negro, 1550–1812* (Chapel Hill: University of North Carolina Press, 1968); Serge Daget, "Le mot esclave, nègre et noir et les jugements de valeur sur la traite négrière dans la littérature abolitionniste française de 1770 à 1845," *Revue française d'histoire d'outre-mer* 60, no. 4 (1973): 511–48; Pierre Boulle, "In Defense of Slavery: Eighteenth-Century Opposition to Abolition and the Origins of Racist Ideology in France," in *History from Below: Studies in Popular Protest and Popular Ideology*, ed. Frederick Krantz (London: Basil Blackwell, 1988), 219–246. Louis Sala-Molins, *Misères des Lumières. Sous la raison, l'outrage* (Paris: Robert Laffont, 1992); Michèle Duchet, "Au temps des philosophes," *Notre Librairie* (October–December 1987) no. 90, Images du noir, 25–33.
7 *Archives Parlementaires*, 1st ser. vol. 8 (session of 3 July 1789), 186.
8 Michèle Duchet, *Anthropologie et histoire au siècle des Lumières* (Paris: Maspero, 1971), 157. Emphasis added. On anticolonialism in France, see Yves Benot, *La*

51

Révolution française et la fin des colonies (Paris: La Découverte, 1987); *La Démence coloniale sous Napoléon* (Paris: La Découverte, 1992).

9 David Geggus, "Racial Equality, Slavery, and Colonial Secession during the Constituent Assembly," *American Historical Review* 94, no. 5 (December 1989): 1290–1308; Daget, "Le mot esclave"; Sala-Molins, *Misères*.

10 Raynal, Guillaume-François, *Histoire des deux Indes, 7* vols. (The Hague: Grosse, 1774). Michèle Duchet, *Diderot et l'Histoire des deux Indes ou l'écriture fragmentaire* (Paris: Nizet, 1978); Yves Benot, *Diderot, de l'athéisme à l'anti-colonialisme* (Paris: Maspero, 1970), *La Révolution française*.

11 Duchet, *Diderot et l'Histoire;* Michel Delon, "L'Appel au lecteur dans l'Histoire des deux Indes," in *Lectures de Raynal. L'Histoire des deux Indes en Europe et en Amérique au XVIIe siècle,* (eds.) Hans-Jürgen Lüsebrink and Manfred Tietz (Oxford: Voltaire Foundation, 1991), 53–66; Yves Benot, "Traces de l'*Histoire des deux Indes* chez les anti-esclavagistes sous la Révolution," in *Lectures de Raynal,* 141–154.

12 Louis Sala-Molins, *Le Code noir ou le calvaire de Canaan* (Paris: PUF, Pratiques Théoriques, 1987), 254–261. In Benot's apt phrase, autonomy was "fatally white" whenever it came up in the *Histoire* (Benot, "Traces de l'*Histoire*," 147).

13 Serge Daget, "Le mot esclave, nègre et noir," 519.

14 Yves Benot, *Diderot*, 316. Emphasis added.

15 Pierre Bourdieu, *Le Sens pratique* (Paris: Minuit, 1980), 14. [. . .]

16 There is no term in the vocabulary of the times either in English or in French that would account for the practices—or encapsulate a generalized notion—of resistance. I use resistance here in the rather loose way it appears nowadays in the literature. [. . .]

17 [. . .] Mercier, *L'An 2440*, xxii, in Bonnet, *Diderot*, 331.

18 Whether Louverture himself had read Raynal in 1791 and was convinced of his own future role in history is unproven and beside the point.

19 In Benot, *Diderot*, 214; Duchet, *Anthropologie et histoire*, 175. Emphasis added.

20 "Ces fers dès longtemps préparés . . . pour nous . . . / C'est nous qu'on ose méditer/ De rendre à l'antique esclavage" etc. (*La Marseillaise*).

21 *Archives Parlementaires*, vol. 9 (session of 22 October 1789), 476–478.

22 Lucien Jaume, *Les Déclarations des droits de l'homme, Textes préfacés et annotés* (Paris: Flammarion, 1989).

23 Actually, the two remarkable exceptions I am willing to concede are Jean-Pierre Marat and Félicité Sonthonax.

24 To be sure, there were oral and written texts of which the philosophical import became increasingly explicit as the Revolution advanced, from the speeches reportedly given at the gatherings that preceded the insurrection to the Haitian Constitution of 1805. But these are primarily political texts marking immediate goals or recent victories. Up to the first post-independence writings of Boisrond-Tonnerre, there were no full-time intellectuals to engage in speech acts one step removed from the political battles, as in the French and the American revolutions, the later anticolonial struggles of Latin America, Asia, or Africa, or the revolutions that claimed a Marxist ancestry.

25 [. . .] See Julien Raimond, *Observations sur l'origine et les progrès du préjugé des colons blancs contre les hommes de couleur* . . . (Paris: Belin, 1791); Michel-Rolph Trouillot, "Motion in the System: Coffee, Color and Slavery in Eighteenth-Century Saint-Domingue," *Review* 5, no. 3 (A Journal of the Fernand Braudel Center for the Study of Economies, Historical Systems and Civilizations): 331–388; Michel-Rolph Trouillot, "The Inconvenience of Freedom: Free People of Color and the Political Aftermath of Slavery in Dominica and Saint-Domingue/Haiti," in *The Meaning of Freedom: Economics, Politics and Culture after Slavery*, ed. F. McGlynn and S. Drescher (Pittsburgh: University of

Pittsburgh Press, 1992), 147–182; Geggus, "Racial Equality," 1290–1308. On the rejection of racial prejudice by mulatto leader André Rigaud, see Ernst Trouillot, *Prospections d'Histoire. Choses de Saint-Domingue et d'Haïti* (Port-au-Prince: Imprimerie de l'Etat, 1961), 25–36.

26 *Archives Parlementaires,* vol. 34 (session of 30 October 1791), 521; see also 437–38; 455–58; 470, 522–531.

27 Robin Blackburn, *The Overthrow of Colonial Slavery* (London and New York: Verso, 1988), 133.

28 Cited by Cauna, *Au temps des isles à sucre,* 223. Emphasis added.

29 Blanchelande, *Précis de Blanchelande sur son accusation* (Paris: Imprimerie de N.-H. Nyon, 1793); Anonymous, *Extrait d'une lettre sur les malheurs de SAINT-DOMINGUE en général, et principalement sur l'incendie de la ville du CAP FRANCAIS* (Paris: Au jardin égalité pavillon, 1794); Anonymous, *Conspirations, trahisons et calomnies dévoilées et dénoncées par plus de dix milles français réfugiés au Continent de l'Amérique* (Paris: 1793); [Mme. Lavaux], *Réponse aux calomnies coloniales de Saint-Domingue . . .* (Paris: Imp. de Pain, n.d.); J. Raimond et al., *Preuves complettes [sic] et matérielles du projet des colons pour mener les colonies à l'indépendance, tirées de leurs propres écrits* (Paris: De l'imprimerie de l'Union, n.d. [1792]).

30 *Cobbett's Political Register,* vol. 1 (1802), 286.

31 Benot, *La Démence.*

32 Historically, of course, the respective denials of the Haitian Revolution, of the relevance of slavery, and of the Holocaust have quite different ideological motivations, social acceptance, and political impact.

33 See chap. 2. See also David Nicholls, *From Dessalines to Duvalier: Race, Colour and National Independence in Haiti* (London: Macmillan Caribbean, 1988); and Michel-Rolph Trouillot, *Haiti: State against Nation. The Origins and Legacy of Duvalierism* (New York and London: Monthly Review Press, 1990).

34 The Haitian Revolution sparked the interests of abolitionists in the United States and especially in England, where there were a few calls for support. But even British abolitionists showed much ambivalence toward the Haitian people and their forcibly acquired independence. Blackburn, *The Overthrow of Colonial Slavery,* 252–52; Geggus, "Racial Equality."

35 Trouillot, *Haiti: State against Nation.*

36 One of the rare studies of the Polish legions in Saint-Domingue is Jan Pachonski and Reuel Wilson, *Poland's Caribbean Tragedy. A Study of Polish Legions in the Haitian War of Independence, 1802–1803* (Boulder: East European Monographs, 1986), unfortunately marred by a number of mistakes. Hobsbawm mentions the Haitian Revolution once in the notes, twice in the text: the first time to say, in passing, that Toussaint Louverture was the first independent revolutionary leader of the Americas—as if that was not important; the second time (in parentheses) to note that the French Revolution "inspired" colonial uprisings. See Eric J. Hobsbawm, *The Age of Revolutions, 1789–1848* (New York: New American Library, 1962), 93, 115. [. . .]

37 Blackburn, *The Overthrow of Colonial Slavery,* 251, 263.

38 An increasing number of historians are also exposing the silence. Geggus, "Racial Equality," 1290–1291; Benot, *La Révolution française,* 205–216; Tarrade, "Les colonies et les principes de 1789," 9–34.

39 These collective works include notably, François Furet and Mona Ozouf, *Dictionnaire critique de la Révolution française* (Paris: Flammarion, 1988); Jean Tulard, Jean-François Fayard et Alfred Fierro, *Histoire et dictionnaire de la Révolution (1789–1799)* (Paris: Robert Laffont, 1987); Michel Vovelle, ed., *L'Etat de la France pendant la Révolution* (Paris: La Découverte, 1988). In such arid land, this last compilation has the merit to attribute a few pages to colonial issues,

53

written by U.S. historian Robert Forster and the indefatigable Yves Benot. On the celebrations, see Sala-Molins, *Les Misères des Lumières*.

40 E.g., Yvan Debbasch, "Le Marronage: Essai sur la désertion de l'esclave antillais," *L'Année sociologique* (1961): 1–112; (1962): 117–195.

41 One example among others. David Geggus and Jean Fouchard agree in suggesting that a royalist conspiracy could have provoked the revolt of 1791. But Fouchard notes this possibility in a book that remains one of the epic monuments of Haitian history. Geggus, in turn, concludes that if royalist participation is proved, "the autonomy of the slave insurrection will find itself considerably diminished." Robin Blackburn, who notes this disparity between the two authors, rightly finds Geggus's conclusion "curious" (Blackburn, *The Overthrow of Colonial Slavery*, 210). See Jean Fouchard, *The Haitian Maroons: Liberty or Death* (New York: Blyden Press, 1981; original printing, 1972).

42 See Julius S. Scott III, "The Common Wind: Currents of Afro-American Communications in the Era of the Haitian Revolution" (Ph.D. diss., Duke University, 1986).

43 See Robert Stein, *Léger Félicité Sonthonax: The Lost Sentinel of the Republic* (Rutherford: Fairleigh Dickinson, 1985); Benot, *La Révolution*.

44 Stein, *Léger Félicité Sonthonax*; Cauna, *Au temps des isles*; David Geggus, *Slavery, War and Revolution: The British Occupation of St. Domingue, 1793–1798* (Oxford: Oxford University Press, 1982). The "revolution" in Geggus's title is the *French* revolution. He has since extended his use of the word to include Haitian achievements.

45 Eugene Genovese, *From Rebellion to Revolution* (New York: Vintage, 1981 [1979]). Blackburn, *The Overthrow of Colonial Slavery*.

46 Thomas Madiou, *Histoire d'Haïti*, 7 vols. (Port-au-Prince: Henri Deschamps, 1987–89 [1847–1904]); A. Beaubrun Ardouin, *Études sur l'histoire d'Haïti* (Port-au-Prince: François Dalencourt, 1958). See Catts Pressoir, Ernst Trouillot, and Hénock Trouillot, *Historiographie d'Haïti* (Mexico: Instituto Panamericano de Geografia e Historia, 1953); Michel-Rolph Trouillot, *Ti difé boulé sou istoua Ayiti* (New York: Koléksion Lakansièl, 1977); Michel-Rolph Trouillot, *Haiti: State against Nation*.

47 See Carolyn Fick, *The Making of Haiti: The Saint Domingue Revolution from Below* (Knoxville: University of Tennessee Press, 1990); Claude B. Auguste and Marcel B. Auguste, *L'Expédition Leclerc, 1801–1803* (Port-au-Prince: Imprimerie Henri Deschamps, 1985). Fick remains much too close to the epic rhetoric of the Haitian tradition. Her treatment of resistance is overly ideological and skews her reading of the evidence in the direction of heroism. Nevertheless, her book adds more to the empirical bank on Saint-Domingue than most recent works in the epic tradition. David Geggus's ongoing research remains empirically impeccable. One wishes that it would continue to move further away from the discourse of banalization and would spell out explicitly, one day, some of its hidden assumptions. The work by the Auguste brothers on the French expedition comes closer to finding a tone that treats its material with ideological respect without falling into a celebration or extrapolating from the evidence. It is well grounded into archival research, yet it does not make concessions to the banalizing discourse.

48 Fernand Braudel, *Civilization and Capitalism*, 3 vols. (New York: Harper & Row, 1981–1992); Eric R. Wolf, *Europe and the People without History* (Berkeley: University of California Press, 1982); Marc Ferro, *Histoire des colonisations. Des conquêtes aux indépendances, XIIe-XXe siècles* (Paris: Seuil, 1994).

2

SLAVE RESISTANCE

(Excerpt from *The Making of Haiti: The Saint Domingue Revolution From Below*)

Carolyn E. Fick

Through repression and terror the white masters managed to erect a system of social control to contain and regiment the half million black slaves whose labor created their wealth, but they could not annihilate the slave's human spirit.

Slave resistance to the brutality and human degradation of the system took many forms, not all of them overt, and some of them even self-destructive. Similarly, not all slaves resisted to the same degree or in the same ways, depending upon their place in the ranks of slavery, their treatment as a slave, their cultural background or, simply, their individual level of tolerance and capacity to endure. It was well known, for example, that Ibo slaves were more inclined to suicide, even collectively, as a response to slavery than slaves of other nations. Of the Ibos, Moreau de Saint-Méry wrote that they had to be closely watched, as "feelings of chagrin or the slightest dissatisfaction pushes them to suicide, the idea of which, far from terrifying them, seems rather to offer something alluring because they believe in the transmigration of souls."[1]

Suicide, however, was certainly not limited to the Ibos. One reads time and again throughout the literature how slaves often preferred death to a lifetime of slavery.[2] [. . .]

In response to those who sought to justify the slave trade by claiming that they were saving the blacks from a life of hunger, misery, and mutual destruction in primitive Africa, a white colonist, himself Creole, remarked with astonishment:

> If the blacks were so undernourished and so miserable [in Africa] . . . how is it that they are so well-proportioned, strong and in such vigorous health when they arrive in the colonies? And how is it that at the end of one year here, their health diminishes, they become weak, thin and unrecognizable–a state from which, if they do not die, they never completely recover? . . . Likewise, if

> the blacks were so miserable and without feeling in their native
> land, why are they driven by despair to commit suicide. [. . .][3]

Indeed, the first instance of resistance, and of suicide as resistance, occurred aboard these slave ships, most often while still at port, in the initial stage of what was to become for most a long and tortuous journey toward a life of perpetual bondage in the colonies. For those unable to escape before being boarded as captives, suicide was a fatal affirmation of their refusal to accept the conditions of bondage imposed on them. [. . .][4]

While some captives succeeded in throwing themselves into the sea, often with chains still attached, others would knock their heads against the ship or hold their breath until they suffocated; still others would attempt to starve themselves aboard the ships, hoping to die before the end of the voyage. To force recalcitrant slaves to eat, some ship captains would have the slaves' lips burned by hot charcoal; others would try to make them swallow the coals if they persisted. To set an example, one captain even reportedly went to the extreme of having molten lead poured into the mouths of those who stubbornly refused all food.[5] [. . .]

Once sold and introduced into the plantation system, slaves continued to resist individually and collectively by means of suicide. Death was seen not only as a liberation from the extreme conditions of slavery but, according to popular African beliefs, as a means of escape permitting the dead to return to their native land.[6] However, feelings of despair or, conversely, of outraged dignity and pride were not the only factors provoking suicide. By the beginning of the eighteenth century, contemporary observers became aware of a calculated motive on the part of slaves who committed suicide either individually or collectively to inflict serious economic damage, if not ruin, upon the master. Regarding slave suicides, Père Labat wrote in 1701: "They destroy themselves, they off-handedly slit their throats for trivial reasons, but most often, they do this to cause damage to their masters."[7] [. . .] As a means of resistance, then, suicide was also an offensive measure that could go beyond purely personal considerations and, in the same blow, aim at the economic base of the planter.

Slave women often resorted to abortion and even infanticide as a form of resistance rather than permit their children to grow up under the abomination of slavery. [. . .] One slave woman from the Rossignol-Desdunes plantation in the district of Artibonite admitted having poisoned or killed [. . .] over seventy children in order to spare them the pains of slavery.[8] Although other considerations may have played an additional role in the motivation of such acts–vengeance against a master for cruel treatment, the desire to inflict pain upon a master when the slave child was in fact his own, jealousy, retribution–in all instances, the net result was the near decimation of a potential work force. [. . .]

Equally as characteristic of slave resistance, however, was its opposite, outwardly aggressive or assertive, rather than self-destructive, nature.

One slave captain complained before arriving to unload his captive cargo: "The older ones are uncontrollable; they turn fugitive. Not only are they of little use in the colony, but they are even dangerous."[9] Aboard this particular ship they broke out in revolt. Armed revolts were actually not unusual during the first stages of captivity and, in fact, occurred far more frequently aboard slave ships along the African coast or during the voyage than in the colony itself. [. . .][10]

But if slave revolts were far more recurrent aboard the ships at harbor and during the voyages than in Saint Domingue itself, it may be that, outside of desperate and propitious revolt at the one end, or suicide by diverse means at the other, alternative modes of resistance aboard ship were few and far between. An organized slave society no doubt afforded more varied, and perhaps even more effective, long-term ways and means of resisting or protesting one's conditions than open revolt. Significantly, the revolts and conspiracies to revolt that did occur in Saint Domingue were nearly all situated in a relatively early period of the colony's economic and sociopolitical development, the very first one occurring in 1522 while the island was still under exclusive Spanish rule.[11] Within the twenty-five years between 1679 and 1704, four other armed conspiracies had been planned by slaves in different parts of French Saint Domingue, all aimed at the massacre and annihilation of their white masters.[12] In the end, however, they were localized affairs that the authorities quickly crushed, and so collective armed revolt remained at this time a limited form of slave resistance with minimal chances of success. With the one notable exception of the Makandal conspiracy in 1757, no other organized slave revolt was conceived before the revolution in 1791. [. . .] But then the conspiracy of 1757, as well as the revolt of 1791, which dramatically opened the black revolution, occurred within a context substantially different from that of the earlier revolts. The revolt that was planned by Makandal in the North, and which subsequently was to have spread to "all corners of the colony," was both conceived and organized in marronage. Also, some evidence exists to suggest that marronage may indeed have contributed to the basic groundwork and general form of the massive outbreak of 1791.[13]

Of the many and diverse forms of resistance, marronage proved in the end to be the most viable and certainly the most consistent. From the very beginning of the colony under Spanish rule, throughout its long history under the French, until the abolition of slavery in 1793–94, slaves defied the system that denied them the most essential of social and human rights: the right to be a free person. They claimed that right in marronage. But it was not until 1791 that this form of resistance, having by this time acquired a distinctively collective characteristic, would converge with the volatile political climate of the time and with the opening of a revolution that would eventually guarantee that right. That marronage had become an explosive revolutionary force in 1791 was due as much to the global context of revolutionary events as to the persistent traditions of resistance which, necessarily, remained narrower in scope.

Prior to the revolution, colonial observers who bothered to question the motives of slaves who left the plantation to eke out an existence for themselves in the mountains or in other secluded, inaccessible areas, or on the fringes of plantation society where they risked being recaptured, almost invariably invoked undernourishment, cruel treatment, or overwork as the chief causes; in short, the living and working conditions of slavery. While all of these factors contributed to the slaves' decision to escape, it leaves the question unanswered as to why reputedly humane masters often had as many fugitives as the cruel ones.[14] For the planters to voluntarily accede that fugitive slaves had fled to become free persons, that they had the ability to consciously and materially negate the condition of perpetual bondage imposed upon them by slavery, would be to undermine the ideological foundations of slavery itself. More than that, such an admission would require both a fundamental reevaluation and a consequent rearrangement of the entire economic base of their wealth and power, thus jeopardizing the viability of the slave system to which their own survival was irrevocably tied. No ruling class does this gratuitously. They convinced themselves, rather, that it was merely a recurrent manpower problem, which in part it was.

On the other hand, contemporary literature and administrative correspondence (especially in the two decades preceding the revolution) reveal a tendency, both implicit and explicit, to see in marronage not only the individual will of the slave to be a free person, but a force that, if left unchecked, threatened to destroy the colony. In an extract from the register of the Upper Council of le Cap, one finds this statement, written in 1767: "The slave . . ., inconstant by nature and capable of comparing his present state with that to which he aspires, is incessantly inclined toward marronage. *It is his ability to think*, and not the instinct of domestic animals who flee a cruel master in the hope of bettering their condition, that compels him to flee. That which appears to offer him a happier state, that which facilitates his inconstance, is the path which he will embrace" (italics mine).[15] [. . .] On the one hand, the colonists tried, if not to eliminate, at least to control, marronage through a long series of rigorous punitive laws, even the death penalty. On the other hand, some planters preferred a more humane treatment of their slaves. Regardless of the measures taken, and in spite of them, marronage persisted as a means of resisting slavery.

[. . .]

Marronage was practiced both collectively and individually, in small groups as well as in larger established communities, in organized armed bands or by slaves as free persons with a trade in the urban centers. When slaves left the plantations, they left with no knowledge of what their future would be, nor did they know how long their marronage would last, nor whether they would be recaptured. While some may have fled to escape punishment or cruel treatment and returned in a plea for clemency, others had made a consciously planned and determined break from slavery, from the master and the plantation regime, and were prepared to face the unknown. They carried out their escape with the bare minimum of clothing and food, often taking with them a few tools, a horse, a mule, or a canoe and, not uncommonly, arms of some sort. Rarely, if ever, did the African-born slave live in marronage alone. Many went off to join other slaves already established and subsisting in bands in the heavily wooded mountains, often living in entrenched camps closed off by walls of woven liana and surrounded by ditches of some twelve to fifteen feet deep and eight or ten feet wide, lined at the bottom with sharpened stakes.[16] Others, fortunate enough to find some long-abandoned piece of property in an isolated region, attempted to assure their survival off the land. Once established, some even risked their newly acquired freedom by going back to the plantation at night to secure the escape of their wives or children, left behind under circumstances that rendered impossible the collective flight of the family.[17]

The most frequent refuge for the field slave was in the Spanish part of the island, the colony of Santo Domingo, or in the extensive range of mountains in the South, extending eastward to form the border between the two colonies. Here, since the beginnings of slavery, slaves had formed permanent and collective maroon communities. [. . .] The authorities of Saint Domingue had attempted, since the beginning of the eighteenth century, to reach an accord with the Spanish for the return of the fugitives from the French colony and to join efforts in capturing and dispersing the maroons along the border, all without much success. In 1785, the French authorities finally comprehended the futility of their aims and yielded. A peace treaty was signed granting pardon and according independence to the remaining maroons. Each family would receive a small plot of land and provisions for eight months to assure their subsistence until their farms became productive.[18]

In addition to these long-established and well-known communities, other bands in various parts of the colony, smaller in number and perhaps lesser known, waged similar struggles throughout the colonial era in defense of their precariously acquired freedom. Establishing themselves in the forests or in the thickly wooded foothills of the mountains, they maintained a marginal but independent existence. They, too, had their chosen leaders whose decisions governed the organization and functioning of the group. When conditions no longer permitted them to subsist off the land, it became necessary for them to descend at night upon neighboring plantations in organized raids, pillaging, ransacking, sometimes even devastating the plantation to secure food, animals, additional arms, or other necessary supplies for their survival. These marauding maroon bands often created such terror as to cause certain planters in relatively isolated areas to sell out or simply to abandon their holdings.

[. . .]

It was precisely the aggressive and intrepid aspects of marronage that necessitated, from the beginning of slavery, the adoption of repressive and punitive measures to eliminate what many contemporaries came to consider a continual plague and a danger to the security of the colony.[19] The first comprehensive legislation dealing with marronage appeared in the Black Code of 1685. Slaves of different plantations were now forbidden to assemble together, be it in celebration of a marriage, to organize a calenda, or for any reason whatsoever, under punishment of the whip or the burning brand of the *fleur de lys*. For those who persisted, it could mean death.[20] [. . .] Planters were now permitted to shoot on sight any slave they believed to be a fugitive, a provision that incidentally caused innocent slaves mistaken for fugitives to be recklessly killed.[21]

In 1741, following a maroon attack on the town of Mirebalais, additional punishments for marronage were imposed. Captured fugitives were put in public chain gangs for a specified period of time, sometimes for life. Two years later, the punishment for maroons caught with arms of any kind was death.[22] In spite of these restrictions, as well as subsequent ordinances of similar consequence, marronage remained a well-entrenched mode of resistance to slavery. In fact, official estimates in 1751 had brought the number of French slaves living in marronage in the Spanish colony alone to nearly three thousand.[23] [. . .]

But this type of collective marronage, of fugitive slaves living in small groups, forming armed bands or even large, organized communities, constituted only one of its aspects. It predominantly involved the African-born, non-creole field slaves and certainly characterized its more openly aggressive form. The domestic slave, on the other hand, profited from the numerous avenues of escape available to those slaves whose particular position in the plantation system afforded them greater mobility and freedom of movement than that of the field slave.

Many took advantage of the situation when sent by the master on a daytime errand, and never came back. Others, having learned to read and write, fabricated their own passes indicating that they were on an errand for the master. The practice had become so common that it was nearly impossible for the authorities to distinguish, at the marketplace, in the streets, at the crossroads, between the free blacks and those who, using passes to escape from the plantation, gave themselves out to be free. [. . .] To escape detection, some slaves would carefully change names; most were dressed in their best clothing to project the outward appearance of a free black. Some even pushed their audacity to the extreme and attached a pair of stolen pistols in fine holsters onto the saddle of a stolen horse as a surer guarantee that they would be recognized as a free black, especially since slaves were forbidden to own or ride a horse.[24] They fabricated false documents of enfranchisement, baptismal certificates, or any other type of attestation to legitimize their assumed status.[25] Others, having stolen a horse or mule upon leaving the plantation, would travel considerable distances to reach an isolated town or bourg where they were unknown, sell the animals, and establish themselves in the community as free. [. . .]

Engendered by the social and economic relations of slavery itself, marronage had become an irreversible feature of Saint Domingue slave society. [. . .]

As a constant reality, then, the impact of marronage upon the slaves could be felt in a number of ways. First, the mere existence of fugitive slaves in a plantation slavery society offered an alternative, although a treacherous one, to accommodation and perpetual submission. It meant that avenues of escape did exist–perhaps they were no less perilous than life under slavery, in any case–and whether or not the individual slave decided to resort to them was as much a matter of choice as the force of circumstance. Marronage offered no guarantees, but its continued exist-ence in colonial society was testimony that slavery was not an irrevocably closed system. Second, a contingent relationship necessarily developed between the fugitives and their plantation counterparts, who often shel-tered them, gave them food, helped them steal for provisions, and, aware of the goings-on in the master's house, could advise and warn them.[26] Reciprocally, the impact of armed maroons who audaciously raided nearby plantations and occasionally even attacked white colonists, forcing them to organize night vigils, could be highly disruptive of the plantation slaves.[27] Although it was strictly forbidden for slaves to carry arms of any sort, exception was made by the colonial administrators for the slave *commandeurs*, "in order to defend the slaves' quarters and keep guard of their animals and crops against the outrages of the maroons."[28]

If a certain complicity, tacit or otherwise, existed between the fugitive and the plantation slaves, it also existed between the fugitive and the free blacks. A royal ordinance of 1705 revealed that the punishments estab-lished in the Black Code of 1685 "against free blacks who facilitate the means by which slaves may become maroons or commit acts of theft did not stop them from sheltering such maroons in their homes, from concealing their thefts and sharing the booty with them." Consequently, any free black who committed one of these acts "would lose his freedom and be sold into slavery along with his immediate residing family." [. . .][29] And so, here again, one finds evidence of reciprocal relations between two sectors of the black population, the one not so far removed from slavery itself. Through repressive and discriminatory legislation, the free coloreds were to serve as a buffer to protect white supremacy and buttress the slave system, but their mere presence as free persons in colonial slave society could also facilitate avenues of marronage and flight for slaves. Conversely, however, the repercussions of this contact with fugitive slaves could dras-tically influence both the status and social conditions of the free blacks, who themselves risked becoming slaves.[30]

In this vein, one ought perhaps to be cautious of succumbing to the tendency to classify the maroons as a type of separate entity that existed entirely outside of the system. [. . .] The maroons, one ought to remember, were still slaves and, when caught, were subject to the laws and practices governing slavery. Though they existed on the fringes of the plantations, they were nonetheless an integral element of slave society generally. Thus to see them simply as a distinct or separate group might be to suppose that fugitive slaves, once punished, were never reintegrated into the plantation amongst the others, or that they never repeated their acts of defiance to turn fugitive again, or that the hard-working and apparently accommodating plantation slave who stayed on to bide his time never turned fugitive himself. Significant relations did exist between maroons and other elements of the larger society, and it is perhaps from this dynamic that the practical consequences of marronage and, ultimately, its potential for popular revolutionary organization and activity in Saint Domingue might best be understood.

Similarly, reciprocal relations existed between marronage as a mode of slave resistance, in itself, and other forms of resistance for which marronage provided conditions that allowed these to pervade. Among them was Vodou. As one of the first collective forms of resistance, it was both a cultural and, in its practical applications, a politically ideological force. Since it was severely outlawed in the colony and therefore forced into clandestinity,[31] its development and proliferation were reinforced in the general context of marronage. The maroon leaders of African origin were almost without exception either Vodou priests or, at least, Vodou devotees.[32] And, of course, the case has generally been made for the perpetuation, or at least reconstitution within a New World context, of African ways in marronage.

Characteristically, it was in the Vodou ceremonies that African traditions: language, dance, religion, world view, and medicine were all evident. Indeed, the words of the sacramental Vodou hymns were almost all, if not exclusively, of African origin.[33] In a sense, then, the various African languages constituted in themselves a form of cultural protest against the colonial order, as well (as we have seen) as a means of reinforcing a self-consciousness and a cultural identity independent of the white masters. Vodou as generally practiced in Saint Domingue (and especially its linguistic diversity) constituted, in effect, a broad synthesis of the various religious beliefs and practices of all the African nations forming the slave population.[34] One of the most famous Vodou hymns, chanted in unison for the initiation of a neophyte, according to Moreau de Saint-Méry, is the following:

Eh! eh! Bomba, hen! hen!
Canga bafio té
Canga moune dé lé
Canga do ki la
Canga li[35]

It is of Congolese origin; more specifically it is in the Kikongo language and might be translated this way:

Eh! eh! Mbumba [rainbow spirit = serpent]
Tie up the BaFioti [a coastal African slave-trading people]
Tie up the whites [i.e., Europeans]
Tie up the witches
Tie them.[36]

The significance not only of the words but of the levels of meaning is to be found both within the African society and culture of the Kongo, or Bakongo, and the New World setting of Saint Domingue. For if, as Moreau de Saint-Méry observed, the incantation was used for the initiation of a neophyte, then it may pertinently involve the creation of a *nkisi* charm, whereby one symbolically "ties up," or gathers together, the enumerated powers by tying a string around the combined elements. Mbumba may be Mbumba Luangu, the rainbow serpent invoked in adoration in the coastal Kongo initiation society, Khimba.[37] Bafioti, meaning "the coastal people," more than likely referred to the coastal Fioti, who were slave traders that hunted down and captured people of the Kongo interior to trade them as slaves to the Europeans, or the white man, the Mundele. The Fioti were thus feared and believed capable of using their powers, not the least of which was witchcraft.[38] And so, the tying up of the *ndoki*, or witches, may refer as much to these slave traders, the Fioti, as to any other person believed to be an evil spirit causing hardship, taking other people's goods, making animals disappear, making the earth sterile, killing in mysterious ways, or, more pertinently, being responsible for the slaves' bondage.[39]

By the eve of the 1791 slave revolt in the North, in a changing context of war and armed slave rebellion, it may perhaps not be too presumptive to infer an even more literal connotation to the "tying up" of the white man, as in the physical act of capturing and tying up the enemy, and thereby conquering those powers. But in the context of slavery, the chant was generally used to initiate a newcomer into the rite of Saint Dominguean Vodou, and in this sense it was most certainly an invocation of protection from the dreaded powers ranged against the slaves. Here, then, we find a culturally specific Congolese ritual contained within an overall religious structure with rules, procedures, hierarchy, and general principles that Moreau himself distinctly described as Dahomean, or more generally, Arada.[40] [. . .]

By the eve of the revolution the Congolese were certainly among the most numerous of the ethnic groupings composing the African-born slave population, and although reputedly well-adjusted to slavery, they constituted the predominant nation among the maroons.[41] Their preponderance by the end of the colonial period also helps explain the considerable cultural input of this grouping into a religion embraced and informed by the ethnically diverse African slave masses.[42] It was precisely this plural-istic nature of Saint Dominguean Vodou and its disinclination to separate into ethnic cults, as was the case in Brazil, for example, that allowed it to function as a far-reaching collective force. Not surprisingly, it was from the Vodou tradition that the African-born maroon leaders generally emerged. Almost exclusively, if not Vodou priests, they were at least fervent Vodou devotees of one rite or another, whether rada, congo, or petro.[43] And so, a popular religion on the one hand, Vodou constituted, on the other, an important organizational tool for resistance. It facilitated secret meetings, as well as the initiation and the adherence of slaves of diverse origins, provided a network of communication between slaves of different plantations who gathered clandestinely to participate in the cere-monies, and secured the pledge of solidarity and secrecy of those involved in plots against the masters. [. . .]

By far the most extraordinary and awesome of these prerevolutionary "Vodou" maroon leaders was François Makandal. According to a contem-porary source, he was born in "Guinea" into an illustrious family that undertook his education at a very early age.[44] [. . .] At the age of twelve he was captured as a prisoner of war, sold as a common slave to the European traders, and shipped to Saint Domingue. [. . .] According to one version, Makandal turned fugitive after his hand was amputated, having caught it in the machinery of the sugar mill while working the night shift.[45] Another, however, attributes his marronage to the consequences of a dispute between himself and his master over a young and beautiful Negress. Apparently, Makandal's master had, out of vengeance, ordered him to receive fifty lashes of the whip, whereupon Makandal refused this humili-ation and precipitously took to the woods.[46] Here he began his long and notorious career, one that spanned nearly eighteen years, as a prerevolu-tionary maroon leader.

Operating from his mountain retreat during these years, he carefully built an extensive network of resistance with agents, as one account goes, in nearly all points of the colony.[47] [. . .] His ultimate weapon was poison. Having acquired considerable knowledge of herb medicine, a talent that his master recognized very early, he instructed his followers in its uses and developed, according to the above account, an "open school of this execrable art."[48] [. . .]

His qualities of leadership, his sense of organization, his stature as a religious cult leader, his eloquence as an orator, not only rivaled that of the European orators of the day, but surpassed it in strength and vigor, affording him an immeasurable influence and command over the slaves in his following.[49] [. . .]

In this vein, the observations of de Vaissière appear singularly lucid: "Makandal was more than simply a leader of maroon bands. Not that he disdained the pillaging and ransacking of plantations, or the theft of cattle and other ordinary exploits of fugitive slaves; but he seemed at the same time to have sensed the possibility of creating out of marronage a center of organized black resistance against the whites."[50] More than that, he had a solid understanding of the racial origins and development of Saint Domingue, as well as their broader implications. To illustrate this before a large gathering of slaves, he had a vase full of water brought to him, in which he placed three scarves–one yellow, one white, and one black. Pulling out the yellow scarf first, he told his listeners: "This represents the original inhabitants of Saint Domingue. They were yellow." "These," he said, pulling out the white scarf, "are the present inhabitants. Here, finally, are those who will remain masters of the island; it is the black scarf."[51]

For the first few years, he remained completely unknown to the white masters (except his own who, after a number of years, most likely gave him up for dead) and, with extraordinary audacity, went from plantation to plantation to proselytize and stir up the zeal of his partisans, often under cover of the anonymity afforded by calendas and other nocturnal slave gatherings or festivities. During the next twelve years of marronage, he and his followers pursued their ultimate plan with a constancy and ingenuity, as one report goes, that "one would almost be tempted to admire."[52] Finally, the day and the hour were set when the water of all the houses in le Cap was to be poisoned. Within the core of his band he had disciplined agents–captains, lieutenants, and various other officers– operating and organizing on the plantations. He knew the names of every slave on each plantation who supported and participated in his movement. He had an exact list of those slaves who, once the poison had struck panic throughout the town, were to organize in contingents from le Cap and spread out into the countryside to massacre the whites.[53]

The aim was to overthrow the white regime, whereby the blacks would become the new masters of Saint Domingue. It was the first real attempt in the long history of slave resistance at disciplined, organized revolt aiming not only at the destruction of the white masters and of slavery, but at the political notion of independence, albeit historically premature and rhetorically expressed in messianic overtones. The final goals of the conspiracy were not achieved, and unfortunately we have no way of knowing what the outcome might have been. It was, ironically, an inopportune and unfortunate carelessness on the part of Makandal that led to his capture.[54] He managed to maneuver a spectacular but short-lived escape and was promptly recaptured when dogs were finally sent upon his trail. He was summarily tried and burned at the stake.

But for many blacks, Makandal was still alive and would return some day to fulfill his prophecies.[55] For others, his memory was sufficient to nourish the long and bitter struggle that would one day lead to their emancipation. As a legendary figure, his name became identified with almost all forms of fetishism, with poisoning, sorcery, and slave dances. Thereafter, the *houngan*, or Vodou priests, were often referred to as "makandals"; to possess certain powers or simply to practice Vodou was to be a "makandal."[56] [. . .]

Who were the slaves who followed Makandal, who joined him in marronage, who poisoned their masters and members of their family, who poisoned other slaves that could not be trusted? [. . .]

Among those arrested for crimes relating to poison was Assam, a young slave woman belonging to the planter M. Vallet of la Souffrière, and Pompée, a free black and farmer on the plantation of Sieur Deseuttres [des Gentres?], who served as intermediary. The official interrogation of Assam, dated 27 September 1757, offers certain insights into the attitudes and motives, as well as the methods used by slaves in their covert undertakings.[57] Upon reading and evaluating the interrogation, it seems clearly evident, in spite of her protests to the contrary, that Assam knew full well it was a death-inducing potion she administered to two slaves of the plantation who had fallen ill and finally died shortly after her treatments. [. . .]

In addition to the countless fatalities resulting from the use of poison as a weapon of slave resistance, this practice contributed greatly toward maintaining the master class in a state of fear from which there appeared to be little effective recourse. Through the uses and abuses of poison, the slaves themselves placed the masters in a position of uncertainty and dependence, for, in the final count, their economic survival, as well as their own life or death, were matters that could equally be determined by those they oppressed. [. . .]

Makandal's final plan was a premature attempt at revolution. The component elements comprising its general framework were those found within the material and historical parameters of mid-eighteenth-century slave society in Saint Domingue: poison, Vodou, marronage.[58] It was nevertheless a forecast of what would come in full force some thirty years later. It signaled what had become an incipient movement among the masses, at this stage fragmentary and incohesive and not yet conscious of its revolutionary potential, but one that tended toward the eventual destruction of slavery and one whose avowed goal, despite the messianic overtones and African outlook of its leaders, was nonetheless the independence and mastery of Saint Domingue.

[. . .]

In the end, the Makandal affair was not simply an isolated episode in the history of slave resistance. On the one hand, 1758 marked the climax of slave resistance by means of poison, facilitated by marronage (especially of the chief leaders) and reinforced by the powerful influences of colonial Vodou. But the use of poison as a weapon against slavery hardly began, nor did it end, here. Throughout the eighteenth century, planters were periodically plagued by the ravages of poison on their plantations, and if they believed they had rid themselves of the problem with the wave of executions and repressive legislation after Makandal's death, they proved singularly shortsighted.[59]

[. . .]

Slave resistance had spanned several centuries and was expressed or carried out by the slaves in many ways. Partial revolts, conspiracies, plots to kill the master, suicide, infanticide, Vodou, poisonings, marronage with its long and diverse history, all bore witness to the slaves' human spirit and capacity to assert an independent will. If undercurrents of a consciousness harboring the eventual destruction of slavery and the master class had become evident in the half-decade or so before the revolution, it was not until 1791 that this consciousness became substantively collective, when, beginning in the North, entire plantations of slaves deserted in rapid succession to join what had become a massive revolutionary army. And what was unique about this slave revolt, in addition to its highly disciplined and broadly based organization, was the widespread (and alarming) extent of popular participation and support. Although somewhat fragmentary, there is even evidence to suggest that, in fact, a few of the early leaders of the revolt, notably Boukman and Jean-François, had an acquired experience of popular marronage.[60]

For nearly three years, between 1789 and 1791, the slaves of Saint Domingue witnessed the revolts of the propertied classes. The white colonists began by claiming their rights and demanding the abolition of the economic and commercial restrictions laid upon them by the Ancien Régime. They were followed by the *affranchis*, who demanded an equal footing with the whites. New forces had burst open in the colony. Talk of "liberty, equality, and fraternity" fell upon the receptive ears of domestic slaves, who interpreted these slogans in their own way as they perfunctorily served their white masters. One colonist writes in 1789: "What preoccupies us the most at this time are the menaces of a revolt. . . . Our slaves have already held assemblies in one part of the colony with threats of wanting to destroy all the whites and to become masters of the colony."[61] Another lucidly observes: "Everyone has made a habit of arming himself and of grouping together to patrol the roads and the large savannas. These precautions seem to make an impression on the slaves, but the work is going badly, and it is easy to perceive that something is being conspired and will break out in mutiny on one plantation: This will be the signal for all the others."[62]

It was the French Revolution that provided the opportunity for that revolt.

NOTES

1 M. L. E. Moreau de Saint-Méry, *Description . . . de la partie françoise de l'isle Saint-Domingue*, 3 vols. (1797, repr., Paris, 1959), 1:51. [. . .]

2 M.-R. Hilliard d'Auberteuil, *Considérations sur l'état présent de la colonie française de Saint-Domingue*, 2 vols. (Paris, 1776–1777), 1:141 ; Jean Mettas, *Répertoire des expéditions négrières françaises au XVIIIe siècle*, 2 vols., ed. Serge Daget (Paris, 1978, 1984), 2:752.

3 Milscent, *Du régime colonial* (Paris, 1792), 26–27, 39. The above-cited passage was kindly forwarded to the author by J. Fouchard in personal correspondence.

4 See Robert L. Stein, *The French Slave Trade in the 18th Century: An Old Regime Business* (Madison, 1979), 94.

5 M. Frossard, *La cause des esclaves nègres*, 2 vols. (Lyon, 1789), 1:263. For a description of conditions aboard the slave ship, see ibid., 261–306. See also Lucien Peytraud, *L'esclavage aux Antilles françaises avant 1789* (Paris, 1897), 95–121, as well as Gaston-Martin, *Histoire de l'esclavage dans les colonies françaises* (Paris, 1948), 50–80, and, recently, the exhaustive work of Jean Mettas on the eighteenth-century French slave trade, cited in Fick, *The Making of Haiti*, ch. 1, n 59. Additionally, Stein's *French Slave Trade* provides a description of daily life aboard the ships (101–3). [. . .]

6 Albert Savine, *Saint-Domingue à la veille de la révolution* (Paris, 1911), 94.

7 Cited in Pierre de Vaissière, *Saint-Domingue: La société et la vie créoles sous l'Ancien Régime 1629 – 1789* (Paris, 1909), 230.

8 M. E. Descourtiltz, *Histoire des désastres de Saint-Domingue* (Paris, 1795), 185. [. . .]

9 In Mettas, *Répertoire*, 2:223.

10 Stein, *French Slave Trade*, 103. In this vein, the actual number of slave revolts (like the actual frequency of other types of resistance) reported by ship captains in Mettas's *Répertoire* may well be far below reality. [. . .]

11 A narrative account of this revolt is cited in Jean Fouchard, *Les marrons de la liberté* (Paris, 1972), 467–69. In his book, Fouchard has provided an exhaustive chronological synopsis of slave resistance in Saint Domingue from 1499 to 1793 (445–557) based on primary, as well as secondary, source materials, passages from which are often quoted in full.

12 Presumably these would be considered "restorationist" movements in purely Genovesean terms since they were pre-eighteenth/nineteenth-century. [. . .] But the fact that they did not succeed in destroying slavery and white slave society has more to do with the historical and material limitations of the period–as opposed to conditions in 1791–than with some intrinsically "restorationist" outlook.

13 See n. 60 below and the discussion of marronage in the context of the August 1791 revolt in Ch. 4 of Fick, *Making of Haiti*. Also, on the relationship of marronage to the revolutionary participation of the slaves in the West province, see Ch. 3 in Fick, *Making of Haiti*.

14 See G. Debien, *Les esclaves aux Antilles françaises* (Basse-Terre, 1974), 465.

15 AN, Arch. Col., C9^A 131.

16 De Vaissière, *La société*, 234–35.

17 Fouchard, *Marrons de la liberté*, 390.

18 AN, Arch. Col., C9^B 35. See Fick, *Making of Haiti*, 289n47.

19 In fact, the first official report dealing with the problem of marronage among black slaves as a threat to the colony appeared in 1503, under the Spanish governor, Ovando, merely a decade after the arrival of Columbus. Fouchard, *Marrons de la liberté*, 464.

20 Moreau de Saint-Méry, *Loix et constitutions des colonies françaises de l'Amérique sous le vent*, 6 vols. (Paris, 1784), 2:36–37; 3:159–60.

21 Ibid., 2:27; 6:253, 528, 718.

22 Ibid., 3:728–29.

23 R. P. A. Cabon, *Histoire d'Haïti*, 4 vols. (Port-au-Prince, 1920–1940), 1:206. Although it is impossible to ascertain the exact number of maroons in Saint Domingue at any given time, figures running into the thousands [. . .] do not

seem entirely unrealistic. See, however, the brief discussion of the problem in D. Geggus, "Slave Resistance Studies and the Saint Domingue Revolt: Some Preliminary Considerations," Occasional Papers Series, no. 4 (Miami: Latin American and Caribbean Center, Florida International University, 1983), 6–7.

24 AN, Arch. Col., C9^B 15. Diverse decrees forbidding slaves to be in possession of a horse date back to the 1690s, shortly after the armed revolt at Port-de-Paix in 1691, and recur throughout the eighteenth century. Moreau de Saint-Méry, *Loix et constitutions*, 1:622–23; 2:11, 660–61.

25 The practice had evidently become significantly widespread for colonial authorities to pass an ordinance forbidding the inscription of the title *"libre"* [free] on the baptismal certificates of children of the *affranchis* without due proof of the mother's freedom. Ibid., 5:802–3; 807–8.

26 Moreau de Saint-Méry, *Loix et constitutions*, 2:25.

27 Ibid., 2:209–10.

28 Ibid., 2:568–69.

29 Ibid., 2:36–37.

30 While the 1705 ordinance designates the free blacks specifically in this respect, both the initial 1685 Code and a subsequent decree of 1726 use the term *affranchis*, presumably implying a potential loss of liberty to enfranchised mulattoes, as well. Ibid., 1:421; 3:159.

31 In fact, an ordinance of 1758 ordered slaves to be punished by whipping, and masters by a fine of three hundred livres, the former for having participated in, and the latter for having tolerated this slave dance. H. Trouillot, *Introduction à une histoire du Vaudou* (Port-au-Prince, 1970), 84. Needless to say, these laws were to no avail.

32 Ibid., 42, 48. See also by the same author "La guerre de l'indépendance d'Haïti: les grands prêtres du Vodou contre l'armée française," *Sobretiro de Revista de América* 72 (julio-dic., 1971): 261–327. Along these lines, see the recent work by Pierre Pluchon, *Vaudou, sorciers, empoisonneurs: de Saint-Domingue à Haïti* (Paris, 1987), where the author explores the diverse relationships between certain maroon leaders (notably Makandal), Vodou, and sorcery, generally, within the context of slave poisonings in eighteenth-century Saint Domingue society.

33 Trouillot, *Introduction*, 10–17. See esp. Fouchard, *Marrons de la liberté*, 188–89.

34 Ibid., 189.

35 Cited in Moreau de Saint-Méry, *Description*, 1:67; also cited in Mgr. J. Cuvelier, *L'ancien royaume de Congo* (Brussels, 1946), 290. [. . .] The sometimes-cited translation (from Drouin de Bercy in the French) of "We swear to destroy the whites and all that they possess; let us die rather than fail to keep this vow," is highly inconsistent, literally speaking, with the original African words, and thus quite inaccurate. On this point, see Pluchon, *Vaudou*, 112, 114.

36 The author is most deeply grateful to anthropologist John M. Janzen for this translation (personal correspondence). Professor Janzen's knowledge of Kikongo was acquired over the many years he spent studying Congo coastal societies. It is the language used in the region where, from the beginning of the slave trade that caused such major disruptions in coastal African society, there developed an important, socially therapeutic and integrative "cult of healing, trade and marriage relations," known as Lemba, which sought to "calm" or mediate the tensions and conflicts brought about in this region by three centuries of slave trading. Janzen has studied, in great depth and with much perspicacity, the development and role of this cult (in its bio-social, political, economic, cultural, and humanistic dimensions) in response to these disruptive forces in his challenging and fascinating book, *Lemba, 1650–1930: A Drum of Affliction in Africa and the New World*. There are also many similarities between Lemba and

the Haitian petro rites to which Janzen has devoted an entire chapter. See Fick, *Making of Haiti*, Ch. 1, n129.

37 Janzen, Personal Correspondence. Also, *Lemba*, 53. On the significance of "tying up" the elements composing a talisman, see also Fick, *Making of Haiti*, 292n88.

38 Janzen, Personal Correspondence. The present writer assumes responsibility, however, for any linguistic oversights or interpretive errors in judgment in attempting to explain the cultural significance and potentially "revolutionary" implications of this invocation in colonial Saint Domingue slave society. (While the word *mundele*, or "whiteman," is indeed derived from *mu + nlele*, or "person of cloth" [Janzen, personal correspondence], it should not be assumed [cf. Geggus, "Slave Resistance Studies," 16] that the colonial priests or the churches should have been objects of the slaves' vengeance at the outbreak of the revolt in 1791. The very first "whitemen" to come into contact with the African coastal peoples of the Kongo, it should be remembered, were Portuguese missionaries–Europeans, whites, and outsiders–and it was the "whiteman," the *mundele*, who transported them into bondage in the New World. In the context of the "Eh! Mbumba!" chant, *mundele* clearly refers to the white European masters, be they planters or traders.)

39 See the definition of *ndoki* as "sorcerer" or *kindoki* as "witchcraft" in Cuvelier, *Ancien royaume de Congo*, 88–89.

40 See Fick, *Making of Haiti*, Ch. 1, n133. Also, Moreau de Saint-Méry, *Description*, 1:64, 68. On the significance and predominance of "Guinée," as opposed to other rites in Haitian Vodou today, see S. Larose, "The Meaning of Africa in Haitian Vodu," in I. M. Lewiss, ed., *Symbols and Sentiments* (London, 1977), 85–116. Also, A. Métraux, *Voodoo in Haiti* (London, 1960), 29.

41 See especially Fouchard, *Marrons de la liberté*, 187; G. Debien, J. Houdaille, R. Massio, and R. Richard, "Les origines des esclaves des Antilles," *Bull. de l'IFAN* 29 (3–4):549–58; Debien, *Esclaves aux Antilles*, 466–67; Moreau de Saint-Méry, *Description*, 1:53.

42 Fouchard, *Marrons de la liberté*, 187.

43 See n. 32.

44 M. de C, "Makandal, histoire véritable: extrait du *Mercure de France* 15 septembre 1787," RSHHGG 20 (janv. 1949): 21–22. Also T. Madiou, *Histoire d'Haïti*, 2nd ed. (Port-au-Prince, 1922), 1:35; Trouillot, *Introduction*, 46.

45 Cited in Fouchard, *Marrons de la liberté*, 492.

46 M. de C, "Histoire véritable," 22–23.

47 AN, Arch. Col., C9^B 29. Extrait d'un mémoire sur la création d'un corps de gens de couleur levé à Saint-Domingue, mars 1779.

48 Ibid.

49 AN, Arch. Col. C9^B 29. Extrait d'un mémoire. ISL, Relation d'une conspiration trainée par les nègres dans l'isle de Saint-Domingue, n.d. [1758?]. Moreau de Saint-Méry, *Description*, 2:629–31. Also, AN, Arch. Col. F^3 136. Moreau de Saint-Méry, "Notes historiques," 198, cited in Fouchard, *Marrons de la liberté*, 495–97. M. de C, "Histoire véritable."

50 De Vaissière, *La société*, 237.

51 AN, Arch. Col., F^3 136. Moreau de Saint-Méry, "Notes historiques," 198, cited in de Vaissière, *La société*, 237, and in Fouchard, *Marrons de la liberté*, 495.

52 AN, Arch. Col. C9^B 29. Extrait d'un mémoire.

53 Ibid.

54 He was denounced by a slave (or by several slaves) while attending a calenda on the Dufresne plantation in Limbé. While Madiou claims he was discovered by means of a trap set by some slaves whose women Makandal had stolen (1:36; also, M. de C, "Histoire véritable," 27–28), Moreau de Saint-Méry simply

states that "a young male slave, perhaps taken by the impression of this colossal presence," warned the surveyor and the owner's father-in-law, M. Trévan, who thereupon gave out plenty of tafia to everyone and then captured Makandal (2:630). A third version, in a letter dated June 1758 (ISL, Relation), claims that it was a female slave [. . .] who "provided the means by which to capture Makandal who was their leader."

55 Having convinced his followers that he was immortal, Makandal had once declared that if ever the whites captured him, it would be impossible for them to kill him, for upon breathing his final breath, he would escape in the form of a mosquito, only to return one day more terrifying than ever. AN, Arch, Col., $C9^B$ 29. Extrait d'un mémoire.

56 Trouillot, *Introduction*, 45. [. . .]

57 Translated and edited by author in Appendix A of Fick, *Making of Haiti*.

58 In reference to these slaves, C. L. R. James wrote in 1938: "An uninstructed mass feeling its way to revolution usually begins by terrorism, and Mackandal aimed at delivering his people by means of poison." *The Black Jacobins; Toussaint L'Ouverture and the San Domingo Revolution*, 3rd ed. (London, 1980), 21.

59 See de Vaissière, *La société*, 238–39.

60 Geggus, "Slave Resistance Studies," 10. See also Fouchard, *Marrons de la liberté*, 526–27. Where Geggus agrees that "a connection can be established between the revolutionary leadership and an experience of marronage," especially in reference to Boukman and Jean-François, he nevertheless expresses doubt that marronage was directly related to the outbreak of the 1791 revolt by asserting that the two leaders were not associated with already established, separately constituted bands: "It very much seems that [the revolution] was organized from within the system and not from outside it" (10). Although these are only preliminary considerations, one does find here again the fixed notion that the only maroons worthy of the definition were those who formed independent bands. It seems rather an oversimplification to assume that fugitive slaves (and Geggus offers some evidence that Boukman and Jean-François were apparently often fugitive) were not true maroons simply because they did not belong to a maroon band; or that maroons did not return to the plantations and become slaves again (were they ever anything else?); or that on subsequent occasions they would not once again take flight. These short periods of marronage (possibly for motives manifestly different from those which habitually characterized *petit* marronage in the colonial period) may in the long run have proved more effective an organizational tool for preparing a revolt than the existence of external autonomous bands. The evidence permitting, it seems equally plausible that the 1791 revolt was organized *both* from within *and* from outside the system. In fact, Makandal, who nevertheless *was* an independent maroon with a band of followers, always worked in close connection with slaves inside the plantation system, many of whom were often occasional maroons. This was his mainstay as well as his distinguishing feature as a maroon leader (see Fick, *Making of Haiti*, 292n81, and especially the testimony of the slave Haurou, a distributor of poison, and the association that Pluchon himself derives from the evidence between poisoning and occasional marronage [*Vaudou*, 191, 193]; also Fick, *Making of Haiti*, Appendix A, n11).

61 Cited in Fouchard, *Marrons de la liberté*, 524.

62 In M. Begouën-Demeaux, *Mémorial d'une famille du Havre: 1743–1831*, 4 vols. (Le Havre, 1957), 2:137.

3

SAINT-DOMINGUE ON THE EVE OF THE HAITIAN REVOLUTION

David P. Geggus

The Haitian Revolution is an event of global significance partly because of where it took place. Eighteenth-century Saint-Domingue represented the apogee of the European colonizing process begun three centuries earlier. In the late 1780s, it was the world's major exporter of sugar, coffee, and, till shortly before, of indigo as well. These were not the cheap bulk commodities they later became but were valuable staples, the lifeblood of Atlantic commerce. Saint-Domingue's exports were worth far more than the gold of Brazil or the silver of Mexico, and they kept an entire navy in business.[1] The colony's enslaved population was then almost as large as that of the United States south of the Potomac. It had become the single main destination of the Atlantic slave trade. When the French Revolution broke out, Saint-Domingue was home to almost half a million slaves, about 30,000 white colonists, and a roughly equal number of free people of color.

The French and Haitian Revolutions' simultaneity and intertwined narratives inevitably have led historians to ask in what degree the colonial revolution was caused by the metropolitan one. Had there been no upheaval in France, might Haiti be nowadays a French *département?* Or was the Saint-Domingue of the 1780s hurtling toward its destruction whatever might happen in France?

Those colonists who gathered in Paris in 1789 were warned by the marquis de Mirabeau that they were sleeping at the foot of a volcano. One of them, the marquis de Rouvray, had himself written a few years earlier that, as slave-owners, they "walked on barrels of gunpowder." Another stated in a government report that "sooner or later" Saint-Domingue's overworked and underfed slaves would "rush headlong into the horror of terminal despair." Raynal's already famous *Histoire des deux Indes* had predicted a black Spartacus, and the triumph of such a figure was foreseen in Louis-Sébastien Mercier's frequently republished 1771 novel, *L'an 2440.* Even proslavery writers were willing to respond that if their own reform projects were ignored, such predictions might come true.[2]

To my mind, such premonitions raise some doubt about categorizing the Haitian Revolution as an "unthinkable event," as Rolph Trouillot memorably called it.[3] It is particularly difficult to explain the widespread fears of slave revolt that struck colonists, merchants, and officials at the very beginning of the French Revolution if contemporaries were incapable of imagining a massive or successful rebellion.[4] Yet it is certainly true that those commentators (mostly physiocrats) who, from the 1750s, had forecasted or approved a future separation of France and Saint-Domingue generally envisaged secession as being carried through by the planter class, not the enslaved.[5] Both slaves and slave-owners, therefore, were seen in some quarters as potential threats to the colonial status quo.

Of course, such prognostications were rare. Predictions of environmental ruin were perhaps more common.[6] The surviving correspondence of colonists is largely filled with family matters, work, and weather. The major preoccupations of Saint-Domingue's administrators in these years were administrative, judicial, and fiscal reform; trade regulation; and public works. They did not see the slave revolution coming, even if they did not exclude the possibility. Whether we think they should have been more attentive to the rumblings of the volcano partly depends on how much smoke we can detect at its summit when looking through the lens of the historical record. Personally, I do not find the view very clear.

Let us start with slave rebellions. Although Saint-Domingue possessed the Caribbean's largest slave population for most of the eighteenth century, historians have been hard put to discover rebellions and conspiracies prior to that of 1791. Pierre de Vaissière, one of the few historians to work through the full range of pre-revolutionary administrative archives, believed that there were none after 1704. Charles Frostin, another such historian, concluded contentiously that Saint-Domingue's whites were the most rebellious part of the population.[7] Yet there are references here and there in eighteenth-century sources to localized revolts or plots, and we need to know more about them. Nonetheless, it is obvious that Saint-Domingue was not like Jamaica with its long record of collective violent resistance. Some colonists attributed this difference to the colony's authoritarian government, others to its large free colored militia.[8]

Perhaps more plausibly, the paucity of rebellions might be related to the feasibility on this large island of escaping from slavery, especially across the frontier into sparsely populated Santo Domingo. The study of such "maroonage" has been a battleground, notably between Haitian scholars who have read it as a protorevolutionary development in which Haitian independence was already implicit and European empiricist historians who seek to delimit its dimensions and generally see it as a safety valve within the system. Each side has accused the other of either romanticizing or "banalizing" the subject–and with good reason.[9] Maroonage certainly was banal, in the sense of being an everyday event, although the short-term and localized *petit marronage* was infinitely more common than the eye-catching activities of armed bands that novelists and Caribbean nationalists have found so appealing. On the other hand, all fugitives risked brutal retribution and had to live by their wits, be it for years or just days. Behind every banal statistic was a personal drama.

For our purposes, the following points seem most relevant.[10] Clashes between maroon communities of more than a hundred people and major expeditions continued, even in the densely settled North Province of Saint-Domingue, into the mid-1770s, but they were always a frontier phenomenon, and ten years later they were a thing of the past everywhere in the rapidly developing colony. The total number of fugitives undoubtedly continued to increase with the slave population, but plantation documents generally suggest that the proportion missing at any given time was about 1 percent; maybe one in thirty or forty adult slaves went missing in any year, and the great majority returned or were recaptured in a few weeks or months. Proportionately, the colonial garrison lost far more of its soldiers to desertion.[11] Not all of those missing were outside the system: some passed as free in the towns, others were employed under conditions resembling the exploitation of illegal immigrants today. Finally, the common claim that the main leaders of the 1791 uprising were maroons is, with one important exception, demonstrably untrue.

That exception was the dashing young coachman Jean-François, who became the slave revolution's main leader. We know he had been a fugitive for the previous four years, though we do not know if he lived in a maroon community.[12] Although his fellow leaders Biassou, Jeannot, and Boukman were not maroons, one can find a few lesser figures who were and who subsequently played minor roles in the uprising.[13] This might be a promising line of investigation and could substantiate Robin Blackburn's and Carolyn Fick's argument that the experience gained in *petit marronage* contributed to the revolution's success. It is unlikely, however, that most of those who took up arms in 1791 had ever been fugitives.

The likeliest connection between maroonage and the uprising might in fact be a negative one. The rapid clearing of mountain forests in Saint-Domingue that made it progressively more difficult to become a successful maroon may have made outright rebellion more likely. In this view, maroonage was an alternative to violent revolt rather than a precursor.

A similar argument can be made about Vodou and whether it defused anomic tensions in the slave population as much as it contributed to the coming revolution.[14] That contribution came in several forms but especially through providing leadership and an organization that overcame the ethnic divisions of slave society. Faulty translations of surviving religious chants have exaggerated the specifically anti-white nature of an association that primarily promised its followers protection. Belief in the protective power of amulets, however, was to prove a powerful mobilizing device. As with maroonage, many revolutionary leaders have been unjustifiably claimed as Vodou priests, but contemporary evidence does exist in the case of Boukman and, less certainly, Jeannot, although modern claims about a network of Vodou priests are very implausible.[15]

Above all, we do not really know when the umbrella structure of the present-day religion came into existence and thus united the different ethnically based religions that were its components. It is possible that it was forged by the unifying experience of participating in a successful revolution rather than being a major element in that revolution's causation. Ethnic identities, and tensions, certainly continued until after independence. Pre-revolutionary evidence is largely limited to the accounts of the colonists Moreau de Saint-Méry and Drouin de Bercy. Mixing Kongo chants with apparently West African blood oaths and snake worship, these accounts may simply conflate different stories their authors had heard. Yet it is tempting to see in them the first concrete evidence that by the 1780s slaves from different religious traditions were worshipping together in the same forum.

Moreau de Saint-Méry also testifies to the recent appearance in Saint-Domingue of the violent, conflict-centered Petro cult, which colonists regarded as particularly dangerous. It was evidently linked with the growing numbers of Kongolese in the colony and, because of its apparent association with the famous Bois-Caïman ceremony that preceded the slave uprising, it may be regarded as at least a shower of sparks shooting from the colonial volcano.[16]

According to C. L. R. James, the slaves' main weapon of resistance was poison.[17] Most histories of the Haitian Revolution tell the story of the charismatic sorcerer Macandal, who was executed in 1758 for distributing poison and who quickly became a legend. Many writers quote the novelette-like account of his life published thirty years later in the *Mercure de France*, but few have used the report by the judge that examined Macandal's case. Historian Pierre Pluchon interpreted the contemporary sources as revealing no revolutionary conspiracy. Instead, he found a network of sorcerers and clients that spanned several parishes (not the colony) that killed many more blacks than whites and for personal, not political, motives.[18] Since panic-stricken colonists confused both disease and sorcery with poison and gathered evidence by using torture, distinguishing fact from fiction in the affair may be impossible. Room certainly remains for interpretation, and what is perhaps most important about Macandal is that by 1789 he had already become a mythical figure, remembered by slaves, as Moreau de Saint-Méry tells us, for his supernatural powers. The terrible poisoning scares of the period 1757–1779 appear to have abated in the pre-revolutionary decade. This reflected the growth of a more modern mindset among colonists, who became more willing to interpret livestock epidemics as natural events and less inclined to believe confessions extracted with torture. Trends in the actual use of poison, however, are impossible to discern.

Pre-revolutionary developments in slave resistance, therefore, offer no strong clues about the approach of the 1791 uprising. What about changes in colonial demography or the conditions under which slaves lived? Do we find there signs of destabilization, weakening social control, or mounting pressures?

Saint-Domingue's demography leads one immediately into a thicket of contradictory statistics and questionable sources, at both the plantation and colonial levels. Simply identifying official census figures for a given year can be an impenetrable mystery, let alone assessing their reliability or estimating more arcane figures such as contraband slave imports or birth and death rates.[19] Fortunately, as the "hardest" data available concern the legal slave trade, we do know that more than 220,000 enslaved Africans arrived in Saint-Domingue during the postwar economic boom years of 1784–1790. During the five years before the uprising, the colony absorbed nearly two-fifths of all the Africans being brought to the Americas, breaking all records for the Atlantic slave trade. Then, in the year 1790, imports jumped by 45 percent above their already high level, and close to 20,000 Africans arrived in just the single port of Cap-Français, which the following year became the center of the zone of insurrection. The proportion of young males among them was higher than ever before.[20] The figures are so compelling that it might seem that one need look no further than the demography of the slave trade to understand why there was a Haitian Revolution.

However, this upsurge in immigration did not greatly change the overall shape of Saint-Domingue's already populous society. Because the white and free colored populations also grew rapidly in this period, the balance between slave and free and between black and white remained fairly stable and within the norms of the non-Hispanic Caribbean. The remarkable population growth reported in the late colonial censuses was partly due to improved record-keeping. Saint-Domingue underwent an extraordinary boom, but other slave societies (Cuba, Guadeloupe) knew similar spurts of growth and several Caribbean colonies (Grenada, Antigua, Tobago, Suriname) had even more unbalanced populations,[21] although the combination of a highly unbalanced *and* a rapidly expanding population was much more unusual.

One need also note that the fastest-growing of Saint-Domingue's three provinces in the 1780s was not the North, the home of the 1791 uprising, but the underdeveloped South Province.[22] Between the 1775 and 1789 censuses, the North grew far more slowly than both the South and West.[23] The great majority of new migrants, moreover, were absorbed into the rapidly expanding coffee sector and went to live in the mountains of Saint-Domingue,[24] precisely those areas that were drawn most slowly into the Haitian Revolution. This was especially true of the Kongolese, whom John Thornton has arrestingly depicted as exiled soldiers.[25] While this depiction significantly reshapes understanding of the 1791 insurgents, it is not evident that such military captives were more prominent in the slave trade of the 1780s than earlier. Most important, the slave revolt of 1791 broke out amid the most creolized part of the slave population and was led by locally born slaves. Thus it remains far from clear that the rapid expansion of the slave trade made the Haitian Revolution more likely.

One could argue that the demographic ratio most relevant to social control was that between slaves and the European soldiers of the garrison. Although the logic is perhaps a little too elementary to appeal to all scholars, the colonial garrisons were the last line of defense against revolts, and an extensive body of evidence shows that slave conspiracies and rebellions in the Americas often occurred at times of declining garrison strength.[26] The French Caribbean was more strongly garrisoned than the British until the mid-1780s. Saint-Domingue's peacetime garrison apparently maintained a ratio close to 100 slaves for every soldier, and in wartime it was far lower.[27] During the American Revolutionary War more than 8,000 French troops as well as Spanish forces were stationed in the colony.[28] In the British West Indies, troop levels were maintained after the war and then increased, but the concentration of soldiers in Saint-Domingue was abruptly dispersed in the mid-1780s, just when the slave population was growing most rapidly.

The ratio of slaves to soldiers shot up to more than 150 to 1, even with a garrison at full strength, and began climbing sharply. In January 1788, the garrison was in fact 16 percent under strength.[29] Furthermore, although the slave population roughly doubled during the 1770s and 1780s, the number of rural police (200) remained unchanged.[30] The situation became even more precarious after the outbreak of the French Revolution, when the garrison had difficulty maintaining its numbers. It is true that the South was always the most lightly garrisoned part of Saint-Domingue. Yet the greatest absolute and relative declines in troop levels, the most likely to encourage slaves' reassessment of the balance of power, occurred in the North. This took place in the mid-1780s when the wartime military buildup, which was concentrated in that province, came to a belated end. Even before the disruption of the French Revolution, therefore, slaves in the North Province had good cause to feel that the prospects for successful resistance were improving.

Access to freedom through legal channels, on the other hand, was clearly diminishing in the late ancient régime. Manumission, the freeing of slaves by legal instrument, has often been regarded as a safety valve for slave regimes that encouraged compliance by offering hope. In Saint-Domingue, however, alarm at the growth of the free black population caused the administration after 1775 to make the freeing of slaves more difficult, and after brief improvements in 1779 and 1785, the number of manumissions declined precipitously on the eve of the revolution (see Table 3.1).[31]

Although the odds of being freed were good compared with those of a modern lottery, the great majority of those emancipated were women and children of white fathers. Black males, including children, made up merely 14 to 16 percent of the manumitted. They had never been favored for

Table 3.1 Official Manumissions

Year	Total Freed	Female Percent	Black Percent
1785	739	65	45
1786	411	64	na[1]
1787	273	na	na
1788	297	67	43
1789	256	63	41

[1] na = "not available."

Sources: C9A/159, f. 183, C9A/158, f.37, C9A/156, manumission statistics for 1785 (corrected), and C9B/37, letter of January 16, 1787, all in CAOM; Barbé-Marbois, *État des finances* (Port-au-Prince, 1789), table 5; Proisy, *État des finances* (Port-au-Prince, 1790), 31 and table 4.

manumission, but black slaves' access to freedom was evidently being limited by increasing competition from those of mixed racial descent.[32] Scarce regional data suggest that slaves in the North Province had similar chances of being freed to those in the rest of the colony but that the situation there for men, after improving somewhat, declined sharply. In 1789, only seven black males were freed out of a regional population of more than 190,000.

How important this trend may have been in disappointing the expectations of the enslaved depends on whether this restriction of official manumission encouraged masters to de facto free slaves without paying the fees that legalized the change of status. Slave-owners may have increasingly evaded the requirement. It is also plausible that the rising cost of slaves in these years discouraged all types of manumission.[33] Uncertainty about the extent of unofficial emancipation mandates caution, therefore. Yet it would seem that if manumission did strengthen the slave regime in Saint-Domingue, it was through co-opting enslaved women, typically domestic servants, who hoped that they or their children would one day be freed. It had much less impact on the black males who made up the majority of the slave population, and insofar as it was a safety valve, it appears to have been almost closed shut before the outbreak of the revolution.

Changes in other aspects of slave treatment are much harder to discern. The historians who assert that conditions on Saint-Domingue's plantations worsened in the late colonial period collectively make three assertions: that atrocities increased in response to fears caused by population imbalance; that workload also increased, in response either to soil exhaustion or to booming demand; and that food supplies became inadequate for the growing population. The reasoning is always *a priori* and without supporting evidence. Empirical investigation of these issues in a colony with 8,000 plantations is, however, a daunting task and fraught with methodological problems. At a very general level, it is unlikely that, by Caribbean standards, Saint-Domingue was an exceptionally deadly place for slaves. By 1790, it had imported about as many Africans as had neighboring Jamaica (and its African immigrants had a man-to-woman ratio that was less favorable to reproduction than that of Jamaica's African immigrants), yet it had a much larger slave population.[34] This, however, does not exclude the possibility that conditions worsened through time.

Insofar as a trend can be perceived in the incidence of atrocities against slaves, it was apparently toward diminution. Contemporaries remarked that by 1770 they were becoming less common as slave-owners' mores became more civilized.[35] Official executions were fewer and the administration was, according to some, more willing to intervene against "private justice."[36] Heinous acts of cruelty persisted, without any doubt, but the gradual humanizing of European culture in these decades (and perhaps the rising price of slaves) make it unlikely that atrocities were really more common, especially as no contemporary seems to have thought so.

Two general reasons for doubting that the conditions of slave life worsened after 1750 are the increasing percentage of locally born slaves in the population and the increasing proportion that worked on coffee and cotton plantations. Creoles lived healthier and socially more complete lives than transplanted Africans, and their growing numbers progressively brought down the imbalance between men and women from 18 to 10 in 1730 to about 12 to 10 in the 1780s.[37] Coffee and cotton, the colony's main growth sectors after 1750, were considerably less demanding on their workforces than sugar, which by 1791 employed less than one-third of the enslaved population.[38] Technological advances, moreover, went some way in these years toward eliminating the most exhausting tasks in both coffee and indigo production.[39] The growth of these secondary crops also increased the presence of resident owners among the planter class, which colonists and historians have generally thought positive for slaves. Certainly the grueling labor involved in creating new plantations offset these factors, to an unknowable degree, but by the 1780s land clearance had become a diminishing proportion of the slaves' work.[40]

Table 3.2 Trends in Workload on Sugar Plantations

Region	Time Period	Acres of Caneland per Slave	Number of Plantations
North	1770s	1.77	(24)
	1780s	1.66	(43)
	1790–91	1.53	(9)
West and South	1770s	1.41	(13)
	1780s	1.34	(27)
	1790–91	1.31	(11)

On sugar estates an increasing ratio of slaves to caneland seems to indicate that workloads were diminishing in the last two decades of slavery,
but it may simply reflect the long-term trend toward producing semi-
refined sugar, which demanded more workers in the manufacturing stage
than did muscovado. It may also reflect a tendency to replant cane more
frequently and ratoon less frequently.[42] These factors may explain the
seemingly higher workload on northern estates. However, the generally
lower fertility rates of enslaved women on northern estates suggest that
the work regime there was harsher and that it perhaps grew worse during
this 20-year period (see Table 3.2).

Low fertility, of course, can be related to poor nutrition as well as overwork. Although there is reason to believe that slaves were better fed in the
north than elsewhere in Saint-Domingue, pressure on locally grown food
supplies was most likely to be felt on Northern Plain estates because they
had the smallest reserves of new land and were the most affected by soil
depletion. Most had highland provision grounds, but soil erosion and
declining rainfall were already impacting the northern mountains, and
the 1787 and 1788 censuses show a 5 percent decline across the colony in
the acreage devoted to food crops, although the reliability of these
statistics is admittedly dubious.[43] The opening of new free ports brought
improved access to imported foodstuffs, particularly at Cap-Français,
but contemporaries disagreed about whether this was an adequate
solution.

Besides population pressure and environmental decline, natural disasters were the other main threat to the food supply. These were, however, a
regular feature of Caribbean life. In Saint-Domingue, the most drought-
prone plantation zones (the northeast and northwest) were not the most
prompt to rebel in the 1790s. It may be significant, even so, that the drought
of 1790 was the worst in living memory. As in 1776 and 1786, some
slaves were left to fend for themselves, to scavenge and seek out odd

Table 3.3 Trends in Fertility on Sugar Plantations

Region	Time Period	Mean Fertility Index[1]	Median Fertility Index	Number of Plantations
North	1770s	.309	.314	(21)
	1780s	.328	.300	(38)
	1790–91	.221	.236	(8)
West and South	1770s	.357	.341	(8)
	1780s	.369	.297	(14)
	1790–91	.408	.443	(6)

[1] Fertility index = children 0–4 years/women 15–44 years.
Sources: Personal database.[41]

jobs in return for food. Such abandonment in the basic matter of subsistence must have undermined whatever paternalist claims were made by the slave-owners concerned.[44] It would also have facilitated contact between slaves over a wide area and thus the mobilization of the discontented.

Gabriel Debien devoted the final chapter of his *magnum opus* on French West Indian slavery to the question of whether the slave regime became less harsh during the years after 1770. He found evidence of better treatment of new arrivals, the sick, pregnant women, and newborns, but he concluded that such improvements were piecemeal and affected only a minority of plantations.[45] Such a scenario of scattered improvements might have encouraged a sense of relative deprivation among the majority of slaves who did not benefit and thus increased levels of discontent.[46] The same is perhaps true of the royal government's attempted reforms of 1784–1785, which created a storm of protest among colonists and a flurry of strike action by slaves and apparently remained a dead letter.[47] This effort by the late ancien régime administration to intervene between slave and slave-owner is perhaps most important, however, for its having created a plausible basis for the royalist ideology that the slave insurgents would adroitly use in 1791, when they claimed to be acting in the name of the king.

This brings us to the white population of Saint-Domingue. While it seems appropriate to devote most attention to the slaves, the Haitian Revolution began nonetheless at the apex of colonial society as a pursuit of self-government and free trade by both resident and absentee sections of the planter class. White settler autonomism had a long history in the colony. The 1670s, 1720s, and 1760s had each seen brief rebellions against the agents of royal authority. The 1780s brought much to encourage and alarm wealthy slave-owners who identified with the French *pays d'état* and envied British colonists their cheap slaves and self-government. The independence of the United States had shown that a colonial rebellion could be successful and respectable, and trade relations with the new mainland republic expanded in the postwar period, when Yankee merchants opened businesses in Le Cap and Port-au-Prince. Probably only the wildest dreamers imagined that an easily blockaded island whose colonists were greatly outnumbered by slaves could emulate the mainland colonies' secession, but to others a British protectorate may have seemed feasible.[48]

In some quarters, the cultural adaptation of planters to the tropical milieu perhaps reinforced the sense of separate identity forged by divergent interests. So many young whites spoke Creole better than French that a newspaper editor suggested replacing the Latin Mass with a French one to teach them the mother tongue. Some colonists preferred cassava to wheaten bread. Young white women copied women of color in dress and mannerisms.[49] But all this is easily exaggerated.

A far more immediate threat to imperial ties was the battery of reforms launched by the late ancient régime government that alienated a wide spectrum of the white population. Slave-owners and plantation employees were angered by the 1784–1785 decrees and bursts of judicial activism and administrative intervention that sought to limit their abuse of slaves and punish atrocities.[50] The abolition of the Cap-Français appeal court, whose role paralleled that of the *parlements* in France, earned the enmity of its numerous lawyers and was a blow to all North Province colonists.[51] Mercantilist trade laws were relaxed somewhat, but efforts to combat smuggling were stepped up. Finally, the intendant Barbé-Marbois (1785–89) reclaimed a mountain of debts from lax officials, ran roughshod over the colonists' few fiscal privileges, and initiated reform of sensitive issues such as debt law and land grants. A paragon of vigorous efficiency, he became one of the revolution's first casualties.[52]

This conflict between the administration and colonial whites fits quite well with R. R. Palmer's concept of an "aristocratic reaction." The revolution would take a democratic turn in 1789 only because of the explosive militancy of the *petits blancs*, the artisans, clerks, seamen, and plantation personnel of European origin. They burst on the scene, in the minds of some observers, "as if from underground."[53] As the main colony of Europe's most populated country, Saint-Domingue had always attracted indigent young males seeking employment, but migration seems to have surged with the economic crisis in France of the late 1780s. The net inflow of passengers (which was 85 percent male) together with deserting seamen exceeded 1,950 in the period 1788–1789, and the rate of arrival increased in the first half of 1790.[54] This presumably explains why some contemporaries (and later historians) were surprised at the later prominence in the revolution of the white working class and unemployed.

The role they played was marked by an extreme hostility to the free people of color, the colony's third major population group, with whom they competed for jobs. These *gens de couleur libres* grew rapidly during the decades before the revolution, not just in numbers but also in wealth. Although many historians have exaggerated their ownership of land and slaves, they were exceptional by American standards for including a substantial group of middling planters as well as urban proprietors.[55] They stood out all the more in Saint-Domingue because the wealthiest whites were absentees. The government's response to this upward mobility was a growing body of discriminatory legislation and an increasingly punctilious policing of the color line. After 1760, race relations quickly lost the flexibility they had once had. Banned from certain jobs and from wearing certain clothing and segregated in public venues, people of color also suffered extralegal harassment that ranged from petty humiliation to vicious assaults.[56]

This combination of upward mobility confronted by repression was potentially explosive because free men of color made up about half of the colonial militia by 1789 and most of the rural police. During the War of American Independence, two free colored battalions had seen service overseas, which provided military experience to several future revolutionary leaders. The experience encouraged some of the wealthiest men of color to lobby the colonial ministry about reforming the regime of racial discrimination. Their arguments were sympathetically heard by the minister, de Castries, but officials in Saint-Domingue continued to discourage any innovation through the 1780s. Debate went on in the corridors of power whether a policy of humiliating or co-opting free people of African descent would do least to destabilize the slave regime.[57] As white opinion was not monolithic, it is uncertain how that debate would have developed.

Also uncertain is how explosive the racial question was in Saint-Domingue. Some contemporaries thought harassment of *gens de couleur* was worsening. But Dominique Rogers has recently argued that the overall picture was one of increasing integration.[58] Moreover, although their numbers and sense of identity were growing, the free people of color were a very diverse and fragmented group, and they would behave with similar diversity in the revolution.

* * *

Separate channels of lava beneath the colonial volcano, free colored activism, white settler autonomism, and slave resistance all had complex prehistories quite independent of the French Revolution. Their explosive potential seems obvious in hindsight, as it did to many eighteenth-century observers. But that potential was realized only through the seismic tremors that issued from revolutionary France. How we read the balance between stress and stability in late colonial Saint-Domingue will ultimately depend on our individual susceptibility to materialist and idealist arguments and to local and external factors. Regrettably, the facts do not suggest a coherent picture of either mounting pressure or steady equilibrium.

Were it possible to construct a "misery index" for the slave population, it is debatable whether it would have been higher in 1789 than in 1750. There are, nevertheless, several indications that if slaves were being worked harder than in the past and going hungrier, it was probably in the Northern Plain. Moreover, if objective conditions were not worse in the aggregate, the scattered attempts some planters made to improve conditions may have provoked a sense of relative deprivation among slaves. The ineffective reform efforts of the administration may have produced a similar result and may have revealed cracks in the power structure that could be exploited. On the other hand, the revolutionary potential of the slave population's dramatic growth is not as obvious as it first seems, although its relation to the military component of social control and to trends in manumission warrant further investigation.

Slave resistance, in my view, was chiefly important for keeping alive a spirit of contestation. The popular picture of massing bands of maroons linked to a network of Vodou priests is entirely mythical, although of the four main leaders of the 1791 uprising, one was a maroon and perhaps two were Vodou priests. The documentary evidence does hint at a religious organization that was bringing together different ethnic groups before the revolution, but as long as it promoted magical rather than political remedies to real-world problems, its revolutionary potential was limited. Maroon band activity clearly diminished in the 1780s, and it may be that decreasing opportunities for maroonage made armed revolt more likely.

If the French Revolution had occurred two or three decades earlier, one might wonder if the slave, or indeed white, populations would have behaved any differently than in 1789. Only among free people of color, then a community in embryo, might a different reaction have been expected. Even so, the autonomist leanings of the planter class were undoubtedly strengthened by the United States example and the late ancien régime's program of colonial reform. By the time the French state went bankrupt in the summer of 1788, colonists were already concerting opposition to the colonial administration, drawing inspiration from the reform movement in France, and they quickly picked up the demand for representation in the States-General that was to link the colonial and metropolitan revolutions inextricably.

NOTES

1 Despite considerable uncertainty about price levels and the dimensions of contraband commerce, there can be little doubt that exports were worth at least 22 million dollars, easily twice as much as the private bullion shipped from Brazil or Mexico, i.e. excluding royal taxes, and were equivalent to the average annual amount of silver coined in Mexico around 1790. See David Geggus, "Urban Development in Eighteenth Century Saint Domingue," *Bulletin du Centre d'Histoire des Espaces Atlantiques* 5 (1990): 228; Fernando A. Novais, *Portugal e Brasil na crise do antigo sistema colonial (1777–1808)* (São Paulo, 1979), 306–390; John Fisher, *Commercial Relations between Spain and Spanish America in the Era of Free Trade, 1778–1796* (Liverpool, 1985), 61; Leslie Bethell, ed., *Colonial Spanish America* (Cambridge, 1987), 139–141; David Brading, *Miners and Merchants in Bourbon Mexico* (Cambridge, 1971), 131.

2 Jean Philippe Garran Coulon, *Rapport sur les troubles de Saint-Domingue*, 4 vols. (Paris, 1797–1799), 4:18; Paul Vaissière, *Saint-Domingue: la société et la vie créoles* (Paris, 1909), 174, 230; Yves Benot, *La Révolution française et la fin des colonies* (Paris, 1987), 26–29; Paul Ulric Dubuisson, Julien-Antoine Dubuc-Duféret, *Lettres critiques et politiques sur les colonies et le commerce des villes maritimes de France, adressées à G.T. Raynal* (Geneva, 1785).

3 Michel-Rolph Trouillot, *Silencing the Past* (Boston, 1995), ch. 3 [*Editor's note: refers to Trouillot's essay "An Unthinkable History," reprinted in this volume*].

4 For an example of each: Commission des Colonies, *Débats entre les accusateurs et les accusés dans l'affaire des colonies*, 9 vols. (Paris, 1795), 1:100–103; entry for September 5, 1789, C 4364, Archives départementales de la Gironde, Bordeaux;

letters of October 1789, C9A/162, Centre des Archives d'Outre-mer, Aix-en-Provence (hereafter CAOM).

5 Benot, *La Révolution française*, 26–27; Prosper Boissonnade, "Saint-Domingue à la veille de la Révolution," *Mémoires de la Société des Antiquaires de l'Ouest* 29 (1905): 555–556.

6 Jacques-François Dutrône de Couture, *Précis sur la canne* (Paris, 1790), 343–346; *Les j'ai vu d'un habitant du Cap. Nouvelle édition* (Cap-Français: 1790), 2; *Histoire des désastres de Saint-Domingue* (Paris, 1795), 17–18, 81–85; Gabriel Debien and Charles Frostin, "Papiers des Antilles III," *Cahiers des Amériques Latines* 1 (1968): 203.

7 Vaissière, *Saint-Domingue*, 232–234.

8 "Réflexions sur la position actuelle," F3/192, CAOM (also in John Carter Brown Library, Providence, Codex Fr 19); *Histoire des désastres*, 52.

9 David Geggus, *Haitian Revolutionary Studies* (Bloomington, 2001), ch. 5.

10 This section draws on many collections of plantation papers; see below, note 41. Relevant published studies include Geggus, *Haitian Revolutionary Studies*, ch. 5; Geggus, "Une famille de La Rochelle et ses plantations de Saint-Domingue," in *France in the New World*, ed. D. Buisseret (East Lansing, 1998), 119–136; Bernard Foubert, "Le marronage sur les habitations Laborde à Saint-Domingue dans la seconde moitié du XVIIIe siècle," *Annales de Bretagne* 95 (1988): 277–310 (whose figures I have adjusted).

11 Regimental statistics in CAOM: D2C/99 and 105 (1786–1791), C9B/37 (1787), and F3/160, f. 116 (1765).

12 See the "wanted" ad in *Affiches Américaines, Feuille du Cap*, November 3, 1787.

13 For example, one source identifies as a maroon François Dechaussée, who participated in the Lenormand plantation meeting and subsequent attack on the Chabaud estate in August 1791: Limbé municipality report, Government Papers 8:5, Fisher Collection, New York Public Library.

14 David Geggus, "Haitian Voodoo in the Eighteenth Century: Language, Culture, Resistance," *Jahrbuch für Geschichte von Staat, Wirtschaft und Gesellschaft Lateinamerikas* 28 (1991): 21–51; Geggus, *Haitian Revolutionary Studies*, ch. 5.

15 *Procès-Verbaux des Séances et Journal des Débats* (Cap-Français), November 15, 1791. Historians have failed to recognize that the leader known as Médecin-Général was not Toussaint Louverture but Jeannot. Vodou was still acephalous in the twentieth century.

16 However, the significance of the Bois-Caïman ceremony of August 1791 has been much exaggerated, and according to West African historian Robin Law was not necessarily a Petro ceremony: Geggus, *Haitian Revolutionary Studies*, ch. 6.

17 C. L. R. James, *The Black Jacobins* (New York, 1963), 16.

18 Pierre Pluchon, *Vaudou, sorciers, empoisonneurs: de Saint-Domingue à Haïti* (Paris, 1987), 165, 170–182, 208–219, 308–315; M.-R. Hilliard d'Auberteuil, *Considérations sur l'état présent de la colonie française de Saint-Domingue*, 2 vols. (Paris, 1776–1777), 1:137–138.

19 Geggus, "The Major Port Towns of Saint Domingue in the Late Eighteenth Century," in *Atlantic Port Cities*, ed. Franklin Knight and Peggy Liss (Knoxville, 1991), 101–104.

20 Geggus, "The French Slave Trade: An Overview," *William and Mary Quarterly* 58 (2001): 119–138; David Eltis, *Voyages: The Trans-Atlantic Slave Trade Database*, available at http://www.slavevoyages.org/tast/index.faces.

21 These comments hold true even for high estimates of the slave population of up to 600,000, which I believe are exaggerated.

22 Report of June 28, 1789, C9A/163, CAOM, which shows a growth rate nearly 50 percent higher there than in the rest of the colony. The figures for 1788 and

1789 in the introduction to Ducoeurjoly, *Manuel des habitants de Saint-Domingue* (2 vols. [Paris, 1802]), show 4 percent growth in the north and 9 percent elsewhere.

23 By 50 percent as compared to 78 percent. See G1/509, CAOM; Vincent-René de Proisy, *État des finances de Saint-Domingue* (Port-au-Prince, 1790), table 10.

24 Morange to Foäche, July 19, 1789, 505 Mi 85, Archives Nationales, Paris (hereafter AN); Félix Carteau, *Soirées bermudiennes* (Paris, 1802), 299; *Histoire des désastres*, 81–85.

25 John Thornton, "African Soldiers in the Haitian Revolution," *Journal of Caribbean History* 25 (1993): 58–80.

26 David Geggus, "The Enigma of Jamaica in the 1790s," *William and Mary Quarterly* (1987): 292–299. For additional data, see Geggus, "Slavery, War, and Revolution in the Greater Caribbean," in *A Turbulent Time: The French Revolution and the Greater Caribbean*, ed. D. Gaspar and D. Geggus (Bloomington, 1997), 35n31; Jean-Claude Nardin, *La mise en valeur de l'isle de Tabago (1763–1783)* (Paris, 1969), 211.

27 A scattering of (sometimes contradictory) military data from the 1720s onward can be found in F3/160, f. 109–117, CAOM; 195 Mi 1, dossier 8/16, AN; M. L. E. Moreau de Saint-Méry, *Description ... de la partie françoise de l'isle Saint-Domingue*, 3 vols. (1797, repr., Paris, 1958), 2:1006–1007, 1013; and Beauvais Lespinasse, *Histoire des affranchis de Saint-Domingue*, 143–144, 159–160, 168–170, 180–183. Colonial censuses are in G1/509, CAOM.

28 195 Mi 1, dossier 8/16, AN. According to J. Abeille, *Essai sur nos colonies* (Paris, 1805), 42, the total reached between 15,000 and 20,000 troops. Some, expelled from the east Caribbean, stayed only briefly.

29 Garrison statistics, C9A/161, CAOM.

30 Stewart King, *Blue Coat or Powdered Wig: Free People of Color in Pre-Revolutionary Saint Domingue* (Athens, 2001), 59. King notes that the *maréchaussée* compensated by using unpaid supernumerary troopers, who could number six per regular *cavalier*. In the North, however, they were rare, "impossible to find," according to Moreau de Saint-Méry, *Description*, 1:441.

31 Barbé to Castries, January 16, 1787, and Barbé to Montmorin, December 13, 1787, C9B/37, CAOM. For reasons unknown, Peytraud, *Esclavage*, 492, gives a slightly higher figure for 1785 manumissions, and Moreau de Saint-Méry, in *Considérations présentées aux vrais amis du repos et du bonheur de la France* (Paris, 1791), 36, states that 1,765 (instead of 1,976) people were freed in 1785–1789. The peak in 1785 was partly due to the decision of the departing intendant, de Bongars, to waive the manumission tax for numerous administrative colleagues. Although a subset of the total, the 1,630 notarized acts of manumission from the period 1776–1789 studied in Dominique Rogers, "Les libres de couleur dans les capitales de Saint-Domingue: fortune, mentalités et intégration à la fin de l'Ancien régime (1776–1789)" (Thèse de doctorat de l'université, Université de Bordeaux III, 1999), 69–80, 274–289, are particularly valuable.

32 See the samples of manumittees from earlier periods in Gautier, *Les soeurs de Solitude* (Paris, 1985), 172; John Garrigus, "A Struggle for Respect: Free Coloreds in Pre-Revolutionary Saint Domingue" (Ph.D. diss., Johns Hopkins University, 1988), 422–423; King, *Blue Coat or Powdered Wig*, 44, 108; and Rogers, "Les libres de couleur," 71. Service with the *maréchaussée*, nonwhite militia, and the Chasseur battalions of 1779 and 1780 did offer men an exclusive avenue to freedom and helped boost the male percentage of manumittees around 1780.

33 The average price of Africans disembarked from slave ships rose by 28 percent to 2,134 livres from 1783 to 1789. See Geggus, "The French Slave Trade," note 38; La Luzerne, *Mémoire envoyé le 18 juin 1790* (Paris, 1790), 70. The manumission tax for women was 2,000 livres.

34 This assumes that 15,000 Africans reached Saint-Domingue in the seventeenth century and that the inter-island trade supplied an additional 10 percent beyond the data in David Eltis, Stephen Behrendt, David Richardson, and Herbert Klein, *The Transatlantic Slave Trade: A Database on CD-ROM* (Cambridge, 1999); and David Eltis, *The Rise of African Slavery in the Americas* (Cambridge, 2000).

35 F3/90, f. 155, 268, CAOM; "Remarques sur la colonie" (ca. 1780), Ms. 3453, f. 36–37, Bibliothèque Mazarine, Paris; Peynier and Marbois to La Luzerne, September 25, 1789, C9A/162, CAOM; Vaissière, *Saint-Domingue*, 192–194.

36 F3/150, f. 78–83, CAOM.

37 Censuses 1681–1788, G1/509, CAOM; "Tableau de la population. . . 1789," Special Collections, University of Florida. Overall sexual imbalance was lower, since censuses tended to omit the elderly (who were mostly women).

38 The author of *Histoire des désastres* is unusually critical of coffee plantations for their negligent planters and inhospitably cold climate but still accepts that the work regime was worse on sugar estates (pp. 65–66). He is conspicuously weak on demography.

39 On the grinding and winnowing mills that extracted coffee beans, see Carteau, *Soirées bermudiennes*, 297; *Histoire des désastres*, 105–106. On the mechanical paddles used in indigo basins, see Geggus, "Indigo and Slavery," in *Slavery without Sugar*, ed. Verene Shepherd (Gainesville, 2001), 21.

40 This is probably the main reason the premium paid for adult male slaves declined after the 1760s.

41 [*Editor's note: This table and the references in this note were updated by the author in 2011 for publication in this volume*]. Most of the sources are listed in Geggus, "Sugar and Coffee Cultivation in Saint Domingue and the Shaping of the Slave Labor Force," in *Cultivation and Culture: Labor and the Shaping of Slave Life in the Americas*, ed. Ira Berlin and Philip Morgan (Charlottesville, 1993), 95–96, and Geggus, "The Sugar Plantation Zones of Saint Domingue and the Revolution of 1791–1793," *Slavery & Abolition* 20 (1999): note 8. Additional sources include: Archives municipales de Bordeaux, 210 S 112 (Menoire de Beaujau); Archives départementales de l'Eure et Loire, Chartres, 24 J art. 145 (Peyrac); Archives Nationales, Paris, 300 AP I 144 (D'Orléans); 92APC/5/16 (Gérard), Notsdom 405 (Des Varrennes), Notsdom 866 (Collot), Notsdom 934 (De Luynes), Notsdom 1396 (Minière de Tressain), Notsdom 1712, d.14 (Chantelot), and Notsdom 1713 d.7 (La Serre), all in CAOM; Public Record Office, London, HCA 30/273 (Caillau/D'Orlic and Laugardière); University of Florida, Gainesville, Jérémie Papers, Greffe 3:17 (Foäche); University of Florida, Slavery and Plantations in Saint Domingue Collection (Rocheblave, and Molie/Villeneuve); *Affiches Américaines* (Port-au-Prince), July 1786 (Dubreuil de Fontroux), Apr. 1787 (Duburqua/Durocher), and Aug. 1787 (Audubon); Bernard Foubert, "L'Habitation Leroux," *Revue de la Société Haïtienne d'Histoire* 212 & 213 (2002) (Leroux); Jean-Louis Donnadieu, "Entre Gascogne et Saint-Domingue" (Thèse de doctorat, Université de Pau, 2006) (Noé).

42 Geggus, "The Sugar Plantation Zones of Saint Domingue," 31–46. Using the erroneous equivalence of 1 *carreau* = 1.137 hectares (it should be 1.292 hectares), colonial historians, including myself, have hitherto understated land areas. The error, which may have resulted from confusing the English foot and the French *pied*, apparently derives from the 1958 edition of Moreau de Saint-Méry, *Description*, 1:16, which has misled two generations of scholars. Ratoon canes grew from the roots of harvested canes. They yielded less than "plant canes" but obviated the back-breaking work of planting.

43 C9A/160, f. 335–336, CAOM. According to Mats Lundahl, *The Haitian Economy: Man, Land, and Markets* (New York, 1983), the environmental impact of food crops is particularly deleterious.

44 James C. Scott argues that access to subsistence and reciprocity between subordinate and dominant classes have been central to peasants' sense of social justice (*Moral Economy of the Peasant: Subsistence and Rebellion in Southeast Asia* [New Haven, 1976], 157–160, 165–179) and that the gap between ideology and reality prevents the achievement of hegemony and stimulates resistance (*Weapons of the Weak: Everyday Forms of Peasant Resistance* [New Haven, 1985], 317, 336–338).

45 Gabriel Debien, *Les esclaves aux Antilles françaises aux XVIIe et XVIIIe siècles* (Basse Terre, 1974), 471–495.

46 Although the concept of relative deprivation as an explanation for group behavior fell from academic favor after T. R. Gurr's controversial *Why Men Rebel*, it has since regained popularity. See Iain Walker and Heather Smith, eds., *Relative Deprivation: Specification, Development, and Integration* (Princeton, 2001).

47 Letters of March-November 1785, 505 Mi 85, AN; F3/126, f. 417–418, CAOM.

48 Gabriel Debien, *Les colons de Saint-Domingue et la Révolution française: essai sur le Club Massiac* (Paris, 1953); Charles Frostin, " 'L'Histoire de l'esprit autonomiste colon à Saint-Domingue aux XVIIe et XVIIIe siècles" (Thèse de doctorat d'état, Université de Paris I, 1972).

49 *Affiches Américaines, Feuille du Port-au-Prince*, July 1790; Ms 3453, f. 71, Bibliothèque Mazarine; Justin Girod de Chantrans, *Voyage d'un Suisse dans différentes colonies d'Amérique*, ed. Pierre Pluchon (Paris, 1980), 152–155.

50 Pierre Pluchon, *Nègres et juifs au XVIIIe siècle* (Paris, 1984), 164–188; Malick Ghachem, "Sovereignty and Slavery in the Age of Revolution: Haitian Variations on a Metropolitan Theme" (Ph.D. diss., Stanford University, 2001), 120–142, 156–170, 255–298; note 47 above.

51 The court's abolition in 1787 looks like a dry run for the government attack on the *parlements* the following year. It was touted twenty years later as a model for future metropolitan reforms in Guillaume Lamardelle, *Réforme judiciaire* (Paris, 1806).

52 See especially letters of February 17, May 4, September 11, and December 23, 1788, C9A/161, CAOM.

53 Robert R. Palmer, *The Age of the Democratic Revolution*, vol. 1 (Princeton, 1959); Geggus, *Slavery, War and Revolution* (Oxford, 1982), 34–35; Anne-Louis Tousard, *Tousard, Lieutenant-colonel* (Paris, 1793), 8; Lincoln to Stanislas Foäche, July 5, 1792, 505 Mi 80, AN.

54 Shipping statistics in *Affiches Américaines*, 1788–1790; Gabriel Chastenet-Destère, *Considérations sur l'état présent de la colonie française de Saint-Domingue* (Paris, 1796), 47.

55 They were almost entirely absent from the sugar sector. As coffee planters, they appear in the notarial archives infrequently, usually as very small-scale proprietors. However, a study of the Artibonite plain, where free coloreds were numerous, is critically needed.

56 Yvan Debbasch, *Couleur et liberté: le jeu du critère ethnique dans l'ordre juridique esclavagiste* (Paris: Dalloz, 1967); King, *Blue Coat or Powdered Wig*; John Garrigus, "Colour, Class and Identity on the Eve of the Haitian Revolution: Saint Domingue's Coloured Elite as *Colons Américains*," in *Against the Odds: Free Blacks in the Slave Societies of the Americas*, ed. Jane Landers (London, 1996), 20–43; letters of March 11 and September 25, 1786, C9B/36, CAOM.

57 John Garrigus, "Catalyst or Catastrophe? Saint Domingue's Free Men of Color and the Battle of Savannah," *Revista/Review Interamericana* 22 (1992): 109–125; Debbasch, *Couleur et liberté*, 108–131.

58 T650/1/5, f. 9, AN; Rogers, "Les libres de couleur," 589–594.

4

"I AM THE SUBJECT OF THE KING OF CONGO"

African Political Ideology and the Haitian Revolution*

(*excerpts*)

John K. Thornton

Shortly after a body of rebellious slaves had sacked Le Cap François (now known as Cap Haitien) in June 1793 at the behest of the republican commissioners, their leader, known as Macaya, retreated to the hills and swore allegiance to the king of Spain, who had supported the rebellion for some time. When the commissioner Étienne Polverel tried to persuade him to return to the republic, Macaya wrote back: "I am the subject of three kings: of the King of Congo, master of all the blacks; of the King of France who represents my father; of the King of Spain who represents my mother. These three Kings are the descendants of those who, led by a star, came to adore God made Man."[1]

These sentiments, seconded by other revolutionary leaders from time to time, have led many analysts of the Haitian revolution, from the venerable Thomas Madiou onward, to consider that the rebel slaves were inveterate royalists.[2] Some scholars have proposed that royalism was a product of the slaves' African background, where kings were the rule.[3] Nor was this observation confined to modern historians: the same civil commissioners who were rebuffed by Macaya wrote to Pierrot, one of his associates, at about the same time begging him to consider "the lot which you are preparing for the blacks [*nègres*] who surround you. . . . They follow the banner of kings and therefore of slavery. Who sold you on the coast of Guinea? It was the kings." They continued, "Who is it that gives you freedom? It is the French nation . . . that has cut off the head of its king who sells slaves."[4] A bit later they returned to the same theme: "You know our intentions, they are pure, they are favorable to the unfortunate ones whom the kings of Guinea sold to the white kings."[5]

In a larger context, Eugene Genovese has viewed slave revolts in the Americas in a similar way. Earlier revolts, he argues, were largely backward-looking and restorationist, seeking to recreate an African past in the

Americas, including its kings. On the other hand, perhaps ignoring this piece of evidence, Genovese sees the Haitian revolution as ultimately the product of the dissemination of "bourgeois-capitalist" ideas diffusing from Europe and eventually reaching even the slaves.[6] C. L. R. James, whose classic treatment of the revolution was fired by both republican and socialist thought, saw the royalism of the slaves as an inherent problem of their African background, from which heroes like Toussaint Louverture gradually and patiently weaned them.[7] In both scholars' view, backwards Africa confronted forward-looking Europe in the origins and ideology of the Haitian revolution.

However one views the Haitian revolution in its totality, there is no question that many of the revolutionary leaders expressed royalist sentiments, that their followers carried royalist banners and called themselves *gens du roi*, and that they even demanded the restoration of the monarchy.[8] These as well as other elements of the slaves' outlook may well reflect their African background. It is worthy of consideration, after all, that perhaps as many as two-thirds of the slaves in Saint-Domingue (Haiti) on the eve of the revolution had been born, raised, and socialized in Africa.[9] Attention to the ideological orientation of the mass of the slaves might be important even if many of their leaders were creoles with no immediate African background, since they would still have to appeal to their followers in terms that resonated with their ideology. Taking this into consideration, Carolyn Fick, whose recent history of the revolution focuses on the mass participation of the slaves, proposes that much could be learned about the revolution and the slaves' background by studying the eighteenth-century Kongo, from which a large number ultimately hailed.[10]

The African Background: Kongo in the Late Eighteenth Century

It is appropriate, as Fick suggests, to start with the ideology of the kingdom of Kongo, the central African state to whom Macaya was referring in his celebrated reply to Polverel. Kongo is a particularly good starting point both because it is an extremely well-documented kingdom (including texts dealing with political philosophy) and because it provided thousands of slaves to the island colony of Saint-Domingue on the eve of the revolution. These slaves were exported in large measure as a result of civil war in the kingdom of Kongo. People enslaved through war or as a result of the decline of public order created by constant warfare and resulting brigandage were sold to local merchants, who brought them to the coast for resale.[11] [. . .]

Slaves from this region made up the majority of those imported into Saint-Domingue for the last twenty years before the revolution.[12] David Geggus has studied plantation inventories and concluded that in the 1780s "Congos" made up 60 percent of the slaves in North Province, where the revolution began, and about the same percentage in the south.[13] They were common enough among the rebels that *Congo* became a generic term for the rank and file of the slave insurgents.[14] That Macaya was a Kongolese[15] might be inferred from his name, which can be attested as a personal name in Kongo from the late seventeenth century.[16] [. . .]

Kongolese Political Ideology

The role of Kongo is also important because it can be seen as a source of revolutionary Haiti's ideology—not just its royalism, as an archaic throwback to obsolete political forms, but also its positive movement toward a better society. In this way, Kongo might be seen as a fount of revolutionary ideas as much as France was, even though the idiom of Kongolese ideology was royalist and, being alien to most researchers, has been overlooked.

Indeed, it was to political philosophy that Kongo owed its late eighteenth-century participation in the slave trade. The civil wars that punctuated most of the eighteenth century were fought at least in part to resolve constitutional issues and determine who was the king of Kongo and what were his powers. Many of those enslaved and eventually sent to Saint-Domingue had served in Kongo's civil wars or were caught up by them. The issues that shaped the civil wars in Kongo might well have shaped a different civil war in the Caribbean.

Civil war in Kongo can be analyzed through the two questions of who was to be king and what were the king's powers. The first issue, although of significance to partisans in Africa, is of less importance to those interested in Haiti than the second one, for ultimately it was the type of king (or government) rather than the specific person that would count. It is in the matter of the duties and role of kings that the ideological issues of leadership and political structure were shaped in Haiti.

Ever since the battle of Mbwila on 29 November 1665, the culmination of war with Portugal, Kongo had been torn by civil war. For much of the period the wars matched partisans of two great family-based alliances, the Kimpanzu and the Kimulaza. Although some kings, like Pedro IV in the early eighteenth century, managed to win general recognition,[17] the unity was fragile and often fell apart, as several families contended incessantly and generally indecisively for the royal title.[18] A long and devastating round of these wars that began in 1779, first matching partisans of King Pedro V against those of José I (pre-1779–1781), and then breaking out again upon the death of José's successor and brother Afonso V (1785–94),[19] contributed substantially to the export of Kongo slaves that fueled the surge of imports of Kongolese into Saint-Domingue recorded in the same period.[20]

If the Kongolese could not agree on who was the king of Kongo, they also disagreed on his exact powers. It is generally true that African states were ruled by kings, or at least by executive figures who could be called kings, but this may not be a particularly helpful statement. African states possessed a bewildering variety of constitutions: monarchs might be hereditary or elected, and they might exercise direct and fairly untrammeled power or be seriously checked by a variety of other institutions. Kongo was no exception. Although it was always ruled by a king, his powers and the basis for his authority were never static or fixed.

In common with many other political systems, Kongo political philosophy alternated between two opposing concepts: an absolutist one that granted the king full powers and the right to manage all the affairs of the country (at least in theory), and a much more limited one that required the king to rule by consent of the governed and to make decisions only after consultation with at least some of those he governed.

Like eighteenth-century Europe, Kongo thus had both an "absolutist" and a "republican" tendency in its political thought. Which one prevailed depended very much on who exercised power, in both Africa and Europe, though at most times there was a dynamic tension between the two. The interplay of these ideas shaped ideological struggle in Africa as in Europe. Major turning points of European political history, such as the French revolution, the Napoleonic empire, the Restoration, and the revolutions of 1830 or 1848, all were exercises in working out the contradictions of these opposed ideas. Ultimately, the triumph of republican forms of government and democracy resulted in the acceptance of one of these traditions, though even after this victory the authoritarian concept remained and resurfaced from time to time.

Kongo also possessed such opposed traditions, though there was no question of dispensing with kings, as European republicanism proposed. Rather, it was a question of the nature of the king's rule. Analysis based on an understanding of European ideology has difficulty comprehending this dynamic because its idiom was substantially different from that of Europe. It is necessary, therefore, to examine Kongolese political philosophy in order to see how it might have contributed to the African side of the ideology of the Haitian revolution.

If political idiom was often different between Kongo and Europe, there was one point of contact: Christianity. Kongo had been a Christian kingdom since the late fifteenth century, when Portuguese missionaries had baptized King Nzinga a Nkuwu[21] as João I on 3 May 1491.[22] [. . .] By the eighteenth century, Christianity was the source of Kongo identity, and virtually all the population participated in and knew its rites and tenets. [. . .] Christianity shaped Kongo political ideology as, in one way or another, it shaped European ideology.

Thus, Macaya's elaborate description (quoted above) of the three kings he served as the descendants of the Magi was not as farfetched as it might first appear. Kongolese ideologues had reworked Christian concepts in a similar way for many years. [. . .]

These imported Christian ideas combined with central African concepts to form the dynamic of power in Kongo. Kongolese viewed kings in much the same way as English, Dutch, or northern European thinkers did: as necessary but as potentially limited in their powers, thus being compatible with republican and even democratic ideas. Kongolese looked back to the foundation stories of the kingdom to explain basic political philosophy, much as eighteenth-century Europeans looked back to republican or imperial Rome for their own ideas. As the Kongolese understood it, the character of the founder formed a charter for the proper governance of the state.

In some versions of the story, the founder was described as a conqueror. Such kings exercised absolute power and could not be controlled by society; they could act with complete impunity. One symbolic statement of this sort of power appeared in tales of kings who killed people arbitrarily. According to one of the starkest versions of this story, recorded by the Capuchin priest Giovanni Cavazzi da Montecuccolo about 1665, the founder stabbed his pregnant aunt through the womb for refusing to pay a crossing toll, thus committing a double homicide. He went unpunished for this heinous crime, and was even admired; followers flocked to his standard, allowing him to conquer Kongo and establish his rule.[23] [. . .]

Such stories were appropriate to a highly centralized and autocratic kingdom, such as Kongo was from the time it first came into contact with Portugal in 1483 until the civil wars of the mid- to late seventeenth century. But in the civil war period, a new version of Kongo history began to emerge, especially as King Pedro IV (ruled 1694–1718) attempted to reunite the kingdom through a policy of reconciliation. Unlike the conqueror king of the centralized state, the new founder needed to be a more republican sort of ruler, one who recognized the rights of numerous families and local powers and ruled by consensus and consent.[24] Hence, the stories of Kongo's foundation told in Pedro's court presented the founder as a blacksmith king.

A memorial of about 1710 originating in Pedro IV's court described the royal family as descendants of a "wise and skillful blacksmith" who "gathered the Congolese People as their arbitrator of their differences and suits."[25] Modern anthropologists recognize the widespread central African image of the blacksmith as a conciliatory figure who resolves conflict and is gentle, generous, and unselfish.[26] To emphasize the gentleness of blacksmiths, they were associated with women. Furnaces were often decorated as women with breasts to heighten the imagery. [. . .]

The contrasting constitutional principles were cross-cut by larger moral ideas of political philosophy, which held that whatever powers kings might have, they should use them in the public interest. Thus, no matter how absolute his rule, a Kongolese king was expected to rule fairly and to share unselfishly in his wealth and power. [. . .]

Selfishness in private life was often seen as witchcraft, though only the individual witch or selfish person had to answer for it. But public greed or selfishness might be divinely punished by public disaster. [. . .]

These principles, with their emphasis on the ruler's responsibility to be unselfish and to support the public interest, were difficult to maintain in a centralized, absolutist polity. Rulers of such polities might be seen as witches because of the behavior of the founders of the states, who had killed freely and without reproach. But they could still be seen as morally correct if they used the power that derived from their absolutist origins in the public interest. Kongolese were not anarchists who disapproved of authority, and thus the king's power to kill or use violence was seen abstractly as the state's power which should be used in the public interest, specifically to counteract evil behavior and witchcraft. The idea of witchcraft could therefore be applied in the political realm only when kings or other political authorities used exploitation or corruption to pursue private wealth or power, and not simply because power was centralized.

[. . .]

Kongolese did not regard kings or soldiers as being intrinsically selfish or committed to useless war, even if some rulers or generals more or less surrendered to these ideas and adopted their religion accordingly. Kongolese political thought still accepted kings and accorded them the rights to kill and to rule. These powers were matched, however, by responsibilities to be generous and especially to show no signs of selfishness.

[. . .]

The struggle over centralization, the power of the leader to command followers, and the role of harmony and witchcraft in political philosophy were no doubt critical in the minds of the many soldiers who fought in these wars and were encouraged or inspired by one or another vision of Kongo.

Kongolese in Saint-Domingue

These ideas did not vanish when those unfortunate soldiers who served in the civil wars were captured and transported to Saint-Domingue, nor did they cease to operate when the conspiracy of 1791 resulted in the slave revolution in Saint-Domingue that eventually led to the independence of Haiti. In the environment of the New World, however, they combined with other ideas to constitute an ideological undercurrent of the revolution. The ideas did have to be translated to fit a new environment, since the social structure of Saint-Domingue was different from that of Kongo. There were, however, ideologically identifiable similarities between the two.

Political Power in the Slave Society

The original leaders of the conspiracy were probably not recently enslaved Kongolese from the civil wars, and indeed they may well have been moved as much by ideas of the French revolution as by those of the Kongo civil wars. According to testimony of the time, the original conspiracy was led by some 200 men, all of whom were *commandeurs d'atelier*, or the leaders of slave gangs.[27] Such men were privileged among slaves in Saint-Domingue, forming a distinct class in a highly unequal slave society. [. . .] These slaves, born in the colony, were more in touch with the local and European ideological environment than with events in Africa. [. . .]

These creole and mulatto supervisors and managers exercised authority in the society of prerevolutionary Saint-Domingue largely through the estate organization. Although they viewed the masters and the white overseers (*économes*) as opponents, much of the revolution from their point of view involved replacing leadership in the plantation, but not necessarily replacing the plantation system itself.

The slaves, especially the common field hands, while certainly required to obey the men their masters had appointed over them, did not necessarily confer legitimacy on them. Their goals certainly included the end of the plantation economy and forced labor, and thus they and the creoles could not share the same ultimate vision for postrevolutionary society.

The newly arrived African field hands often looked to organizations formed by their "nation"—a loose grouping of people from the same part of Africa or the same ethnolinguistic group—to provide leadership and perform mutual aid functions. One way of maintaining leadership of nations was through the election of kings and queens.[28] These elections were widespread in the society of Afro-American slaves in all parts of the Americas.[29] [. . .] In Saint-Domingue, where colonial legislation made open ceremony by national leadership illegal in the interests of security, national leadership was vested in the heads of secret societies.[30] Moreau de Saint-Méry's description of the secret societies on the eve of the revolution notes that they were often nationally organized, while their leaders were selected on a religious basis but served both as oracles and as arbitrators of slave society.[31]

These secret societies, with their kings and queens and their religious orientation, and perhaps also with their potential to form what people might have considered a legitimate government, had strong links to the ideology of African societies. They were also capable of organizing plots, since members of the same nation were typically scattered across many plantations and could be mobilized through the national element of the society. The closest Caribbean analogy to the Haitian revolution in terms of size and scale of mobilization, the Jamaica revolt of 1760, was organized through Akan (Coromanti) national organizations, including an elected king and queen.[32]

Two principles therefore competed in the making of the revolution: the estates headed by creole leadership and relying on the hierarchical organization of plantations for authority, and the nation with a looser but more popular organization. But the two types of organization could not operate independently, for the creoles could not stage a revolt alone. They had to obtain the support of the masses of slaves, and any ideology had to take their beliefs into account. The interesting dual meeting, first between creoles and then among field hands, that started the Haitian revolution was but the first manifestation of the alliance and difficulties between the two groups.[33]

Social Tension Among Rebel Slaves

The common slaves had the numbers of people necessary to conduct the revolt. In addition, many were ex-soldiers and prisoners of war who had the military experience and skills to carry the revolution forward, attributes that creole *commandeurs d'atelier* often lacked.

The military experience of many slaves may well explain the striking military success the rebels enjoyed in the early days of the revolution.[34] [. . .]

Historians have only a vague idea of who commanded these bands, how they were recruited and organized, and how they operated. But it is likely that linkages made through the African nations provided some of the organization and leadership. According to the historian Thomas Madiou, who collected his research material in the mid-nineteenth century and could still obtain recollections of veterans of the old wars, many units were organized by African nationality.[35] [. . .]

Macaya was a leader whose authority may have derived as much from his position in the national organization of Kongolese as from any role he might have played in the plantation economy. From contemporary accounts, his following seems to have been a large one.[36] [. . .]

National units might well have been commonplace since, as Jean-François and Biassou noted in 1791, the average soldier did not speak "two words of French," and thus communication within the band would have had to take place in an African language. If, as they implied, the units were indeed composed of veterans of African wars, there may also have been common organizational and tactical principles that members of the same nation would understand in forming their bands, in addition to the solidarity that probably went back to well before the revolution of conationals.

[. . .]

African Ideology in the Revolution

[. . .] For Macaya and his Kongolese followers, as for other leaders of nationally organized groups, the revolution and its aftermath raised in a new context the same issues that had divided Kongolese in Africa. Was the new society to be an authoritarian state where the plantation economy continued with or without slavery? Or was it to be a more egalitarian society of smallholders where estates were broken up and redistributed? Clearly the Kongolese ideology of blacksmith versus conqueror kings and related ideas could serve in this context as well as republican or imperial ideas of Europe.

Although explicit evidence is lacking, there are hints that at least some of the generals and elite presented themselves as conqueror kings or leaders. These are found in the innumerable atrocity stories that fill whole cartons in the archives and were the stock in trade of travelers, journalists, and analysts of the time.[37] Of course, atrocities can have many explanations that have nothing to do with ideology or revolution. The brutality of the slave regime and the excesses of those suppressing it could easily create a cycle of increasingly bloody acts of revenge that fueled the atrocity stories. Such stories might even be made up to secure the sympathies of a French public that might be moved from its support for the rebels by revelations of their inhumanity.

Whether they were consciously invoking the conqueror king or not, many of the early leaders exercised an iron discipline over their troops and followers, often enforced by horrible atrocities.[38] [. . .]

Military commanders, however, were not the only leaders created by the revolution. From the beginning kings and queens were elected in various areas whenever the insurgents succeeded in gaining political control. These elections harked back to the older kings and queens of national organizations, which in Saint-Domingue had been the secret societies.

L'Acul, Macaya's original base of operations, seems to have been organized in just this way shortly after the outbreak of the revolution, perhaps by the Kongo nation. A detailed diary of a French militiaman from the start of the revolution noted that the rebels chose a king for each quarter that they had captured.[39] [. . .]

The election of kings upon establishing their own government was not restricted to the rebels of the Plaine du Nord. [. . .] Their presence as elected leaders in the areas occupied in the early days of the revolution may represent a tentative movement in the direction of a local limited monarchy based on African ideological views, though surely tempered by the military necessities of the moment and the power this gave to more ruthless and less democratic men, who seem to have often held or taken the title of king.

That there may have been a tendency toward limited government or a democratic strain in the ideology of the national societies that favored Macaya and other such leaders is suggested by an important chant that was recorded on the eve of the revolution by Moreau de Saint-Méry. It was sung in Kikongo and thus provides a link to the ideological concepts of the Kongolese who made up such a large proportion of Saint-Domingue's society. The chant might have inspired a leader like Macaya:[40]

Eh! Eh! Bomba, hen! hen!
Canga bafio té

Canga moune dé lé
Canga doki la
Canga li.

The chant can be translated as follows:

Eh! Eh! Mbomba [Rainbow] hen! hen!
Hold back the black men[41]
Hold back the white man[42]
Hold back that witch
Hold them.

Contemporary observers, as well as many modern historians, who did not know the language of the chant (which is clearly Kikongo),[43] proposed fanciful translations, most of which echoed their understanding that as a revolutionary anthem, it must involve killing the whites.[44]

In fact, translating the chant is not an easy task, for much of its vocabulary has multiple interpretations, depending on context and dialect. [. . .] Although many commentators have sought to provide the chant with revolutionary content by changing its translation, others, notably Pierre Pluchon and David Geggus, have taken the translation as given and sought to deprive it of revolutionary content. They have argued that in fact the chant was not particularly revolutionary; rather, it was simply a part of initiation into a Voodoo society in which the sectarian hoped to find personal protection against the witchcraft, often worked by fellow slaves, that was rampant in prerevolutionary Haiti. Moreover, they question its role as some sort of anthem, suggesting that later writers, who had read Moreau de Saint-Méry, assumed its application by the revolutionary leaders.[45]

Much of the ambiguity in the text and the debate among would-be translators revolves around the correct translation of *kanga* [. . .] , a verb that has multiple meanings in different dialects. Certainly the eighteenth-century meaning of the word was "to stop or bind" in all dialects,[46] although among Christians from Kongo, paradoxically, it might also mean "to save, protect, or deliver" in a Christian religious sense.[47]

Although salvation, protection, and prevention might stress personal meaning, African political ideology used this sort of idiom in a public as well as a political sense. [. . .]

This chant therefore needs to be seen in terms of the political meaning of witchcraft, rather than the personal one, if we are to respect the belief of the colonists that the chant had revolutionary overtones even if they could not translate it. Its general terms of address, to blacks (*bafiote*) and whites (*mundele*) alike, and the invocation of *Mbumba* suggest that it had a social as much as a personal significance. Furthermore, the invocation of *Mbumba* also suggests that it expressed the spirit of harmony and peace as an alternative to personal greed and witchcraft that was rampant in prerevolutionary Haiti. As such it could serve as a sort of shorthand expression of a particular revolutionary creed that sought to restore justice and harmony to all, as expressed in Kongo politico-religious ideology. [. . .]

The present investigation has focused on Kongo ideas about monarchy, but Kongolese were not the only Africans in Saint-Domingue, nor were they the only African group to have ideas of tempered monarchy, nor the only ones among whom disputes and struggle over the powers of kings took place. The larger Yoruba-Aja group of people in Lower Guinea (modern Bénin, Togo, and Nigeria) had strong traditions of limiting monarchical power, over which they eventually became involved in civil war. The Yoruba civil wars in the late eighteenth and nineteenth centuries, like their equivalents in Kongo, concerned constitutional issues and fueled the slave trade.[48] Careful study of ideological issues in other parts of Africa may well add further texture to the ideas presented here, for both the Old World and the New.

NOTES

* [. . .] I am grateful to Carolyn Fick, Linda Heywood, and David Geggus for substantial criticism of earlier drafts, and also to Donna Eveleth for locating and copying sources for me at the Archives Nationales, Paris. [. . .]

1 François-Joseph-Pamphile de Lacroix, *Mémoires pour servir à l'histoire de la révolution de Saint-Domingue*, 2 vols. (Paris, 1819), 1:25, quoting original correspondence.

2 Thomas Madiou, *Histoire d'Haiti* (Port-au-Prince, 1947), p. 104.

3 For similar discussions in another context, see Michael Craton, *Testing the Chains: Resistance to Slavery in the British West Indies* (Ithaca, 1982), pp. 109–10, 122–24; and more generally, Eugene Genovese, *From Rebellion to Revolution: Afro-American Slave Revolts in the Making of the Modern World* (Baton Rouge, 1979), both of whom see the royalism as archaic and backward-looking. Also see David Geggus, *Slavery, War and Revolution: The British Occupation of Saint Domingue, 1793–1798* (Oxford, 1982), pp. 38–40, 182, 414 n.60, and 442 n.165, for speculations that the royalism was related to the African background and counterrevolutionary ideas.

4 Archives Nationales de France (hereafter cited as AN), section D-XXV, carton 43, dossier 415 (hereafter cited as AN, D-XXV, 43, 415), Civil Commissioners to Pierrot, 13 July 1793.

5 AN, D-XXV, 43, 415, Civil Commissioners to Pierrot, 17 July 1793.

6 Genovese, *Rebellion to Revolution*.

7 C. L. R. James, *The Black Jacobins: Toussaint L'Ouverture and the San Domingo Revolution*, 2nd ed. (New York, 1963).

8 Jean-Philippe Garran de Coulon, *Rapport sur les troubles de Saint-Domingue, fait à nom des Comités de Salut Public, de Législation et de Marine réunis*, 5 vols. (Paris, An V), 2:193 and 4:47–48; P. R. Roume, *Rapport de P. R. Roume sur sa mission à Saint-Domingue* (Paris, 1793), pp. 47–48.

9 Louis Médéric Elie Moreau de Saint-Méry, *Description topographique, physique, civile, politique et historique de la partie française de l'isle de Saint-Domingue* (Philadelphia, 1796), 3 vols., 1:44.

10 Carolyn Fick, *The Making of Haiti: The Saint Domingue Revolution from Below* (Knoxville, 1990), p. 321 n.103.

11 For the general outlines of these operations, see Phyllis Martin, *The External Trade of the Loango Coast, 1570–1870* (London, 1972). [. . .]

12 Imports calculated on the basis of Jean Fouchard's careful study of arrivals of ships from colonial newspapers and checked by the fraction of Kongos reported in notices of runaways. See Fouchard, *The Haitian Maroons: Liberty or Death*, trans. A. Faulkner Watts (New York, 1981).

13 David Geggus, "Sugar and Coffee Cultivation in Saint Domingue and the Shaping of a Slave Labor Force," in Ira Berlin and Philip Morgan, eds., *Cultivation and Culture: Work Process and the Shaping of Afro-American Culture in the Americas* (forthcoming); and Geggus, "The Composition of the French Slave Trade," in P. Boucher, ed., *Proceedings of the 13th/14th Meetings of the French Colonial Historical Society* (Lanham, Md., 1990). I thank David Geggus for supplying me with these references.

14 The term was used derisively by Europeans and the upper classes of Haiti, for example, when Dessalines was referred to as a Congo by a French agent, writing to the Ministry of Marine about 1800: AN, AF-iv, 1212, quoted in Robert Heinl and Nancy Heinl, *Written in Blood: The Story of the Haitian People, 1492–1971* (New York, 1978), p. 95. It is unlikely that Dessalines was actually from Kongo.

15 Modern anthropologists use the term *Bakongo* to describe these people, a term I have abandoned in favor of *Kongolese* (but spelled with a *k* to distinguish them from citizens of the modern Republic of Congo, some but not all of whom are Bakongo). *Bakongo* refers to the entire group of people speaking various dialects of the Kikongo language, while my references are specifically to subjects of the king of Kongo, who controlled only a portion of this speech community.

16 It was, for example the name of the son of King António I (d. 1665), Francisco de Menezes Nkanka Makaya (Canca Macaia), as recorded around 1695. See Marcellino d'Atri, "Giornate apostoliche fatta da me . . . nelle Messioni de Regni d'Angola e Congo . . .," published with original pagination marked in Carlo Toso, ed., *L'anarchia congolese nel secolo XVII: Le relazione inedite di Marcellino d'Atri* (Genoa, 1984), p. 55. Elsewhere, however, d'Atri calls him "Canca Macassa," p. 37. The word *makaya* in Kikongo means "leaves."

17 On the origin of the first civil wars and Pedro IV's restoration, see John Thornton, *The Kingdom of Kongo: Civil War and Transition, 1641–1718* (Madison, 1983).

18 For a general chronicle-type survey, based closely on original documents, see Graziano Saccardo [da Leguzzano], *Congo e Angola con la storia del missione dei cappuccini*, 3 vols. (Venice, 1982–84). An analytical study of the eighteenth and nineteenth centuries is available in Susan H. Broadhead, "Beyond Decline: The Kingdom of Kongo in the Eighteenth and Nineteenth Centuries," *International Journal of African Historical Studies* 12 (1979): 615–50.

19 The first phase of these wars (until 1788), their development, and their relation to the slave trade are all explained in detail in the lengthy eyewitness report of the missionary Rafael de Castello de Vide, who resided in Kongo from 1780 to 1788. See Academia das Ciências (Lisbon), MS Vermelho 296, Castello de Vide, "Viagem do Congo do Missionario Fr. Raphael de Castello de Vide . . .," *passim*.

20 See John Thornton, "The Kongo Civil Wars and the Slave Trade: Demography and History Revisited, 1718–1844," paper presented at the Canadian African Studies Association meeting, Montreal, 15–17 May 1992.

21 In writing this name and other Kikongo words and phrases, I have adopted basically the Zairian orthography of Kikongo, which reflects the grammatical

relationship rather than precisely how the words are pronounced. I have favored this orthography over that adopted officially in Angola or Congo-Brazzaville, more technical ones created by modern linguists, or the older orthographies of the seventeenth and eighteenth centuries. This name might be pronounced "Zingan kuwu."

22 For an interpretation of the role of the church in Kongo, see John Thornton, "The Development of an African Catholic Church in the Kingdom of Kongo, 1491–1750," *Journal of African History* 25 (1984): 147–67.

23 Giovanni Antonio Cavazzi da Montecuccolo, *Istorica descrizione de' tre regni Congo, Angola ed Matamba* (Bologna, 1687), book 2, para. 86; these references permit comparison with the modern Portuguese translation of Graziano Maria da Legguzzano, 2 vols. (Lisbon, 1965).

24 On the politics of the restoration, see Thornton, *Kingdom of Kongo*, pp. 97–113.

25 [Francesco da Pavia], "Memoria sopra alcune cose che domanda il Re del Congo," n. d. [c. 1710], Archivio de Propaganda Fide, Scritture riferite nel Congressi, Africa, Congo, vol. 1, fol. 141.

26 Pierre de Maret, "Ceux qui jouent avec le feu: La place du forgeron en Afrique centrale," *Africa* (London) 50 (1980): 263–79.

27 Garran de Coulon, *Rapport*, 2:211–12.

28 For a fuller discussion of the national organization as a mutual aid system and a vehicle for plotting against the masters, see John Thornton, *Africa and Africans in the Making of the Atlantic World, 1400–1680* (Cambridge, 1992), pp. 201–205 (for the earlier period); and, for later periods, Thornton, "African National Organizations and American Societies," paper presented at the conference "Transatlantic Encounters," Vanderbilt University, Nashville, Tennessee, 8–10 October 1992.

29 On the early history of these organizations and their kings, queens, and shadow governments, see John Thornton, *Africa and Africans*, pp. 202–205.

30 On the colonial legislation that made virtually all slave organizations illegal, see Pierre Pluchon, *Vaudou, sorciers, empoisonneurs de Saint-Domingue à Haïti* (Paris, 1987), pp. 29–49.

31 Moreau de Saint-Méry, *Description*, 1:64–69. On the role of ethnicity in general, see two articles by David Geggus: "La cérémonie du Bois-Caïman," *Chemins critiques* 2 (1992): 71; and "The Bois Caïman Ceremony," *Journal of Caribbean History* 25 (1991): 50.

32 The revolt and its details are described fully in Edward Long, *History of Jamaica*, 3 vols. (London, 1774), 2:450–63. On the role of ethnicity in revolts in general, see Craton, *Testing the Chains*.

33 For a thorough examination of the two meetings, see Geggus, "Cérémonie," and "The Bois Caïman Ceremony."

34 For a fuller development of this theme, see John Thornton, "African Soldiers in the Haitian Revolution," *Journal of Caribbean History* 25 (1991): 58–80.

35 Madiou, *Histoire d'Haiti*, p. 105.

36 AN, D-XXV, 23, 231, letters of Macaya, 4 September and 9 September 1793.

37 For example, Brian Edwards, *An Historical Survey of the French Colony on the Island of St. Domingo*, vol. 4 of *The History Civil and Commercial of the British Colonies in the West Indies* (Philadelphia, 1806), pp. 74, 79, and *passim*. Reports contain these tales as well: see, for example, AN, D-XXV, 62, 619, Rouvray to Blanchelande, 8 June 1792; 628, Assemblée Générale, 28 January 1792; 626, Commissioners of Assemblée Coloniale to Commissioners (1792); 627, Commissioners' letters, 28 January and 27 February 1792.

38 AN, D-XXV, 56, doc. 555, Discours, cited in Fick, *Making of Haiti*, p. 111.

39 "San Domingo Disturbances," published in the Philadelphia *General Advertiser*, no. 322, 11 October 1791, diary entry of 5 September. The diary was published

in installments in nos. 321 (10 October 1791), 347 (9 November 1791), 348 (10 November 1791), 349 (11 November 1791), 350 (12 November 1791), and 351 (14 November 1791). [. . .]

40 Moreau de Saint-Méry, *Description*, 1:67.

41 The word is plural.

42 This term is singular; the plural was *mindele*.

43 It is not clear, however, which dialect of Kikongo it is. There are diagnostic differences in phonology and word choice between the Solongo and Zombo dialects, both of which can be documented in the eighteenth century. This text, however, is not sufficiently linguistically sophisticated or long enough to warrant speculation about the dialect.

44 The history of the translation of the text is provided in Geggus, "Haitian Voodoo in the Eighteenth Century: Language, Culture, Resistance," *Jahrbuch für Geschichte von Staat, Wirtschaft und Gesellschaft Lateinamerikas 28* (1991): 24–32.

45 Geggus, "Haitian Voodoo," pp. 42–50; Pluchon, *Vaudou*, pp. 89, 112–16. Fick and Geggus disagree on its use as a revolutionary hymn specifically with regard to its quotation in a modern account that claims to use nonextant documentation and puts it in the mouths of rebels in 1791.

46 The Dictionary of 1774, Biblioteca dei Cappuccini da Genova, using the Solongo dialect from north of the Zaire (a non-Christian area), gives *"kanga, kangezi* [the perfect form] attacher" and adds that "kanga zita" meant "faire un noeud" (p. 68). Geggus adds a longer commentary on the word, noting that it has special meaning in witchcraft terminology of the north bank of the Zaire in the early twentieth century: "Haitian Voodoo," pp. 28–29. Geggus concludes: "Thus, in the chant in question 'canga' doubtless does mean 'stop' but with the particular connotation of 'rendering harmless by supernatural means.' " Its meaning as "to tie" or "to bind" in the Zombo or São Salvador dialect of Christians is attested since the seventeenth century in the Dictionary of 1652, Biblioteca Nazionale da Roma, Vittorio Emmanuele, 1896, MS Varia 274, "Vocabularium latinum, hispanicum et congoese . . .," fol. 51v: *ligo as atar* (Latin "to tie") is *cucanga*; and fol. 116v, *vinculo as entregar en cadenas* (Latin "to tie up" or Spanish "to tie in boxes") is *cucanga quiconi* among other definitions. Bernardo da Cannicatí (Cannecattim), missionary at Bengo from 1779 to 1800, who had information from both the Solongo and São Salvador dialects, gives cánga as the meaning of *atar: Diccionario abbreviado da Lingua Conqueza . . .* (Lisbon, 1805), p. 164.

47 See MSS Araldi (documents in possession of the Araldi Family of Modena), Giovanni Antonio Cavazzi da Montecuccolo, "Missione evangelica al regno de Congo," Vol. A, Book I, pp. 83-86; and Cadornega, *História* 3:223-24. Jesus was also known in Kikongo as Mucangui or Savior. This specific meaning was still retained in the late eighteenth century, for Cannecattim gives *Gánga* (probably a misprint for *cánga*) as the Kikongo for *livrar* in his *Diccionario*, p. 191.

48 On constitutional issues in Yoruba areas, see Robin Law, *The Oyo Empire, 1600–1822* (Oxford, 1977).

Section II

INDEPENDENT HAITI IN A HOSTILE WORLD
Haiti in the Nineteenth Century

The dramatic events of the Haitian Revolution and the political turbulence of the twentieth century in Haiti have often overshadowed the history of the nineteenth century. However, a mounting appreciation of the importance of this period has spurred many recent works. In addition to French-language studies by Haitian and French scholars, a growing literature relating to nineteenth-century Haiti has been produced by Anglophone and Hispanophone scholars of Atlantic, American, Caribbean, Latin American and French history, as well as of Francophone literary studies.

For scholars within Haiti, the early nineteenth century is a critical part of their national past; interest among Haitians in nineteenth-century nation-builders is akin to American interest in the Founding Fathers. Since the fall of the Duvaliers, scholars in Haiti have had renewed freedom to write about the Haitian past – and its connection to the present – without camouflaging their meaning.[1] Yet, as the country's transition to democracy has dragged since 1986, finding the historical roots of twentieth-century authoritarianism has become an urgent preoccupation. The nation's earliest decades seem to many Haitian scholars a logical place to consider: *Why didn't the Haitian Revolution result in an egalitarian society? How did Haiti move from the idealism of its founding to the persistence of authoritarianism in the twentieth century? Do negative aspects of contemporary Haitian politics stem from the nation's early years?*

An excellent overview of Haitian historiography on the nineteenth century can be found in a state-of-the-field collection edited in 2009 by two of Haiti's leading scholars, Michel Hector and Laënnec Hurbon: *Genèse de l'État haïtien, 1804–1859* [Origin of the Haitian State, 1804–1859]. The work, which has not been translated into English, contains essays on many aspects of the long nineteenth century. One of its many useful features is a periodization proposed by Hector. Hector divides the period after the state's gestation (1791–1803) into one phase from 1804 to 1820 and another from 1820 to 1859.[2] The first phase starts with Dessalines' proclamation of Haitian independence in 1804, and also includes the 1806 assassination of Dessalines and the subsequent split of Haiti into two competing regimes, a Northern state led by Henri Christophe and a Southern military republic led by Alexandre Pétion. Tensions between *anciens libres* (the people of color who had been free and relatively wealthy even before the Revolution) and *nouveaux libres* (the slaves freed by the Revolution) persisted. Although these groups were intermingled around the country, the leaders of Christophe's regime tended to be *nouveaux libres* (primarily black), while *anciens libres* (mostly mixed-race) populated the highest ranks of Pétion's government. In 1811, the North became a monarchy when Christophe declared himself King Henry I; in 1818, Pétion died and was replaced by Jean-Pierre Boyer. As civil war between the two states raged in 1820, Christophe committed suicide; within a few weeks, Boyer conquered the North and reunified Haiti.

Even as internal struggles raged in Haiti during its two decades, another prominent feature of the period was a climate of international hostility. As Michel-Rolph Trouillot's article (Section I) indicates, the Haitian Revolution aroused fear throughout the Atlantic world. The facts of the Haitian Revolution – that slaves violently seized their freedom, defeating one of the world's strongest powers and sometimes killing whites in the process – sent shockwaves throughout the New World and back to the European metropoles. After 1804, France refused to recognize Haitian independence. Meanwhile, exiled colonists who had fled to metropolitan France pressed authorities to reconquer the island and regain their property. Other slaveholding countries in the Atlantic world, most notably the United States, also refused to recognize Haiti. Under Thomas Jefferson's administration, the United States imposed an embargo on the island. Throughout the Americas, slavery became even more repressive, as slaveowners fearing copycat revolts crushed any sign of resistance.

The next period of Haitian history, in Hector's model, begins with the unification of Haiti in 1820 and extends until 1859. It includes the Haitian conquest of the Eastern part of Hispaniola (the present-day Dominican Republic), which lasted from 1822 to 1844; the Revolution of 1843, which brought down Boyer's regime; the Piquet Rebellion, a series of peasant uprisings, in 1844; the ascension in 1847 of General Faustin Soulouque, who named himself Emperor Faustin I in 1849 and the toppling of Faustin in 1859 by a revolution led by Fabre Geffrard. Hector's periodization might be modified only by distinguishing between the years before 1825 (when Haiti was largely isolated internationally[3]) and after 1825 (when France agreed to recognize Haitian independence in exchange for an indemnity of 150 million francs). Although this agreement technically allowed Haiti to enter the community of nations, the staggering sum, which lay far beyond Haiti's means, turned Haiti's *de facto* independence into a crippling financial dependency.[4] Compounding matters, the United States continued to refuse to recognize Haiti even after France did. As Senator Robert Y. Hayne of South Carolina argued in 1825, "With nothing connected with slavery can we treat with other nations. Our policy with regard to Hayti is plain. We can never acknowledge her independence."[5]

Haiti's struggles to nation-build in this context have received a great deal of attention in recent years from both Haitian and foreign scholars. One reason why scholars have concentrated on the early nineteenth century is to understand: *Why did Haiti end up much poorer than its Caribbean neighbors?* Hector notes that Haiti faced a triple challenge after independence: simultaneously founding a new state, reinserting itself into the international community and establishing a new economic system to succeed slavery. From 1804 to 1825, Haitian leaders expended considerable effort trying to end the isolation that was crippling their economy.[6] Even after France recognized Haiti and trade restrictions eased, Haitian leaders struggled to induce freed slaves to return to their plantations; like Sonthonax and Polverel (see Section I), they sought to resume the sugar and coffee production that had generated Saint-Domingue's wealth. To escape a compulsory labor system that was only slightly more humane than slavery, many Haitians fled to interior parts of the state to try to farm small plots of land, out of reach of the government.

Rebuilding the state presented a special set of obstacles. Hector has pointed to the fact that other Caribbean countries entered their post-emancipation phases still colonized – that is, without a "radical rupture with the past" like the Haitian Revolution. Whereas on other islands preexisting colonial institutions eased the transition to a post-emancipation economy, Haiti had to build a new government and a new economy at once. Moreover, as Claude Moïse has underscored, the wars of the Haitian Revolution not only devastated the land that had been used for cultivation, but also ejected the dominant colonial classes, leaving only the state to fill the void. The state's overarching power in Haiti since the nineteenth century stems from this fact, Moïse argues.[7]

Hector identifies yet another key difference between Haiti and other Caribbean societies after emancipation: a lack of capital. Following emancipation on other islands, Hector notes, metropoles indemnized colonists for their loss of slave property and funded new industries to replace sugar cultivation. In contrast, Haiti was permitted to enter the community of nations only after paying out of its own meager funds (and taking out loans) to indemnize French former slaveowners. The Haitian scholar Benoît Joachim has referred to the indemnization agreement as a "castration of national capital."[8] Rather than being able to fund new industries, an enormous amount of Haiti's GDP was sent abroad to pay interest on this debt. Haitian leaders thus began their independence years under constraints that would have thwarted even the best-designed policies.

The final stage of Hector's nineteenth-century periodization goes from 1859 to 1915 (the start of the first U.S. occupation of Haiti). Hector distinguishes between two segments of this period: 1859–1889 and 1890–1915. The former began, he argues, as a relatively good era in Haitian history. Under the presidency of Fabre Geffrard (1859–1867), republicanism returned to Haiti. Coffee production flourished alongside subsistence farming; agricultural revenues built a surplus large enough that Haiti could make substantial payments toward its indemnity debt. In the 1860s, Haitian leaders – following global trends in the industrial age – began their first steps toward modernization. The United States finally recognized Haiti in 1862, ending Haiti's isolation from what had been its major trading partner; the first U.S. diplomat (an African-American named Ebenezer Bassett) arrived in Port-au-Prince in 1869. However, just as independent Haiti was poised to overcome the obstacles it had faced since independence, a civil war broke out during the presidency of Sylvain Salnave (1867–1869), with the central government having to deal with rebels known as *cacos* in the North and continuing rebellions by *piquet* rebels in the South. Salnave was executed, and the state effectively split into three entities (North, South and central government). Violent conflicts broke out again between 1870 and 1883, leading to further instability. As Haitian leaders sought international credit at the end of the century (primarily from France), international financial institutions entered the country, but began speculative crises that enriched only themselves.

1890–1915 represents a second phase of this period, characterized by heightened international meddling. This period saw even greater instability and a succession of short-term presidents. After 1890, the international economy entered a downswing, the peasant economy collapsed and international banks (whether French, German or American) became Haiti's *de facto* rulers. Even when the global economy picked up after 1896, local instability prevented Haiti from benefitting from it. Meanwhile, Haitian elites, anxious not to seem backward to the foreigners circulating on the island, flaunted their modernity by consuming foreign fashions and industrialized products. Rather than making productive local investments or seeking to better the lot of the poor, they used their capital to buy foreign consumer goods. Any surplus generated by peasant agriculture now paid not only for interest on the indemnity debt (and on new debts contracted with French banks in 1875 and 1896), but also for "the sumptuous life of local oligarchies."[9]

Meanwhile, as the United States sought to build an empire to rival that of the British and the French, Americans began coveting a Haitian harbor called Môle St. Nicolas that seemed an ideal home for a naval base. Frederick Douglass (who had served as the U.S. ambassador to Haiti from 1889 to 1891) warned in a famous 1893 speech that the U.S. should cease interfering in Haiti and not try to seize Môle St. Nicolas. Although he acknowledged internal conflict in Haiti, Douglass protested that U.S. interference magnified it. Haiti, he argued, has all the conditions essential to a noble, prosperous and happy country. Yet, there she is, torn and rent by revolutions, by clamorous factions and anarchies; floundering her life away from year to year in a labyrinth of social misery. . . . The fault is not with the ignorant many but with the educated and ambitious few. Too proud to work, and not disposed to go into commerce, they make politics a business and are forever plotting to get into their hands the large revenues of their country. . . . They have allies in the United States. . . . It so happens that we have men in this country who, to accomplish their personal and selfish ends, will fan the flame of passion between the factions in Haiti. . . . [M]en in high American quarters have boasted to me of their ability to start a revolution in Haiti at their pleasure.[10]

Despite Douglass's appeal, foreign business interests continued to meddle in Haiti, and a new destabilizing crisis began in 1910 that was even worse than those of the 1840s or 1867–1870. Haiti had seven presidents between 1911 and 1915, some who were overthrown or assassinated and others who died under mysterious circumstances.

In contrast to the earlier phases of the century, this latter period (1860–1915) has received much less scholarly analysis. For one thing, the major works of reference that scholars use for the nineteenth century, those by the Haitian historians Thomas Madiou (1814–1884) and Beaubrun Ardouin (1796–1865), were written mid-century and lack coverage of later decades. In addition, though English-language surveys of Haitian history offer some coverage of this period, they generally do so without the same level of detail as on the Revolution, early independence years and the twentieth century.[11] The other major monographs and articles on this period are in French. The most indispensable of these are the first three volumes of Roger Gaillard's seven-volume series *La république exterminatrice* (the first volume of which was completed posthumously by Gaillard's daughter Gusti-Klara Gaillard-Pourchet, an accomplished historian of Haiti in her own right).[12]

In English, studies on the late nineteenth century have tended to focus on intellectual life rather than politics.[13] However, interest in other aspects of the period is growing. New work by Thorald Burnham challenges the notion of Haitian isolation in the nineteenth century by focusing on immigration to Haiti from 1850–1871, particularly from other parts of the Caribbean. Another important new study, which discusses government persecution of Vodou in the late nineteenth century, is Kate Ramsey's *The Spirits and the Law: Vodou and Power in Haiti*. Some specialists in American and African-American history have also started to work on the last third of the century, whether with regard to U.S. attempts to intervene in Haiti, Haitian efforts to court favor in the United States or African-American efforts to lobby their government on Haiti's behalf.[14]

* * *

The essays reprinted in this section, all penned by Anglophones, proceed from slightly different premises than the work of Hector and other Haitians who have written about the period in French. For Haitians, studying nineteenth-century Haitian history is a quest both to understand the aftermath of the Revolution and to locate roots of their society's current flaws. Anglophone scholars, in contrast, have frequently been attracted to Haiti more by general interests in comparative Atlantic history, the history of slavery in the Americas or the postcolonial condition. Despite their differing impulses, recent Haitian and Anglophone works on the period share much in common, and not only because they both tend to focus on the century's first half. Indeed, the articles in this section demonstrate a fundamental truth also underlying the work of Haitian scholars: *Haitian nation-building cannot be studied without reference to the international context in which Haiti operated; both internal and external factors have to be taken into account in understanding Haiti's development.*[15] While world history scholarship emphasizes that all history is a balance between local and global forces, the particular circumstances of Haiti's history make it important to underscore this point. Consequently, the essays in this section look at both international reactions to Haiti's independence and at the nation-building strategies that Haitian leaders adopted within this climate. The articles cover events from Louverture's and Dessalines' regimes (White, Ferrer, Nicholls and Sheller) through those of Boyer, Geffrard and Salnave (Sheller, Alexander and Nicholls, respectively).

The opening essay in this section considers: *How did the Founding Fathers and others in the U.S. react to the Haitian Revolution, and what impact did their actions have on Haiti?* For many years Americans ignored Haiti, prompted by the kind of animosity charted by Michel-Rolph Trouillot (Section I). During the U.S. occupation of Haiti (1915–1934), American historians became more interested in the history of U.S.–Haitian relations, and several studies were devoted to the topic. In the last thirty years, interest in Atlantic history, the history of race and the history of migration have brought new generations of Americanists to the subject.[16]

One of the leading figures in this recent wave of scholarship is Ashli White, a specialist in the early national United States and its connections to the larger Atlantic world. White's essay "The Politics of 'French Negroes' in the United States" examines how news of the Haitian Revolution was received in U.S. cities. Where previous scholars of the Haitian Revolution's impact in the United States have often focused on elites such as the Founding Fathers, or on reactions to the Revolution in a particular region, White charts the complex reactions to events in Saint-Domingue by multiple groups in the early United States; she focuses particularly on white and non-white refugees from Saint-Domingue. It has become a truism of recent Atlantic historiography that the Haitian Revolution incited fear in the United States as it did elsewhere in the Atlantic world.[17] White nuances this idea by suggesting that U.S. reactions to the Haitian

Revolution were diverse and complex. Furthermore, White argues, contrasts with Saint-Domingue and the rest of the Caribbean played a critical role in the formation of American national identity.

At first, White notes, U.S. slaveowners acted as if there was nothing to fear from the violence in Saint-Domingue; they reassured themselves that their own slaves, unlike those in the Caribbean, were well-treated and would never think of revolting. As time went on, however, slaveowners and others in the U.S. viewed the Haitian Revolution with increasing alarm. States banned the arrival of "French Negroes" (blacks or people of mixed-race coming from Saint-Domingue), out of fear that they would corrupt American slaves. White also notes American policy-shifts toward Saint-Domingue. As U.S. relations with France worsened in the late 1790s, the idea of an independent Saint-Domingue gained a certain appeal to Americans such as John Adams; it seemed a buffer against French encroachment on the United States. Thomas Jefferson's administration was much more hostile to Saint-Domingue, banning commerce with the island completely.[18] While White's focus is on the American reception of the Haitian Revolution, she also touches upon the issue of how Haitian leaders such as Louverture maneuvered in this difficult international climate.

Ada Ferrer's article "Talk About Haiti: The Archive and the Atlantic's Haitian Revolution" looks at a parallel topic elsewhere in the Atlantic: *How was the Haitian Revolution discussed and understood in Cuba?* Ferrer's essay is part of a larger body of recent work that has traced the effects of the Haitian Revolution throughout Latin America and the Caribbean.[19] In other essays, Ferrer (a specialist in Cuban history) has looked in greater detail at how the Haitian Revolution affected Cuba, strengthening its slave system as Cuban sugar production rose to fill the void left by the collapse of Saint-Domingue's plantation system.[20] In this essay, Ferrer uses the Cuban example to test and refine the conclusions of Trouillot on the Revolution's "unthinkable" nature (Section I). Ferrer pushes us to consider: *Were efforts to silence the Haitian Revolution successful? Do archives really conceal the histories of the less powerful?*

Ferrer agrees with many aspects of Trouillot's essay; however, noting that events in Haiti were discussed persistently throughout the Atlantic, she comments that "If this was silence, it was a thunderous one indeed." Ferrer maintains that scholars need to "move beyond" the idea of silencing to understand how the Haitian Revolution was seen by multiple populations (white, enslaved, and free people of color) in the Atlantic world. Ferrer arrives at a different way of thinking about history and historical memory than did Trouillot. She applauds his observation that archives typically contain elites' perspectives on history. At the same time, she argues, if we approach historical archives creatively, we can see "the traces of the operation of [their] own power"; we can understand how "silences and narratives are created, reformulated, sustained, and broken."[21] Ferrer's article also reminds us of the interconnectedness of Haitians and neighboring peoples.

The section's next article, "Sword-Bearing Citizens: Militarism and Manhood in Nineteenth-Century Haiti," takes us back to Haiti itself, but does not disregard international hostility toward the new nation. It helps us think about: *Why wasn't Haiti able to become the egalitarian society that its Revolution seemed to promise?* The piece is authored by Mimi Sheller, a historical sociologist who has produced some of the most innovative recent work on Haiti and the Caribbean. In one sense, Sheller's essay differs from nearly all previous scholarship on the nineteenth century: she concentrates on constructions of gender in Haitian political culture. The role of women is not wholly absent from other works on the period. As David Nicholls' essay in this section indicates, it would be difficult to discuss the turmoil under Salnave without speaking of the crowds of women who supported him. Patrick Bellegarde-Smith has identified a woman among the leaders of the 1844 Piquet Rebellion, and Joan Dayan has done seminal work on the role of gender in nineteenth-century Haitian history and religion.[22] Nevertheless, gender analysis has been much more common for eighteenth-century Saint-Domingue (see Section I introduction) than for the nineteenth century. Moreover, even as new studies are examining twentieth-century Haitian women's lives (see Section III introduction), this work has not been done in detail for the nineteenth.

Despite its originality in this regard, Sheller's work parallels existing scholarship on the nineteenth century in a fundamental way: like Haitians who study the period, she is very much thinking about modern-day Haiti. Sheller speaks of a "political paradox which still plagues Haiti: the egalitarian and democratic values of republicanism were constantly undercut by the hierarchical and elitist values of militarism." She therefore seeks to trace "authoritarian presidentialism" back to the nineteenth century. She considers: *How did discourses of masculinity in early Haitian political culture work to disenfranchise both women and the poor?* Sheller highlights a double exclusion, where both women and *nouveaux libres* peasants were marginalized by hierarchical power structures modeled after military ones. Sheller also demonstrates the intertwining of Haitian choices and the international climate. It was precisely because Haiti faced a persistent threat of foreign invasion, Sheller indicates, that Haiti needed to "remain on a military footing long after the revolution ended." Moreover, since Europeans often portrayed blacks as immature children incapable of governing themselves, Haitian men felt compelled to "prove their manhood." "Building black masculinity," Sheller contends, "became a central task in the construction of Haitian national identity."

Sheller's training in gender theory has led her down paths that scholars in Haiti have not yet pursued. Her essay is one that leading Haitian scholars would applaud, however, if only they were aware of it.[23] Hurbon and Hector lament that gender analysis is essential for understanding the construction of the Haitian state, but that the topic has not yet been tackled for the nineteenth century.[24] Even with Sheller having undertaken this initial foray on the subject, much more can still be learned about both gender ideas and women's roles in nineteenth-century Haiti.

Like Sheller's essay, David Nicholls' article "Rural Protest and Peasant Revolt, 1804–1869" aims to identify the roots of authoritarian tendencies in Haitian politics. Although Nicholls died in 1996, his pioneering research has, in many ways, still not been surpassed. There is no other work in English on nineteenth-century Haiti as comprehensive as his *From Dessalines to Duvalier: Race, Colour and National Independence in Haiti*, which is also seen as seminal by Haitian scholars.[25] In that book (as in *Haiti in Caribbean Context*, the work from which "Rural Protest" is excerpted), Nicholls writes with the Duvalier regime in mind; he looks backwards to find its roots.

Nicholls begins by invoking the *tontons macoutes*, the vicious militia used by the Duvaliers to eradicate opposition. Noting that François Duvalier was a student of Haitian history, Nicholls argues that Duvalier coopted earlier traditions of peasant revolts against elites. Nicholls considers: *What were these traditions of revolt and what motivated them?* His essay offers a helpful overview of the various regimes in Haiti from 1804–1869, while chronicling three rural protest movements in that timeframe. Nicholls notes that while Haitian historians such as Roger Gaillard, Kethly Millet and Alain Turnier had studied peasant movements on the eve of the 1915 U.S. occupation of Haiti, earlier movements had been neglected by scholars.[26] Nicholls examines the demands of nineteenth-century protesters much more thoroughly than in previous works, and finds that their goals were often not revolutionary but "reformist . . . or even conservative." Those involved in such protests, generally black landowners with tiny to medium-sized properties, wanted mainly to "maintain property rights [and] to resist government taxation."

While analyzing such protests, Nicholls asks: *What was the main driver of conflict in nineteenth-century Haiti: social class or skin color?* In general, Nicholls sees these protests as economically motivated. However, he challenges conventional Marxist historiography by insisting that color is an independent variable that sometimes trumps class. Throughout his work, Nicholls has emphasized the enduring divisions, even after independence, between the light-skinned descendants of the *anciens libres* and the poorer black *nouveaux libres*. Nicholls notes that conflict between these groups was aggravated by the United States, which tended to send arms and assistance to support light-skinned elites against revolts by black peasants. Nicholls' focus on racial conflict in Haiti has not been without controversy. Several scholars have seen this emphasis as overstated; Matthew Smith recently offered an extended critique of Nicholls' model. Nevertheless, as Smith has noted, Nicholls' arguments remain very important in the field, even after his death.[27]

The final essay in this section is Leslie Alexander's article on the African-American emigration movement to Haiti " 'The Black Republic': The

Influence of the Haitian Revolution on Northern Black Political Consciousness, 1816–1862". How African-Americans viewed Haitian independence is a profoundly important subject, one that has inspired a growing literature.[28] On one level, Alexander (a specialist in nineteenth-century African-American history) considers a question that belongs more to U.S. history: *What did Haitian independence mean for African-Americans?* However, even as Alexander discusses African-American views of Haiti, her work also concerns policy initiatives by Haitian leaders.

Alexander examines how, in the face of hostility from whites in the United States and elsewhere, Haitian leaders in the 1810s and 1820s turned to free blacks in the northern U.S. for support. On the one hand, Haitian leaders vigorously contested white views of Haitians as barbarians, by suggesting that Haiti could be a beacon of civilization for African-descended people worldwide. They also sought support from African-Americans in the form of immigration: a new nation required teachers, farmers and sailors – and a nation under threat of attack needed soldiers. Talk of Haiti pervaded African-American communities, as African-Americans hoped that they could escape the sting of American racism by moving to a country "where a dark complexion will be no disadvantage." While other scholars have discussed this emigration movement and its ultimate failure (when conditions in Haiti proved harsher than imagined), Alexander also focuses on a second, lesser-known emigration movement in the 1850s, one that failed in large part because of the advent of the U.S. Civil War. Although these emigration movements were short-lived, Alexander notes that independent Haiti's existence remained a powerful symbol for African-Americans, especially as racism persisted in the U.S. Indeed, African-American interest in Haiti's fate has helped to shape U.S. policy toward Haiti into the twenty-first century.[29]

The topics covered in the essays in this section are not the only subjects of recent scholarship on nineteenth-century Haiti. Looking back at issues such as *how have natural disasters shaped Haitian history?*, Matthew Smith has been examining the social impact of the Haitian earthquake of 1842.[30] New work has appeared on topics ranging from nineteenth-century religious policy to relations with the Dominican Republic.[31] In addition, scholars have begun reconsidering the reputations of leaders such as Dessalines and Christophe. Madison Smartt Bell's forthcoming biography of Dessalines aims to reconcile the many competing views of his legacy; those outside Haiti frequently depict him as a barbaric butcher, while many within Haiti view him as a hero and others see him as responsible for the nation's enduring pariah status. Bell's study will be especially valuable since there has never been an English-language biography of Dessalines, in contrast to many on Toussaint. With regard to Christophe, Hector has suggested that the Southern republic's ultimate victory left him with a worse reputation than he merited. Where scholars have tended to praise the establishment of republicanism in Haiti and depict Christophe as a harsh and luxury-loving ruler, Hector argues that republican leaders in Haiti have hardly avoided using violence against their enemies; moreover, Christophe put greater effort into promoting economic and cultural advancement by the Haitian masses than did republican oligarchs. Hector thus feels that it is too simplistic to applaud the republic's victory over Christophe's monarchy; he asks whether the latter might have led Haiti to a more prosperous place.[32]

Recent works have also applied postmodern ideas of self-fashioning to the study of Haitian leaders. Deborah Jenson's new study looks at Toussaint's and Dessalines' efforts to "spin" the Haitian Revolution to the Haitian public and to foreign media. Karen Salt has begun new research on Boyer's efforts to entice African-American immigrants. Bringing in approaches from ecology and marketing, she speaks of Boyer's efforts to "publicly re-brand Haiti as a haven for African Americans" even as his "cultivation strategy built on the labor of these newly minted African American-Haitian citizens."[33]

There are some aspects of the nineteenth century that would still benefit from increased research. The French reaction to Haitian independence is one such topic. In contrast to the growing scholarship on reactions to the Haitian Revolution in the Americas, scholars in France have tended to write about colonial Saint-Domingue to a far greater extent than about post-independence Haiti. Unlike in the American case, the Haitian Revolution was a direct blow against the French nation and was thus best forgotten. As recently as 1991, there were no courses offered in any French university on Haitian history or culture. With growing awareness of the Haitian Revolution among French scholars and an increased willingness to study topics related to race or colonialism, a number of new studies have appeared in the last decade on aspects of the French reaction to Haitian independence.[34]

In addition to this new work on French–Haitian relations, there are many other topics about which we could learn more. One is the attitude toward Haiti of the Bourbon Restoration monarchs (Louis XVIII and Charles X, who ruled after the fall of Napoleon, from 1814 to 1830). Why exactly did Charles X decide to recognize Haiti in exchange for indemnification? While the agreement was no prize for Haiti, it permanently acknowledged France's military defeat, angering ex-colonists who felt that the King should wage war against Haitian "murderers" instead of "rewarding" them for stealing French property. Given the flowering of scholarship on the reintegration of the *pieds noirs* (former French colonists in Algeria) into the French mainland after Algerian independence, it would also be valuable to learn more about how France's first post-colonial refugees, the colonists of Saint-Domingue, adjusted to their new life in a France that was foreign to many of them. In addition, more research could be done on the ex-colonists' activities after recognition, as they continued to denounce the indemnity agreement; and, from the

Haitian side, on how Haitians responded to such propaganda. More work could also be undertaken, especially in English, on foreign meddling in Haitian affairs during the final decades of the nineteenth century (particularly of Germans, which has been less studied than of Americans or the French). Finally, further research on women's experiences and on gender ideas in nineteenth-century Haiti would be welcome.

In its totality, recent work has offered a complex picture of nineteenth-century Haiti's relationship with other nations. It has revealed the external challenges facing Haiti's first leaders, while not neglecting internal social divisions in Haiti. It has also provided a glimpse into the turmoil that produced repeated regime changes over the course of the century (especially after 1843). Nineteenth-century Haiti remains a fascinating field, one that would benefit greatly from continued research. Such work would be valuable not only for enriching our understanding of contemporary Haiti, but also for helping us appreciate the general challenge of nation-building in the wake of a traumatic decolonization.

NOTES

1 On the Duvalier regime's effect on historiography, see M.-R. Trouillot, "Historiography of Haiti," in B. W. Higman, ed., *General History of the Caribbean*, vol. 6: *Methodology and Historiography of the Caribbean* (London: Unesco, 1997), pp. 471–473. On the evolution of history-teaching in Haiti since the Duvalier era, see Delné (2000).

2 See Hector, "Jalons pour une périodisation," in Hector and Hurbon (2009), pp. 31–47. All further references to Hector's periodization are drawn from this article. For a parallel but slightly different periodization, see L. Manigat (2001–2003), I: 42–46.

3 The main exceptions to Haiti's diplomatic isolation in the period were relations with Latin American revolutionaries who took inspiration from Haiti's struggles and with European abolitionists such as Henri Grégoire. On the former, see Verna (1980), Bushnell and Langley (2008) and Bassi (2012); on the latter, see Sepinwall (2005), ch. 8. See also Julia Gaffield's forthcoming work on Haiti's commercial relations during this period.

4 On the indemnity, see especially Joachim (1975); Stein (1984); Blancpain (2003b, 2003c) and Gaillard-Pourchet (2003).

5 Cited in Montague (1940), pp. 53–54.

6 Hector, "Problème du passage à la société postesclavagiste et postcoloniale (1791–1793/1820–1826)," in Hector and Hurbon (2009), p. 93; and Hector and Hurbon, "Introduction," in Hector and Hurbon (2009), p. 21.

7 Hector, "Jalons pour une périodisation," in Hector and Hurbon (2009), p. 35 and Moïse, "Création de l'État haïtien/Constitutions: continuités et ruptures," in Hector and Hurbon (2009), p. 51.

8 Hector, "Problème du passage," in Hector and Hurbon (2009), p. 111 (quotation by Joachim on p. 112).

9 Hector, "Jalons pour une périodisation," p. 38.

10 See Frederick Douglass, *Lecture on Haiti* (1893), reprinted in Jackson and Bacon (2010), p. 205.

11 See however J. N. Léger (1907); M.-R. Trouillot (1989), which includes a substantial discussion of late nineteenth-century governments; Nicholls (1996),

pp. 108–141 and most recently Dubois (2012), which includes two helpful chapters on the period (chs. 4 and 5).

12 Other important studies on the late nineteenth century include Adam (1982) on the Salnave regime; Moïse (1988) on constitutional history; Turnier (1989) on political corruption; G. Gaillard (1990) on the "plundering" of the country's coffee production to pay foreign debt; Blancpain (2001) and Berloquin-Chassany (2004) on foreign domination of Haitian commerce; Delisle (2003) on Catholicism; and Hoffmann and Middelanis (2007) on Soulouque. See also L. Manigat (2001–2003), Denis (2004) and Péan (2005).

13 See Dolce, Dorval and Casthely (1983); Firmin, trans. Charles (2000); Dash (2004) and Magloire-Danton (2005).

14 See for instance Pamphile (2001), Polyné (2010), Salt (2011), and Glen McLish's essay on Frederick Douglass in Jackson and Bacon (2010).

15 On Haitian scholars' interest in their country's early foreign relations, see A. Léger (1930), Gouraige (1955), Turnier (1955), Lubin (1968), Auguste (1979), Etienne (1982), Latortue (2001) and Saint-Louis (2003, 2006).

16 For a fuller analysis of historiography on the American reaction to the Haitian Revolution, see Sepinwall (2003, 2009).

17 See for instance Hunt (1988), Geggus (2001), Geggus and Fiering (2009) and Gomez (2010).

18 For more on Jefferson's attitude toward Haiti, see Zuckerman (1993), Matthewson (2003) and the other works cited in Sepinwall (2003). For an extended version of White's argument, see White (2010).

19 See for example Gaspar and Geggus (1997); Geggus (2001); Fischer (2004); Casimir, Hector and Bégot (2006); Lasso (2007) and Geggus and Fiering (2009).

20 See Ferrer (2003) and Ferrer, "Speaking of Haiti: Slavery, Revolution and Freedom in Cuban Slave Testimony," in Geggus and Fiering (2009), pp. 223–242.

21 For another analysis that extends but aims to nuance Trouillot, see Fischer (2004). On how fiction has silenced the Revolution's memory, see the forth-coming work of Claudy Delné, "Le bâillonnement de la Révolution haïtienne dans l'imaginaire occidental à travers des textes fictionnels des 19e et 20e siècles," Ph.D. diss., French Dept., CUNY, expected 2012.

22 Bellegarde-Smith (2004), p. 41; Dayan (1995); also Bouchereau (1957).

23 While Jean Casimir's contribution in Hector and Hurbon (2009) cites Sheller's *Democracy After Slavery*, the essay of hers reprinted here is not referenced in that volume.

24 See remarks by Hurbon in Hector and Hurbon (2009), p. 313, 319.

25 For a recent reappraisal of Nicholls, see Smith (2007).

26 Studies of nineteenth-century peasant revolts written after Nicholls's seminal work include Hector (2000) and Sheller (2000).

27 Smith (2007); see also L. Manigat (2001–2003), I: 279–291.

28 See Dixon (2000), Pamphile (2001), Clavin (2010) and Jackson and Bacon (2010), along with other works cited in Sepinwall (2003).

29 On African-Americans and Haiti in the twentieth century, see the works by Brenda Plummer cited in Section III; Polyné (2010) and the references to African-American lobbying in Fatton's essay in Section III.

30 See Smith, "Une histoire sous les décombres," *Revue de la société haïtienne d'histoire et de géographie*, forthcoming.

31 See for instance Hurbon, "Les religions dans la construction de l'État (1801–1859)," in Hector and Hurbon (2009), pp. 181–195; J. M. Théodat, "État et territoire: la question de la naissance de la République dominicaine," in Hector and Hurbon (2009), pp. 297–309; Théodat (2003); Venator Santiago (2004) as well as the classic works by Price-Mars (1953) and Moya Pons (1978, 1985).

32 Information on Bell's project communicated by the author; on Christophe, see Hector, "Une autre voie de construction de l'État-nation: l'expérience christophienne (1806–1820)," in Hector and Hurbon (2009), pp. 243–272.
33 Jenson (2011), Salt (2011).
34 For a fuller overview of scholarship on the impact and memory of the Haitian Revolution in France, see Sepinwall (2009). On the memory of the Revolution in France, see also Chris Bongie's essay in *Yale French Studies*, no. 107 (2005), Dorigny (2005), Miller (2008) and Pascal Blanchard's comments on French television following the earthquake (at www.dailymotion.com/video/xbxbzr_la-france-haiti-et-l-amnesie-coloni_news). Other recent studies not discussed in Sepinwall (2009) include the essays by Hélène Servan and Danielle Bégot in Casimir, Hector and Bégot (2006); Itazienne Eugène, "La normalisation des relations franco-haïtiennes (1825–1838)," in Dorigny (2003); Hoffmann and Middelanis (2007); Aliano (2008); Brière (2008) and Kwon (2010). On the absence of courses on Haiti in French universities, see Barthélemy and Girault (1993), p. 9.

FOR FURTHER READING

Adam, André-Georges. *Une crise haïtienne, 1867–1869: Sylvain Salnave*. Port-au-Prince: H. Deschamps, 1982.

Aliano, David. "Revisiting Saint Domingue: Toussaint L'Ouverture and the Haitian Revolution in the French Colonial Debates of the Late Nineteenth Century (1870–1900)." *French Colonial History* 9 (2008): 15–35.

Ardouin, Beaubrun. *Etudes sur l'histoire d'Haïti suivies de la vie du général J.-M. Borgella*. Paris, 1853; reprint, Port-au-Prince: F. Dalencour, 1958.

Auguste, Yves L. *Haïti et les États-Unis: 1804–1862*. Sherbrooke, Québec: Éditions Naaman, 1979.

Barthélemy, Gérard. *Le pays en dehors: essai sur l'univers rural haïtien*. 2nd ed. Port-au-Prince: H. Deschamps, 1989.

Barthélemy, Gérard. *Créoles – bossales: conflit en Haïti*. Petit-Bourg, Guadeloupe: Ibis rouge éditions, 2000.

Barthélemy, Gérard, and Christian A. Girault, eds. *La République haïtienne: état des lieux et perspectives*. Paris: Karthala, 1993.

Bassi, Ernesto. "Between Imperial Projects and National Dreams: Communication Networks, Geopolitical Imagination, and the Role of New Granada in the Configuration of a Greater Carribbean Space, 1780s–1810s." Ph.D. diss., University of California, Irvine, 2012 [ch. 5 on Jamaica and Haiti].

Bellegarde-Smith, Patrick. *Haiti: The Breached Citadel*. 2nd ed. Toronto: Canadian Scholars' Press, 2004.

Berloquin-Chassany, Pascale. *Haïti, une démocratie compromise, 1890–1911*. Paris: Harmattan, 2004.

Blancpain, François. *Un siècle de relations financières entre Haïti et la France, 1825–1922*. Paris: L'Harmattan, 2001.

Blancpain, François. *La condition des paysans haïtiens: du code noir aux codes ruraux*. Paris: Karthala, 2003a.

Blancpain, François. "L'ordonnance de 1825 et la question de l'indemnité." In *Rétablissement de l'esclavage dans les colonies françaises: Aux origines de Haïti*, edited by Yves Benot and Marcel Dorigny, 221–230. Paris: Maisonneuve et Larose, 2003b.

Blancpain, François. "Note sur les 'dettes' de l'esclavage: le cas de l'indemnité payée par Haïti (1825–1883)." In *Haïti: première république noire*, edited by Marcel Dorigny, 241–245. Paris: Société française d'histoire d'outre-mer, 2003c.

Bouchereau, Madeleine G. *Haïti et ses femmes: une étude d'évolution culturelle*. Port-au-Prince: Les Presses Libres, 1957.

Brasseaux, Carl A. and Glenn R. Conrad. *The Road to Louisiana: The Saint-Domingue Refugees, 1792–1809*. Lafayette: Center for Louisiana Studies, University of Southwestern Louisiana, 1992.

Brière, Jean-François. *Haïti et la France, 1804–1848: le rêve brisée*. Paris: Karthala, 2008.

Brown, Gordon S. *Toussaint's Clause: The Founding Fathers and the Haitian Revolution*. Jackson: University Press of Mississippi, 2005.

Burnham, Thorald M. "Immigration and Marriage in the Making of Post-Independence Haiti." Ph.D. diss., York University, 2006.

Bushnell, David, and Lester D. Langley, eds. *Simón Bolívar: Essays on the Life and Legacy of the Liberator*. Lanham, MD: Rowman & Littlefield, 2008 [esp. essays by J. Ewell and D. Bushnell].

Casimir, Jean, Michel Hector, and Danielle Bégot, eds. *La révolution et l'indépendance haïtiennes: autour du bicentenaire de 1804, histoire et mémoire [actes du 36e colloque de l'Association des historiens de la Caraïbe, Barbade, mai 2004]*. Gourbeyre: Archives départementales, 2006 [esp. essays by H. Servant, L. Abenon, B. Brereton, M. Denis, G.-K. Gaillard-Pourchet and C. Fergus].

Césaire, Aimé. *The Tragedy of King Christophe, a Play*. Translated by Ralph Manheim. New York: Grove Press, 1970.

Clavin, Matthew J. *Toussaint Louverture and the American Civil War: The Promise and Peril of a Second Haitian Revolution*. Philadelphia: University of Pennsylvania Press, 2010.

Corvington, Georges. *Port-au-Prince au cours des ans*. 3rd ed. 7 vols. Port-au-Prince: H. Deschamps, 1992–1994 [III: *La métropole haïtienne du XIXe siècle, 1804–1888*; IV: *La métropole haïtienne du XIXe siècle, 1888–1915*].

Dash, J. Michael. "Nineteenth-Century Haiti and the Archipelago of the Americas: Anténor Firmin's Letters from St. Thomas." *Research in African Literatures* 35, no. 2 (2004): 44–53.

Daut, Marlene. "Un-silencing the Past: Boisrond-Tonnere, Vastey, and the Re-writing of the Haitian Revolution." *South Atlantic Review*, 74, no. 1 (2009): 35–64.

Dayan, Joan. *Haiti, History, and the Gods*. Berkeley: University of California Press, 1995.

De Pena, Gustavo Antonio. "The Siblings of Hispaniola: Political Union and Separation of Haiti and Santo Domingo, 1822–1844." M.A. Thesis, Vanderbilt University, 2009 [available at http://etd.library.vanderbilt.edu/available/etd-03272011-220809/unrestricted/DePena.pdf].

Delisle, Philippe. *Le catholicisme en Haïti au XIXe siècle: Le rêve d'une "Bretagne noire," 1860–1915*. Paris: Karthala, 2003.

Delné, Claudy. *L'enseignement de l'histoire nationale en Haïti: état des lieux et perspectives*. Montreal: CIDIHCA, 2000.

Denis, Watson R. "Miradas de mutua desconfianza entre dos repúblicas americanas: el expansionismo marítimo de los Estados Unidos frente a la francofilia haitiana (1888–1898)." Ph.D. thesis, Universidad de Puerto Rico – RPR, 2004.

Dessens, Nathalie. *From Saint-Domingue to New Orleans: Migration and Influences.* Gainesville: University Press of Florida, 2007.

Dillon, Elizabeth. "The Secret History of the Early American Novel: Leonora Sansay and Revolution in Saint Domingue." *Novel* 40, no. 1–2 (2006): 77–103.

Dixon, Chris. *African America and Haiti: Emigration and Black Nationalism in the Nineteenth Century.* Westport, CT: Greenwood Press, 2000.

Dolcé, Jacquelin, Gérard Dorval, and Jean Miotel Casthely. *Le Romantisme en Haïti (la vie intellectuelle 1804–1915).* Port-au-Prince: Éditions Fardin, 1983.

Dorigny, Marcel, ed. *Haïti: première république noire.* Paris: Société française d'histoire d'outre-mer, 2003.

Dorigny, Marcel. "Aux origines: L'indépendance d'Haïti et son occultation." In *La fracture coloniale: la société française au prisme de l'héritage colonial,* edited by Pascal Blanchard, Nicolas Bancel, and Sandrine Lemaire, 47–57. Paris: La Découverte, 2005.

Dubois, Laurent. "The Haitian Revolution and the Sale of Louisiana." *Southern Quarterly* 44, no. 3 (2007): 18–41.

Dubois, Laurent. *Haiti: The Aftershocks of History.* New York: Metropolitan Books, 2012.

Dun, James Alexander. "Dangerous Intelligence: Slavery, Race, and St. Domingue in the Early American Republic." Ph.D. diss., Princeton University, 2004.

Etienne, Eddy V. *La vraie dimension de la politique extérieure des premiers gouvernements d'Haïti (1804–1843).* Sherbrooke, Québec: Éditions Naaman, 1982.

Ferrer, Ada. "La société esclavagiste cubaine et la révolution haïtienne," *Annales: Histoire, Sciences Sociales,* no. 2 (2003): 333–356.

Ferrer, Ada. "Haiti, Free Soil, and Antislavery in the Revolutionary Atlantic." *American Historical Review,* 117, no.1 (2012): 44–66.

Fick, Carolyn. "Emancipation in Haiti: From Plantation Labour to Peasant Proprietorship." *Slavery and Abolition* 21, no. 2 (2000): 11–73.

Firmin, Joseph-Anténor. *The Equality of the Human Races: Positivist Anthropology.* Translated by Asselin Charles, introduction by Carolyn Fluehr-Lobban. New York: Garland, 2000.

Fischer, Sibylle. *Modernity Disavowed: Haiti and the Cultures of Slavery in the Age of Revolution.* Durham, NC: Duke University Press, 2004.

Gaffield, Julia. "Complexities of Imagining Haiti: A Study of National Constitutions, 1801–1807." *Journal of Social History* 41, no. 1 (2007): 81–103.

Gaillard, Gusti-Klara. *L'expérience haïtienne de la dette extérieure, ou, Une production caféière pillée: 1875–1915.* Port-au-Prince: H. Deschamps, 1990.

Gaillard-Pourchet, Gusti-Klara. "Aspects politiques et commerciaux de l'indemnisation haïtienne." In *1802. Rétablissement de l'esclavage dans les colonies françaises: Aux origines de Haïti,* edited by Yves Benot and Marcel Dorigny, 231–237. Paris: Maisonneuve et Larose, 2003.

Gaillard, Roger. *La république exterminatrice.* Port-au-Prince: R. Gaillard, 1984–1998. Vols. I and II (*Une modernisation manquée [1880–1896]* and *L'Etat vassal [1896–1902]*) [vol. numbers reflect their original print designation; Gusti-Klara Gaillard-Pourchet amended the numbering when she completed *Le cacoïsme bourgeois,* covering the earliest material in the series].

Gaillard, Roger, and Gusti-Klara Gaillard-Pourchet. *Le cacoïsme bourgeois contre Salnave, 1867–1870* [written by Gaillard, finished posthumously by Gaillard-Pourchet]. Port-au-Prince: Éditions Fondation Roger Gaillard, 2003 [designated by Gaillard-Pourchet as vol. I in the *La république exterminatrice* series].

Gaspar, David Barry, and David Patrick Geggus, eds. *A Turbulent Time: The French Revolution and the Greater Caribbean*. Bloomington: Indiana University Press, 1997.

Geggus, David. "Haiti and the Abolitionists: Opinion, Propaganda and International Politics in Britain and France, 1804–1838." In *Abolition and its Aftermath: The Historical Context, 1790–1916*, edited by David Richardson, 113–140. Totowa, NJ: F. Cass, 1985.

Geggus, David, ed. *The Impact of the Haitian Revolution in the Atlantic World*. Columbia: University of South Carolina Press, 2001 [includes essays on the reaction to the Haitian Revolution in the United States, Cuba, Colombia, Guadeloupe and elsewhere].

Geggus, David Patrick and Norman Fiering, eds. *The World of the Haitian Revolution*. Bloomington: Indiana University Press, 2009 [esp. sections III and IV on the international impact of the Revolution].

Gómez, Alejandro. "Le syndrome de Saint-Domingue. Perceptions et représentations de la Révolution haïtienne dans le Monde atlantique, 1790–1886." Doctoral thesis, EHESS-Paris, 2010.

González-Ripoll, Dolores, Consuelo Naranjo, Ada Ferrer, Gloria García and Josef Opatrný, eds. *El rumor de Haití en Cuba: temor, raza y rebeldía, 1789–1844*. Madrid: Consejo Superior de Investigaciones Científicas, 2004.

Gouraige, Ghislain. *L'indépendance d'Haïti devant la France*. Port-au-Prince: Imprimerie de L'État, 1955.

Griggs, Earl Leslie and Clifford H. Prator. *Henry Christophe and Thomas Clarkson: A Correspondence*. New York: Greenwood Press, 1968.

Hector, Michel. *Crises et mouvements populaires en Haïti*. [Montreal]: CIDIHCA, 2000.

Hector, Michel, and Laënnec Hurbon, eds. *Genèse de l'état haïtien (1804–1859)*. Paris: Maison des sciences de l'homme, 2009.

Hoffmann, Léon-François, and Carl-Hermann Middelanis. *Faustin Soulouque d'Haïti: dans l'histoire et la littérature*. Paris: L'Harmattan, 2007.

Hunt, Alfred N. *Haiti's Influence on Antebellum America: Slumbering Volcano in the Caribbean*. Baton Rouge: Louisiana State University Press, 1988.

Jackson, Maurice, and Jacqueline Bacon, eds. *African Americans and the Haitian Revolution: Selected Essays and Historical Documents*. New York: Routledge, 2010.

Jenson, Deborah. *Beyond the Slave Narrative: Politics, Sex, and Manuscripts in the Haitian Revolution*. Liverpool: Liverpool University Press, 2011.

Jenson, Deborah, ed. *The Haiti Issue: 1804 and Nineteenth-Century French Studies* [*Yale French Studies*, no. 107 (2005), including essays by D. Jenson, N. Nesbitt, C. L. Miller, C. Bongie, D. Kadish, D. Desormeaux, M. Krueger Enz, and A. Valdman].

Joachim, Benoît. "L'indemnité coloniale de Saint-Domingue et la question des répatriés." *Revue Historique*, 246, no. 2 (1971): 359–376.

Joachim, Benoît. "La reconnaissance d'Haïti par la France (1825): Naissance d'un nouveau type de rapports internationaux." *Revue d'histoire moderne et contemporaine*, 22, no. 3 (1975): 369–396.

Joachim, Benoît. *Les racines du sous développement en Haïti*. Port-au-Prince: Henri Deschamps, 1979.

Kwon, Yun Kyoung. "Remember Saint Domingue: Accounts of the Haitian Revolution by Refugee Planters in Paris and Colonial Debates under the Restoration, 1814–25." In *France's Lost Empires: Fragmentation, Nostalgia, and La*

Fracture Coloniale, edited by Kate Marsh and Nicola Frith, 17–30. Lanham, MD: Lexington Books, 2010.

Lacerte, Robert K. "Xenophobia and Economic Decline: The Haitian Case, 1820–1843." *Americas* 37, no. 4 (1981): 499–515.

Lacerte, Robert K. "The First Land Reform in Latin America: The Reforms of Alexander Petion, 1809–1814." *Inter-American Economic Affairs* 28, no. 4 (1975): 77–85.

Lasso, Marixa. *Myths of Harmony: Race and Republicanism During the Age of Revolution, Colombia 1795–1831*. Pittsburgh: University of Pittsburgh Press, 2007.

Latortue, François. *Haïti (ex Saint-Domingue) et la Louisiane: leurs liaisons passées et leurs rôles dans l'émergence du Colosse américain*. Port-au-Prince: Imprimeur II, 2001.

Léger, J. N. *Haiti, Her History and Her Detractors*. New York: Neale Pub., 1907.

Léger, Abel Nicholas. *Histoire diplomatique d'Haïti*. Port-au-Prince: Impr. Aug. A. Héraux, 1930.

Logan, Rayford W. *The Diplomatic Relations of the United States with Haiti, 1778–1841*. Chapel Hill: The University of North Carolina Press, 1941.

Lubin, Maurice A. "Les premiers rapports de la nation haïtienne avec l'étranger." *Journal of Inter-American Studies* 10, no. 2 (1968): 277–305.

Lundahl, Mats. "Defense and Distribution: Agricultural Policy in Haiti during the Reign of Jean-Jacques Dessalines, 1804–1806." *The Scandinavian Economic History Review* 32, no. 2 (1984): 77–103.

MacLeod, Murdo T. "The Soulouque Regime in Haiti, 1847–1859: A Reevaluation." *Caribbean Studies* 10, no. 3 (1970): 35–48.

Madiou, Thomas. *Histoire d'Haïti*. Port-au-Prince, 1848; reprint, Port-au-Prince: Impr. E. Chenet, 1922–3.

Magloire, Gérarde. "Haitian-ness, Frenchness and History: Deconstructing the History of the French Component of Haitian National Identity." *Journal of Haitian Studies* 5/6 (2000): 30–43.

Magloire-Danton, Gérarde. "Anténor Firmin and Jean Price-Mars: Revolution, Memory, Humanism." *Small Axe* 9, no. 2 (2005): 150–170.

Manigat, Leslie F. *Eventail d'histoire vivante d'Haïti: des préludes à la Révolution de Saint Domingue jusqu'à nos jours, 1789–1999*. 3 vols. [vol. I: *La Période Fondatrice (1789–1838)* and II: *La société traditionnelle épanouie: sa nature, son évolution et son profil de maturité, 1838–1896*]. Port-au-Prince: CHUDAC, 2001–2003.

Manigat, Leslie F. *La révolution haïtienne de 1843: essai d'analyse historique d'une conjoncture de crise*. Port-au-Prince: Média-Texte, 2007.

Matthewson, Tim. *A Proslavery Foreign Policy: Haitian-American Relations During the Early Republic*. Westport, CT: Praeger, 2003.

Miller, Christopher L. *The French Atlantic Triangle: Literature and Culture of the Slave Trade*. Durham, NC: Duke University Press, 2008 [esp. ch. 10, "Forget Haiti: Baron Roger and the New Africa"].

Moïse, Claude. *Constitutions et luttes de pouvoir en Haïti, 1804–1987*. 2 vols. Montreal: CIDIHCA, 1988 [esp. vol. I, *La faillité des classes dirigeantes, 1804–1915*].

Montague, Ludwell Lee. *Haiti and the United States, 1714–1938*. Durham, NC: Duke University Press, 1940.

Moya Pons, Frank. *La dominación haitiana, 1822–1844*. 3rd ed. Santiago: República Dominicana, UCMM, 1978.

Moya Pons, Frank. "The Land Question in Haiti and Santo Domingo: The Sociopoliitcal Context of the Transition from Slavery to Free Labor, 1801–1843."

In *Between Slavery and Free Labor: The Spanish-Speaking Caribbean in the Nineteenth Century*, edited by Manuel Moreno Fraginals, Frank Moya Pons, and Stanley L. Engerman, 181–214. Baltimore: Johns Hopkins University Press, 1985.

Nicholls, David. "A Work of Combat: Mulatto Historians and the Haitian Past, 1847–1867." *Journal of Interamerican Studies and World Affairs* 16, no. 1 (1974): 15–38.

Nicholls, David. *Haiti in Caribbean Context: Ethnicity, Economy, and Revolt*. New York: St. Martin's Press, 1985.

Nicholls, David. *From Dessalines to Duvalier: Race, Colour and National Independence in Haiti*. 2nd ed. New Brunswick, NJ: Rutgers University Press, 1996.

Pamphile, Leon D. *Haitians and African Americans: A Heritage of Tragedy and Hope*. Gainesville: University Press of Florida, 2001.

Pauléus Sannon, H. *Essai historique sur la révolution de 1843*. Cayes: Impr. Bonnefil, 1905 [full-text available on Google Books].

Péan, Leslie J. R. *Haïti: économie politique de la corruption*. 4 vols. Paris: Maisonneuve et Larose, 2005 [vol. I: *De Saint-Domingue à Haïti, 1791–1870*; and vol. II: *L'état marron, 1870–1915*].

Pierce, Jennifer. "Discourses of the Dispossessed: Saint-Domingue Colonists on Race, Revolution and Empire, 1789–1825." Ph.D. diss., Binghamton University, 2005.

Price-Mars, Jean. *La République d'Haïti et la République dominicaine . . .* [1492–1953]. Port-au-Prince, n.p.: 1953.

Polyné, Millery. *From Douglass to Duvalier: U.S. African Americans, Haiti, and Pan Americanism, 1870–1964*. Gainesville: University Press of Florida, 2010.

Racine, Karen. "Imported Englishness: Henry Christophe's Educational Program in Haiti, 1811–1820." In *Imported Modernity in Post-Colonial State Formation*, edited by Eugenia Roldán Vera and Marcelo Caruso, 205–230. New York: Peter Lang, 2007.

Ramsey, Kate. *The Spirits and the Law: Vodou and Power in Haiti*. Chicago: University of Chicago Press, 2011.

[Republic of Haiti]. *The Rural Code of Haïti, in French and English*. London: B. McMillan, 1827 [full-text available on Google books].

Saint-Louis, Vertus. "Relations internationales et classe politique en Haïti (1789–1814)." *Outre-mers: revue d'histoire*, no. 340/341 (2003): 155–175.

Saint-Louis, Vertus. *Aux origines du drame d'Haïti: droit et commerce maritime (1794–1806)*. [Port-au-Prince]: Bibliothèque nationale d'Haïti, 2006.

Salt, Karen. "The Haitian Question." Ph.D. diss., Purdue University, 2011 [esp. ch. 2 on Jean-Pierre Boyer, forthcoming as "Haitian Soil for the Citizen's Soul," in *American Studies, Ecocriticism, and Citizenship: Thinking and Acting in the Local and Global Commons*, eds. Joni Adamson and Kimberly Ruffin (Routledge); and other chapters on Haiti's participation in the 1893 Chicago World's Fair].

Scott, Julius Sherrard. "The Common Wind: Currents of Afro-American Communication in the Era of the Haitian Revolution." Ph.D. diss., Duke University, 1986 [ch. 2 published as " 'Negroes in Foreign Bottoms': Sailors, Slaves and Communication." In Laurent Dubois and Julius S. Scott, eds. *Origins of the Black Atlantic*, 69–98. New York: Routledge, 2010].

Sepinwall, Alyssa Goldstein. "La révolution haïtienne et les États-Unis: Étude historiographique." In *1802. Rétablissement de l'esclavage dans les colonies françaises: Aux origines de Haïti*, edited by Yves Benot and Marcel Dorigny, 387–401. Paris:

Maisonneuve et Larose, 2003 [includes bibliography of English-language primary sources on early U.S.-Haitian relations].

Sepinwall, Alyssa Goldstein. *The Abbé Grégoire and the French Revolution: The Making of Modern Universalism*. Berkeley: University of California Press, 2005 (esp. ch. 8, "Exporting the Revolution: The Colonial Laboratory in Haiti").

Sepinwall, Alyssa Goldstein. "The Specter of Saint-Domingue: American and French Reactions to the Haitian Revolution." In *The World of the Haitian Revolution*, edited by Norman Fiering and David Geggus, 317–338. Bloomington: Indiana University Press, 2009.

Sheller, Mimi. *Democracy after Slavery: Black Publics and Peasant Radicalism in Haiti and Jamaica*. Gainesville: University Press of Florida, 2000.

Sheller, Mimi. *Consuming the Caribbean: From Arawaks to Zombies*. New York: Routledge, 2003.

Sheller, Mimi. *Citizenship From Below: Erotic Agency and Caribbean Freedom*. Durham, NC: Duke University Press, 2012.

Smith, Matthew J. "From *Dessalines to Duvalier* Revisited: A Quarter-Century Retrospective." *Journal of Haitian Studies* 13, no. 1 (2007): 27–39.

Stein, Robert. "From Saint Domingue to Haiti, 1804–1825." *Journal of Caribbean History* 19, no. 2 (1984): 189–226.

Stinchcombe, Arthur L. "Class Conflict and Diplomacy: Haitian Isolation in the 19th-Century World System." *Sociological Perspectives* 37, no. 1 (1994): 1–23.

Théodat, Jean-Marie Dulix. *Haïti, République dominicaine: une île pour deux, 1804–1916*. Paris: Karthala, 2003.

Trouillot, Hénock. *Dessalines, ou, La tragédie post-coloniale*. Port-au-Prince: Éditions Panorama, 1966.

Trouillot, Michel-Rolph. *Nation, State, and Society in Haiti, 1804–1984*. Washington: Woodrow Wilson International Center for Scholars, 1985.

Trouillot, Michel-Rolph. *Haiti, State Against Nation: The Origins and Legacy of Duvalierism*. New York: Monthly Review Press, 1989.

Turnier, Alain. *Les États-Unis et le marché haïtien*. Washington: n.p., 1955.

Turnier, Alain. *Quand la nation demande des comptes*. Port-au-Prince: Impr. Le Natal, 1989.

Vastey, Pompée-Valentin, Baron de. *An Essay on the Causes of the Revolution and Civil Wars of Hayti* . . . Exeter: Western Luminary Office 1823; reprint editions from 2007 and 2010 available from Nabu Press and Kessinger Publishing [includes translations of primary sources by Pétion, Christophe and other Haitian leaders].

Venator Santiago, Charles R. "Race, the East, and the Haitian Revolutionary Ideology: Rethinking the Role of Race in the 1844 Secession of the Eastern Part of Haiti." *Journal of Haitian Studies* 10, no. 1 (2004): 103–119.

Verna, Paul. *Pétion y Bolívar: una etapa decisiva en la emancipación de Hispanoamérica, 1790–1830*. 3rd ed. [Caracas]: Ediciones de la Presidencia de la República, 1980.

White, Ashli. *Encountering Revolution: Haiti and the Making of the Early Republic*. Baltimore, MD: Johns Hopkins University Press, 2010.

Zuckerman, Michael. "The Power of Blackness: Thomas Jefferson and the Revolution in St. Domingue." In *Almost Chosen People: Oblique Biographies in the American Grain*, 175–218. Berkeley: University of California Press, 1993.

5

THE POLITICS OF "FRENCH NEGROES" IN THE UNITED STATES[1]

Ashli White

When slaves on the French Caribbean island of Saint Domingue set fire to their masters' plantations in August 1791, U.S. newspapers carried gruesome reports about what, in their opinion, was a "calamitous event." That "event" grew into a revolution that ravaged the wealthiest colony in the Americas for the next thirteen years. Taking advantage of the political upheaval among ruling white colonists caused by the French Revolution, Saint Dominguan slaves carried out a campaign for freedom that European armies failed to quell. By 1804 black forces had succeeded in dismantling French colonial control and abolishing slavery. In January the black leader Jean-Jacques Dessalines proclaimed the independent nation of Haiti.[2]

As Americans struggled to comprehend how and why the insurrection in Saint Domingue occurred, one of the issues that most troubled them was the role of slaves. Accounts in American newspapers depicted the rebels as agents of death and destruction, but generally denied that the slaves were the authors of the revolution. Instead, contemporary commentators looked to other groups—French republicans, colonists and anti-slavery activists among others—to explain the uprising. In all these scenarios black Saint Dominguans were seen as agents of corrupt whites rather than creators of their own revolution.[3]

Although white participants and bystanders tried to redirect discussion away from the slaves, it was impossible to extricate them from the debate. The difficulty of doing so arose, in part, from the ways in which the French and Haitian revolutions unfolded. When the French National Assembly abolished slavery in February 1794, the goals of metropole republicans and insurgent slaves became officially intertwined. But even before 1794 Saint Dominguan slaves remained central to debates about the Haitian Revolution. For, almost as soon as the insurrection began, slaveholders throughout the Atlantic world worried about the potential for rebellion on their own plantations. White onlookers analyzed circumstances in the French colony hoping to discover a means to avoid a similar situation.

Masters were also concerned that migrating black Saint Dominguans would encourage slaves elsewhere to revolt. As black and colored Saint Dominguans began to turn up in other colonies and nations, white residents were forced to consider the possible consequences of having the rebels in their midst. They were often unable to convince themselves of the minimal and mindless role of Saint Dominguan slaves in revolution.

This was particularly true in the United States where scholars estimate that at least 5,000 black and colored refugees arrived everywhere from New York to Charleston in the 1790s.[4] White locals called these immigrants "French negroes," and although such nationalized terms for slaves were not uncommon in the Atlantic world, "French negro"—in the American context—came to mean something more than simply a slave from the French West Indies. With the advent of the Haitian Revolution, white Americans applied the label almost exclusively to exiled black and colored Saint Dominguans and attributed to them a spirit of rebellion.

Given available sources, it remains difficult to learn much about the intentions of black and colored Saint Dominguan exiles in the United States. But Americans based their responses to the "French negroes" not on the migrants' aims and actions, but on what they were perceived to be. From their preconceptions about the nature of Caribbean slavery and the revolt, white Americans created the stereotype of the subversive "French negro" that persisted for decades. This characterization produced an array of reactions within the population, ranging from terror to admiration. The ambiguous—and sometimes contradictory—discussion surrounding "French negroes" illustrates how, from the 1790s to the Civil War, white Americans struggled to cope with the tremendous impact of the Haitian Revolution on slavery in the United States. While revolution formed the first republic in the New World, revolution in Saint Domingue threatened to overwhelm America's delicate boundaries. The enduring debates over "French negroes" elucidate this tension between American national interests and the larger Atlantic nature of New World slavery.

"That Hell of the Negroes, the West-India Islands"

When first learning of the slave rebellion in Saint Domingue, white Americans tried to distance their situation from that of their Saint Dominguan counterparts. Initial reports in U.S. newspapers attributed black Saint Dominguans' enthusiasm for insurrection to the viciousness of the Caribbean slave system. According to observers, living in "that hell of the negroes, the West-India islands" conditioned "miserable slaves" to revolt.[5] Indeed, since the colonial period, white Americans had cultivated the opinion that slavery in the Caribbean was harsher than its U.S. equivalent. With the advent of the Haitian Revolution, this point of view became even more popular.[6] A number of poems, anecdotes and articles lamented

124

the cruelty of West Indian slaveowners, with Saint Domingue often singled out as a place with particularly barbarous master-slave relations.[7]

When military action intensified, it became more difficult to see black Saint Dominguans as victims. Both northern and southern newspapers ran article after article detailing atrocities committed by the rebels. A writer for Philadelphia's *Pennsylvania Gazette* maintained that the devastation caused by the fighting was unrelated to the slaves' desire for freedom: "They are spurred on by the desire of plunder, carnage, and conflagration and not by the spirit of liberty, as some folks pretend." Boston's *Columbian Centinel* published a letter from a man in Jérémie, a port in southern Saint Domingue, who admitted that black insurgents fought for their liberty, but declared that the ensuing mayhem showed their lack of preparation for it: "Great is our desolation; endless are our woes; and all that, because the offspring of ourang outangs strive to become men."[8]

Reports in the press increasingly accentuated the insurgents' "bad character" which was described as savage, treacherous and tenacious. Guerrilla tactics, it was reported, frustrated European soldiers, who complained that "the Negroes keep themselves embodied in different places, and when attacked, they immediately fly and scatter. This method of theirs harasses our troops in such a manner that, without effecting any thing essential, they get quite worn out, and are obliged to be immediately relieved."[9] Tales circulated that the insurrectionists needed little sustenance to survive: "They break the cane at the joint, and drink the juice like new milk; this makes them as fat and as sleek as the best provisions." Reports further indicated the insurgents were fearless; the sight of compatriots hanging dead in the trees did not check their resistance: "These punishments. . . do not seem to intimidate them, as they . . . meet their fate with the greatest unconcern."[10]

When the French National Assembly abolished slavery in February 1794, the situation in the colony failed to improve. The war escalated as former slaves battled, on the one hand, recalcitrant pockets of French colonists, and on the other, invading British forces that sought to take control and reestablish slavery. For many white Americans the ongoing war bolstered their unfavorable opinion of black and colored Saint Dominguans. From this, many extrapolated generalizations about the effects of a possible emancipation in the United States. Their observations had significant ramifications for debates about the future of American slavery.

Avoiding the "Horrors of St. Domingo" at Home

After 1794 Americans interpreted events on Saint Domingue in ways that exhibited both white fear of black insurrection and confidence in the domestic slave society. For example, in 1796 St. George Tucker, a professor of law at the College of William and Mary and a judge on the Virginia

General Court (the highest tribunal in the state), contended that the Haitian Revolution proved the folly of immediate abolition and the wisdom of gradual manumission. He also invoked the example of Saint Domingue to argue that with slavery's end, black and white could not live side by side.[11] In Tucker's view the protracted war in Saint Domingue resulted from an emancipation that foolishly attempted "to smother those prejudices which have been cherished for a period of almost two centuries." Americans needed to realize that "the early impressions of obedience and submission, which slaves have received among us, and the no less habitual arrogance and assumption of superiority, among the whites, contribute, equally, to unfit the former for *freedom*, and the latter for *equality*." However, the example of Saint Domingue indicated that emancipation was necessary. Tucker argued for eradicating "the evil, before it becomes impossible to do it, without tearing up the roots of civil society with it." He proposed gradual manumission, but without full rights of citizenship. Freedmen would be excluded from holding office, bearing arms and owning property; hopefully these indignities would encourage them to migrate elsewhere.[12]

For other Americans the Haitian Revolution strengthened their resolve to fight against abolition. The specter of race war loomed too large to entertain a plan of emancipation—even a gradual and limited one.[13] In some states fear of the consequences of large-scale, public emancipation influenced views on private manumissions. North Carolina even passed legislation restricting a slaveholder's prerogative to free his slaves.[14]

Most slave states, however, did not outlaw private manumission until the 1850s. The lack of legislation restricting American masters suggests that in the 1790s states worried more about external than internal menaces to plantation society—most significantly, "French negroes," who threatened to infiltrate and overthrow order. Although one commentator writing in May 1792 hoped that "the ocean which surrounds Hispaniola will check the extension of the spirit of revolt," only days afterwards, an account from Jamaica dashed such wishful thinking.[15] Authorities in Kingston reported the arrest of a black man named Ferror, "lately from Hispaniola, and [who] performed a very active part in the late dreadful outrages in the vicinity of St. Marc."[16] The execution of a "horrible plot" was narrowly averted in Martinique, while in 1795 a rebellion in Cuba was attributed to the influence of Haitian revolutionaries.[17]

Putative insurrectionary activity by migrating Saint Dominguans was not limited to the West Indies. As early as 1792 white Americans saw the "insidious" work of "French negroes" in their midst, and concern grew as the numbers of refugees swelled in 1793. In the fall of that year a white Charlestonian expressed anxiety about his city's circumstances: "the negroes who have come here with the French people, have said so much about the insurrections at *St. Domingo*, that we have every reason to apprehend one here."[18] White trepidation seemed justified by the detection of the Secret Keeper Plot, a coordinated revolt planned by free and enslaved blacks in the Carolinas and Virginia. A white resident reported that "two letters have been intercepted, by which it appears that the negroes and mulattoes intended to serve us as the inhabitants of Cape-François were served: They had heard so much from the French negroes about it, and liberty and equality."[19] An article in the *Boston Gazette* stated that "emissaries were expected from St. Domingo, to assist and even to take the lead in this infernal business."[20] In 1797 the *Pennsylvania Gazette* informed its readers that another plot was discovered in Charleston in which "seventeen French negroes intended to set fire to the town in different places, kill the whites, and probably take possession of the powder magazine and the arms." At least two "French negroes" involved in the plan were executed and another two expelled.[21]

Episodes of this sort were not limited to areas below the Mason-Dixon line. Northerners also linked rebellious activity among local African-American communities to the presence of "French negroes." Hearsay alleged that black Saint Dominguans had set a series of fires in New York City in the mid-1790s. In a rumored conversation overheard on the street, a few "French negroes" told their American counterparts: "Ah, you Americans are animals; you do not know how to set fire—we at the Cape know better."[22] This comment suggests that whites perceived the presence of "French negroes" as a dual threat. They might not only take insurrectionary action, but also corrupt the "good character" of black Americans.

These examples also show how, during the 1790s, the presence of "French negroes" provided a means for explaining away any real or perceived rebellious activity on the part of African-Americans. As their critiques of West Indian slavery illustrated, whites prided themselves on the "good" slaves produced by a supposedly beneficent mainland slavery. Of course, many black Americans were inspired by events in the French colony and by the tales told by newly arrived black Saint Dominguans. But they were not, as their white counterparts implied, incapable of independently conceiving and carrying out defiant gestures.

Given notions about "French negroes" and their corruptive powers, white residents tried to banish them from various states. In October 1793 William Moultrie, governor of South Carolina, mandated that all free black and colored Saint Dominguans leave within ten days of his decree; all incoming migrants, whether free or enslaved, were to "remain under the guns at Fort Johnson" until they could be escorted out of the state.[23] The same year Georgia forbade entry of slaves from the West Indies, and in 1795 North Carolina prohibited the admission of Caribbean slaves over the age of fifteen. Early in the decade Maryland had permitted French subjects to bring their personal slaves into the state, but outlawed the concession in 1797. Northern states passed similar laws. In 1798 Governor Mifflin of Pennsylvania, upon hearing that shiploads of Saint Dominguans had arrived in Philadelphia's harbor, issued a proclamation that prohibited "French negroes" from landing. He encouraged President Adams to urge adjacent states to adopt analogous measures.[24]

State governments met with some success in the enforcement of these acts. South Carolina, the most aggressive, reported a few incidents in which black Saint Dominguans were hunted down and expelled. In May 1794 a committee of citizens notified the public through the *City Gazette and Daily Advertiser* that a privateer had recently landed a cargo of 65 slaves. Most of them were "from the island of St. Domingo and of bad character," and so the committee sought to find and then transport them "to some foreign port."[25] A few months later twenty-two "French negroes" were detained on their arrival in Charleston. Seventeen were placed in the workhouse, while the other five, "consisting of two free women and their children," were placed in the custody of a captain who promised to sail within the week.[26]

Nevertheless, white Americans were willing, on occasion, to look the other way. In the early stages of the rebellion this leniency perhaps derived from the belief—on the part of both Americans and Saint Dominguans— that the refugees' stay would prove temporary. Accounts from the island encouraged such suppositions with frequent claims about the restoration of order. For example, a little over a month after Cap Français was reduced to ashes, a Boston newspaper reported that "a number of whites still remain peaceably in town" and that "several of the French exiles were preparing to return."[27] White American sympathy for refugees also may have contributed to leniency in regard to exclusionary laws. Tales of death and destruction on the island filled American newspapers, and in the eyes of white locals, the exiles made a pitiable sight. As their wills and inventories demonstrate, many escaped with little property, bringing only easily moved possessions. These items usually included silver, textiles, currency and slaves. Denying entry to the latter would have eliminated an important means of subsistence, for many exiles rented out or sold their slaves.[28]

To garner sympathy, white Saint Dominguan exiles told harrowing accounts that focused on the brutality of rebellious slaves. At the same time, however, they claimed slaves were not responsible for the revolution, but simply the tools of reckless malcontents. White refugees blamed antislavery advocates in France, the *gens de couleur* (free people of color), Britain and Spain; but most often they accused French republicans of destroying the colony. This allegation received an enlarged reception when, in the second half of the 1790s, relations between France and the United States soured. Infuriated by the Jay Treaty of 1795, a trade agreement between the United States and Great Britain, France authorized privateers to prey on American vessels in the Caribbean. In light of these actions, anti-French sentiment flourished during the Adams administration and was fed by diplomatic disasters. The XYZ Affair galvanized American anti-French resolve. As a result, many Americans turned against

French republicans, and especially the Jacobins, who earlier had been celebrated as proponents of liberty. In particular, Adams' party, the Federalists, lambasted Jacobinism as the expression of lawless, bloodthirsty, godless men. Fear of internal subversion and foreign threats led to the idea that "French negroes" were a potent weapon in the Jacobin arsenal.

Although the association of "French negroes" with Jacobins resulted, in part, from late eighteenth-century American party politics—Federalists railed against the French while Republicans defended them and the course of their revolution—certain developments played to fears. In early 1797, a wave of arson swept across the country, striking cities from New England to Georgia. That fall the *Pennsylvania Gazette* reprinted an article from a London newspaper claiming that Sonthonax's agents had set the fires.[29] Gabriel's rebellion of 1800 seemed to demonstrate further the reality of the alleged connection when slaves in and around Richmond, Virginia organized to fight for their freedom. The plot ultimately unraveled, and two slaves confessed at the trial that "two white French Men were the first instigators of the Insurrection." A contributor to a Fredericksburg newspaper maintained that the conspiracy stemmed from "some vile French Jacobins, aided and abetted by some of our own profligate and abandoned democrats."[30]

Many American merchants overcame any fears they may have harbored about importing insurrection and traded with Saint Domingue throughout the insurrection. After the American Revolution, merchants had taken advantage of newly acquired access to French colonial ports and built a flourishing business in the French West Indies and with Saint Domingue in particular. They outfitted their vessels with provisions and returned from the island laden with coffee, sugar and other lucrative products. By 1790 Saint Domingue was second only to Great Britain in terms of U.S. foreign trade. During the tumultuous 1790s American ships braved the privateer-infested waters of the Caribbean and continued their commerce. The risks were high, but the profits enormous.[31]

These ships were often staffed with black seamen, and scholars estimate that thousands voyaged to Saint Domingue/Haiti between 1790 and 1830.[32] Black sailors were vital links in the information networks that crisscrossed the Atlantic. They collected news on their travels which they then distributed to black Americans along their routes.[33] In the age of the Atlantic revolutions, the French and Haitian upheavals were the hottest news topics, and black sailors spread the word about events in Saint Domingue and France to African-American communities. Yet, even though white Americans recognized the role of black seamen as sources of possibly subversive information, in the 1790s states passed little, if any, legislation restricting their mobility.[34]

As American merchants tried to sustain their business with Saint Domingue during the rebellion, rumors circulated that they were trading with the insurgents. [. . .] American merchants did in fact cultivate commercial ties with Toussaint Louverture's army a few years later. [. . .]

While many American merchants might not at first have been comfortable trading with the black leader, strained relations with France in the late 1790s made commerce with Toussaint Louverture and his forces more palatable. Southerners feared that France would use Saint Domingue to launch an attack against the United States, and they clamored in Congress for greater military protection in their states.[35] Adams and his agents chose instead to nurture friendly relations with Louverture. Secretary of State Timothy Pickering suggested optimistically that the black Saint Dominguans, under Louverture's lead, might soon "declare themselves independent and . . . erect the island into a sovereign State,—to which he seems to think it would not be inconsistent with the interests of America to consent."[36] The administration hoped to transform Saint Domingue from a springboard for ominous French designs into a buffer from them— and make some handsome profits in the process.

Accordingly, the United States did more than trade with Louverture. The administration sought to support the consolidation of his power over the island. Although he had ousted British forces in 1797–8, Louverture still had internal rivals with which to contend, especially André Rigaud, a mulatto who had emerged as the leading general in southern Saint Domingue. In negotiations with both American and British emissaries, Louverture agreed to open trade in return for supplies and support for his military endeavors against Rigaud. The United States complied and significantly assisted Louverture's campaign. The frigate *General Greene* cut off Rigaud's supply vessels near Jacmel and bombarded his forts during the final attack. When Rigaud fled the island in October 1800, the American schooner *Experiment* captured him.[37] Only a month after the detection of Gabriel's conspiracy, Adams' government was treating Saint Domingue as a potential diplomatic partner. In the eyes of some Americans, black Saint Dominguans operated as both useful instruments and potential incendiaries.

Unruly Rebels or Reliable Servants?

The election of Thomas Jefferson to the American presidency in 1800 brought a shift in U.S. policy toward Saint Domingue. In 1805, two years after the black rebels had defeated Napoleon's troops, Jefferson and his political allies pushed through Congress a bill prohibiting commerce with the island. Meanwhile, the stereotype of dangerous pariahs came to dominate how black Saint Dominguans—whether in Saint Domingue/Haiti or the U.S.—were perceived. Of the exiles, some certainly aspired to spread rebellion, but their reasons for fleeing the island and seeking asylum in the United States were varied, as were their experiences.

From the perspective of both white and black Americans, three qualities made black and colored Saint Dominguans "French"—their language, religion and appearance. Most of the migrants did not speak English. A few learned the language after their arrival, but most knew French or "French Creole," and of these, some spoke "indifferent" French at best.[38] This linguistic pattern reflected the nature of Saint Dominguan slavery. Unlike the slave population in the United States, most slaves in the French colony were recent arrivals from Africa. Between 1783 and 1792 the island imported, on average, 37,000 slaves per year; by 1789 two-thirds of the approximately half-million slaves were African-born, and they came from all over the continent.[39] A quick survey of runaway notices from a 1791 issue of the *Gazette de St. Domingue* reveals the diverse origins of Saint Dominguan slaves. Owners employed, among others, the following terms to identify their chattel: Mina, Congo, Myaca, Nago, Ibo, Sénégalais, Mozambique and Gambary.[40]

In addition, white Americans saw incoming *gens de couleur* as being as rebellious as refugee slaves. This characterization followed, in part, from narrow American racial classifications and social structure. American society lacked a group similar to the Saint Dominguan *gens de couleur*, who—especially in the southern part of the island—were some of the colony's largest landowners and slaveholders. In the early years of the French Revolution, the *gens de couleur* had agitated for and won political and civil rights, but for themselves only; they had seen no need to abolish slavery. Throughout the Haitian Revolution the *gens de couleur* and slave insurgents often battled. White Americans failed to recognize this difference of interests and assumed that because neither group was white by American standards, black and colored Saint Dominguans were allies if not one and the same.[41]

Both black and colored Saint Dominguans in the U.S. also stood out as "French" because of their religion. The refugees persisted in their practice of Catholicism. The records for Holy Trinity and St. Joseph's Catholic churches in Philadelphia attest to a high level of participation by black and colored Saint Dominguans.[42] [. . .]

White Americans supposed that the exiled slaves came in order to sow the seeds of rebellion, but the reasons behind the "French negroes'" migration reflected a variety of impulses. To some extent, their migration can be explained by the personal relationships that tied masters and slaves together. Owners also intimidated many slaves into accompanying them to the United States, yet some black and colored Saint Dominguans probably wanted to leave the island. For reasons similar to those of white colonists, wealthy land- and slave-owning *gens de couleur* may have sought asylum from the tumult. In addition, even after the French Assembly declared emancipation, freedom was not necessarily guaranteed; the decree met with still resistance throughout the colony, and Spanish and British forces campaigned to reinstitute slavery. Given the uncertainty, one can imagine a number of circumstances in which a slave from Saint Domingue would take the risk of continuing with his or her owner in the United States rather than stay on the war-torn island.

White Americans' view of "French negroes" lacked the subtlety that the newly arrived migrants' experiences reveal. Residents associated black and colored Saint Dominguans with conspiracies and conflagrations in the French colony and the United States, yet these accusations were corroborated by rumors, overheard conversations, and ambiguous reports. For the historian, then, two questions emerge; did some "French negroes" import revolutionary ideas and did African-Americans turn to "French negroes" as role models for subversion? While documentation remains slim, some evidence shows revolutionary sentiment among "French negroes" in the United States and a correlation between rebellious black locals and the example of the Haitian Revolution.

In New York City "French negroes" joined with African-American residents in 1801 to riot in the streets. Word had spread that a white refugee from Saint Domingue, Madame Jeanne Mathusine Droibillan Volunbrun, had arranged to send her twenty slaves to southern states. Such action was illegal according to New York's recently passed gradual emancipation law. Angered by Volunbrun's audacity, a crowd of about 250 black Saint Dominguans and Americans gathered in front of her house in protest until dispersed by members of the town watch.[43] An unusual document suggests another moment of solidarity. In the mid-1790s a group of "citizens of color of Philadelphia" drafted a letter to the French National Assembly, thanking the legislators for passing the "immortal decree" ending slavery in the French colonies. Although the writers made no mention of the rebellion in Saint Domingue, they referred to the slaves in the French possessions as "our brothers."[44] Clearly, the citizens of color in Philadelphia knew what was happening in France and Saint Domingue, and they saw their interests tied to those of French Caribbean slaves.

While these two instances provide evidence of both concrete and symbolic links between black Americans and Saint Dominguans, another case shows how "French negroes" and their arrival in the United States inspired African-Americans. In September 1793 David Harris submitted to the *Baltimore Evening Post* a runaway advertisement for his slave named Tower. After describing Tower's build and clothing, Harris conjectured that the runaway would try to reach Philadelphia. The city was a common destination for enslaved southerners in search of freedom, so white residents, especially in Maryland, vigilantly watched the paths and roads leading to Philadelphia. Harris speculated as to how Tower would evade detection: "as he speaks a little French, and is known to have put a striped ribbon round his hat, it is probable he will attempt to pass as one who lately came in the fleet from Cape-François."[45] Aware of events in France and its colonies, Tower had purposefully sported a "striped ribbon"—most likely a cockade representing the French tricolor—as a way of illustrating his support of the French Revolution.[46] Having lived in Baltimore, Tower had witnessed the arrival of thousands of refugees of all races from the island, and realized that some were free-colored exiles. With these bits of knowledge, a few pieces of ribbon, and a little French as well, Tower made his break for Philadelphia.

The Legacy of "French Negroes" in Antebellum America

The "French negro" provided American slaveowners and their opponents with a potent weapon in their arguments about abolition, for the "horrors of St. Domingo" loomed large in the imaginations of white Americans. Mary Chesnut, an antebellum, elite southern woman, affirmed that stories of the revolution in Saint Domingue were "indelibly printed" on her mind.[47] Antiabolitionists used the memory of Saint Domingue to argue against emancipation, which they equated with race war. A pro-slavery cartoon, "Immediate Emancipation Illustrated," typified the viewpoint. The 1833 image featured three members of the "Anti-Slavery Society" talking about the liberation of slaves. In the foreground sits a statue of a leopard with the following inscription on its pedestal: "Fanaticism . . . may drench America in blood!!" In the background was a vignette, "Insurrection in St Domingo! Cruelty, Lust, and Blood!," in which blacks murdered whites.[48] The stereotype of the "French negro" continued into the century as white Americans sought to explain insurrection among American slaves. On the eve of the Civil War, white southerners asserted that "no attempt at insurrection in the South has ever originated from the domestic negro; but such nefarious designs have always been fomented from other sources—such as Vesey, of St. Domingo, and Northern incendiaries."[49]

Supporters of the Saint Domingue Revolution countered southern claims with an outpouring of pro-Haiti literature during the antebellum period. Some abolitionists, however, were troubled by the violence that marked the Haitian Revolution, and claimed that Haiti was not a template for emancipation, citing the British Caribbean as a counterexample. Others strove to account for the violence that characterized the rebellion and its aftermath. In 1857 the Reverend James T. Holly, an African-American and ardent supporter of Haiti, blamed the bloodiness of the insurrection on the duplicitous French: "if we now see [Dessalines] resume his work of slaughter and death, and hang 500 French prisoners on gibbets erected in sight of the very camp of General Rochambeau, we may see in this the bitter fruit of the treachery of the whites." In his defense of postrevolutionary Haiti, Holly observed that "there is no nation in North America, but the United States, nor any in South America, except Brazil, that can pretend to compare with Hayti, in respect to general stability of government. The Spanish Republics of America will have as many rulers in eight years as Hayti has had in a half century."[50]

During the antebellum era, some black Americans turned to the Haitian republic as a remedy for the oppression they suffered in the United States. Small numbers moved to Haiti in the early 1820s; encouraged by positive reports, thousands followed. 1824 was a high point when between 6,000 to

7,000 black Americans left for the island. The project, however, faltered, and Haitian President Jean Pierre Boyer began to rethink its wisdom. Ultimately, many of the African-Americans who emigrated chose to return to the United States because they found the linguistic, religious and social character of Haiti too foreign.[51]

Some abolitionists hoped for a Haiti in the American south. According to one, "The indignation of the slaves . . . would kindle a fire so hot that it would melt their chains, drop by drop, until not a single link would remain; and the revolution that was commenced in 1776 would then be finished, and the glorious sentiments of the Declaration of Independence . . . would be realized."[52] Such activists reversed southerners' logic concerning the link between race war and emancipation, contending that race war and revolution were the consequences not of emancipation, but of the failure to abolish slavery.

From the 1790s through the Civil War, ideas about rebellious "French negroes" shaped American arguments about slavery and abolition. Pro-slavery advocates used the image of "French negroes" to raise fears about rebellion and strengthen the link forged by Tucker connecting emancipation and race war. At the same time, the specter of "French negroes" provided slaveowners with a scapegoat for explaining defiant activity on the part of their own slaves. For anti-slavery proponents, insurgent "French negroes" were causes for celebration and explanation. While lauding the revolution, they also sought to reconcile its means with its ends in order to discredit pro-slavery claims as well as to resolve, in their own minds, Haiti's ambiguous legacy. This decades-long discussion illustrated how the Atlantic revolutions and New World slavery permeated, both literally and figuratively, the boundaries set by nations, long after the initial tremors of rebellion had subsided.

NOTES

1 Research for this article was supported by fellowships from Columbia University, the John Carter Brown Library, the Library Company of Philadelphia, and the American Philosophical Society. The author thanks Elizabeth Blackmar, Eduardo Elena, Eric Foner, François Furstenberg, Malick Ghachem, Winston James, Herbert Sloan, Billy G. Smith and the participants at the Harvard University seminar on Atlantic Revolutions (August 2001) for their helpful comments and suggestions.

2 On the history of the Haitian Revolution, see Carolyn Fick, *The Making of Haiti: The Saint Domingue Revolution from Below* (Knoxville, 1990); David Gaspar and David Geggus, eds., *A Turbulent Time: The French Revolution and the Greater Caribbean* (Bloomington, 1997); David Geggus, *Slavery, War, and Revolution: The British Occupation of Saint Domingue, 1793–1798* (New York, 1982); C. L. R. James, *The Black Jacobins: Toussaint L'Ouverture and the San Domingo Revolution* (New York, 1938).

3 The most eloquent investigation of this argument comes from Michel-Rolph Trouillot, *Silencing the Past: Power and the Production of History* (Boston, 1995).

4 Gary Nash, "Reverberations of Haiti in the American North: Black Saint Dominguans in Philadelphia," *Explorations in Early American Culture: A Special Supplemental Issue of Pennsylvania History* 65 (1998): 45. On Saint Dominguan refugees in the United States in the 1790s, see Winston C. Babb, "French Refugees from Saint Domingue to the Southern United States, 1791–1810" (Ph.D. dissertation, University of Virginia, 1954); Susan Branson and Leslie Patrick, "Étrangers dans un pays étrange: Saint Domingan Refugees of Color in Philadelphia" in *The Impact of the Haitian Revolution*; Frances Sergeant Childs, *French Refugee Life in the United States, 1790–1800: An American Chapter of the French Revolution* (Baltimore, 1940); R. Darrell Meadows, "Engineering Exile: Social Networks and the French Atlantic Community, 1789–1809," *French Historical Studies* 23 (2000); Morales, "The Hispaniola Diaspora"; Nash, "Reverberations"; and Joseph G. Rosengarten, *French Colonists and Exiles in the United States* (Philadelphia, 1907).

5 *The Universal Asylum, and Columbian Magazine* (Philadelphia: from the press of M. Carey, September 1792), p. 214. Slaveowners in Cuba employed similar arguments to differentiate Cuban from Saint Dominguan slavery. See Matt Childs, "A Black French General Arrived to Conquer the Island: Images of the Haitian Revolution in Cuba's 1812 Aponte Rebellion" in *The Impact of the Haitian Revolution in the Atlantic World*, ed. David P. Geggus (Columbia, 2001).

6 It was even held by some French observers. As the exile Médéric-Louis-Elie Moreau de St. Méry complained in his journal, "Since the misfortunes of the French colonies, it has been the habit in France to praise the attitude of the United States toward slaves." Kenneth Roberts and Anna M. Roberts, trans. and ed., *Moreau de St. Méry's American Journey [1793–1798]* (New York, 1947), p. 303.

7 See, for example, Moreau de St. Méry, "Character of the Creoles of St. Domingo," *The American Museum* (November, 1789), p. 360; Joseph La Vallée, "The Negro Equalled by Few Europeans," *The American Museum* (April 1791), 211n; and [Edward Darlington], *Reflections on Slavery; with Recent Evidence of its Inhumanity. Occasioned by the Melancholy Death of Romain, a French Negro* (Philadelphia: printed for the author by R. Cochran, 1803).

8 *Pennsylvania Gazette*, 9 November 1791; *Columbian Centinel* (Boston), 14 August 1793.

9 *Pennsylvania Gazette*, 12 October 1791.

10 *Pennsylvania Gazette*, 2 November 1791.

11 Fifteen years earlier in *Notes on the State of Virginia*, Thomas Jefferson had predicted that emancipation would lead to "the extermination of the one or the other race," and to Tucker, Saint Domingue proved the sagacity of Jefferson's prophecy. Thomas Jefferson, *Notes on the State of Virginia*, ed. Frank Shuffelton (New York, 1999), Query XIV, p. 145. For more about Jefferson's views on the aftermath of abolition, see Peter S. Onuf, " 'To Declare Them a Free and Independent People': Race, Slavery, and National Identity in Jefferson's Thought," *Journal of the Early Republic* 18 (1998): 1–46.

12 St. George Tucker, *A Dissertation on Slavery: with a Proposal for the Gradual Abolition of it, in the State of Virginia* (Philadelphia: printed for Mathew Carey, 1796), pp. 88, 77, 68, 95–6.

13 Alfred Hunt, *Haiti's Influence on Antebellum America: Slumbering Volcano in the Caribbean* (Baton Rouge, 1988), p. 2.

14 Thomas D. Morris, *Southern Slavery and the Law, 1619–1860* (Chapel Hill, 1996), p. 379.

15 *Pennsylvania Gazette*, 16 May 1792.

16 Reported in *Virginia Herald and Fredericksburg Advertiser*, 5 July 1792, but account dated from May. For an excellent treatment of the situation of slaves in Jamaica during the Haitian Revolution, see David Geggus, "The Enigma of Jamaica in the 1790s: New Light on the Causes of Slave Rebellions," *William and Mary Quarterly* 44 (1987): 274–99.

17 On Martinique, see *Pennsylvania Gazette*, 27 January 1796; on Cuba see José Morales, "The Hispaniola Diaspora, 1791–1850: Puerto Rico, Cuba, Louisiana, and other Host Societies" (Ph.D. dissertation, University of Connecticut, 1986), p. 54.

18 *Columbian Centinel* (Boston), 19 October 1793.

19 *Virginia Chronicle* (Norfolk), 19 October 1793. For more on the Secret Keeper Plot, see Robert Alderson, "Charleston's Rumored Slave Revolt of 1793" in *The Impact of the Haitian Revolution in the Atlantic World*; Douglas Egerton, "The Tricolor in Black and White: The French Revolution in Gabriel's Virginia" in *Slavery in the Caribbean Francophone World: Distant Voices, Forgotten Acts, Forged Identities*, ed. Doris Y. Kadish (Athens, GA, 2000), pp. 96–8; Sylvia R. Frey, *Water from the Rock: Black Resistance in a Revolutionary Age* (Princeton, 1991), pp. 230–1; James Sidbury, "Saint Domingue in Virginia: Ideology, Local Meanings, and Resistance to Slavery, 1790–1800," *The Journal of Southern History* 63 (1997): 531–52.

20 *Boston Gazette*, 11 November 1793.

21 *Pennsylvania Gazette*, 13 December 1797; for more detail on the Charleston plots, see George D. Terry, "A Study of the Impact of the French Revolution and the Insurrections in Saint-Domingue upon South Carolina: 1790–1805" (M.A. thesis, University of South Carolina, 1973), pp. 46–131.

22 Quoted in Shane White, *Somewhat More Independent: The End of Slavery in New York City, 1770–1810* (Athens, GA, 1991), p. 65.

23 *Columbian Herald* (Charleston), 19 October 1793; *City Gazette and Daily Advertiser* (Charleston), 9 October 1793.

24 Davis, *The Problem of Slavery*, pp. 120–1; Frey, p. 232; Hunt, p. 109; Nash, *Forging Freedom*, p. 175; Thompson Westcott, *A History of Philadelphia, From the Time of the First Settlements on the Delaware to the Consolidation of the City and Districts in 1854* Vol. 3 (Philadelphia, 1886), p. 637.

25 *City Gazette and Daily Advertiser* (Charleston), 12 May 1794.

26 *Columbian Herald* (Charleston), 8 September 1794.

27 *Columbian Centinel*, 3 August 1793. Refugees traveled back and forth between Saint Domingue and the United States, eager to recover their lands and businesses despite dangerous circumstances. In her loosely autobiographical novel, *Secret History; or, the Horrors of St. Domingo*, Mary Hassal (also known as Leonora Sansay) described her voyage from the United States to Cap Français in the early 1800s. Mary Hassal (Leonora Sansay), *Secret History; or, the Horrors of St. Domingo, in a Series of Letters, Written by a Lady at Cape François, to Colonel Burr, Late Vice-President of the United States, Principally During the Command of General Rochambeau* (Philadelphia, 1808).

28 In slaveholding areas the plea for allowing "French negroes" to enter proved persuasive; for instance, the Norfolk police admitted that "from motives of humanity," they had suspended enforcement of state laws that prohibited the entry of slaves and freemen from other areas. Scores of advertisements for the services and sometimes sale of "French negroes" also attest to the flexibility of the laws' enforcement. Tommy L. Bogger, *Free Blacks in Norfolk, Virginia, 1790–1860; The Darker Side of Freedom* (Charlottesville, 1997), p. 27.

29 *Pennsylvania Gazette*, 6 September 1797.

30 Quoted in James Sidbury, *Ploughshares into Swords: Race, Rebellion, and Identity in Gabriel's Virginia, 1730–1810* (Cambridge, 1997), p. 129. On the Frenchmen

involved in the plot, see Douglas R. Egerton, *Gabriel's Rebellion: The Virginia Slave Conspiracies of 1800 and 1802* (Chapel Hill, 1993), pp. 182–5.

31 On U.S. trade with Saint Domingue, see Donald Hickey, "America's Response to the Slave Revolt in Haiti, 1791–1806," *Journal of the Early Republic* 2 (1982): 362–3. On the dynamics between greed and fear of slave insurrection, see David Brion Davis, "Impact of the French and Haitian Revolutions" in *The Impact of the Haitian Revolution*.

32 W. Jeffrey Bolster, *Black Jacks: African American Seamen in the Age of Sail* (Cambridge, 1997), p. 145.

33 For example, see ibid; Peter Linebaugh and Marcus Rediker, *The Many-Headed Hydra: Sailors, Slaves, Commoners, and the Hidden History of the Revolutionary Atlantic* (Boston, 2000); Julius Scott, "A Common Wind: Currents of Afro-American Communication in the Era of the Haitian Revolution" (Ph.D. dissertation, Duke University, 1986); and Sidbury, "Saint Domingue in Virginia."

34 Bolster, p. 147.

35 Hunt, p. 87; Stanley Elkins and Eric McKitrick, *The Age of Federalism: The Early American Republic, 1788–1800* (New York, 1993), pp. 645–6.

36 Quoted in Elkins and McKitrick, p. 654. For more on the American diplomacy with Saint Domingue during the Adams administration, see Rayford Logan, *The Diplomatic Relations of the United States with Haiti, 1776–1891* (Chapel Hill, 1941), chapter 3; Mats Lundahl, "Toussaint L'Ouverture and the War Economy of Saint-Domingue, 1796–1802," *Slavery and Abolition* 6 (1985); 122–38; and "Letters of Toussaint Louverture and of Edward Stevens, 1798–1800," (in Documents) *American Historical Review* 16 (1910): 64–101.

37 Elkins and McKitrick, p. 659; David Brion Davis, *Revolutions: Reflections on American Equality and Foreign Liberations* (Cambridge, 1990), pp. 25–6.

38 See, for example, the *Baltimore Daily Intelligencer*, 2 April 1794.

39 Fick, pp. 22, 25.

40 Supplement to *Gazette de St. Domingue*, 12 January 1791. A few runaway notices posted in the United States also noted the assorted African origins of "French negroes." For example, see *Gazette française et americaine* (New York), 16 September and 30 October 1795 [slaves from the Congo nation]; and 1 January 1796 [slave from Mozonbie]; *Baltimore Daily Intelligencer*, 3 December 1793 [slave from nation Nago].

41 Opinion about the "rebelliousness" and alliances of free people of color was also influenced by negative portrayals in the press. An article from 1792 claimed that the "mulattoes of St. Domingo" were descended from greedy, shameless white men who, having "no immediate objects of gratification presented, but the enslaved African female," peopled "the island with a progeny, who were neither European nor African, and felt no attachment to either." While noting that some fathers sponsored the education of their illegitimate offspring, the author warned that schooling bred discontent among the *gens de couleur* with their subordinate social position. He then argued that their aspirations led to upheaval in Saint Domingue: "they allied themselves to the blacks, whom they heretofore held in contempt, and have carried fire and sword through the territories of the white inhabitants." Anonymous, *The American Museum* (July 1792), p. 39.

42 F.X. Reuss, trans. and ed., "Baptismal Records from Holy Trinity Church, Philadelphia," *Records of the American Catholic Historical Society* 22 (1911): 1–20; Reuss, "Marriage Registers for Holy Trinity Church, Philadelphia," *Records of the American Catholic Historical Society* 24 (1913): 140–61; Reuss, "Marriage Registers for St. Joseph's Church," *Records of the American Catholic Historical Society* 20 (1909): 22–48; Reuss, "Sacramental Registers of St. Joseph's Church,

Philadelphia, *"Records of the American Catholic Historical Society* 15–17 (1904–06), pp. 1–32, 53–68, 202–23, 289–313, 314–43, 322–47, 361–90, 454–75.
43 White, pp. 144–5.
44 Draft of a letter by "Les Citoyens de couleur de Philadelphie à L'Assemblée Nationale," 1793. John Carter Brown Library, Providence, RI. Although dated 1793, this letter—because of its reference to the abolition decree of February 1794—might be later. There is no indication as to whether this letter was actually sent or who wrote it.
45 *Baltimore Evening Post*, 18 September 1793.
46 On cockades and who wore them, see Simon P. Newman, *Parades and the Politics of the Street: Festive Culture in the Early American Republic* (Philadelphia, 1997), chapters 4 and 5.
47 Quoted in Hunt, 73n.
48 "Immediate Emancipation Illustrated," 1833. Print Collection. Library Company of Philadelphia, Philadelphia, PA.
49 Quoted in Hunt, p. 142.
50 James Theodore Holly, *A Vindication of the Capacity of the Negro Race for Self-Government and Civilized Progress, as Demonstrated by Historical Events of the Haytian Revolution; and the Subsequent Acts of that People since their National Independence* (New Haven, 1857), pp. 33, 40.
51 Nash, *Forging Freedom*, p. 244; Chris Dixon, *African America and Haiti: Emigration and Black Nationalism in the Nineteenth Century* (Westport, CT, 2000), pp. 26, 39–42.
52 William Wells Brown, *St. Domingo: Its Revolutions and its Patriots. A Lecture Delivered Before the Metropolitan Athenaeum, London, May 16, and at St. Thomas' Church, Philadelphia, December 20, 1854* (Boston, 1855), p. 38.

6

TALK ABOUT HAITI

The Archive and the Atlantic's Haitian Revolution

Ada Ferrer

In thinking about the legacies of the Haitian Revolution in the Atlantic World it is tempting to think in binaries. The revolution produced fear and terror among whites, hope and inspiration among slaves and free people of color. The revolution resulted in the radical end of slavery in Saint-Domingue; elsewhere (for instance, in Cuba, southeastern Brazil, and parts of the southern United States) it served as a catalyst to further enslavement. And in postcolonial Haiti itself the promise of radical revolution went unfulfilled as the despotism and mass poverty of colonial servitude were reconfigured in the postcolonial period.

The same kind of double structure is present when we think of another legacy of the Haitian Revolution, namely the construction of a powerful silence around the Haitian Revolution. Among the most important and persuasive expressions of this critique are Michel-Rolph Trouillot's 1995 essays "An Unthinkable History" and "The Three Faces of Sans Souci."[1] In these works, Trouillot argued that contemporaries were incapable of apprehending a revolution made by enslaved men and women. Limited by that incapacity, they reverted to explanations about the decisive role of outside agitators, the pernicious effects of French Revolutionary ideology, and the miscalculations of slaveowners and statesmen. Rarely if ever did they consider the power or consciousness of slaves themselves. According to Trouillot, this contemporary inability to understand the Revolution helps explain the relative absence of the Haitian Revolution in the production of historical knowledge. Unprecedented and unmatched in its challenge to slavery and colonialism, radical in its outcome, it remains little known compared to other world revolutions. Though more studied in the last decade than ever before, it still easily earns the label penned by Trouillot in 1995: "the revolution the world forgot."[2]

But if Trouillot has provided a much-needed and powerful condemnation of the relative silence that has surrounded the Haitian Revolution to the present, other authors have shown that at the time, as news of the slaves' actions erupted onto the world stage, everyone seemed to be talking and thinking about events in Saint-Domingue. As Julius Scott has amply demonstrated, from South America to New England news of the Revolution spread across linguistic, geographic, and imperial boundaries. And even in Europe, according to Susan Buck-Morss, the events were known to "every European who was part of the bourgeois reading public," who apprehended the Revolution as "the crucible, the trial by fire for the ideals of the French Enlightenment."[3] If this was silence, it was a thunderous one indeed.

My purpose in this essay is not to refute the idea—now so powerful in the literature—of a silencing of the Haitian Revolution, but rather to get inside and move beyond that claim. I contend that before we can understand the meanings of Haiti, we must first explore the ways in which Haiti was talked about as it was created. What news circulated? Through what specific points of contact? Among whom? With what language and images? And with what kinds of resonance? As these kinds of questions suggest, our focus is not only on the content of Haitian news, but also on the social and physical networks that helped produce, circulate, and transform rumor and observation into news and eventually into historical narrative and explanation.

To engage in this kind of exploration, I ground this study in Cuba, a neighboring island where consciousness of Haiti and its revolution was particularly strong. The easternmost point of the island was only about fifty miles away from Haiti. Early in the Revolution, slaveowners from the French colony arrived by the thousands, carting slaves, seeking refuge, and telling stories of black vengeance and physical desolation. Throughout the decades following Haitian independence, there were continuous scares and rumors about imminent Haitian invasions into scarcely populated eastern territory. So, in many ways, in Cuba the Haitian Revolution felt immediate and urgent. That urgency, however, derived not only from physical proximity or patterns of migration, but also from the fact that Cuba was in a sense beginning to supplant Haiti. In terms of sugar production, it was coming to occupy the place formerly held by French Saint-Domingue. Cuban planters, merchants, and bureaucrats were highly conscious of this; and, in fact, they explicitly saw themselves as following in the footsteps of, and eventually surpassing, their once-prosperous French counterparts in Saint-Domingue.[4] One of the immediate effects of the Revolution on this neighboring island was thus the importation of an ever-growing number of enslaved Africans, to work the sugar that was finally making Cuba the most profitable of colonies. Here, then, the Revolution produced a potentially powerful contradiction: at the same time that it created a heightened consciousness of slave rebellion and power, it also produced a massive rise in the actual number of slaves. It is in this setting that I explore the material and quotidian links between a revolution that was dramatically dismantling slavery in Saint-Domingue and a colonial society that was at the same moment erecting a profitable and growing slave system in Cuba.

In what follows I will focus on two distinct streams of information entering Cuba from revolutionary Saint-Domingue. I chose these two in particular for several reasons. First, because they are in many ways unexpected and surprising. Second, because they highlight on the one hand how rich and detailed was the information arriving and on the other hand the diversity of the social actors it reached. And, third, because an examination of both routes encourages one to reconsider some of the broad categories that scholars have used in talking about the Revolution's impact in the Atlantic World and to reflect more generally on the way historical knowledge is produced.

Witnessing Revolution

In Cuba, word of the slaves' uprising in Saint-Domingue arrived just days after it started. A stream of almost continuous information would follow over the next thirteen years. Letters of private French citizens, addressed to French and non-French residents of Cuban cities, circulated from hand to hand, sometimes reaching local Spanish authorities. Copies of printed proclamations, reports, and newspapers arrived with letters or smuggled aboard ships. Official pleas from authorities in Saint-Domingue reached Spanish officials in Cuba and elsewhere. Subsequent ones arrived, under very different circumstances, from other officers of France, for instance from the mulatto general André Rigaud, as he did battle against the forces of Toussaint Louverture, the principal black leader on the island. But Louverture, as well, was in communication with the Spanish governor of Santiago de Cuba, in at least one instance even offering his aid to the embattled provincial governor whose city was lacking in basic foodstuffs and receiving little sustenance from the capital.[5] In Cuba, then, communications arrived regularly from central players of the Revolution.

Indeed, sometimes the very players arrived, relaying news and opinions in person. French officers and troops leaving Saint-Domingue for France often did so by way of Cuban cities such as Santiago and Havana. When Vézien Desombrage, French commander of Jérémie, evacuated the colony in 1793, he stopped in Santiago, providing the governor there with extensive information on the state of the French colony. Several years later, in 1800, when the officers, soldiers, and families of the forces of André Rigaud evacuated Saint-Domingue after their defeat by the forces of Toussaint Louverture, they chose the same route. Their presence in Santiago de Cuba, said the governor of that city, had become widely known among the local population.[6] At the end of the war, defeated French troops, now in greater number, also evacuated by way of Santiago. Informed of the massive arrival of French soldiers, the captain general in Havana ordered the provincial governor in Santiago to confine these troops to their ships so as to avoid all contact with Spanish subjects. But these measures did not prevent local residents from seeing and learning of the evacuating soldiers, leaving their once prosperous colony in the hands of men of color, many of them formerly enslaved.

If one source of news was French soldiers passing through Cuba en route from Saint-Domingue to France, another—more important for our purposes—was the Spanish and Cuban soldiers and officers who experienced firsthand the revolution in Saint-Domingue. Recall that during the war between France and Spain from 1793 to 1795, the theater of war and revolution was not limited to the French side of the island. Spanish forces claimed French territory, and Spanish commanders mobilized and collaborated with the leaders of former French slaves, such as George Biassou, Jean François, and, most famously, Toussaint Louverture. Spanish forces thus had regular contact with the slave revolution that would make Haiti. And, as it turns out, many of these Spanish forces were composed of men who had come directly from Cuba and who then returned to Cuba with that experience and those stories in mind.

The Cuban regiments began arriving in Spanish Santo Domingo during the summer of 1793, approximately two months after Spanish governor Joaquín García pacted for the services of armed French slaves, who came to be known as the black auxiliaries. The soldiers arrived under the command of Matías de Armona, who from exhaustion and utter frustration at having to embody and make material the alliance between the Spanish monarchy and the slave forces of Saint-Domingue, grew ill and was replaced by another Cuban, Juan Lleonart. Upon arriving, both officers seemed perplexed and disturbed by this alliance, which they understood as one between a legitimate army and bands of runaway slaves. Their discomfort deepened as they gradually came to see Spain's complete reliance on these forces. By April 1794, Spain held a large swath of territory formerly belonging to France, controlling such cities as Gonaïves, Marmelade, Petite Rivière, Fort Dauphin, and Mirebalais. But the commanders of the Cuban regiments insisted repeatedly that this control was illusory. To hold these towns, they were completely reliant on the black auxiliary forces, the allegiance of whom was, at best, painful and, at worst, transitory.

The tables seemed to have been turned. The Spanish depended on former slaves for military victories and relied on their magnanimity for their continual survival. Armona complained that the black forces saw the Spanish ones as tributaries who were obligated to supply them with food, drink, money, and other resources in order to preserve any sense of security. He complained that the auxiliaries gave themselves military ranks and titles, that they wore imposing military and royal insignia, that they tried to act like men, acting "with a certain air of superiority, as if *we* needed them and *we* have to please them."[7] The correspondence between the auxiliary forces and these Spanish-Cuban commanders gives a sense

142

of this inversion. White officers wrote to former slaves addressing them as friends and exuding deference even as they called for obedience. New black officers wrote with demands, their documents stamped with images of trees of liberty topped with crowns sustained by naked black men.[8]

In military ritual and ceremony, the inversion was given material form and official sanction. Toussaint and Biassou were regaled in San Rafael in early 1794, each receiving a gold medal from the king of Spain in honor of their services as his loyal vassals. At the ceremony, it was the officers of two Cuban infantry units who awarded the medals. It was men from the Cuban regiments who gathered to witness the concession of this highest honor, who played the military music, who paraded with the medal recipients, and who joined the two black officers in a lavish two-hour meal prepared in their honor.[9]

In an examination of the contact between Haitian leaders and these men from Cuba, one thing that emerges powerfully is the attempt of the latter to apprehend and in a sense classify the political, military, and social landscape that lay before them. To do this, the Cuban officers engaged in a two-pronged interpretation of their new allies. On the one hand, they observed them closely and tried to read into their behavior larger designs. They watched carefully and imputed significance to the way black commanders approached their camps, the way they announced their arrival, the composition of their guards, and many other things, all to make predictions about black loyalty or treachery. But if circumstances required this kind of close reading of allies' behavior, in practice the Cuban commanders just as often engaged in what might be called a kind of "intuitive sociology," where the form and protagonists of events were thought to be knowable almost intuitively, with little reference to events and facts on the ground.[10] So, when the commanders began predicting black auxiliary attacks on the Spanish and Cuban forces, they did so principally with reference to what they saw as the inherent character of the rebels. These white Cuban and Spanish observers could close their eyes and not refer to anything specific, and still feel confident predicting what they saw as the inevitable outcome of a military and political alliance with former slaves.

On an even more basic level, we see how these officers, confronted with a large army of rebel slaves only nominally under their command, struggled to apprehend and classify the situation before them. How, for example, were they to approach the black commanders on which they now depended? They knew the black rebels were officially auxiliaries, but they often noted that really they were "runaway slaves." The officers' reports sometimes seemed to acknowledge that their own system of classification did not correspond with that of the slave rebels. Armona, for example, routinely recorded such discrepancies. "They," he said, referred to their positions as encampments, but he called them "*palenques*." He mentioned that they referred to themselves as generals, brigadiers, and lieutenants. He seemed about to record a difference in the way the Spanish named these same leaders, but then added, sheepishly almost, that they called them that, too. His discomfort suggests that the situation—that is the power of the forces led by black rebels—was making old labels (such as maroons) inappropriate, and new ones (such as general for a former slave) plausible, but still not so natural as to go unmarked.[11]

The alliance between the two groups ended in 1795, when Spain lost the war to France and ceded Santo Domingo. At that point, these Cuban and Spanish officers returned to Havana with physical artifacts from the war, many with slaves purchased or taken from the scenes of upheaval in Hispaniola, and all with firsthand accounts of revolutionary turmoil. On separate ships, roughly at the same time, Spanish authorities in Santo Domingo also embarked the black auxiliaries for Cuba. The Marqués de Casa Calvo, another Cuban-born officer from a very prominent Havana family who was then commander of Bayajá, where Jean François had staged a massacre of approximately seven hundred white French residents then living under Spanish rule, witnessed this embarkation. Faced with the certainty of seeing the perpetrators of this massacre headed for his native Havana (where his family was making a fortune on sugar worked by slaves), he decided to intervene. He wrote the governor of Havana a letter that was pained and urgent. It was pained because he confessed how agonizing he had found it to have to establish "a perfect equality" with a "Black man who though he called himself a General, did not escape from that sphere to which his birth and his origins in slavery had relegated him." The letter was also urgent, because he was imploring the Cuban governor to turn away the black forces and to forbid their entry in Havana. He begged him,

> not [to] lodge or settle in the bosom of the flourishing island of Cuba, loyal and faithful to her King, nor within the boundaries [recinto] of Havana, these venomous vipers. . . . I am almost an eyewitness to the disgraceful day of the 7th [of July], I am as well of the desolation of this whole Colony, and I have stepped on the vestiges of their fury. These are, even if painted with different colors, the same ones who assassinated their Masters, raped their Mistresses, and destroyed all who had property on this soil at the beginning of the insurrection. Why more reflections, if with these alone the human heart is horrified.[12]

In truth, Calvo had nothing to worry about, since Las Casas, without having been an eyewitness to the massacre, had already voiced strong objections to his superiors in Madrid. He prevented Jean François and Biassou, or any of the seven hundred members of their entourage, from disembarking in Havana, though the ships were moored in the harbor some time. In opposing the settlement of black leaders Jean François and Biassou, Las Casas argued that they were dangerous and that they horrified a white population that counted so many slaves and free people of color in their midst. He even stated that the very names of Jean François and Biassou already resounded in Cuba like the names of great conquerors. He may not have been exaggerating. In several Cuban slave conspiracies uncovered in the period and aftermath of the Haitian Revolution, slave witnesses spoke to the significance and appeal of the figure of Jean François. In 1812, for example, during the Aponte Rebellion, one of the largest and most interesting rebellions in the history of the island, numerous enslaved and free witnesses made ample references to the 1795 visit of the two black generals, despite Las Casas's refusal of permission to disembark.[13]

The claim, and indeed the scattered evidence, that the reputations of these two black generals were already well known on the island is of course important. It suggests that all kinds of news—not just official news—was circulating. Moreover, it suggests that this news circulated not just among colonial authorities or soldiers or a well-connected elite, but rather that the population as a whole was coming into contact with news of black rebellion against enslavement and eventually against colonialism.

Reading the Revolution

If the historical record seems to portray a Cuban world in which Haitian news reached a wide cast of characters, it also strongly suggests that this cast included people of color, slave and free—people who were sure to give such news very different spins than, say, a planter turned commander. Surviving records give us precisely this sense, as they allow us to explore some of the routes by which people of color learned of Haiti and the ways they thought about it.

The very first news of the Saint-Domingue slave insurrection appears to have arrived in Cuba on August 27, 1791, when a French officer appeared in Baracoa, Cuba's easternmost city and the one closest to the French colony. He arrived with a clear description of events and an urgent plea for aid.[14] The first indication that the news had reached the population of color comes almost as early, but—unfortunately—is significantly less clear. Here I am referring to a very brief, very vague entry in the meeting minutes of the Havana city council, an entry moreover the main subject of which is ostensibly a city butcher shop and not enslaved or free black people. In the entry, dated September 9, 1791, city council members tried to explain a sudden shortage of pigs at the city butcher shop for pork. The only explanation they proferred—and one they did not like—seemed to be that the shop was short of pork because people of color in Havana had begun sacrificing pigs in honor of insurgents in foreign colonies. A council member then went on to lament the potential influence of foreign blacks on their own slaves.[15] So just over two weeks after the start of the slave revolution in Saint-Domingue, people of color in Havana appeared to know of their acts. The entry further suggests that local blacks sought to honor the rebels and that they may have done so by sacrificing pigs. Here, of course, we cannot help but think of the Bois Caïman ceremony in which Haitian revolutionaries probably took blood oaths and sacrificed a black pig in preparation for the war they were about to commence.[16]

The question of how to interpret this brief mention of Haiti in the documentary record is of course a challenging one. The white official's confidence in alluding to the existence of pig sacrifices among Havana blacks made to honor or benefit foreign insurgents combined with the knowledge that pig sacrifices occurred in preparation for slave rebellion in Saint-Domingue tempts us to take the official at his word. It encourages us to conclude, or at the very least to suggest, that blacks in Havana (whether slave or free we cannot know) had certain knowledge of the Haitian Revolution days after it began and organized ceremonies which resembled the very ceremonies of their slave counterparts in the Northern Plain of Saint-Domingue. That suggestion, of course, leads us to further ones: the possibility that the pig sacrificers in Havana—those descendents of Ethiopia as they are described in the record—felt a powerful affinity, a shared sense of belonging, and a common purpose, with enslaved men and women engaged in the process of making themselves free in what would become Haiti.

But the record itself is highly ambiguous. In the official minutes of the Havana City Council meetings, the pig sacrifice and the Haitian Revolution are explicitly linked—though of course the latter cannot yet be named in that way. But the link is asserted only here and only on the basis of unspecified rumor and speculation. Reading backwards and forwards from that particular meeting, we see that the question of meat and pig shortages in the city was a fairly routine matter of business. The fact of a shortage in August or September 1791 is far from exceptional. The claim that the cause of that shortage was linked to local black solidarity with the revolution was. What is interesting, however, is that another version of that same meeting is available in the documentary record. When in 1794, colonial officials wrote to Madrid to plead that black prisoners from Saint-Domingue not be brought to Cuba to be sold as slaves, they referred to and reproduced the partial minutes from that original September 9, 1791, meeting. But in this later transcription, there was no mention of pig sacrifice. Here, the same colonial official shares instead the news of the arrival of a French ship from Saint-Domingue carrying 292 slaves and fresh information of a massive slave insurrection. News of the arrival of the ship is immediately followed by the same lament that appears earlier about the likelihood that foreign insurgents will corrupt and incite Cuban slaves to rebellion. Thus one written version of the meeting begins with speculation of pig sacrifice, the other with the news of rebellion arriving aboard a French slave ship.[17]

It is impossible to say with any degree of certainty what accounts for the significant discrepancy in the two versions of the meeting. We cannot even say if the difference was one of design or of error in transcription. The records remind us again—in a very tangible way—just how fragmentary and inscrutable can be the traces of slaves' political vision that have survived in the documentary record. Yet for all that inscrutability, both versions of the event suggest that white elites were perceiving and fearing the possibility of precisely that vision. They imagined that slaves in one locale would act in support of fellow slaves elsewhere for a goal that was shared across lines geographical and imperial.

Other records suggest that whether or not actual bonds of practical support ever came to exist, people of color in Cuba clearly had the desire to imagine them. In casual street encounters between free urban blacks and local whites, in confrontations between masters and slaves, in heated exchanges between black suspects and white interrogators, Cuban people of color regularly referred to the Haitian Revolution as something they respected and hoped to emulate. They referred by name to men such as Toussaint Louverture, Dessalines, Christophe, and Jean François. They even said among themselves that they wanted to be captains or leaders precisely like these men. Their testimony, on numerous occasions, explicitly refers to the "feats" of slaves in Guarico, the Spanish colonial name for Cap Français—slaves they now referred to as their "compañeros." Slaves recruited others to conspiracy by urging them to do as their counterparts had done in Saint-Domingue, where blacks were now "absolute masters of the land."[18]

While the regular invocations of Haiti by slaves and free people of color leave no doubt that they learned and used knowledge of revolutionary events, on their own these references do not tell us how and from what sources they acquired that knowledge.[19] In what follows, I focus on one source, which according to the captain general of Cuba, the Márques de Someruelos, was of notable importance in informing Cuba's people of color about the unprecedented events of the Haitian Revolution. The source is a surprising one: an official Spanish newspaper—the *Gaceta de Madrid*, a biweekly publication of the Spanish government in Madrid.[20] What is perhaps surprising in examining this newspaper is that, for all the government efforts to curtail the flow of information, the source with most information on events in Saint-Domingue circulating in Cuba was not a foreign newspaper, but the official newspaper of its own metropole. According to the captain general, the problem this posed was significant. He lamented that the newspaper was so readily available: "It is sold to the public, and everyone buys it, and it circulates well among the blacks," who, he added, read it, discuss it, and analyze its contents "with considerable liveliness."[21] What worried the governor so profoundly was that in the pages of this gazette, Cubans of color encountered substantial and animated news of black rebellion in what had been an orderly and prosperous sugar colony just miles away. Here were stories of the revolutionary terror in Paris, of abolitionist debates in Britain, of war in Europe. And in regular installments, often reprinted from French, British, and U.S. newspapers, stories of the Haitian Revolution unfolded.

The *Gaceta's* coverage of the Revolution began in November 1791, with the first reference to the rebellion of the slaves in the North.[22] Coverage continued, with articles on other attacks and massacres, on the abolition of slavery in Paris in 1794, and on Spanish and English attacks on French territory in Saint-Domingue. In 1796, readers first encounter the figure of Toussaint Louverture (though he is not explicitly identified as black until 1800).[23] Although coverage of Haitian events is regular and fairly frequent, we see, not surprisingly, that at certain moments of the Revolution, the coverage intensified. This was clearly the case with the Leclerc expedition which began leaving France in the final months of 1801. The expedition was devised by Napoleon, commanded by his brother-in-law Leclerc, and meant to contain what authorities in Paris saw as the evils and excesses that had taken root in their once-prized colony. The *Gaceta* covered this event in exceptional detail. In almost every number, news appeared of the expedition: readers learned of so many ships gathering for the journey from Brest to Saint-Domingue, of the number of troops and arms to be transported by each. The impression given by the regular dispatches was of an imminent and massive invasion of the colony by metropolitan forces.

Coverage intensified still more with the arrival of the expedition on the coasts of Saint-Domingue in February 1802. Then, readers of the gazette began learning of the reactions of former slaves and their leaders. Arriving at the Couleuvre ravine near Gonaïves, the expedition encountered resistance, cannon shots and hand-to-hand combat from Toussaint's men. When fresh forces arrived at Le Cap, the black leader Christophe refused to grant them entry without the previous authorization of Toussaint. In Port-au-Prince, the rebels set fire to the town before French troops could disembark. Alongside the detailed descriptions of such encounters were reprinted extracts from official reports by Leclerc and Rochambeau (governor of Saint-Domingue) to the Overseas Minister. All this was published in the pages of the newspaper and read, as we know from Someruelos, with much interest in Cuba.[24]

The frequency and nature of the reports turned the news into something like a serialized novel. Little by little, the number of ships leaving Brest grew and grew; little by little the reactions of rebel slaves became clearer and clearer. And as in a novel, sometimes the details of the unfolding events were quite intimate. So for example, the gazette published a quite detailed description of the reunion between Toussaint's wife and her two sons (both of whom had been sent to France to study and who now accompanied the expedition on Napoléon's request). We learned of her embrace, her tears, and the maternal love she displayed. Longer still was the gazette's description of Toussaint's own meeting with his sons shortly thereafter.[25]

In fact, as news of the expedition unfolded, the key questions soon came to center around Toussaint himself—how would he receive the expedition, what would his attitude be, what would his destiny be? The ultimate answer came, of course, with news of his deportation to France in June 1802.[26] Even with Toussaint out of the picture, however, the gazette's readers may have soon begun to surmise that his plans were perhaps bearing fruit. Gradually, more and more articles began appearing about the mounting deaths of French soldiers. They learned of Leclerc's death, and the death of many other officers who only a few weeks earlier had appeared in the gazette's pages as the dogged persecutors of Toussaint and his allies. By the end of the year, almost every number of the gazette seemed to provide evidence of the weakness of the French and the growing power of black leaders such as Dessalines and Christophe.[27]

But the gazette spoke not only of black military victories, it also published articles that gave some insight into the desires and the ideas of Haitian rebels. It published the words of black leaders. The issue of the gazette that had prompted the complaint by Cuban Captain General Someruelos, in fact, contained two translated proclamations by black Haitian leaders: one signed by Dessalines and another by Dessalines, Christophe, and Clerveaux. In both documents, the black leaders invited refugees who had fled the colony to return and live peacefully under the new system being erected. But their invitation also entailed a clear and explicit threat. Speaking of the refugees, the three leaders declared:

> The God who protects us, the God of free men, commands us to extend toward them our victorious arms. But those who, intoxicated with a foolish pride, ... [those who] think still that they alone form the essence of human nature, and who pretend to think that they are destined by heaven to be our owners and our tyrants, [we tell them] never to come near the island of Santo Domingo, because if they come, they will find only chains and deportation.[28]

This was the proclamation that had so worried Someruelos—a proclamation in which were manifest the power of new black leaders, who forbade the return of Saint-Domingue to its colonial ruler and who were willing to admit only those refugees who deigned to live under a government of former slaves and in a society without slavery.

Just one week after Someruelos penned his attack on the publication and circulation of this document, a new proclamation appeared in the pages of the gazette. This time it was the Haitian declaration of independence, signed by Dessalines on January 1, 1804, and published in the gazette six months later on June 1. We know that other copies of the Haitian declaration of independence had already arrived in Cuba, aboard French ships, for example, and that authorities on the island had done their best to have them confiscated, translated, and sent to Madrid.[29] But in spite of their attempts to limit its circulation, in June we see the declaration now translated, published, and circulating, even among black Cubans, who Someruelos argued were able to acquire the gazette with little difficulty. So, we know that people of color in Cuba were able to read the Haitian declaration of independence, a proclamation of former slaves who had vanquished their masters by force of arms.

Now we can understand more profoundly the discomfort of Someruelos upon recognizing that these words and ideas, that these examples of a new kind of presence and power in Haiti, of a new liberty by and for black people, were circulating in his own colony. It was not only that people of color learned of Haitian news, for according to the gazette itself there was not one black person who did not already know these stories by memory.[30] It was also that with repetition and circulation, the example acquired more and more substance.

Archives, History, and the Haitian Revolution

Through the pages of the *Gaceta de Madrid*, through contact with soldiers formerly stationed in the theater of war and revolution, and through other multiple routes not traced here, people in Cuba received interesting, detailed, and sometimes intimate news of the world's first black revolution. We know now that whatever sense of fear or hope may have been sparked in Cuba by the example set by Haitian events did not have to be imagined out of whole cloth, but would have likely drawn on ample raw material, on detailed narratives, and suggestive stories available to residents of Cuba regarding those events. So, for example, when alleged slave conspirators in Bayamo relayed the name of Jean François to Spanish authorities, or when during the Aponte conspiracy in Havana in 1812, slaves and free people invoked the names of Jean François, Christophe, and others, both the tellers of and the audiences for those stories would have had ample opportunity to learn of the real Jean François and his exploits. The oft-repeated assertion that Cuban Creole elites feared that any attempt at political liberation would stir the population of color, perhaps makes more sense when we know that members of that elite had firsthand experience in Santo Domingo with unsuccessful attempts to mobilize and contain armed former slaves in support of elite political goals. Cuban men had been defeated by some of those slave forces in 1794–95. Cuban residents had opportunities to witness defeated whites evacuate the French colony and then to read the proclamations of their black victors. The fears or hopes allegedly inspired by the Haitian Revolution would have been shaped by these very concrete contacts and experiences.

The proliferation of substantial, detailed, even intimate talk of the Haitian Revolution does not, however, require that we abandon the important notion of "silence" discussed at the outset of this paper. Rather, it compels us to try to understand more deeply the ways in which such silences (and mentions) were constructed, sustained, and challenged, and the ways particular kinds of historical knowledge and narratives became ascendant.

In 1995, Michel-Rolph Trouillot brilliantly and persuasively argued that the silence that has tended to surround the Haitian Revolution is explained in part by the inability of contemporary observers to understand or narrate the events of the Revolution—and particularly the aspirations and actions of slave rebels—with the language and categories available at the time, or even now. For Trouillot this is a silence in which the archive itself is implicated, as an institution of power that selects, gathers, organizes, and legitimates certain kinds of documents and facts in ways that reinscribe the power already at play in the historical act itself.[31]

I would suggest, however, that a grounded analysis of the ways in which people regularly spoke, heard, learned, and wrote about the Revolution as it unfolded, encourages us to approach the archive in a different way: not as transparent depository of transparent documents, but neither simply as obstacle for historian and accomplice to state power. A more fruitful approach, rather, invites us to see the archive as also containing the traces of the operation of its own power. There, we can trace the processes by which certain silences and narratives are created, reformulated, sustained, and broken. And in the archive, Haiti emerges simultaneously in multiple forms: as a place about which detailed, complex, dense, and unruly stories circulated, and as a name that served as loaded key word, black-and-white image, a brief cautionary (or inspirational) invocation. Indeed, if we focus on the sources themselves, we see these dual uses competing even in the same documents. We see at work, in other words, the very process of silencing, the process of what Trouillot calls archival power itself. It is as if we could see the tug of war, the efforts of narrators to contain events in categories that will not allow them to fit.

We see this, for example, even in the archival use or absence of the very term *Haiti*. Haiti, of course, was the name given to colonial Saint-Domingue immediately after independence. It was the Arawak-Taino name for the island; it signified mountainous or high lands; and supposedly it was the name "on everyone's lips" and the name "enthusiastically welcome[d]" when it came time to name the new country.[32] But though the state became Haiti in name, colonial and metropolitan authorities seemed loathe to use that title; to use it, they must have surmised, would be to recognize the victory of slaves and former slaves and the defeat of European rule. Thus, for example, in Cuba and in the Spanish-speaking world in general, the name Haiti makes only scattered archival appearances in the decades after it was created. Spanish authorities continued using the name Santo Domingo for newly independent Haiti, even when this was the source of great confusion. When officials forbade (yet again) the entry of people from Haiti shortly after independence, they did so without naming Haiti, referring simply to Santo Domingo. The move, of course, caused predictable confusion when local authorities confronted refugees from the formerly Spanish part of the island still called Santo Domingo and were unsure if they also were included in the prohibition.[33] It is revealing irony that those Haitians who helped Simón Bolívar win his anticolonial bid against Spain are identified in the historical record as "*franceses*" rather than Haitians.[34]

The same disconnect between the categories and names deployed by narrators and the complex and unprecedented realities on the ground are evident as well in the ways in which colonial and metropolitan authorities struggled to deal with black heads of state, a category of person unknown to them just years or months earlier. So Captain General Someruelos facing letters from black authorities, opts to seek advice from the metropole. He seems at a loss not only about what political strategies to follow, but even about what language to use, what titles, what tone, and with what consequences.[35] Here the Captain General seemed to echo the Cuban officers discussed earlier in the paper, who arrived in Spanish Santo Domingo, and knew not what to name the troops of former slaves who served as their "auxiliaries," calling them "maroons" and "skirmishers," even as they admitted that they were "the all" of the war.[36]

But the writings of Spanish officials also explicitly acknowledge this struggle to name and narrate the scenes before them with words that could not be made to correspond. In doing so, they left for our archives intriguing traces of the struggle between competing ways of naming the history represented by Haiti. In one revealing exchange between Santiago governor Sebastián Kindelán and the Haitian leader Alexandre Petión, we see in fact two discordant regimes of classification. The Haitian letter refers to the "time of the French" and to the Haitians; meanwhile the letter of the colonial official cannot admit such a reality. Here Haiti even in the postindependence year of 1809 continues to be named as "a foreign colony."[37] In these day-to-day documents of empire, and in exchanges such as these, are revealed the conflicts between different visions of Haiti—Haiti as newly independent nation, and Saint-Domingue as permanent turbulent colony. Such examples—and there are many in the historical record—encourage us to move beyond seeing the archive as an institution that only works to silence particular narratives and legitimate those associated with the victors of history. It is more interesting, challenging, and productive to imagine the archive as a place that may also contain—if we choose to read it that way—traces of the conflicts between competing histories and their would-be tellers.

Take, for instance, the following exchange dating from the final months of the revolution in 1803. By midyear, with the conflict in Saint-Domingue now clearly a war of independence, French troops and white residents began (again) fleeing from the colony and arriving by the boat loads in eastern Cuba. The local governor wrote almost daily letters to his supe-riors informing them of the number of ships and people arriving constantly to his territory. He had each captain of each ship formally interviewed, and each solicited "hospitality" from the Spanish. In one such request for hospitality, the French officers stressed the fact that England and France were now again at war and that their town was under threat of British invasion. The governor hearing this request showed little compassion and was inclined to deny refuge. If the threat was merely from the attack of a British enemy, then why not flee to another point in the colony? It was not, he added, as if they were threatened by black troops or black rule. Having expressed this doubt and having voiced a familiar—if at the moment alternative—narrative, he overdetermined the nature of the narrative that would ultimately be produced. Formally requesting hospitality days later, that is, stating the official reason for their flight, the refugees' petition now requested hospitality in a more urgent and conformist language. "We left of absolute necessity," they wrote, "because we were about to be killed by black rebels."[38] Here we see clearly how the power and authority of the governor, and perhaps the very exigencies of producing routinized docu-ments of empire, shaped the record of the archive and turned several possible narratives—for example, of imperial war between Britain and France, or of anticolonial struggle between black rebels and their metropole—into a much simpler, starker story of blacks violently sacri-ficing whites.

In such sources we can see the multiple disjunctures in the way contem-poraries wrote and heard about Haiti—the gap between the proliferation of detailed information and the simultaneous emergence of vulgarized, key-word type references to Haiti, as well as the incompatibility between the terms and categories available to narrators and the unprecedented realities and outcomes on the ground. Such inconsistencies serve to illu-minate the processes by which a particular kind of historical narrative and a particular kind of historical knowledge becomes ascendant. In these disjunctures we are able to observe colonial power trying to convert the Haitian Revolution, among the most radical and significant of the modern world, into a mere warning, a cautionary tale in black and white, a carica-ture with only suppressed traces of the will and thought of the black and mulatto men and women who made the Revolution. But if the historical record shows anything at all, it is that that suppression was far from total.

NOTES

I thank Doris Garraway for the opportunity to be part of this volume [*Editor's note: Tree of Liberty* (Virginia, 2008), ed. Doris Garraway] and of the lively conference at Northwestern University from which it emerged. In addition to the Northwestern audience, I thank audiences at the John Carter Brown Library, the Rutgers Black Atlantic Seminar, the University of Pittsburgh Atlantic History Seminar, the University of Michigan-University of Windsor joint conference on Slavery and

Freedom in the Atlantic World, and the graduate students in my Haitian Revolution colloquium at NYU in spring 2004. For comments on earlier versions, I'd like to thank Laurent Dubois, Sibylle Fischer, Mimi Sheller, Herman Bennett, Rebecca Scott, Jean Hébrard, Fernando Martinez, Michael Zeuske, Julius Scott, Gloria García, Reinaldo Funes, Consuelo Naranjo, Manuel Barcia, Walter Johnson, and Doris Garraway. A shorter and earlier version of some of this material appeared in Spanish as "Noticias de Haití en Cuba," *Revista de Indias* 63 (2003): 675–93.

1 Michel-Rolph Trouillot, *Silencing the Past: Power and the Production of History* (Boston: Beacon, 1995).
2 Ibid., 71. For important recent work on the Revolution, see especially, Laurent Dubois, *Avengers of the New World: The Story of the Haitian Revolution* (Cambridge: Harvard University Press, 2004); Carolyn Fick, *The Making of Haiti: The Saint-Domingue Revolution from Below* (Knoxville: University of Tennessee Press, 1991); and David Geggus, *Haitian Revolutionary Studies* (Bloomington: Indiana University Press, 2002).
3 Julius Scott, "The Common Wind: African American Communication in the Era of the Haitian Revolution," (PhD diss., Duke University, 1986); and Susan Buck-Morss, *Hegel, Haiti and Universal History* (Pittsburgh: University of Pittsburgh Press, 2009).
4 On the Cuban sugar boom in this period, see especially Manuel Moreno Fraginals, *El ingenio: complejo económico social cubano del azúcar*, 3 vols. (Havana: Editorial Ciencias Sociales, 1978); Rolando Ely, *Cuando reinaba su majestad el azúcar* (Buenos Aires: Editorial Sudamericana, 1963). For an important conceptual discussion of this boom and the emergence of a "second slavery" in the aftermath of the Haitian Revolution and British abolitionism, see Dale Tomich, "Spaces of Slavery, Times of Freedom" and "The 'Second Slavery,'" both in his *Through the Prism of Slavery: Labor, Capital, and World Economy* (Lanham, MD: Rowman and Littlefield, 2003).
5 In a letter to Someruelos, Sebastián Kindelán translates and transcribes Toussaint's communication. Governor of Havana Sebastián Kindelán to the Marqués de Someruelos, Captain General of Cuba, 29 April 1800, in Archivo General de Indias, Seville (hereafter AGI), Cuba, legajo 1534.
6 Kindelán to Someruelos, 31 August 1800, in AGI, Cuba, legajo 1534.
7 Matías de Armona to Joaquín García, Captain General of Santo Domingo, San Rafael, 12 August 1793, in Archivo General de Simancas, Simancas, Spain (hereafter AGS), Sección Guerra Moderna (GM), legajo 6855. Emphasis added. Unless otherwise noted, all translations are mine.
8 The reference to the stamp of the tree of liberty appears in Armona to García, San Rafael, 14 August 1793, in AGS, GM, legajo 6855. For a discussion of slave royalism and the on-the-ground compatibility of royalist and republican motifs, see Laurent Dubois, *Avengers of the New World*, 106–8.
9 "Continuación de la noticias de la Ysla de Sto Domingo asta 25 de Marxo de 94" in file "Relación de lo ocurrido en la Ysla de Santo Domingo con motivo de la guerra con los franceses, 1795. D. Antonio Barba," Servicio Histórico Militar, Madrid (hereafter SHM), Colección General de Documentos, Rollo 65, doc. no. 5-4-11-1. The document mentions that General Jean François had received the same honor earlier.
10 The term "intuitive sociology" is borrowed from Arlette Farge and Jacques Revel, *The Vanishing Children of Paris: Rumor and Politics before the French Revolution* (Cambridge: Harvard University Press, 1993), 53.
11 Armona to García, San Rafael, 12 and 14 August 1793. In folder "Correspondencia del Brigadier Dn. Mathías de Armona desde 19 de Junio hasta 10 de Septiembre de 1793" in AGS, GM, legajo 6855.

12 Marqués de Casa Calvo to Luis de las Casas, Captain General of Cuba, 31 December 1795, in AGI, Cuba, legajo 1474.

13 "Testimonio de la criminalidad seguida de oficio contra el negro Miguel, Juan Bautista y José Antonio sobre la conjuración que intentaban contra el Pueblo y sus moradores [Bayamo]," 25 August 1805, in AGI, Cuba, legajo 1649. On Aponte, see Matt Childs, "'A Black French General Arrived to Conquer the Island': Images of the Haitian Revolution in Cuba's 1812 Aponte Rebellion," in David Geggus, ed., *The Impact of the Haitian Revolution in the Atlantic World*, (Columbia: University of South Carolina Press, 2001), 135–56; and Jose Luciano Franco, *Las conspiraciones de 1810 y 1812* (Havana: Editorial de Ciencias Sociales, 1977).

14 See Ignacio Leyte Vidal, Tte. Gob. de Baracoa, to Luis de las Casas, 27 August 1791, in AGI, Cuba, legajo 1435; and 28 August 1791, in Archivo Nacional de Cuba, Havana (hereafter ANC), Asuntos Políticos, legajo 4, exp. 33.

15 Archivo del Museo de la Ciudad de la Habana, (hereafter AMCH), Actas Capitulares del Ayuntamiento de la Habana Trasuntadas, Enero 1791 a Diciembre 1791, folio 247, 9 September 1791.

16 For an interesting and persuasive discussion of the Bois Caïman ceremony and the controversy that has surrounded it in the literature, see David Geggus, "The Bois Caïman Ceremony," in *Haitian Revolutionary Studies*, 81–92.

17 Cabildo extraordinario 12 February 1794, appended to Las Casas to Pedro de Acuña, 19 February 1794, in AGI, Estado, legajo 14, no. 73.

18 See Ada Ferrer, "La société esclavagiste cubaine et la révolution haïtienne," especially 346–56.

19 Julius Scott's pathbreaking work first raised this question and offered a brilliant analysis of the currents of communication among people of color, in which sailors figure very prominently. See Scott, "Common Wind."

20 Larry R. Jensen, *Children of Colonial Despotism: Press, Politics, and Culture in Cuba, 1790–1840* (Gainesville: University Press of Florida, 1988), 6. The gazette was, in fact, one of only two newspapers allowed to operate in the metropole after censorship legislation in February 1791 clamped down on the peninsular press in an effort to prevent the spread of French revolutionary currents.

21 Someruelos to Sec. de Estado, 25 May 1804, in Archivo Histórico Nacional, Madrid (hereafter AHN), Estado, legajo 6366, exp. 78. A transcription of the letter also appears in Someruelos to Sec. de Estado, 13 August 1809, in AGI, Estado, legajo 12, exp. 50.

22 *Gaceta de Madrid* (hereafter *GM*), 25 November 1791, 856.

23 On the emancipation decree, see *GM*, 8 April 1794, 394; on the Spanish victory in Bayajá, *GM*, 1 April 1794, 363–71; on British victories, *GM*, 24 January 1794, 103–4, and 26 August 1794, 1006–7. The first mention of Louverture that I have found in the periodical is from 2 December 1796 (1024), though he does not appear to be identified as black in the journal until 18 January 1800 (50). Coverage of the conflict between Louverture and Rigaud begins 15 October 1799 (894). For his appointment as prefect, 4 August 1801 (816).

24 *GM*, 1801: 1 December, 1214; 8 December, 1230; 18 December, 1236; 22 December, 1278; *GM*, 1802: 5 January, 12; 23 March, 270; 26 March, 283; 2 April, 313–16; 6 April, 326–29; 9 April, 338–41; 20 April, 376–77; 23 April, 385–86; 18 May, 477–79. Someruelos's letter is the one cited above (AGI, Estado, legajo 12, exp. 50).

25 Both appear in *GM*, 21 May 1802, 489–91.

26 See *GM*, 1802: 23 March 270; 2 April, 312; 6 April, 328–9; 13 April, 348–50; 20 April, 376–77; 18 May, 477–79; 21 May, 389–91; 1 June, 528; 22 June, 606–8; 6 July, 650–52; 9 July, 664–5; 27 July, 736; 6 August, 780; 10 August, 789; 28 September, 971.

27 On disease and death among French troops, see *GM* in 1802: 17 August, 817–8; 20 August, 831–2; 19 October, 1054–55; 14 December, 1241–2; 24 December, 1269; and in 1803: 25 January, 67–8.

28 *GM*, 23 March 1804, 267–8.

29 Marqués de Someruelos to D. Pedro Cevallo, 14 March 1804, in AHN, Estado, legajo 6366, exp. 70.

30 *GM*, 18 May 1804.

31 Trouillot, *Silencing the Past*, passim, but especially 48–53. For other important and generative work on thinking about the archive, see especially Arlette Farge, *Le goût de l'archive* (Paris, Seuil, 1997).

32 Thomas Madiou, *Histoire d'Haïti*, quoted in Geggus, *Haitian Revolutionary Studies*, 207.

33 AGI, Cuba, legajo 1549.

34 See Robin Blackburn, *The Overthrow of Colonial Slavery* (London: Verso, 1989), 345.

35 Someruelos to Junta Suprema, 26 December 26, 1808, in AGI, Estado, legajo 12, exp. 57.

36 Armona to García, San Rafael, 10 September 1793. In folder "Correspondencia del Brigadier Dn. Mathías de Armona desde 19 de Junio hasta 10 de Septiembre de 1793" in AGS, GM, legajo 6855.

37 AGI, Estado, legajo 12, exp. 54.

38 Kindelán to Someruelos, 15 August 1803, with enclosed "Testimonio de los autos obrados sobre la arribada que han hecho a este Pto. de Stgo. de Cuba 5 Goletas y una balandra francesas . . . con varias familias de la misma nación pidiendo hospitalidad," in AGI, Cuba, legajo 1537A. See also J. A. Caballer, Consejo de Indias, 21 February 1804, in Archivo del Ministerio de Asuntos Exteriores, Madrid, Politica, República Dominicana, legajo 2372.

7

SWORD-BEARING CITIZENS

Militarism and Manhood in Nineteenth-Century Haiti

(excerpts)

Mimi Sheller

From the slave uprising of 1791 to declaration of independence in 1804, the Haitian Revolution shook the slave-owning European powers to their core. Throughout the Atlantic world the young Republic of Haiti became a powerful symbol of black liberation and racial equality, a harbinger of African emancipation, and a beacon of hope for the anti-slavery movement. Revolutionary self-emancipation, however, also carried with it a burden of self-defense from the embittered slave-holders whose navies circled Haiti's shores and controlled regional trade routes. Facing a continuous threat of invasion over many decades, an ongoing civil war, and the refusal by France, Britain, and even the United States (which, after all, shared a revolutionary republican origin) to recognize Haitian independence, the Haitian state had to remain on a military footing long after the revolution ended. In these difficult circumstances of state-formation, a martial image of the male citizen took on special salience; indeed, building black masculinity became a central task in the construction of Haitian national identity.

In seizing the reins of power and constructing a militarized and masculine model of citizenship the victors of this slave revolution created a political paradox which still plagues Haiti: the egalitarian and democratic values of republicanism were constantly undercut by the hierarchical and elitist values of militarism. The paramount sign of this fundamental contradiction, I suggest, is the historical exclusion of women from the wholly masculine realms of state politics and citizenship; even as it destroyed some forms of domination, the process of social change that occurred in the post-independence period replicated others.

Through an analysis of the language of citizenship in official documents, newspapers, and intellectual writings (including perceptions of Haiti by European contemporaries), I argue that the exclusion of women

157

from full citizenship aided in the construction of an elitist, coercive, and autocratic state in Haiti, to the detriment of the ideals of freedom and equality that underpinned the revolution and that continued to resurface in episodic peasant resistance against the state. After briefly reviewing the historiographic background for a gendered political history of Haiti, I trace the masculine rhetoric of Haitian citizenship to three sources: (a) the revolutionary republican tradition of armed egalitarianism, transposed into the heroic figure of the rebel slave and the black general; (b) the post-independence institution of male rights to land based on participation in armed defense of the nation; and, (c) the influential political network of freemasonry, with its patriarchal brotherhood and its constitutive exclusion of women. The republican veneration of arms-bearing males in a brotherhood of manly civic duty—along with a devaluation of women's work and social contributions—helped to create an authoritarian and statist political system that privileged military elites and significantly undermined the radical democratic premises of the Haitian Revolution. A political discourse of male-centered familial relationships served to uphold non-democratic state structures, with damaging long-term consequences for the freedom the Haitian people had won.

In the second half of the article I turn to the place of women in nineteenth century Haitian society, and the relationship between institutional structures and masculine identities after slavery. I demonstrate that although Haitian women played a significant economic role in both agricultural production and market trading, and benefited from unusually egalitarian legal rights, they were literally and metaphorically excluded from the terms of nationhood and citizenship. Haitian women's high labor-force participation and predominant role in market trading—public roles that were lambasted and criticized by many European commentators of the Victorian era, and that became the subject of much anthropological speculation in the modern era—remained distinct from any recognition of their political citizenship or equality with men. Female economic independence in Afro-Caribbean societies, I argue, is associated not with women's empowerment, but with post-slavery cultures that place a high *symbolic* value on prestigious male-defined occupations, whether military or civil. Thus, female marketing can be explained by the same causal mechanism whether found in militarized settings, like Haiti in the nineteenth century, or in non-militarized settings like neighboring Jamaica: freed men gained status by monopolizing authority positions from which women were excluded, whether political, military, religious, or civil. Agricultural labor, domestic labor, and petty commerce were low-status occupations associated with control by landowners and dependence on creditors, and were thus avoided by those men who could find more prestigious positions; the social ambivalence of women's work contributed to freed women's ongoing subordination in the public realm.

This research suggests that the symbolic construction of the nation, the prevalent discourses of citizenship, and the actual social structure in post-independence Haiti were all entwined in the celebration of military ideals which legitimated the empowerment of a small elite. These mutually reinforcing patterns of development have had long-lasting impact on Haitian political culture. The relationships between family rhetoric, militarism, and masculine identities after slavery, I suggest, are crucial not only to understanding the authoritarian path of political development taken in nineteenth-century Haiti, but also to critically evaluating the extent to which the current Haitian democratization movement will succeed in enabling the majority of the population to share in the redefinition and exercise of a non-militarized and inclusive citizenship. The "masculinization" of power was historically—and remains presently—incompatible with the egalitarian values that inspired the Haitian Revolution.

Foundations for a Gendered Political History of Haiti

Rods, swords, scepters, staffs, sharpened sticks, flags: these are the symbols of power identified by Richard D. E. Burton as central to nineteenth-century "Afro-Creole" cultures of opposition. Burton perceptively argues that "the rod in its multiple manifestations becomes the symbol of both power and popular opposition to power in the Caribbean." It is these phallic symbols that are wielded both in the playful spirit of opposition and in the hard play of political power. As he hastens to point out, though, this is a "male-dominated culture of reputation and play" from which women have historically been absent; moreover, this oppositional culture has the quality of a "double-edged sword" which can be turned back upon its wielder since it both "challenges and reinforces the status quo."[1] It is precisely this double-edged nature of Afro-Creole masculine cultures of opposition that I seek to point out in the formation of the Haitian Republic. In what ways did the military struggles of revolution, war of independence, civil war, and national defense become institutionalized in a way that inadvertently turned armed force back upon the Haitian people, thus replicating a colonial culture of domination?

My analysis of gender and power in Haiti draws on two streams of recent theorizing on the subject. On one hand, feminist historiography has shown how symbols of gender and actual structures of sexual differentiation inform systems of power at the level of the nation state. As Joan W. Scott argued a decade ago, gender is "a primary way of signifying relationships of power." Whether in authoritarian or democratic regimes, she suggests,

> [p]ower relations among nations and the status of colonial subjects have been made comprehensible (and thus legitimate) in terms of relations between male and female. The legitimizing of war—of expending young lives to protect the state—has variously taken

159

the forms of explicit appeals to manhood (to the need to defend otherwise vulnerable women and children), of implicit reliance on belief in the duty of sons to serve their leaders or their (father the) king, and of associations between masculinity and national strength. High politics itself is a gendered concept, for it establishes its crucial importance and public power, the reasons for and the facts of its highest authority, precisely in its exclusion of women from its work.[2]

Of particular relevance for understanding Haiti in this regard are recent arguments concerning the masculinist practices of republicanism in France and the United States, and the exclusion of women from the bourgeois public sphere;[3] Haiti drew on the same philosophical sources in constructing its own republicanism, and comparison with other cases suggests similar rhetorical strategies and exclusions at work. Other Caribbeanists have begun to focus on the gendering of power relations and national struggles over gender and its moral meanings. Cultural historians, for example, have shown how symbolic struggles over race, class, and gender constitute the politics of national identity and inform popular oppositional cultures.[4] Yet there has been little research into the gendered symbolism of power within Haiti itself. [. . .] More thorough analysis of the construction of gender in Haitian political discourse is surely overdue.

At the same time, I also draw on the recent interest in the construction of masculinity in labor history, and of black masculinity in particular. [. . .] African-American labor history now increasingly acknowledges the centrality of male gender identities to the formation of a black working class, and these insights might fruitfully be extended to the Caribbean, where far more research has focused on female gender identities.[5] [. . .]

These strands of scholarship are very suggestive for interpreting the meaning of masculinity in nineteenth-century Haiti, but there are few previous studies in this area.[6] [. . .] Unlike its Latin American neighbors, Haiti also has a long history of female fieldwork and women's predominance in market trading. Any study of masculinity in Haiti, then, must grapple with the specificity of its sexual division of labor, as well as its Afro-Creole culture of opposition.

Another line of historical research has focused on the "feminization" of the Antilles and of the black race in the writing of Europeans during the colonial period, yet there has been little analysis of gender discourses within Haiti.[7] Did Haitian leaders employ appeals to manhood, elicit the obedience of sons, or associate national strength with masculinity, and, if so, what effect did such rhetoric have on the construction of citizenship and the nation in the post-slavery period? Were women excluded from high politics, and if so, how did their exclusion distort the meaning of freedom and citizenship? Perhaps Haitian historians have avoided such questions because there are few primary sources to guide one in answering them; women were indeed marginalized from the public sphere and are thus largely absent from the archives which were written by men, for men, and mostly about men. In consequence, macro-historical approaches have usually focused on Haitian women only to the extent that they constitute a distinct portion of the labor force; diplomatic histories or studies of "high politics" often ignore gender altogether, since women seldom appear as major actors in the historical record; and even histories more attuned to broader political culture pay far more attention to constructs of race and class than to those pertaining to gender.[8] Concern with gender has been more prevalent in the ethnographic study of contemporary Haitian culture, but micro-level studies of local practices or family structures have generally not been connected to the macro-construction of power relations at the level of the state.[9]

A major problem facing the historian of gender in Haiti is the meager range of primary sources available for the nineteenth century. Many of the original archives of the Haitian state were destroyed over the years, thus there is great dependence on the writings of a few Haitian historians like Thomas Madiou or Beaubrun Ardouin, or the records kept by hostile foreign consulates and the (often racist) publications of European visitors.[10] Moreover, since the bulk of the population were illiterate and largely excluded from everyday political participation, any understanding of power relations drawing on *written* sources is unavoidably filtered through the prism of a few elite men's perceptions. Nevertheless, this should not deflect us from pursuing these questions, as the sources are rich in their way and demand further interrogation. Above all, rather than searching for rare accounts of women and their political actions—proverbial but always precious needles in the haystack—why not also turn to the wealth of material on the symbolic construction of masculinity? How was masculinity envisioned and invoked in post-independence Haiti? What kinds of male heroes and actors were celebrated? Do sex, gender, and familial relationships find their way into the historical record in unexpected places?

[. . .] To explore these areas, I draw on four kinds of pertinent sources: (a) Haitian official documents, including laws, codes, and government proclamations; (b) publications by Haitian intellectuals, including historians, newspaper contributors, and publicists; (c) European official documents, including consular papers and other foreign office correspondence; and (d) publications by European and American observers, visitors, or commentators.[11] Since none of these sources has previously been used to shed light on the significance of *gender* to power relations, this should be taken as a preliminary attempt. [. . .] I turn to them now with an important caveat: the written record is far removed from the lives, ideas, language, and practices of the bulk of the Haitian population. Additional tools and contributors will be needed to unearth what James Scott calls the "hidden transcript."

The Masculine Symbolism of Haitian Nationhood

The first generation of Haitians who abolished slavery and threw off European domination were infused with a strong sense of civic duty and military patriotism, leading them to symbolize the citizen as soldier, and the soldier as citizen. The first constitution of 1805 institutionalized these republican military traditions in its vision of a fraternal brotherhood-in-arms of all men of African descent. [. . .] Thus a fundamental aspect of the Haitian nation-building project was the elevation of the black man out of the depths of slavery into his rightful place as father, leader, and protector of his own people. Familial imagery was closely allied with a masculine call to arms and a depiction of women as grateful recipients of male protection, as we shall see in the rhetoric of each of the early consolidators of state power.

Making Haitian Citizens: Militarism and Masculinity

Popular figures of African masculinity and military prowess served a significant function in materially achieving and symbolically marking the transition from slavery to freedom in many parts of the Americas. Violence anointed manhood in many post-slavery contexts, but especially in Haiti where freedom was won by force of arms. At least since the days of Makandal and Boukman—leaders who are thought to have drawn on African martial arts and Vodou ritual to give rebel slaves mystical powers in warfare—the male warrior has been venerated in Haiti.[12] Women too celebrated these war heroes: Thomas Madiou reports that on the first of January, 1804, during independence celebrations, "women and young girls, richly attired, were mixed among the warriors whom they exalted with their patriot songs."[13] [. . .] To begin to interrogate the ways in which various governments have used these popular images should in no way be seen as a criticism of the men who fought for freedom, nor as a judgment on this mode of emancipation. Nevertheless, I will argue that the rhetorical construction of gender identities in Haitian nationalist discourse was cynically manipulated by ruling elites in order to contain the currents of democratization that were surging through the Atlantic world in the first half of the nineteenth century.

Throughout its first decades, the Haitian state suffered diplomatic isolation, ongoing external threats, and civil war up until 1820, necessitating military government and a strong executive commander of the armed forces.[14] From the very beginning, plantation workers did not necessarily benefit from the "freedom" they had won; even Toussaint L'Ouverture, the great hero of the revolution, created a system of military enforcement of agricultural production that some suggest was not much different from slavery.[15] Facing a hostile world, governing regimes used familial imagery to bind competing regions, classes, and colors together. In the

162

first Constitution of General Jean-Jacques Dessalines, for example, the nation was envisioned as a family, the emperor as its father, and all the people as of one color: "All distinctions of color among the children of one and the same family, of which the Head of State is the father, necessarily ceasing, the Haitians will henceforth be known only by the generic denomination of blacks [noirs]."[16] The comparison of citizens to children and the one-father/one-color ideology defused tensions between the mostly mulatto *anciens libres* and the black *nouveaux libres* by making all citizens equal. Paternalism enforced the authority of the chief of state as father of this new nation, while republican fraternalism reinforced unity and military solidarity.

Although they proclaimed the egalitarian values of revolutionary republicanism, early Haitian leaders also seem to have valued hierarchical power structures modeled on the patriarchal family and on military discipline. Ever since the revolution, most Haitian leaders have been military men. As Michel Laguerre argues, "the existence of the indigenous army preceded that of the nation and, in effect, made possible the state and the first government of the republic. After independence in 1804, the military, in addition to providing internal security and defense against foreign aggressors, was also the government."[17] Indeed, Article Nine of the first constitution stated, "No one is worthy of being a Haitian if he is not a good father, a good son, a good husband, *and above all a good soldier*" [emphasis added], foreshadowing the militarization of the state, the marginalization of women, and the depiction of citizens as male protectors of family and nation. The consequences of this, Laguerre continues, were "the lack or weakness of civilian institutions on which democracy could flourish, the militarization of civilian institutions, military paternalism, the institutionalization of corruption, and the transformation of the role of the military as the permanent government of the land."

As a result, armed force was used against the civilian population and against political oppositions. [. . .]

If the good *Haïtien* was a soldier, what of good *Haïtiennes*? The constitution made no mention of mothers, daughters, wives, or female workers, farmers, or traders—except for purposes of taxation. Civic worthiness was a matter of manliness, and arms meant freedom. In fact, freedom had always had different connotations for men than for women. Throughout the Americas there was a strong link between male emancipation and military service; male slaves were manumitted in return for risking their lives by almost every colonial power during most outbreaks of major warfare in the Americas.[18] Within the power structure of slave societies, freed men's armed service connoted respectability, citizenship, and public service; *women's* freedom, on the other hand, often came at the price of sexual vulnerability, non-citizenship, and dependence on private relationships, since the majority of women who gained higher status occupations or manumission during slavery often did so via sexual relations with white men, or through familial relations as their offspring. Freed men and freed women thus experienced different kinds of freedom, particularly in regard to the political process. [. . .]

For Haitian men citizenship first took the form of military service, and the army became one of the main avenues of male political participation, as well as a route to land ownership. No sooner had the French land-owners and British and Spanish occupying forces been driven out of the island than military leaders seized the land of the former plantations; land-holding generals quickly dominated government both in the Kingdom of Haiti, which formed in the north, and in the Republic of Haiti in the south.[19] Christophe maintained the big northern estates intact, under the control of a few successful generals who formed a new aristoc-racy; his courtly entourage reinforced the masculine ideal of the noble warrior. When the French tried to negotiate a Haitian protectorate in the post-Napoleonic period, he responded in the language of a proud military tradition: "How dare you speak to us of masters and slaves? To us, a free and independent people; to warriors covered in noble scars won on the battlefields of honor. . . . How dare you propose to men free for twenty-five years, who still hold weapons in their hands, to depose themselves and return to the chains of ignominy and barbarous slavery!"[20] Taking up arms and carrying the scars of warfare entitled this proud nation to its freedom. [. . .]

To legitimize military power, the kingdom celebrated familial ideals. Free Haitian manhood was built on protecting the family and nation, with women and children depicted as grateful dependents. When the birthday of Madame Christophe was celebrated in 1807 with "great pomp," public addresses were made praising her role as "virtuous wife" and "mother of the unhappy, consoler of the afflicted, protector of widows and orphans . . . who fears not to face the miasma of hospitals in order to spread a healthy balm on the wounds of the defenders of the fatherland."[21] Yet the King's title was declared to be "hereditary in the male and legitimate descendants of his family in a direct line, by elder birthright, *to the exclu-sion of females.*"[22] The Queen's role, as she herself put it, was to "delight in being a tender mother" to the Haitian people.[23] [. . .] Encouragement of family life was not only rhetorical, but also found its way into law and social institutions. The *Code Henri* bound proprietors to "treat their respec-tive laborers with true paternal solicitude," outlawed "female licentious-ness," and encouraged childbirth by exempting pregnant women and nursing mothers from field labor.[24] Thus the monarchical state manipu-lated gender relations in the service of state power: good families made good subjects.

In the south, President Alexandre Pétion also rewarded male military service. He distributed land to the veterans of the wars of independence who had fought to liberate the island and end slavery.[25] [. . .] Women received no land. As Lepelletier de Saint-Rémy put it, Pétion's parcellization of the old colonial plantations had "republicanized the soil"; yet it was a republic based on a male obligation to serve the state and female political marginalization. Women were disenfranchised along with "criminals, idiots, and menials."[26]

General Jean-Pierre Boyer, Pétion's successor, quickly won control not only over the northern kingdom, in 1820, but also over the former Spanish colony of Santo Domingo in 1822. Now anyone born in any part of the island could become a Haitian citizen, as could anyone of African or Amerindian descent who chose to emigrate to Haiti. Only whites were barred from owning property or exercising the rights of Haitian citizenship. However, the law did not apply equally to all Haitians; the Civil Code of 1825 specified that a Haitian woman who married a foreigner forfeited her citizenship. This was a way of preventing foreign white men from owning property in Haiti through marriage, but it underlines the constitutional marginalization of women from the republic.[27] [. . .]

With the ongoing threat of French invasion through the early to mid-nineteenth century, the military remained the most significant branch of the executive, while the elected Chamber of Deputies had little power. The British Consul Charles Mackenzie described the situation in 1827: "The government that is now established professes to be purely republican . . . but in practice it may be said to be essentially military."[28] [. . .] The army also essentially functioned as the local government, with each commune under the authority of soldiers. A military spirit pervaded the state, and irrevocably molded the meaning of citizenship. [. . .]

The Use of Familial Symbolism in the Consolidation of State Power

Despite the death or expulsion of most of the white population of Saint Domingue during the revolution and wars of independence, Haiti built on the cultural legacies of Europe as well as those of Africa. Haitian republicanism was in fact even more adamantly virile than French republicanism, which, as Lynn Hunt argues, symbolized revolution as the sons' overthrow of the King-as-father, and, as Joan Landes argues, substituted a masculinist language of fraternity and civic brotherhood in rejecting the effeminacy of ancien régime salons. The gendered symbolism of Haitian politics swung between discourses of republican fraternalism and patriarchal presidentialism, much as Richard D. E. Burton finds in Martinique and Guadeloupe, which shared similar French political traditions:

> the brothers systematically excluded their sisters, mothers, wives, and mistresses from active participation in the wholly masculine procedures, electoral and other, of the Republican confraternity. And before that, of course, the "brothers" had repeatedly quarreled fratricidally amongst themselves, provoking the regular return of patriarchal figures committed to the restoration of order at all costs.[29]

165

Whatever the value of military fraternalism may have been in the revolutionary period and in the self-emancipation from slavery, its institutionalization after independence undermined the complementary revolutionary ideals of liberty and equality. Military republicanism, which initially served the necessary purpose of building a new state and new citizens from scratch, soon became the only *raison d'être* for a state in which there were few civil institutions to balance an overwhelmingly military power. This section will explore how the discursive construction of the male citizen was used to consolidate state power and resist European domination.

In addition to civic republicanism, the Haitian statist model of democratic citizenship also borrowed blueprints from one of the most important elite associations in France and her colonies, the Order of Freemasons. While proud of their independence and freedom, Haitian elites were nonetheless engaged in a "civilising process" of moral education and self-improvement, with an eye to themselves as an example to the world. Freemasonry was crucial to this process and became a significant feature of nineteenth-century Haitian politics. In the lodges men became "citizens" in so far as they wrote constitutions, elected leaders, and ruled themselves through means which simulated democratic governance. The lodge was a "school of civic sociability" and self-cultivation for the bourgeois man, and it laid the foundations for modern civil society. Yet in creating a new secular citizen, freemasonry promoted patriarchy and also presumed that only literate and educated men "could be entrusted to act ethically and to think disinterestedly in the interests of society, government, and improvement."[30] The same class and gender exclusions were replicated in Haiti, despite its national origins in slave revolution.

[. . .]

Haitian freemasonry promoted an ideology of progress based on learning to both direct and to obey one's brothers, and to advance on the basis of merit and virtue; however, [. . .] it also insisted more paternalistically that young men show due respect and veneration for their elders. [. . .] This symbolic genealogy of citizenship, passed from father to son—as well as the outright exclusion of women from participation in all-male masonic lodges—left Haitian women politically invisible and in many cases publicly silenced [. . .].

[. . .]

Haitian citizenship, therefore, forged in revolution and consolidated through the ties of freemasonry, was from the beginning based on a republican fraternity of brothers-in-arms with a streak of loyal filial obedience. Perhaps it is because these features seem so ordinary, so typical of the nineteenth century, that they have seldom been researched or commented on: of course this was a military society, women were excluded from politics, and "universal" suffrage meant adult male suffrage. Yet the outcome was not so straightforward, nor was the rhetoric unopposed. The vast social changes wrought by revolutionary emancipation also set in motion an undercurrent of popular culture which was not so easily shaped to the ends of an elitist military state. It is this other oppositional "Afro-Creole" world that swirled below the surface of power, raising doubts among the powerful and giving hope to the powerless. But before turning to these contradictory forces, let us see how these symbolic representations of gender were normatively invoked.

Haitian intellectuals echoed the masculinist discourse of military republicanism and the paternalistic discourse of freemasonry in their writings on nationhood, in which they exhorted their compatriots to be obedient sons and live up to the example of their fathers. [. . .] The sense of both an obligation to the past and a vision of the future placed a burden on the shoulders of this generation of young men to join together in brotherhood and vindicate their fathers' legacy. A petition of 1843 expressed this sense of historical mission: "Citizens! Dessalines and Pétion call out to you from the depths of their graves; Grégoire watches you from the heights of heaven, Isambert speaks to you: save Haiti, your communal mother; stop her from perishing. . . . Save her. . . ."[31] [. . .]

Women had no place in this construction of the nation and its moral destiny, except as mothers of warriors and symbols of the nation itself, which was envisaged as the great "mother" of the people whom male citizens must venerate and protect. An imagery of the manly duties of citizenship infused the language of Haitian nationhood, and young and old generations of men were called upon as fighters to protect the mother-nation, sometimes inverting the traditional image of France as the mother-nation. Toussaint Louverture was said to have challenged Napoleon's expeditionary force in 1803 by saying "A son owes submission to his mother, but if she unnaturally aims to destroy her offspring, nothing remains but to entrust vengeance to God."[32] [. . .]

Likewise, the Manifeste de Praslin, a key defining text of the liberal revolution of 1843, called forth "all the fathers of families who care for the future of their children" to join the revolution. It referred to the country as "our first mother" and, with a touch of melodrama, demanded the reader to "See miserable Haiti, suffering, dressed in rags, nearly a slave, trembling under the weight of injustice and arbitrary power, degraded under this regime of immorality!"[33] The only direct reference to actual women in the entire revolutionary manifesto is as family members, and even here it is addressed to men, urging them on as paternal protectors:

> See your children deprived of instruction, nourishment of civilized man, last sacrament of the republican; see them menaced with soon becoming victims of tyranny. Plunge your regards into this fearful future for them, if you do not shelter them with your paternal wings. Hear the plaints, laments, reproaches, the just reproaches of your wives, your mothers, your daughters, your sisters, who accuse you of cowardice, pusillanimity, torpor.[34]

Haitian women were part of this symbolic construction of the nation only in the roles of wife, mother and sister—never as citizens in their own right.[35]

[. . .]

Family rhetoric served a conservative function not only in excluding women, but also in avoiding participatory democracy. As in other "organic statist" democracies, conservative elites "portrayed the nation-state as a harmonious, integrated community in which competing class interests could be reconciled and smoothed away by enlightened elders ruling with the best interests of the society at heart."[36] In Haiti this took the form of comparing the people to children in order to justify "enlightened" leadership by their wise elders; mulatto elites denied any conflict of interest between classes or colors, even as they argued that the people were not "ready" to govern themselves.[37] In 1842, for example, conservative senator and historian Beaubrun Ardouin published a newspaper, Le Temps, in which it was suggested that "The boy passes through adolescence before arriving at virility. . . . A young people . . . must not make haste more than it should . . . It does not suffice for such a people, having adopted certain institutions that old nations could procure for themselves only over the succession of centuries, to then believe that they are in a state to put them into practice right away."[38]

This produced an angry retort from Telismon Bouchereau's more liberal newspaper, Le Patriote: "one compares the Haitian Nation to an infant, barely out of diapers. [. . .] What! Do you not see that the child has become a man?"[39] [. . .] It was precisely this cry of "manhood" that was expressed in the liberal revolution of 1843 that soon followed this exchange of views on the readiness of the Haitian people to participate in their own government. A generation of young men challenged their "fathers" to live up to the ideals of the Republic, and succeeded in deposing President Boyer. Boyer himself turned familial imagery against the liberal revolution, calling it "perverse" for "arming citizen against citizen, brothers against brothers, sons against their fathers!"[40] Opposition was seen as a corruption of the sanctity of the civic family, an Oedipal drama on the national stage.

The use of the imagery of childhood to depict political immaturity was prevalent in racist discourse of the nineteenth century, which compared non-white people, slaves, women, and servants to children in order to justify their civil and political subordination. In Haiti, the representative of the British Foreign Office, Charles Mackenzie (himself a man of color), described the Haitians as "young Barbarians."[41] Likewise, the French Ministry of Foreign Affairs gave their representatives, who were in Haiti to negotiate a treaty of recognition, these instructions: "it is a case of showing the superiority of the civilized white over the half-savage negro; one must consider the Haitians as big children, pardon them their stupid blunders, and always show them a kind, indulgent face."[42] In this patronizing setting where Africans and their descendants in the New World were denied "full manhood rights," as they were known at the time, it is not surprising that Haitian independence became a matter of proving their manhood; the relationship between men and women in Haiti thus became implicated in defending the masculinity of the Haitian man. [. . .]

This external "gaze" upon Haitian culture—along with actual military threats and power over the Haitian state—thus insidiously shaped Haitian self-presentation, and demanded a virile model of citizenship. [. . .]

Normative Judgments of Gender Identities in Post-Slavery States

Despite Haitian efforts to politically, militarily, and symbolically prove their masculinity, European observers of Haitian society in the nineteenth century became fixated on women's predominant role in both agricultural labor and marketing. The female-dominated internal marketing system undermined prevalent European cultural notions of private and public, order and disorder, femininity and masculinity, Christianity and barbarism. Many white Europeans attributed black women's hard physical work to the "retention" of a primitive African culture. As gender became a crucial symbolic marker in the defining national narratives of "progress" and "civilization," a fundamental contradiction emerged between the elite ideology of domestic femininity (implicit in the republican calls to protect women as well as in conservative discourses of paternalism and civic incubation), and actual Haitian women's ceaseless economic activities.

If gender distinctions were deeply embedded in the entwined networks of republican militarism and liberal freemasonry that shaped the upper echelons of Haitian political society in the first half of the nineteenth century, there was also an inescapable contradiction created by the prominent role of women in the economy. Militarized masculinity is but one side of the story, for on the other hand we must also consider the "feminization" of trade. Militarism gave men a stake in the state's power, and made armed service the most attractive route to land and wealth. Yet women played a significant economic role in Haiti's labor force and markets, and at times became key political protagonists. How can Haitian women's economic activity and autonomy be reconciled with the masculinist imagery of the state? This combination of masculine political rhetoric and female economic self-sufficiency, I argue, reflects the "statist solution" by which a military-dominated state exploited a disempowered civil society.[43] With no voice in national government or local decision-making, excluded from the military and from public office, women became the most disempowered group within this statist autocracy.

Female Marketing and the Position of Women in Haiti

Let us first review the status of Haitian women in the late eighteenth and early nineteenth centuries. To understand the inequality of women in Haiti, one must begin with the period of slavery. Historians of slavery have shown that status divisions within slave societies tended to give enslaved men more opportunities than their female counterparts to achieve positions of some independence and material reward; emancipation, likewise, was experienced in different ways by each sex, with women facing new forms of subordination.[44] At the height of the Haitian sugar boom of the 1770s and 1780s, according to David Geggus, enslaved "men were eight times as likely as women to escape from the drudgery of fieldwork into a post offering some independence and status." This occurred because "females had much less access than their male counterparts to positions of independence, skill, and prestige. The number of specialist positions open to women was extremely small, and they offered only limited rewards."[45] Barred from becoming sugar boilers, sailors, blacksmiths, coopers, carpenters, etc., black women were left with degrading domestic service and precarious petty marketing as some of the few occupations outside of fieldwork. Thus, from the start, black women occupied the lowest economic and social rungs in the plantation system.

During the colonial period, however, free women of color took advantage of the more open opportunities of thriving urban ports like Cap Français and Port-au-Prince to engage in various kinds of business, ranging from property speculation (both in real estate and slaves), to small retail trading, inn-keeping, and prostitution. "The majority of free women of color," writes Susan Socolow, "certainly led precarious economic lives, but notary transactions suggest that many played important roles in the local economy, acting independently, unlike white women, who were rarely visible acting on their own."[46] Despite their prominent economic role, free women of color were often caricatured in European writing of the period as creatures of sexuality, luxury, and sensuality. Their public, urban, independent roles were linked to images of decadence, disorder, and sin in the colonial imagination [. . .]. The very existence of free urban women of color was seen to threaten the Christian moral foundations of European colonial society.

Women's participation in trade in the Republic of Haiti thus built on patterns established during the colonial period and carried with it the heavy baggage of colonial racial and sexual inequality. Nevertheless, commerce was preferable to field work. In addition to the sheer backbreaking nature of work in the cane fields and coffee hills and the rigorous time-discipline imposed by overseers, another motivating force for women to prefer marketing activities over field work must have been the low wages offered to freed women in comparison to men. James Franklin reported in 1826 that "the wages are from 2½ to 3 dollars a week . . . for an able-bodied cultivator. Women who work in the fields get the same wages as boys about 14 years of age, which is about 1½ dollars."[47] [. . .]

Thus many women found better opportunities as small traders. Female marketing was extended in the post-colonial period, and legally codified by the Rural Code of 1826. [. . .]

A crucial outcome of this legal codification of female marketing was the creation of a segmented economy in which the more profitable export crops (*haut commerce*) such as cotton, coffee, and mahogany were channeled through foreign mercantile houses that were allowed to operate out of eleven open ports, while the less profitable regional internal markets for local food produce (*petit commerce*) were left to Haitian women—and even here they operated on credit extended by foreign merchants, mainly against the coffee crop.[48] [. . .]

Haitian women's economic independence was circumscribed by the inequalities of both the world economy and the local structure of gender relations. Most traders were trapped in a circuit of small trade, which required intense work, returned tiny profits, and left them vulnerable to debt. With a faltering economy and heavy state taxation, women's marketing in the nineteenth century was a labor-intensive, high-risk, and low-return activity (much as it remains today). Despite high levels of participation in agricultural labor and marketing, Haitian women have generally owned less land than men, had less capital to invest, earned lower wages, and enjoyed less autonomy.[49]

On the other hand, Haitian women had access to credit to a degree quite unusual for the time, and unthinkable in Europe, where women were largely excluded from commercial credit. A revision of Haitian civil law in 1840 granted special legal rights to women because of their *de facto* independent financial status, and Article 201 for the first time ensured financial independence for *married* women.[50] [. . .] Ardouin conceded that this legal emancipation of married women was an unavoidable outcome of their already existing financial independence, but he hypothesized that it would disappear as Haiti "advanced in civilization." Haitian civil law not only allowed married women independent incomes, but also allowed female inheritance with none of the restrictions of male primogeniture. [. . .] Modernizing elites complained of this situation, and the 1843 Manifeste de Praslin actually bemoaned the "bizarre civil law" which "eroded marital authority and paternal power."

Nevertheless, a submerged Afro-Creole peasant worldview is recognizable. Despite a paucity of primary evidence, there are nonetheless hints of oppositional popular conceptions of nationhood, citizenship, and freedom.

Contrary to the rhetoric of masculine citizenship, women in Haiti did in fact seize a number of public roles. The fact that Haitian women were central protagonists in several important political events during the 1843 liberal revolution, for example, stands in stark contrast to the rhetorical version of Mother-Haiti protected by her brave sons, but unable to defend herself. [. . .] Thomas Madiou observed that women in Les Cayes composed "a powerful propaganda in favor of the revolution," and contemporary newspapers reported that old people, women, and children came out to cheer the popular army who gathered in Les Cayes.[51] Even more importantly, women actually took part in the fighting. The women of Léogâne, "while singing, dragged two large cannon from fort Ça-Ira into the town, and placed them in a battery facing the plain of Dampuce"; two shots from these cannon killed thirty soldiers.[52] [. . .]

Several sources report that after suffering military desertions and defeats, President Boyer's final defeat came with the intervention of the women of Port-au-Prince. When the president ordered a battalion of *grenadiers* (national guards) to join the battle on foot, "The battalion began to march, but as soon as it arrived at Morne-à-Tuf, it was stopped by an innumerable multitude of women. . . . [Boyer] was assailed by a new disturbance of women, who followed him and cursed him, abusing him in the most scathing manner."[53] [. . .] That evening, he "lost hope" and embarked on a British ship to Jamaica; without the support of the women of Port-au-Prince, many of them *marchandes*, he had no social base for opposing the revolution.

The active role of women in revolutionary mobilizations is not the only indication of a more complex reality behind the gendered rhetoric of both liberal and conservative elites. We have few direct sources from peasant actors in the nineteenth century, since most were illiterate and few government records were preserved from this period; however, the evidence we do have suggests that there were alternative visions of race, class, and gender, as well as a different vision of Haitian nationhood, submerged in a subaltern consciousness. The peasant movement known as the Piquets, led by Louis-Jean-Jacques Acaau, publicly articulated trenchant criticisms of the elite view of Haitian citizenship. [. . .] To begin with, Acaau explicitly denied that the Haitian "family" were all one color; to the contrary, he recognized divisions of color, class, and status, summarized in the famous saying of the Piquet rebellion, "Nègue riche qui connait li et écri, cila mulâte; mulâte pauvre qui connait pas li et écri, cila nègue" [The rich black who can read and write is a mulatto; the poor mulatto who cannot read or write is black].[54] [. . .] It is thought that the Piquet movement included women in roles of leadership, and seems to have rejected the domestic ideology that confined women to the private sphere.[55]

Female Work and Male Honor in Post-Slavery Contexts: A New Hypothesis

Given the paucity of historical sources giving the viewpoint of working women (due to the double silences of both illiteracy and exclusion from the official public sphere), focusing on the views of elite observers can enable us to see the repressed power of working women surfacing in men's fears and self-projections. Both European missionaries and Haitian elites equated women's financial independence with a sexual threat to paternal power. [. . .] The threat of women's control of both trade and sex was explicitly recognized by a number of male writers (both Haitian and foreign), who saw in the system of female marketing not only an emasculation of the patriarch, but also a retrograde step in the progress of civilization.

Many European observers of Haitian society in the mid-nineteenth century lambasted the economic role of *Haïtiennes*, which conflicted with their own ideologies of "public man" and "domestic woman."[56] The reaction of Jonathan Brown, an American who visited Haiti in 1837, is typical, equating female labor with barbarism and lamenting the lack of a male work ethic: "As is the case with all barbarous nations, the females are compelled to perform most of the labor. Those of the country employ themselves in cultivating the soil, while the men spend their time in traversing the country on horseback, in drinking, smoking, and other habits equally unprofitable."[57] Sidney Mintz quotes this account of a *marchande* in 1854, depicting the extent of female financial independence:

> Elsiné [. . .] was a wide-awake, intelligent, amiable and well-conditioned black woman, about forty years of age; Emilien, her faithful consort, was not near as intelligent, nor quite as fat, nor quite as tall, nor quite as dignified as Elsiné. . . . She is the capitalist of the concern, and does all the business. He has no more to do with the direction of affairs, in or out of the house, than if he were her child. She is worth from fifteen to twenty thousand dollars, all of which she has made as a dealer in provisions. [. . .][58]

[. . .] As Mintz observes, the European found this "a strange inversion of the ordinary relations of husband and wife." [. . .] Yet men like Emilien accepted this role, perhaps because they had the consolation of a masculine citizenship that was denied women. The Haitian man's tolerance of female economic independence reveals "that Western conceptions of male 'integrity,' 'dignity,' 'pride,' and 'worth' are much more deeply embedded in notions of male economic dominance than may be generally widely recognized."[59] Perhaps Haitian men did not need economic dominance when they had civil and political dominance. Although *marchandes* exercised a certain degree of financial independence, many were at the mercy of male partners, who could take advantage of their access to credit. [. . .]

Nevertheless, from a Western masculine viewpoint, the commercial success of *Haïtiennes* reflected badly on the country's honor, and was proof of semi-barbarism, African backwardness, and a general lack of civilization. Only when women were in their rightful place, that is, the home, these white commentators imply, would Haiti move forward on the road from barbarism to civilization. Women's roles outside the home (and their sexual counter-power) were thus associated with degradation, not elevation. [. . .]

173

Conclusion

The meanings and practices of gender distinctions within popular culture are topics which require further research, but understanding their symbolic elaboration in the deep founding narratives of nationhood is one starting point. To what extent women (and civilian men) cooperated or resisted in this construction of masculine citizenship and military authority probably depended on specific circumstances and locations. This interpretation raises some interesting questions, for example, about the power relations expressed in the practice of Vodou. In his comparative study of "ecstatic religions" throughout the world, I. M. Lewis argues that women use possession cults as "thinly disguised protest movements directed against the dominant sex"; other downtrodden social groups who have few effective means to press their claims similarly engage in ecstatic religions in what he calls an "oblique aggressive strategy."[60] Religion, in other words, may channel women's protest activities in certain directions. Female devotees' assumption of male personas when "mounted" by the *lwas* may allow them to exercise some degree of masculine authority, without actually challenging the underlying sex/gender system. [. . .]

Women's roles in *informal* religious leadership have been recognized as an important African-American cultural phenomenon throughout the Americas.[61] In Haiti, the Mambo, or Vodou priestess, is a powerful female leader in the religious sphere, yet there is a dichotomy between "Vaudou domestique," practiced in family settings, and the more public practice of powerful male priests, *oungans*, who often have ties to political figures.[62] Karen McCarthy Brown goes so far as to argue that "Haitian culture is a misogynist culture. The ideology of male supremacy is fierce . . . and domestic violence is a frequent occurrence. Vodou has not escaped the influence of this attitude. . . ."[63] [. . .] The historical and contemporary roles of Mambos in civic culture and in politics are topics which require further research. Nevertheless, these observations suggest some of the ways in which the historical construction of symbols of nationhood, discourses of brotherhood, and rhetorics of manhood influenced both political and religious practices in Haiti with long-lasting impact.

An analysis of contemporary Haitian political discourse would no doubt turn up similar sets of symbolic systems and real exclusions at play; women's inequality has certainly been recognized at the grassroots level by groups of self-organized peasant women.[64] Whether the Haitian peasantry and urban poor, men and women alike, will be included in governing their nation, free from intimidation by armed men, remains to be seen. [. . .]

I have tried to demonstrate the masculinist foundations of citizenship in nineteenth-century Haiti. From the revolutionary fathers who cast off the chains of slavery to the republican sons who fought to defend their motherland, Haitian men proved themselves free and worthy, but elevated themselves at the expense of the average worker and to the

174

detriment of women. I have also shown how Haitian women's economic activities may have created some degree of autonomy and power within the household, yet did not translate into social equality. Financial and sexual empowerment were not highly valued attributes in a symbolic system that attached little status to commerce and gave great respect to armed men. The construction of masculine identities (especially of land-owning "*grandans*" or "big men") around positions of authoritarian dominance based on the power to control others originated in Haiti's anti-slavery and anti-colonial entrance on the world stage, but had the unfortunate consequence of creating a state which coercively exploited its own population. The legacy of revolutionary "republican virtue" was thus twisted into a downward spiraling system of authoritarian presidentialism, which in the end destroyed the freedom which the Haitian Revolution had won. Any hopes for democratization in contemporary Haiti must begin not in another military solution, but in building on the deep traditions of resistance and "counter-power" existing within the non-militarized spheres of civil society, just as it existed in the interstices of slave societies.

NOTES

1 Richard D. E. Burton, *Afro-Creole: Power, Opposition, and Play in the Caribbean* (Ithaca and London, 1997), 10–12.
2 Joan Wallach Scott, "Gender: A Useful Category of Historical Analysis" in *Gender and the Politics of History* (New York, 1988), 44, 48.
3 See Joan B. Landes, *Women and the Public Sphere in the Age of the French Revolution* (Ithaca, 1988); Mary P. Ryan, *Women in Public: Between Banners and Ballots, 1825–1880* (Baltimore, 1990); and Nancy Fraser, "Rethinking the Public Sphere: A Contribution to the Critique of Actually Existing Democracy" in Craig Calhoun, ed., *Habermas and the Public Sphere* (Cambridge, Mass., 1992), 109–42.
4 Cf. Brackette Williams, *Stains on My Name, War in My Veins: Guyana and the Politics of Cultural Struggle* (Durham and London, 1991); and Carolyn Cooper, *Noises in the Blood: Orality, Gender, and the "Vulgar" Body of Jamaican Popular Culture* (Durham, 1995).
5 Contributions to analysis of gender, race, and class in the Caribbean include Verena Martinez-Alier, *Marriage, Class and Colour in Nineteenth-Century Cuba*, 2nd ed. (Ann Arbor, 1989); Janet H. Momsen, ed., *Women and Change in the Caribbean* (Kingston, Bloomington, and London, 1993); Verene Shepherd, Bridget Brereton, and Barbara Bailey, eds., *Engendering History: Caribbean Women in Historical Perspective* (London and Kingston, 1995); and Kevin Yelvington, *Producing Power: Ethnicity, Gender and Class in a Caribbean Workplace* (Philadelphia, 1995).
6 Arthur L. Stinchcombe, *Sugar Island Slavery in the Age of Enlightenment: The Political Economy of the Caribbean World* (Princeton, 1996), 300–05.
7 Regis Antoine demonstrates the feminization of the Antilles in French literature in *Les écrivains français et les antilles* (Paris, 1978), as does J. Michael Dash for Haiti [. . .] (*Haiti and the United States: National Stereotypes and the Literary Imagination*, 2d ed. [Basingstoke and New York, (1988) 1997], 1).
8 Otherwise exemplary works that largely ignore gender include Alex Dupuy, *Haiti in the World Economy: Class, Race and Underdevelopment since 1700* (Boulder, 1989); Brenda G. Plummer, *Haiti and the United States: The Psychological Moment*

(Athens, Ga., 1992); David Nicholls, *From Dessalines to Duvalier: Race, Colour and National Independence in Haiti*, 3d ed. (London and Basingstoke, 1996); and Michel-Rolph Trouillot, *Haiti: State Against Nation: The Origins and Legacy of Duvalierism* (New York, 1990).

9 Cf. Melville J. Herskovits, *Life in a Haitian Valley* (New York, [1937] 1964), or Harold Courlander, *The Drum and the Hoe: Life and Lore of the Haitian People* (Berkeley, 1960). More recently, Karen McCarthy Brown, whose work is discussed below, has made efforts to link ethnographic analysis of gender relations in Vodou to issues of political participation and power.

10 It is known that "the earliest archives in Haiti were destroyed in the time of President Boyer. Others were probably lost when the National Palace was blown up on December 18, 1869. It is believed that all of the existing government archives were destroyed by fire during the disturbance of September 22 and 23, 1883." Rayford Logan, *The Diplomatic Relations of the United States with Haiti, 1776–1891* (Chapel Hill, 1941), 459.

11 I deliberately omit Haitian literature and poetry, since the kind of detailed analysis required of novels, poems, and plays would be beyond the scope of this paper. For a partial bibliography of nineteenth-century literary sources, consult Nicholls, *Dessalines to Duvalier*. A feminist interpretation of the "silencing" of Haitian women writers can be found in Myriam J. A. Chancy, *Framing Silence: Revolutionary Novels by Haitian Women* (New Brunswick, 1997).

12 With regard to the historical and symbolic significance of the Maroons of Haiti, the early leader Makandal, and Boukman's ceremony at Bois Cayman, which remains a popular image in Haitian art, see Laënnec Hurbon, *Voodoo: Truth and Fantasy* (London, 1995), 39–43; Wade Davis, *The Serpent and the Rainbow* (New York, 1985), ch. 11; Leslie F. Manigat, "The Relationship Between Marronage and Slave Revolts and Revolution in St. Domingue-Haiti," in Vera Rubin and Arthur Tuden, eds., *Comparative Perspectives on Slavery in New World Plantation Societies* (New York, 1977), 420–73; and Michel-Rolph Trouillot, *Ti Difé Boulé sou Istoua Ayiti* (Brooklyn, N.Y, 1977).

13 Thomas Madiou, *Histoire d'Haïti*, 8 vols. (Port-au-Prince, 1988), III, 102–03 (my translation).

14 On Haiti's isolation, see Brenda Plummer, *Haiti and the United States*; Abel-Nicolas Leger, *Histoire Diplomatique d'Haïti* (Port-au-Prince, 1930); Rayford Logan, *The Diplomatic Relations of the United States with Haiti, 1776–1891* (Chapel Hill, 1941); and Mimi Sheller 'The 'Haytian Fear': International Narratives and Regional Networks in the Construction of Race," forthcoming in Pinar Batur-Vanderlippe and Joe Feagin, eds., *Research in Politics and Society* 6 (Summer 1998).

15 In regard to the slave-like work regimen of this "militarized agriculture," see Trouillot, *State Against Nation*, 43–45.

16 Constitution impériale d'Haïti, 20 mai 1805, an II, Art. 14, in Baron S. Linstant, *Recueil général des Lois et Actes du Gouvernement d'Haïti*, 5 vols. (Paris, 1851–60), vol. 1, 49 (my translation).

17 Michel S. Laguerre, *The Military and Society in Haiti* (Knoxville, 1993), 26.

18 On differing patterns of male and female emancipation throughout the Caribbean, see Barbara Bush, *Slave Women in Caribbean Society, 1650–1838* (London, Kingston and Bloomington, 1990); Barry Higman, *Slave Populations of the British Caribbean, 1807–1834* (Baltimore, 1984); and Marietta Morrissey, *Slave Women in the New World: Gender Stratification in the Caribbean* (Lawrence, Kan., 1989). Slave soldiers were freed during the Haitian Revolution, the United States Civil War, and the Cuban Ten Years' War, among others.

19 Hayti is the name given to the French colony of Saint Domingue after 1804; from 1807 to 1820 it was divided into a northern kingdom and a southern

republic; from 1822 to 1844 it was united with the rest of Hispaniola (subsequently the Dominican Republic).

20 *Pièces Relatives aux communications faites au nom du gouvernement français, au Président d'Hayti par M. le Général Dauxion Lavaysse, député de S.M. Louis XVIII, Roi de France et de Navarre*, enclosing "Procès Verbal des Séances du Conseil Général de la Nation, Cap-Henry, 1814" (New York, 1816) (my translation).
21 Madiou, *Histoire*, IV, 32–33.
22 Act I, Art. I of the Supreme Authority, *Haytian Papers*, Preface and ed. Prince Sanders, Esq. (London, 1816), 128 (my translation, emphasis added).
23 "Narrative of the Accession of Their Royal Majesties to the Throne of Hayti," in *Haytian Papers*, 112.
24 *Code Henri*, Titre I, Ch. I; Ch. II, Art. XIX and XXIII, *Haytian Papers*, vii passim.
25 Robert K. Lacerte, "The First Land Reform in Latin America: The Reforms of Alexander Pétion, 1809–1814," *Inter-American Economic Affairs* 28, no. 4 (1975): 81–83. [. . .]
26 James G. Leyburn, *The Haitian People* (New Haven, 1980 [1966]), 243.
27 Beaubrun Ardouin, *Études sur l'histoire d'Haïti*, 11 vols. (Paris, 1860), IX, 319.
28 Archives Nationales, France (A.N.), CC9a.54, Communications Received at The Foreign Office Relative to Hayti, No. 3, Mackenzie to Canning, 9 September 1827.
29 Richard D. E. Burton, " 'Maman-France Doudou': Family Images in French West Indian Colonial Discourse," *Diacritics* 23, no. 3 (1993): 71. And see Lynn Hunt, *Politics, Culture and Class in the French Revolution* (Berkeley, 1984); and Landes, *Women and the Public Sphere*.
30 Margaret C. Jacob, *Living the Enlightenment: Freemasonry and Politics in Eighteenth Century Europe* (New York and Oxford, 1991), 21, 123. See also Reinhart Koselleck, *Critique and Crisis* (Cambridge, MA, 1988); Jürgen Habermas, *The Structural Transformation of the Bourgeois Public Sphere* (Cambridge, MA, 1989); and Landes, *Women and the Public Sphere*.
31 Madiou, *Histoire*, VII, 507 (my translation).
32 [C.M.B.], *A Glimpse of Haiti, and her Negro Chief* (Liverpool and London, 1850), 83.
33 Madiou, *Histoire*, VII, 415–16 (my translation).
34 Ibid., 415 (my translation).
35 *Le Manifeste*, no. 1, 1ère Année, 4 April 1841, p. 1, signed E***H (my translation).
36 George Andrews and Herrick Chapman, eds., *The Social Construction of Democracy, 1877–1990* (New York, 1995), 20.
37 Cf. Nicholls, *Dessalines to Duvalier*.
38 *Le Temps*, no. 1, 10 February 1842, cited in Jean Desquiron, *Haïti à la Une: Une anthologie de la presse haïtienne de 1724 à 1934*, 2 vols. (Port-au-Prince, 1993), I, 191–2 (my translation).
39 *Le Patriote*, no. 1, 1ère année, 2 March 1842, in Desquiron, *Haïti à la Une*, 199 (my translation). E. Hertelou also responded to *Le Temps* and similarly defended the maturity of the Haitian people in *Le Manifeste*, no. 49, 6 March 1842, and no. 50, 13 March 1842. A year earlier it also printed lengthy debates on the readiness of Haiti for a participatory democratic government (no. 1, 4 April 1841; no. 2, 11 April 1841; no. 26, 26 September 1841).
40 Madiou, *Histoire*, VII, 447 (my translation).
41 Public Record Office, Great Britain, FO 35/3, General Correspondence, Charles Mackenzie to Canning, 6 September 1826.
42 AN, Archives Marines, GGII. 1, papiers de l'Amiral Charles Baudin, Mission d'Haïti, 1837–38 (my translation).
43 This parallels the argument of Michel-Rolph Trouillot, in *Haiti: State Against Nation* (New York, 1990), although he does not analyze the state/society split in terms of gender.

44 Cf. Morrissey, *Slave Women*; Rhoda Reddock, "Women and Slavery in the Caribbean: A Feminist Perspective" in *Latin American Perspectives*, Issue 44, vol. 12, no. 1 (Winter 1985): 63–80; Shepherd et al., *Engendering History*; Jacqueline Jones, *Labor of Love, Labor of Sorrow: Black Women, Work and the Family, From Slavery to the Present* (New York, 1985).

45 David P. Geggus, "Slave and Free Colored Women in Saint Domingue," in D. B. Gaspar and D. C. Hine, eds., *More Than Chattel: Black Women and Slavery in the Americas* (Bloomington, 1996), 262. Similar arguments concerning the lack of skilled occupations for slave women appear in Reddock, "Women and Slavery."

46 This paragraph is based on Susan M. Socolow, "Economic Roles of the Free Women of Color of Cap Français," in Gaspar and Hine, *More Than Chattel*, pp. 279–97.

47 Public Record Office, Great Britain, FO 35/1, Memorandum from James Franklin, enclosed in Horton to Canning, 14 Oct. 1826.

48 On foreign creditors and women's indebtedness, see A. N., CC9a.54, *Communications Received at the Foreign Office Relative to Hayti*, No. 10, Mackenzie to Canning, 30 November 1826; F. O., 35/26, Ussher to F. O., 14 January 1843; and Sidney Mintz, "Black Women, Economic Roles and Cultural Traditions," in Hilary Beckles and Verene Shepherd, eds., *Caribbean Freedom* (Kingston, 1993), 238–44.

49 Serge Larose, "The Haitian Lakou: Land, Family and Ritual," in Arnaud Marks and Rene Romer, eds., *Family and Kinship in Middle America and the Caribbean* (Curaçao, 1975), 482–512.

50 Ardouin, *Études*, XI, 119 (my translation).

51 *Le Patriote*, no. 49, 20 April 1843.

52 Madiou, *Histoire*, VII, 455, 468 (my translation).

53 Madiou, *Histoire*, VII, 468 (my translation); A.N., Archives Marines, GGII.1 Baudin Papers, letter of 29 March 1843; also see Mark Bird, *The Black Man; Or, Haytian Independence* (New York, 1869), 226, on this same incident.

54 Gustave d'Alaux, *L'empereur Soulouque et son empire*, 2nd ed. (Paris, 1860), 112 (my translation).

55 [. . .] According to one historian, a woman named Louise Nicolas "is credited with organizing the [Piquet] movement in 1844" [Patrick Bellegarde-Smith, *Haiti: The Breached Citadel*, (Boulder, 1990), 70]. [. . .]

56 See, for example, discussion of European gender ideologies in Leonore Davidoff and Catherine Hall, *Family Fortunes* (London/Chicago, 1987) and Catherine Hall, *White, Male and Middle Class* (Cambridge, 1992).

57 Jonathan Brown, *The History and Present Condition of St. Domingue*, 2 vols. (Philadelphia, 1837), vol. 2, 281.

58 Sidney Mintz, "Black Women, Economic Roles and Cultural Traditions," in H. Beckles and V. Shepherd, eds., *Caribbean Freedom* (Kingston, 1993), 238–44, quoting J. B., 'Notes of a Tour in Haiti,' *The Evening Post*, LIII (19 May 1854).

59 Mintz, "Black Women," 239.

60 I. M. Lewis, *Ecstatic Religion: A Study of Shamanism and Spirit Possession* (London, New York, 1993), 26–27.

61 For the U.S., where African-American women's leadership has challenged more male-dominated formal organizations, cf. Jones, *Labor of Love*, 67; and Evelyn Brooks Higginbotham, "The Black Church: A Gender Perspective," in Timothy E. Fulop and Albert J. Raboteau, eds., *African-American Religion* (New York and London, 1997), 201–225. For Jamaica, where the title "Mother" or "Queen" is used for female religious leaders, cf. Mimi Sheller, "Quasheba, Mother, Queen: Black Women's Public Roles and Political Protest in Post-Emancipation Jamaica," CAAS Working Paper No. 42, University of Michigan (October 1997).

62 Gérard Barthélemy, *Le pays en dehors: essai sur l'univers rural haïtien*, 2nd ed. (Port-au-Prince, 1989), 31.
63 Karen McCarthy Brown, *Mama Lola: A Vodou Priestess in Brooklyn* (Berkeley, 1991), 459, n. 11.
64 Personal observation, meeting of women's groups of the Mouvman Peyizan de Papaye, Poulie (near Lascahobas), Haiti, June 1996.

8

RURAL PROTEST AND PEASANT REVOLT, 1804–1869

(Excerpt from *Haiti in Caribbean Context*)

David Nicholls

Perhaps the most notorious feature of Haiti under the Duvaliers has been the militia, popularly known as the *tontons macoutes* (after the figure in Haitian folklore who carries off wicked children in his bag). The organisation originated as a private paramilitary group during the election campaign of 1956–7. [. . .] François Duvalier, who had studied the history of Haiti, was fully aware that many of his predecessors had fallen as a result of action by the army and that some counterforce was therefore necessary if he was to survive. He decided to revive an ancient tradition in the country by involving the masses in a paramilitary organisation. From the revolutionary period (1789–1803) to the US occupation (1915–34), large numbers of Haitians had been in possession of firearms, and it was only with the defeat of the *cacos* rebellion under Charlemagne Péralte in 1919 that the people were generally disarmed.

In this chapter I wish to discuss three rural protest movements in the period following the declaration of independence. Little has been written on this aspect of Haitian history[1] and most Haitian writers of the period treated these revolts as unfortunate disturbances to the normal course of events. As Louis Joseph Janvier remarked, 'up to now those who have written the history of the *piquets* were their enemies or their assassins'.[2] Rural movements of this period manifest a certain pattern which was to be repeated in the years immediately preceding the US invasion of 1915 and in the bold military resistance to the occupation led by Péralte and Benoît Batraville.[3] They were centred in the countryside and were, as Léon Laroche observed with respect to the *piquets*, directed largely against the towns.[4] The movements with which we are concerned in this chapter were usually led by black landowners with medium-sized properties, and it is likely that they were supported principally by small-holding peasants rather than by the landless and very poor.

Certain parts of Haiti were particularly prone to such risings. The region around Jérémie in the southern peninsular of Haiti, known as La

180

Grand'Anse, has been the centre of two of the most important revolts. Owing to its physical characteristics the South was the last region to be colonised and developed by the French. Its mountainous terrain was less suitable for the establishment of large sugar plantations than were the plains of the North and West. La Grand'Anse was, then, a region of small coffee plantations, and by 1780 most of the properties were in the hands of the *affranchis*. During the coffee boom of the 1780s, however, they began to sell these properties as their value increased. The plantations were bought largely by *petits blancs*, who by the time of the British occupation of 1793 had become a formidable power in the region. Independent-minded and fiercely racialist, these white coffee farmers feared the return of the mulatto general Rigaud and were among the earliest French colonists to go over to the British. Another significant feature of the region was that among the slave population of La Grand'Anse was a high proportion of *bossals* (African-born slaves) who tended to predominate on the coffee farms of the colony.[5] During the revolutionary years and in the post-independence period large numbers of these blacks established themselves as independent small farmers in the interior. The city of Jérémie, where many of the mulattoes had settled, was known even in colonial times as a centre of the most bitter racial and colour prejudice.

While the rhetoric of the leaders of these movements was frequently revolutionary, the aim of the rank and file seems to have been reformist, to employ a distinction made by Eric Hobsbawm,[6] or even conservative. Their principal concerns were to maintain their property rights, to resist government taxation and to limit the power of urban money lenders and *spéculateurs*. The customary looting which took place does not imply a revolutionary determination to overthrow the economic and social system, but was rather a gesture of defiance towards the authorities. The colour issue was often raised, either by the rebels themselves or by their opponents. This is because of the fact that in Haiti, as in many other parts of the Caribbean, dark colour is the *badge* of low economic status and the rhetoric of protest is commonly formulated in colour terms, though the real issues are economic and social. [. . .]

Finally, while many of these protest movements effected the overthrow of the government in Port-au-Prince their influence on the policy of the succeeding administration was minimal. Only in the revolt led by Goman was an independent state maintained for any length of time.

The Political Background

Haiti had become independent as a result of a bloody colonial war lasting many years and involving several European countries. It was a struggle in which large numbers of Haitians were involved and it might properly be called a war of national liberation. After independence had been declared the principal internal question which confronted the leaders of the country was that of land ownership. Jean-Jacques Dessalines, the first ruler (1804–6), was clearly unhappy about a situation in which a small proportion of the population, the class of predominantly mulatto *anciens libres*, owned large properties while the liberated slaves, *nouveaux libres*, were legally landless, though increasing numbers of them had begun squatting on vacant properties. He made it clear that he intended to rectify the situation, and this is undoubtedly one of the reasons for his assassination. Henry Christophe, ruler of the North, at first attempted to maintain a plantation system, producing crops for export and punishing workers who left their plantations without permission.[7] Later however, he followed Pétion's policy of land distribution. Pétion, who had become president of a republic in the South and West, had began to distribute and to sell state properties soon after his accession to power.[8] While it would be wrong to suggest that this land policy was a 'democratic' move, for the principal beneficiaries were the largely mulatto generals of his army, nevertheless it did lay the foundations for a landowning peasantry, which has been one of the features distinguishing Haiti from other principal islands of the Antilles.[9] The first protest movement we shall be considering occurred during the presidency of Pétion and continued into that of his successor.

Pétion's successor, Jean-Pierre Boyer, a spokesman of the mulatto elite, saw with distress the decline of plantation agriculture and endeavoured to check the trend towards a peasant economy by his rural code of 1826 and other legislation.[10] These efforts were generally unsuccessful. Boyer, who had invaded and occupied the eastern two-thirds of the island in 1822, ruled the whole of Hispaniola until his tenure of office came to an end in 1843. A period of instability followed in which four presidents succeeded each other in rapid succession. It was a time in which the rural black elite, with support from the black masses, particularly in the South, reasserted its position in reaction to the mulatto hegemony. Our second protest movement took place at this time. The shift in the balance of power towards the blacks was to some extent reinforced during the Soulouque era (1847–59) but the overthrow of the empire and the advent of Geffrard (1859–67) did something to re-establish the position of the mulatto elite.[11] This chapter ends with a consideration of the third rural protest movement which took place in the confused period of civil war during the presidency of Salnave (1867–9).

* * *

Goman's Peasant Republic

When a country has secured its liberation by armed struggle, a tradition of violence frequently persists into the period of independence. Haiti's sovereign status was not recognised by France until 1825 and in the two decades which preceded this there was a continual threat of French invasion. Also Napoleon's army remained on the island, at Santo Domingo, until 1809. Large standing armies were therefore maintained by all Haitian governments, in addition to which almost the whole male population over fifteen years of age was ready to take up arms at short notice.[12] Pétion and Christophe had issued fierce assertions of their determination to resist foreign invasions. The former warned that French troops would find nothing in Haiti but 'ashes mingled with dust', while Christophe declared: 'At my voice Hayti will be transformed into a vast camp of soldiers'. A war of ambush and guerrilla tactics would be pursued involving the whole population.[13] French observers who best knew the situation advised against any attempt to reconquer the country by arms.[14] The British consul, Charles Mackenzie, writing in 1826, concurred in this judgement, 'I am disposed to think that no invading European force can ever succeed in conquering Haiti unless through the treachery of the native chiefs' [. . .].[15] In a situation of this kind, when a high proportion of the population is accustomed to carry weapons, it is not surprising that individual generals had considerable autonomy, and that disaffected groups should take up arms against the government from time to time.[16]

The insurrection of La Grand'Anse, which lasted from 1807 to 1819, is at once the most interesting and the least documented protest movement of nineteenth-century Haiti. It was led by a former slave, called Goman, who was a *bossal* from the Congo, well known as a maroon in colonial days. His full name was Jean-Baptiste Dupérier, or Perrier.[17] It is likely that he had been a slave on the Perrier plantation in La Plaine des Cayes. After the revolt on this plantation the mulatto general André Rigaud negotiated in 1792 with slaves and masters for a settlement which included 700 manumissions.[18] Goman, having returned to the plantation, was possibly one of these *affranchis* and was adopted by Rigaud as his 'godson'. Goman was among the considerable number of southern blacks who supported Rigaud against Toussaint in the war of the South (1799–1800). After Rigaud's defeat, Goman returned to work on the Perrier plantation, though during the struggle for independence he took up arms once more. His opposition to Toussaint and later to Dessalines was no doubt reinforced by the hostility which existed at this time between *créole* and *bossal* blacks.[19]

The assassination of Dessalines in October 1806 led to a period of confusion in Haiti. Christophe, heir-apparent, was unprepared to accept the restrictions which rival generals sought to impose upon the new head of state, and civil war broke out. It was at this time that an insurrection occurred in La Grand'Anse. The origins of this outbreak are unclear. It is possible, as Madiou maintained, that the revolt was started by Thomas Durocher, a black officer who was inspector of agriculture for the region, and Bergerac Trichet, the brother of Théodat Trichet a supporter of Pétion. The reason for their discontent was said to be the appointment of General Francisque as commandant of La Grand'Anse. It is probable that they were encouraged in this revolt by Henry Christophe or at least by their belief that the black general would defeat Pétion and soon take control of the whole country.[20] The small black peasant farmers of the region, led by Jason Domingo, Cesar Novelet and Bazile, took to arms, and on 8 January 1807 invaded the mulatto-dominated city of Jérémie. The residents of the city managed, however, to repel the attack. Goman, who was at this time leading the nineteenth battalion at L'Anse d'Hainault, was appointed head of the insurrection by a gathering of rebels held at L'Habitation Fiollé, near Dame Marie, in the following month. Durocher and Trichet (if indeed they had ever been involved in the insurrection, which Beaubrun Ardouin denied[21]) went over to the government side.

From 1807 until 1819, despite repeated attempts by the government to suppress the revolt, large inland areas in the southwest were controlled by Goman and his second in command, Saint Louis Boteau. A general amnesty was proclaimed in April 1807 and, on the advice of Durocher, the prisoners were released and organised into an army of 1500 men known as *éclaireurs*. It was hoped that this group, composed of men who knew the terrain, would lead the regular army in crushing the rebels. Goman successfully resisted, and organised a peasant republic in the area, maintaining close links with a number of collaborators in Jérémie and other coastal towns, from whom he secured supplies of arms and other necessities. He moved his headquarters from place to place, but eventually settled in the mountains about sixty-five kilometres from Jérémie at a village known as Grand-Doco, where he planted large areas in *vivres* (ground provision) and other food crops in order to support his army.

According to Madiou the perennial colour problem was raised by Boteau, who endeavoured to turn the struggle into a war of caste by stirring up the black peasants against the mulattoes on grounds of colour.[22] Swift action by black generals on the government side, including Durocher and Vaval, managed to prevent the struggle from becoming such a caste war and Boteau was obliged to abandon his black power propaganda.

Goman's ability to resist the assaults of the republican forces is partly explained by the fact that Pétion was fighting on two fronts. Most of his energy was taken up in a long war with Christophe's forces; also he was plagued by continual conspiracies from within. The presence of his former rival, General Gérin, in the South led to particular problems which were solved only by the suicide of Gérin in 1809 and by the arrest of Durocher and Trichet as alleged collaborators in an intended *coup*. Soon after these events, however, the tranquility of the republic was further disturbed in April 1810 by the arrival in Les Cayes of André Rigaud, the celebrated mulatto general, from exile in France. He was invited to Port-au-Prince by Pétion where he was received with honours and appointed commander of the forces in La Grand'Anse, charged with suppressing the revolt. Rigaud met his former disciple and godson Goman, who promised to submit to the government, a promise which the peasant leader failed to keep. Then

Rigaud, encouraged by disaffected mulattoes including Bruno Blanchet, Guy-Joseph Bonnet and J.-M. Borgella, declared the independence of the South with its capital in Les Cayes. There were, then, four states in Haiti at this time, apart from the Spanish colony in the eastern part of the island. Whether Rigaud was sent by the French as an agent, as the British feared, or whether he remained a loyal Haitian patriot, as Pétion had maintained,[23] is not clear, but death soon removed him from the scene and in 1811 Borgella led the South back into Pétion's republic.

Goman maintained his independence and was created Comte de Jérémie by Christophe, who had become King Henry 1 in 1811. Goman evidently enjoyed popular support in the region and even Pétion recognised legitimate grounds for peasant discontent in La Grand'Anse. In a letter to General Bazelais, commandant of the region, the president wrote: 'The cultivators, having never been considered as active citizens of the republic, have always been treated with rigour and with more or less injustice. This abject state, this stupid system, is one of the principal causes of the insurrection which is devouring this region.'[24] Goman remained in almost undisputed possession of his domains until after the death of Pétion in 1818. The new president, Boyer, announced in January 1819 a campaign against the rebels. 'The time has come,' he declared, 'when the insurrection of La Grand'Anse must cease.'[25]

The attack on Goman was co-ordinated by Bazelais and included troops under the command of Borgella, Lys and Francisque, together with the national guard from a number of towns. The rebels retreated into the hills, where they were relentlessly pursued by government troops who destroyed the plantations of the rebels as they went. After several months government forces seized Grand-Doco, where Le Comte de Jérémie was living with his wives. He avoided capture but his headquarters were destroyed together with the plantations which had constituted his main source of food. With the exception of Goman himself and two of his officers most of the rebel leaders submitted and by the end of June 1819 the peasant republic had been conquered. The fate of Goman himself is unknown, although Beaubrun Ardouin suggested that he probably died of injuries received in the fighting.[26]

* * *

Boyer and His Legacy

After the death of Christophe in 1820, Haiti was reunited under Boyer, who occupied the former Spanish colony of Santo Domingo in 1822 and ruled the whole island until he was deposed in 1843. These years were marked by a concentration of power in the hands of a small group of mulatto families. It was a time of relative peace and stability, enlivened with only occasional plots and protests, led mostly by black generals.

Rural discontent was, however, widespread owing to Boyer's attempt, enshrined in the rural code of 1826, to reimpose the plantation system and to his efforts to raise money from the peasants to cover the huge indemnity imposed by France as a condition for recognising Haitian independence.[27] Hostility towards France was almost universal and the government was unpopular for having accepted these conditions.[28] Boyer's fall in 1843 came as a result of divisions within the ranks of the mulatto elite gather than from a revolt among the black masses. The new president, Charles Hérard, was no less exclusivist in his policies, and black discontent exploded in the same year.

The most serious and prolonged insurrection was again in the region of La Grand'Anse, though there was also considerable resistance in parts of the North.[29] The southern revolt began under the leadership of the Salomon family, who were rich black landowners in the region of Les Cayes. The rising started in August 1843 and government forces under General Lazare were sent to put it down. It was estimated that Salomon's men were armed with roughly 300 rifles and 500 wooden pikes, from which they derived the name of *piquets*.[30] The revolt was temporarily suppressed and the Salomons were arrested. Leadership then passed into the hands of Louis Jean-Jacques Acaau. Born of a black small-holding family during the early years of the century in the commune of Torbeck, Acaau joined the army at an early age and soon became an officer. He was, in the words of the British consul, 'a man of some instruction for a negro'.[31] Nevertheless, promotion was difficult for blacks in the Boyer era and consequent discontent among black officers was one of the causes of the rising. The principal complaints of the small farmers of the region were about the penalty of imprisonment for debt and the power of bailiffs. According to Madiou though, the unacknowledged objects of the rising were to destroy mulatto dominance in general, to install a black president, and to confiscate land from the rich of all colours, distributing it among the poor.[32] It was Acaau who is said to have first enunciated the well-known *Kréyol* proverb *nèg rich sé mulât, mulât pov sé nèg*.

Acaau's opponents and many foreign observers portrayed the struggle in the South as one of colour,[33] and feeling in the South was indeed such that three black generals told the French foreign minister, in an extraordinary letter, that they would prefer a restoration of French control to a continued domination by *petits mulâtres*. Acaau himself, however, explicitly denied inaugurating a caste war, claiming to defend the interests of the poor of all colours.[34]

Dressed in straw hats, with ragged trousers and jackets, these *piquet* leaders carried large machetes and had pistols in their belts. Acaau's followers proclaimed him *chef des réclamations de ces concitoyens*. 'The population of the countryside,' he declared, 'awaking from the slumber into which it has been plunged, is murmuring in its poverty and is determined to work for the securing of its rights.'[35] Acaau undoubtedly enjoyed widespread popular support, particularly in La Grand'Anse, as Goman had before him. He reinforced his position with claims to supernatural powers.[36] [. . .]

Despite being poorly armed, Acaau's men were able to occupy the cities of Jérémie and Les Cayes and to put considerable pressure on the government. The fall of Charles Hérard and the election of the black General Guerrier did something to pacify the *piquets* and Acaau submitted to the government, being later appointed commandant of L'Anse à Veau. By August 1845 Acaau was named by the British consul as one of the possible successors to President Pierrot. His lieutenants Dugué Zamor and Jean Claude had in the meanwhile also secured official positions. 'These two men', wrote the British consul Thomas Ussher, 'are the terror of the peaceably disposed inhabitants of Aux Cayes. . . . the Government dare not dismiss them'. Many of those involved in the southern revolt were hostile not only to the French but to all foreigners. Pointing to British warships off the coast, General Lazare said to his men, 'There are your real enemies, the white men, beware of them'.[37] Acaau, however, had approached Commodore Sharpe with a request for British protection.[38]

Black Empire and Bourgeois Republic

The period of acute governmental instability which began with the fall of Boyer came to an end with the election of the black general, Faustin Soulouque, in March 1847. The new president was generally believed to be weak and stupid; mulatto politicians, including the Ardouin brothers, had supported his election thinking that they would be able to manipulate him. These men soon learned that this was not to be so. Soulouque proved to be a canny, ruthless and unpredictable leader with a mind of his own. One of the first things he did after his election was to replace many mulatto officers by blacks and build up a paramilitary group called the *zinglins* under the command of Maximilien Augustin, popularly known as Similien.[39] Recruited from the urban sub-proletariat, the *zinglins* were generally feared by the bourgeoisie of all colours.[40]

Acaau, having become disillusioned with the situation, committed suicide, and leadership of the southern *piquets* passed into the hands of Pierre Noir, Jean Denis and Voltaire Castor, though it is likely that the Salomons continued to exercise an influence over them. In 1848 a detachment *of piquets* invaded Les Cayes. The rich blacks, who had collaborated with the mulatto establishment in the city, laid down their arms, confident that their colour would save them. They badly misjudged the situation, however, and eighty-nine of these blacks were put to death, Castor himself killing seventy of them with his own hands. Thus came to pass, in the words of the French consul, the saying of Acaau *nèg rich sé mulât*. A similar event had occurred in the city two years earlier when the *piquets* had put to death 'blacks and mulattoes whom they supposed to be proprietors of anything'.[41]

Soulouque clearly believed that the *piquets* were getting out of hand and he charged Dugué Zamor with the task of suppressing them; Zamor was soon replaced by General André Thélémaque, who was in turn removed by Jean Claude who proclaimed himself commandant of the South. The situation was however brought under control by the government and Pierre Noir was executed in November 1848. In the following year Soulouque felt confident enough to relieve Similien of his duties and have himself proclaimed Emperor Faustin 1. The inauguration of the empire began a period of relative stability which lasted until General Fabre Nicolas Geffrard's successful revolution of 1859. The emperor took refuge in Jamaica, returning to Haiti only with the fall of Geffrard in 1867; he died a short while after at Petit Goâve.

Geffrard was an elite *griffe*[42] and was generally identified with the interests of the mulatto bourgeoisie. Although a change in government certainly led to a shift in the balance of power away from the blacks, the contrast between the regimes of Soulouque and Geffrard has frequently been overstated. While many of the emperor's ministers had been mulattoes, a number of blacks retained their positions under Geffrard; most of the army commanders survived the change.[43] Geffrard suppressed attempted *coups* by black generals from the South in 1862 and 1865, the former being led by members of the Salomon family. More serious was the revolt in Cap Haïtien in 1865 led by General Silvain Salnave, with support from the black politician and writer Demesvar Delorme. This rising, which lasted for several months, had backing from the USA and from elements in the Dominican Republic, but was put down by Geffrard with help from a British gunboat which bombarded the city. Renewed attempts by Salnave, together with a revolt led by General Nissage Saget at St Marc, were successful, and in 1867 sections of Geffrard's crack brigade, *les tirailleurs*, mutinied. In March 1867 the president left for Jamaica, where he died eleven years later. An economic and financial crisis had weakened the government and important elements of the national bourgeoisie had become disaffected, claiming that Geffrard favoured foreign merchants. The charges brought against him by Saget included turning the girls' schools in the country into *'maisons de séduction à son profit'*.[44] The following section of this chapter will consider the armed conflicts of the two succeeding years.

* * *

Salnave and The Cacos War

The period of Salnave's presidency was marked by almost continuous fighting, and according to F. D. Légitime constituted the worst conflagration in Haiti since the war of independence.[45] The president was combating not only the peasant irregulars, known as *cacos* in the northern part of the country, but also groups of *piquets* in the South, both of which were supported by dissident generals of the regular army with their men.

Salnave was himself a handsome, light-skinned mulatto who managed to secure the bulk of his support from the blacks of Cap Haïtien and Port-au-Prince. He was a powerful orator and a populist who had an easy manner with the ordinary Haitian and treated all men (and women) as equals. Even his most bitter critics witnessed to the president's popularity among the urban poor.[46] With the fall of Geffrard a provisional government was set up with Nissage Saget as president and including Victorin Chevalier, a reluctant supporter of Salnave, whose followers called him *chef d'exécution de volontés du peuple*. A constituent assembly was called for 8 April 1867, but it was clear that Salnave's claim to the presidency would be accepted. Popular chants were sung in Salnave's favour and enthusiastic support for him spread throughout the countryside. 'The people', reported the French minister in Port-au-Prince, 'wish only for him and they rise up as one man whenever he appears, from the Cap to Port-au-Prince.'[47] He was, as Firmin observed, 'the idol of the masses.'[48]

Opposition to the new regime was, however, swift to manifest itself. The French minister, Comte Méjan, referred to a revolt of *'cocos'* which broke out in the north-east in May 1867; it was centred at Ouanaminthe near the Dominican border and involved many of the same local chiefs who had opposed Salnave in 1865. They saw his rise to power as constituting a threat to their own established positions. There was also fighting in the region of Jérémie. 'Never has a government,' Méjan reported, 'never has a head of state, lost his popularity more completely or more rapidly.'[49] General Léon Montas, the principal leader of anti-government forces in the north-east was captured and put in prison where, after some months, he was found dead in December 1867. This increased the bitterness of the struggle.

Salnave's government earned the hostility of traders and *spéculateurs* by instituting a state monopoly in coffee and ensured support from the urban masses by the establishment of *magasins d'état* for the sale of necessities at low prices: two steps which Salomon had attempted as finance minister in Soulouque's government. Salnave thus retained his popularity among the urban proletariat and sub-proletariat, particularly with the women. Chevalier claimed that Salnave's government was 'the expression of the needs, the sentiments, the interests of the masses'.[50] In October 1867 demonstrations in favour of the government were held in the capital, with women marching through the commercial centre of the city crying: *'Vive Salnave; à bas les négotiants cacos'*. The violent rhetoric of Salnave's supporters increased. 'The government,' declared the British minister Sir Spenser St John, 'has taken into its pay bands of the lowest negresses to parade the town armed with butchers' knives and threatening with death and with plunder and fire all the respectable inhabitants'. St John, whose hostility to Salnave and support for Geffrard was well-known, denounced the president for having 'turned the Palace into a rendezvous where the scum of the negresses assembled to dance and drink'.[51]

Meanwhile, opposition to Salnave was growing throughout Haiti, and he took personal charge of the army in its campaign against the northern *cacos*. In the spring of 1868 a rising at Gonaïves proclaimed as president General Philippeaux (a government minister under Geffrard). In Hinche a revolt forced the commandant to retreat to the fort. Nissage Saget, whose power base was St Marc, issued a proclamation on 26 April against the government. He was in turn denounced by the president for 'profiting from the brigandage of the *cacos*.'[52] May 1868 witnessed a further rising in the South, which began at Léogane and spread westwards. Three divisions, headed by the Generals Domingue, Faubert and Dubois, declared against the government. Salnave was faced with yet another revolt at Dondon led by Nord Alexis. From May to September, Port-au-Prince was under siege with rebel troops occupying Carrefour, just five kilometres west from the city centre, and Croix-des-Bouquets somewhat further to the east. Salnave countered by encouraging *piquet* leaders in the South to rise up against his enemies. In the countryside around Jacmel, Léogane, Petit Goâve and in La Grand'Anse the *piquets* revolted, thus compelling the armies of Domingue which were besieging the capital to withdraw and defend the cities of the South. From this time on there were effectively three separate states in Haiti: the north with its capital at Saint Marc, under Nissage, the south under Domingue, centred at Les Cayes, and – between the two – the government of Salnave, controlling the capital, some northern cities and (through the *piquets)* considerable parts of the rural South. The civil war led to serious famine and to outbreaks of cholera and yellow fever in the cities of the South and West.

Who were the *cacos*? I have argued elsewhere that the *cacos* came from the middle class of peasants rather than from the very poor, as has been asserted by several writers.[53] The name is probably derived from the fierce little bird called the *taco* and was first used to designate the black guerrillas who harassed the French in 1802. Government forces attacked by the *cacos* in the period prior to the United States invasion of 1915 were known as *zandolites*, after the large lizard which the *taco* finds tasty. Père Cabon, however, claimed that the term *cacos* derives from the *caraco*, a garment worn by peasants.[54] These peasant irregulars took up arms on the initiative of local chiefs, or of disaffected army officers, with the hope of payment or at least opportunities for pillage. When government forces advanced, the *cacos* bands would usually dissolve and the peasants would return to cultivate their land; they would then reassemble elsewhere when the troops had gone.[55] The same was generally true of the *piquets* in the South. One consequence of this mode of operation was that the area within which each band could act effectively was limited by the unwillingness of its members to move far from their properties.[56]

The colour question played a part in the struggles of these years. It was widely believed by peasants in the countryside that Salnave was black and he received considerable support from such *piquet* leaders as Siffra Fortuné, who controlled the region around Baradères in the South. In September 1868 an English observer recorded how Salnave's army which was surrounding the rebel city of Jacmel was mostly composed of 'country people (the true black).'[57] When, according to Janvier, the *piquets* discovered that Salnave was a very clear-skinned mulatto many of them were less keen to support him. Sections of them went over to the black General Michel Domingue, who eagerly exploited his colour advantage, denouncing Salnave for not having a drop of African blood in his veins.[58]

Although, as I have pointed out, much of Salnave's support came from urban blacks, most mulattoes in the capital were also prepared to give him tacit support, owing to their fear of a black head of state taking his place. At least Salnave was the right colour![59] Whether the president practiced voodoo, as his opponents claimed, is not certain, but his policies were undoubtedly anti-clerical and erastian. The president attempted to reinstate some irregular clergy who had ministered in Haiti prior to the *Concordat* of 1860, but who had been deposed by the new hierarchy. Government troops imprisoned a number of priests and others were chased from their parishes by *piquet* leaders loyal to the government. From the days of the *Concordat* onwards the hierarchy of the Roman Catholic church had tended to side with the mulatto elite, while the *noiriste* elite, with which Salnave had associated himself, had frequently practised free-masonry and adopted an anti-clerical stance. Salnave's dispute with the hierarchy culminated in a decree of 28 June 1869 deposing the archbishop of Port-au-Prince, Mgr Testard du Cosquer. The vicar general, Mgr Guilloux, denounced the decree as null.[60]

With the raising of the siege of Port-au-Prince in September 1868 and the arrival of a new government warship from the USA the fortunes of Salnave seemed to be turning. Nevertheless fighting continued in various parts of the country throughout 1869; Gonaïves fell at the end of August, and a decisive development occurred at the beginning of December when the *cacos* seized Cap Haïtien. Then on the night of 18 December Generals Brice and Boisrond Canal invaded the capital from the sea. Salnave remained in the palace until the last moment when he fled to the hills hoping to reach the Dominican border. He was captured and brought back to the capital where he was shot in the following month. Thus came to an end the *cacos* war. Only the *piquets* of La Grand'Anse remained faithful, refusing to believe that Salnave had fallen.[61] As André Adam has convincingly shown,[62] Salnave's defeat was due to an alliance between the bourgeois classes in the towns and large sections of the *classe intermédiaire* in the countryside. These groups were encouraged by French and British consuls and by the Roman Catholic hierarchy. So exhausted was the country that the new president, Nissage Saget, an elite *griffe*, was able to rule in relative peace and was one of the few Haitian heads of state to remain in office for his constitutional term and then retire.

191

Owing to his populism and his anti-clericalism Salnave soon became a hero of the *noiriste* tradition in Haiti and is frequently said to have been the founder of the National Party. He is one of the few mulattoes to receive a favourable report in the writings of Duvalier and his followers.[63] [. . .]

* * *

Conclusion

Our study raises the complicated issue of the relationship between class and colour in rural Haiti and more generally throughout the Caribbean. Class loyalties often supersede colour loyalties, as when the invading *piquets* put to death their fellow blacks from the bourgeois class or when the black proletariat and sub-proletariat of the capital supported Salnave through the most harrowing months of the siege. As we have also seen, however, there are clearly situations when colour must be recognised as a significant and independent variable in explaining the course of events. The case of the rural blacks whose attitude to Salnave changed when they discovered his true colour is not an isolated incident. The black politician Anténor Firmin recorded how his National Party opponents spread the rumour that he was 'a mulatto as clear-skinned as a white,' so that the blacks of the rural North would not vote for him.[64] Domingue's attempt to exploit the colour issue and to convince the poor blacks that their interests were the same as those of the black elite has been imitated by succeeding politicians of the black elite and middle class. Estimé and Duvalier were both denounced by their opponents for exploiting the colour issue in just this way.

It would be true to say though, that colour normally becomes significant in Caribbean politics only when it is reinforced by other factors, real or imagined. The change in attitude towards Salnave on the part of rural blacks who did not know him was due to the fact that in their experience mulatto leaders tended to act in the interests of the urban bourgeoisie, while the black leaders at least knew enough about the countryside to realise that they must take some account of peasant interests. Their belief that they should not support Salnave is therefore understandable in the light of the general coincidence between colour and class in Haiti. Colour prejudice, having come into being for whatever cause, develops a dynamic of its own and often leads men to act in ways which are in conflict with their material interests.

While the protest movements I have been considering have certain features in common there are clear differences between them. In its determination to maintain an independent peasant state, Goman's revolt stands out as peculiar. All three movements were in certain respects conservative. The first two were defending the interests of the small peasants against perceived threats from the urban bourgeoisie. The *cacos* revolt was a movement of peasants with small and medium-sized holdings, in alliance with the urban bourgeoisie against a government which was seen to be acting in the interests of the growing proletariat and sub-proletariat in the towns. In all three movements the principal leaders of the revolts had been regular army officers, but professional soldiers played a much larger part in the two later revolts than in the movement headed by Goman. The personal factor, depending on the charismatic leadership of local chiefs and on a patron–client relationship, was a basic feature of all three movements. Local chiefs who had established such a dependency relationship with the poorer peasants in their region were able to call on their support in time of need. The power of these rural chiefs increased during the latter part of the nineteenth century and contributed in a major way to the political instability of the country in the period prior to the US invasion. Thanks to the work of Haitian historians Alain Turnier, Roger Gaillard and Kethly Millet, we know a good deal about these later peasant movements. The researches of these writers generally confirm the pattern which has emerged from our brief study of the three earlier revolts.

With the defeat of the *cacos* revolt of 1918–19, however, the balance of power shifted from the countryside to the capital. In the years following the withdrawal of the marines all important decisions were made in Port-au-Prince and successful protest movements were invariably centred there. The election of Dumarsais Estimé in 1946 and of François Duvalier in 1957 marked a reassertion of rural claims, though the subsequent policies of their governments have hardly done anything to disturb the hegemony of 'the republic of Port-au-Prince'. Despite the rhetoric, little consideration has been given to the interests of rural Haitians who, after all, still comprise about 90 per cent of the country's population.

One of the methods Duvalier used to recruit support in rural areas and to maintain control throughout the country was by developing the organisation of *tontons macoutes*. 'Excellency,' declared one *macoute* leader in 1960, addressing the president, 'the gun that Sonthonax gave us to defend our liberty and that the American occupation has taken away from us is the gun that, without fear, you have given back to us – be assured that this gun will not be used against you.'[65] Many *macoute* leaders come from that class of medium-sized land owners which provided leadership and much of the rank and file membership of the nineteenth-century movements, some like Zacharie Delva of Gonaïves, were also *houngans*. The notorious slaughter of mulatto families in Jérémie in August 1964 also bears comparison with some of the deeds of the *piquets*. Nevertheless, the difference between the *macoutes* and the groups which we have been considering is clear. The former has become a movement dedicated to preserving a government, like the *zinglins* of Soulouque, rather than for defending the interests of the masses. Perhaps the true successors of the *cacos* and *piquets* of former days are the peasant bands which, following the death of François Duvalier in April 1971, stoned the houses of Delva and other unpopular *macoute* leaders, forcing them to take refuge in the capital.

NOTES

1 Apart from the classical nineteenth-century Haitian historians, Thomas Madiou *fils* and Alexis Beaubrun Ardouin, few writers have dealt with these protest movements [. . .]. Worthy of mention, however, are Camille Large ('Goman et l'insurrection de la Grande Anse', *Revue de la Société Haïtienne d'Histoire et de Géographie*, 12, 1940), Paul Moral (*Le paysan haïtien* [Port-au-Prince, 1959]), H. Pauléus Sannon (*Essai historique sur la révolution de 1843* [Les Cayes, 1905]) and F. E. Dubois (*Précis historique de la révolution haïtienne de 1843* [Paris, 1866]) in addition to the works cited in this chapter. Particularly interesting is the series of articles by F. D. Légitime, a former president of Haiti, on the *cacos* war of 1867–69, in which he took an active part; these appeared in *La Revue de la Société de Législation* in many instalments, beginning in 1907. Also reference should be made to a recent book by André Georges Adam, *Une crise haïtienne, 1867–1869: Sylvain Salnave* (Port-au-Prince, 1982).

2 L. J. Janvier, *Le vieux piquet* (Paris, 1884), p. 4.

3 R. Gaillard, *Les cent jours de Rosalvo Bobo* (Port-au-Prince, 1973); H. Schmidt, *The United States Occupation of Haiti, 1915–1934* (New Brunswick, N.J., 1971), ch. 5; and S. Castor, *La ocupación norte-americana de Haití, 1915–1934* (Buenos Aires, 1971), ch. 7.

4 L. Laroche, *Haïti: une page d'histoire* (Paris, 1885), p. 85n.

5 M. L. E. Moreau de St Méry, *Description topographique, physique, civile, politique et historique de la partie française de l'île Saint-Domingue* (1798; reprint Paris, 1958), 3, p. 1400.

6 E. Hobsbawm, *Primitive Rebels* (New York, 1965), pp. 10f.

7 'Memorandum on Northern Haiti', in H. Popham to Lord Melville, 13 June 1819, Melville Papers (Rhodes House, Oxford), 2/323. The owners of estates were in turn obliged to support the old, injured and infirm (ibid., 2/322).

8 L. F. Manigat, *La politique agraire du gouvernement d'Alexandre Pétion* (Port-au-Prince, 1962); S. Thébaud, *L'évolution de la structure agraire en Haïti de 1804 à nos jours* (University of Paris thesis, Faculté de Droit, 1967); and R. K. Lacerte, 'The first land reforms in Latin America', *Interamerican Economic Affairs*, 28:4, 1975, pp. 77f.

9 On the wealth of some generals see David Nicholls, *Haiti in Caribbean Context* (New York, 1985), 94.

10 There was an English translation of the *Code Rural* published in 1827 with a prefatory letter to Earl Bathurst stating that it would be of concern to those 'most deeply interested in ascertaining the possibility of obtaining regular and steady labour in tropical climates without compulsion' (*The Rural Code of Haiti*, p. iii). By 'peasant economy', in the text, I mean simply a situation in which the emphasis is upon growing crops for local consumption by persons owning their land, in contrast to a plantation economy geared to the cultivation on large estates of one or a few crops for export. [. . .]

11 See David Nicholls, *From Dessalines to Duvalier* (Cambridge, 1979), pp. 76f.

12 Estimates of the size of the armies at this time vary considerably. A French visitor gave the figure, for the republican army, of over 30 000, excluding the militia (A. Rouzeau, *De la république d'Haïti* [Paris, 1818], quoted in *Journal des voyages*, 1821 edn p. 385.) The northern army was thought by Vice Admiral B. S. Rowley to contain nearly 15 000 men together with a national guard of 10 000 (Rowley to J. W. Croker, 12 October 1810, PRO Adm 1/261). The figure for the kingdom of 18 000 was mentioned in the memorandum referred to in n. 7 above.

13 P. V. Vastey (Baron de Vastey), *An Essay on the Causes of the Revolution and Civil Wars of Haiti* (Exeter, 1823), p. lxxxiv; King Henry, 'Discours', *Gazette Royale d'Hayti*, 19 juillet 1815. [. . .]

14 'Reprendre St. Domingue de vive force est impossible', 'Mémoire sur Haïti', 9 février 1820, AAE CPH, 2/19 and A. Rouzeau, De la république, p. 385.

15 C. Mackenzie to G. Canning, 9 September 1826, PRO FO 35/4. Marcus Rainsford (An Historical Account of the Black Empire of Hayti [London, 1805], p. 360) had come to the same conclusion some years earlier.

16 T. Madiou, Histoire d'Haïti (Port-au-Prince, 1847–48), 3, p. 228.

17 See de Vastey, An Essay, p. 76 and C. Mackenzie, Notes on Haiti (London, 1830), 2, p. 77.

18 De Vastey, An Essay, p. 86. I am grateful to David Geggus of the University of Florida for some of these details.

19 C. Ardouin, Essais sur l'histoire d'Haïti (Port-au-Prince, 1865), pp. 106f.

20 Madiou, Histoire, 3, p. 363 and F. Dalencour in A. B. Ardouin, Études sur l'histoire d'Haïti (Port-au-Prince, 1958; first published Paris, 1853–60), 6, p. 111n.

21 A. B. Ardouin, Études, 6, p. 111.

22 Madiou, Histoire, 3, p. 437.

23 A. Pétion à B. S. Rowley, 23 mai 1810, PRO Adm 1/261.

24 S. Linstant (de Pradine), Recueil général des lois et actes du gouvernement d'Haïti (Paris, 1851–65), 2, p. 245.

25 A. B. Ardouin, Études, 8, p. 36.

26 Ibid., 8, p. 92.

27 G. T. Mollière au Baron le Damas, 8 juillet 1827, AAE CCC, Le Cap (Haïti); and R. M. Dimond to J. Forsyth, 2 February 1837, USNA DS, Despatches from US Consuls, Port-au-Prince 1; and Ragueneau de la Chainaye à Damas, 15 septembre 1827, AAE CPH 2/343.

28 Postscript of 3 mai in Ragueneau à Damas, 26 avril 1826, AAE CCC, Les Cayes, f. 51. The US consul also noted hostility between blacks and mulattoes on the one hand and a general antagonism towards France on the other; T. G. Swain to Forsyth, 25 January 1838, USNA DS, Despatches, Port-au-Prince 1.

29 Early in 1844 General Thomas Hector and Député Bazin led a black revolt in the North and in May 1844 the black general Pierrot declared the independence of the North [. . .] (Madiou, Histoire d'Haïti: années 1843–46 [Port-au-Prince, 1904], p. 167.)

30 Le Manifeste, 3 septembre 1843. Leslie Manigat (La révolution de 1843 [Port-au-Prince, n.d.], p. 25) writes 'Le piquétisme était né fruit de la conjonction d'intérêts entre grands et moyens propriétaires noirs et petits paysans parcellaires également noirs. La revendication axée sur la couleur servait de liaison organique.' His further assertion that this movement had a basically 'progressiste' tendency is more contestable and would certainly be disputed by the protagonists of what I have called the mulatto legend of the Haitian past.

31 T. N. Ussher to Lord Aberdeen, 24 May 1844, PRO FO 35/28.

32 Madiou, Histoire . . . 1843–46, pp. 66, 152 and 148.

33 Ussher to Aberdeen, 7 April 1844, PRO FO 35/28, and P. Bridgeman to Sir C. Adams, 23 April 1844, PRO FO 35/29.

34 P. Guerrier et al. à F. P. G. Guizot, 2 juillet 1843, AAE CPH 11/14; L.J.-J. Acaau, République haïtienne. Proclamation au peuple et à l'armée . . ., 6 mai 1844 (n.p., n.d.).

35 Le Manifeste, 26 mai 1844. Acaau's critics denounced him as a communist; see A. B. Ardouin, Études, 1, p. 24n. and G. d'Alaux, 'L'empereur Soulouque et son empire, 3', Revue des Deux Mondes, 9, 1851, p. 322.

36 G. d'Alaux, ibid., p. 322.

37 Ussher to Aberdeen, 18 August 1845 and 17 September 1845, both in PRO FO 35/30; Ussher to Aberdeen, 7 April 1844, PRO FO 35/28; see also Levasseur à Guizot, 14 janvier 1843, AAE CPH 10/190.

38 [. . .] Acaau au Commodore R. Sharpe, 4 mai 1844, PRO FO 35/29. [. . .]

39 M. J. MacLeod, 'The Soulouque regime in Haiti, 1847–1859: a re-evaluation', *Caribbean Studies*, 10:3, 1970; G. F. Usher to J. Buchanan, 23 September 1847, USNA DS, Despatches, Port-au-Prince 2; and J. Bouzon, *Études historiques sur la présidence de Faustin Soulouque* (Port-au-Prince and Paris, 1894), p. 13.

40 Bouzon, *Études*, p. 56; '*La populace de Port-au-Prince insultait et menaçait non plus seulement les mulâtres, mais encore la bourgeoisie noire*' (d'Alaux, 'L'empereur Soulouque . . ., 3', p. 348.)

41 G. d'Alaux, op. cit., p. 336; and Lartigue au Ministre de la Marine, 23 avril 1846, AAE CPH 14/244.

42 The term *griffe* has two connotations in Haiti. It was the name given in colonial times to a person with one black and one mulatto parent [. . .]. The term is also used more popularly to describe a person with dark skin but with European features.

43 J. A. Firmin, *Monsieur Roosevelt, président des États Unis et la république d'Haïti* (New York and Paris, 1905), p. 372.

44 'Manifeste', quoted in Comte Méjan au Marquis de Moustier, 16 mars 1867, AAE CPH 26/23.

45 F. D. Légitime, 'Souvenirs historiques: la présidence de Salnave', *Revue de la Société de Législation*, 18:9, p. 149.

46 A. Thoby, 'Nos constitutions républicaines', *Revue de la Société de Législation*, 6:12, 1899, p. 8.

47 Méjan à Moustier, 4 avril 1867, AAE CPH 26/60; [. . .] Méjan à Moustier, 14 avril 1867, AAE CPH 26/64.

48 Firmin, *Monsieur Roosevelt*, p. 388.

49 Méjan à Moustier, 23 juillet 1867, AAE CPH 26/100.

50 F. D. Légitime, 'Souvenirs historiques, 1867–1870', *Revue de la Société de Législation*, 16:7, 1907, p. 103.

51 S. St John to Lord Stanley, 7 June 1868, PRO FO 35/74; S. St John, *Hayti or the Black Republic* (London, 1889), p. 119.

52 'Adresse', *Le Moniteur*, 29 avril 1868.

53 See Nicholls, *Haiti in Caribbean Context*, 242n20.

54 J. Price Mars, 'Les cacos', *L'Essor*, 25 mai 1921; Gaillard, *Les cents jours*, p. 58n; A. Cabon, *Mgr Alexis-Jean-Marie Guilloux* (Port-au-Prince, 1929), p. 122n.

55 Méjan à Moustier, 23 mars 1868, AAE CPH 26/168.

56 E. de Courthial à Moustier, 4 novembre 1869, AAE CPH 27/35.

57 T. F. Jones to A. Phillimore, 23 September 1868, PRO FO 35/76.

58 L. J. Janvier, *Les constitutions d'Haïti* (Paris, 1886), 2, p. 345; de Courthial à Moustier, 4 novembre 1868, AAE CPH 27/36; M. Domingue, 'Aux citoyens trompés par Salnave', *La Voix du Peuple*, 6 octobre 1868.

59 St John to Stanley, 7 June 1868, PRO FO 35/74.

60 Cabon, *Mgr Guilloux*, p. 158.

61 Doazan à Daru, 8 février 1870, AAE CPH 29.

62 Adam, *Une crise haïtienne*.

63 Nicholls, *From Dessalines to Duvalier*, pp. 195f.

64 Firmin, *Monsieur Roosevelt*, p. 426.

65 B. Diederich and A. Burt, *Papa Doc: Haiti and Its Dictator* (London, 1969), p. 156.

9

"THE BLACK REPUBLIC"

The Influence of the Haitian Revolution on Northern Black Political Consciousness, 1816–1862[1]

(excerpts)

Leslie M. Alexander

On August 30, 1824, Peter Williams Jr., an esteemed leader in New York City's Black community stood before a group of Black migrants as they prepared to embark on a powerful journey: an exodus from the United States, their land of birth, to Haiti, a new land of hope. "You are going to a good country," he exclaimed, "where a dark complexion will be no disadvantage; where you will enjoy true freedom. . . ." For Williams and his supporters, this was a momentous occasion, when the first "pioneers" set sail from the United States destined for a new homeland where they believed they would find liberty, justice, equality, and citizenship – not only for themselves, but for their children and the entire race. As Williams bade them farewell, he concluded: "Go to that highly favored, and as yet only land, where the sons of Africa appear as a civilized, well ordered, and flourishing nation. Go, remembering that the happiness of millions of the present and future generations depends upon your prosperity. . . ."[2]

As Williams' closing remarks revealed, many African Americans in the early nineteenth century viewed Haiti as a beacon of hope, a land full of vitality and potential where people of African descent could build a new republic, free from the bonds of slavery and racism. Enthusiasm about the budding nation was particularly strong among free Black Northerners, who were inspired by Haiti's status as an independent Black republic. Their excitement grew in the 1820s after the country's political leaders began espousing early notions of Pan-Africanism; the Haitian government openly promoted racial solidarity, and urged African Americans to migrate to Haiti where they could help create a powerful, autonomous Black nation. As the exodus from New York City demonstrated, the Haitian emigration movement blossomed during this era and thousands of African Americans fled the US.

However, the early Haitian emigration movement was short lived, and its demise marked a trend away from Pan-Africanism and emigration among African Americans. In the wake of internal political and economic discord in the new island nation, excitement about Haitian emigration waned toward the end of the decade. By 1830, the Black leadership essentially abandoned emigration and colonization schemes, resolving, instead, to fight for justice and equality in the United States. Yet while most scholars end this story at this moment – the Black leadership's decision to focus their energies on the fight for abolition and American citizenship – it is certainly not the end of this important tale. Ultimately, although the reality of Haiti proved somewhat disappointing, Haiti's image as an independent Black nation was still powerfully important to America's free Black population in subsequent decades.

Indeed, despite the decline of the early Haitian emigration movement, Black leaders remained determined to protect Haiti's freedom, and fought to assert its legitimacy in the international political arena. This became a particularly contentious issue after 1825, because although France finally acknowledged Haitian independence, the United States stubbornly refused to extend diplomatic recognition to the new Black republic. The US government's denial of Haiti's autonomy, and its existence as an independent nation, was particularly frustrating to the Black leadership because they clearly understood that such a policy smacked of racism, upheld the system of slavery, and was a decided concession to the pro-slavery South. As a result, from the late 1830s through the 1850s, Black activists consistently pressured the United States Congress to recognize Haitian independence.

Moreover, by the late 1850s, Black activists renewed their support for independent Haiti by re-invigorating the emigration movement. Prominent leaders such as James Theodore Holly, Henry Highland Garnet, and Frederick Douglass openly encouraged African Americans to relocate to Haiti, and aid in the process of building a free Black nation. This movement had substantial support until shortly after the outbreak of the Civil War, when many activists refocused their attention on the domestic front in hopes that the war might finally bring an end to slavery. Ultimately, this era was a time of hope for Black activists; they witnessed the demise of slavery, and the US government finally extended diplomatic recognition to Haiti. Even so, the United States government's discriminatory policies toward Haiti in the early nineteenth century created an unfortunate legacy for the Black republic's political and economic viability throughout the decades that followed, a pattern that painfully mirrored the United States' policies toward the African American community within its own borders.

* * *

In 1804, Jean-Jacques Dessalines announced the formation of Haiti, the first Black republic in the Western Hemisphere, and officially declared their independence from France. This event was profoundly important to African Americans in the United States, and ultimately had both symbolic and tangible ramifications for the Black freedom struggle in the antebellum era. Yet unlike the South, where the influence of the Haitian Revolution was more immediately felt in the form of rebellions, the response in the North was slower and more gradual. By 1816, however, Haiti played a critical role in Northern Black political discourse. Plagued by violence, racism, injustice, poverty, the denial of citizenship, and a tenuous social status, many newly emancipated African Americans wondered if "freedom" was an illusion and grew increasingly doubtful about their future in the United States. By contrast, Haiti represented the culmination of Black political autonomy. During the revolution, enslaved people had thrown off their shackles and declared their right to self-determination. Once Haiti became an independent nation, it appeared to be the ultimate manifestation of what Black activists hoped to achieve. Thus, Black Northerners who feared that they would never receive equality and citizenship in the United States cast their vision to Haiti and eventually formed an emigration movement.

Significantly, the growing enthusiasm about the notion of Black migration to Haiti was not one-sided. From the nation's founding, Haitian leaders actively worked to attract Black migrants from the United States to their burgeoning country. Haiti's first president, Jean-Jacques Dessalines, vigorously recruited African Americans and even offered American ship captains forty dollars for every African American they brought to Haiti. Henri Christophe and Alexandre Pétion, who beginning in 1807 ruled Northern and Southern Haiti respectively, also sought to mold Haiti into a potential destination for African Americans. When Pétion drafted his Constitution in 1816, he included a special clause that granted citizenship to all descendants of Africa who lived in Haiti for one year, a strategy that would have certainly appealed to many African Americans. Although such inducements did not immediately produce a large Black migration to Haiti, their efforts revealed that Haitian leaders felt an emigration movement could be mutually beneficial; Haiti would gain from an influx in population, especially skilled laborers and sailors, and African Americans could find refuge from American racism and obtain citizenship in a new home.[3]

In the latter portion of 1816, the Haitian emigration movement slowly took shape when activist Prince Saunders began extolling the virtues of the Haitian republic in the Black community. Saunders, a teacher at the African School in Boston, first traveled to Haiti in 1815 after British abolitionist William Wilberforce encouraged him to help establish schools there. Shortly after his arrival, Henri Christophe, the ruler of Northern Haiti, appointed Saunders as the Minister of Education and, over the next few years, Saunders recruited teachers and worked to enhance Haiti's educational system.[4] Inspired by his interaction with Christophe and the positive developments he witnessed within the Haitian republic, Saunders soon became an avid supporter of Haitian emigration. In an effort to spark a movement, Prince Saunders published his reflections on Haiti in a pamphlet widely known as the *Haytian Papers*, a document he hoped would effectively promote emigration among African Americans.[5]

Armed with his printed evidence of Haiti's success, Saunders set out on a speaking tour in Northern Black communities. In 1818, Saunders unveiled his plans for Haitian emigration at two important gatherings in Philadelphia [. . .]. His message was well received in both gatherings and, subsequently, he traveled to New York, Boston, Baltimore, and throughout the North, advocating for Haitian emigration. His efforts were quite successful. Haitian Emigration Societies began to appear in many Northern cities [. . .].[6] Despite Saunders' dedication, however, there was only a small trickle of emigration over the next few years, and it appeared that the movement had hit a stand-still.[7]

Yet in the early 1820s, a series of important developments emerged that dramatically accelerated Black migration to Haiti. Following the deaths of both Henri Christophe and Alexandre Pétion, a new leader, Jean Pierre Boyer, assumed control of Haiti. Boyer's presidency was an important turning point because he successfully unified the Haitian republic under his rule and, in 1822, gained control over the entire island of Hispaniola. As Haiti solidified and stabilized during Boyer's regime (at least in the early years), the nation began to attract African Americans' interest and attention. Although a few of Boyer's predecessors had encouraged Black emigration, Boyer was the first to successfully implement a program that resulted in a full-scale migration of African Americans to the island nation.[8]

President Boyer endorsed emigration because he hoped that Black migration would simultaneously bolster the Haitian economy and improve relations between Haiti and the United States. Immediately following the Haitian Revolution, the US government had terminated all relations – commercial and diplomatic – with the new republic. Although the US eventually re-established trade relations, the government patently refused to recognize Haiti diplomatically. Boyer believed that if Black Americans began to migrate, the US government might feel compelled to extend diplomatic relations in order to facilitate the emigration movement.[9] What he did not realize, however, was that the US government's tenacity regarding their non-recognition policy would not be so easily broken.

Regardless, Boyer was initially enthusiastic about Black immigration and began developing an attractive plan in which he wisely implemented two effective strategies; he articulated a political philosophy that reso-nated with Black leaders, and created a proposal that addressed their most fundamental needs. Although Boyer would later come under crushing criticism for his controversial policies and inept leadership, which eventu-ally caused him to resign and flee Haiti in 1843, he earned widespread support among Blacks in the United States during the mid-1820s. His popularity rested, in part, on the fact that he espoused strong Pan-African leanings. He emphasized that all people of African descent would find brotherhood, equality, and citizenship in Haiti, and lamented the harsh and humiliating conditions that his fellow "descendants of the Africans" experienced in the United States. Even more, he expressed a desire to assist his "brethren" in America who were struggling under racial oppression. As Boyer explained, he had a natural "sympathy" for those of "African blood" and yearned to give them refuge in Haiti: "my heart and my arms have been open to greet, in this land of true liberty, those men upon whom a fatal destiny rests in a manner so cruel." For Black leaders in the United States, who were desperately seeking an asylum for their people, Boyer's Pan-African rhetoric would certainly have held tremendous appeal. Even more appealing, however, were the financial inducements that Boyer designed to encourage emigration.[10]

In June of 1824, Boyer dispatched a representative, Jonathas Granville, to travel throughout the United States and unveil his proposal for Haitian emigration: the Haitian government agreed to pay their travel expenses, provide fertile land, tools, schooling and, most importantly, full citizenship. Boyer declared, "Those who come, being children of Africa, shall be Haytiens as soon as they put their feet upon the soil of Hayti."[11] Jonathas Granville was well received in the United States, and was greeted as a celebrity throughout the North. Although his feelings about America were less enthusiastic, particularly because he was outraged by the severity of American racism, he still toiled diligently in the US and worked hard to recruit potential emigrants [. . .].[12]

Granville's message was so convincing that he won the endorsement of African Americans throughout the North during the summer of 1824. In Philadelphia, Haitian emigration enjoyed widespread support, even among well-respected activists such as James Forten and Bishop Richard Allen, the leader of the African Methodist Church. After Allen began corresponding with President Boyer and Haitian Secretary General Joseph Balthazar Inginac, he started recruiting migrants, and eventually both Allen and James Forten formed the Philadelphia Haitian Emigration Society's leadership. Allen even sent one of his sons, John, to Haiti to assess the movement's progress and provide reports about its success. By early 1825, the Haitian Emigration Society published a pamphlet urging free Blacks to consider Haiti as an option since they would never achieve full equality in the United States. [. . .][13]

Granville enjoyed similar success in New York City, where activists excitedly endorsed Boyer's plan. [. . .][14] Black Baltimoreans also embraced Granville's message, and formed an emigration society shortly thereafter [. . .].[15] Even Black leaders in Richmond, Virginia responded warmly to the blossoming republic of Haiti, and passed a resolution expressing thanks and gratitude to Haiti and President Boyer for providing an "asylum" where Black people could find true liberty.[16] Within the first six months after Granville's journey through the North, between 4,000 and 5,000 African Americans departed for Haiti, and thousands more soon followed.[17]

Although free Blacks endorsed Haitian emigration with fervor, American newspapers expressed a wide range of opinion about the movement. The *National Advocate*, for example, praised the notion of Haitian emigration on the grounds that the government, climate, and social environment would likely be more conducive for the Black population than the United States. But the editor also worried about the long-term effects of encouraging the growth of a Black republic in close proximity to the United States. Moreover, he suggested that the departure of "respectable" Black people could have a deleterious effect on the United States, since the "worst part" of the Black community would likely be left behind.[18] Other papers, however, simply took note of the number of migrants who departed from American shores and predicted that the emigration movement would be highly successful. In August of 1824, the *Maryland Gazette* announced there were hundreds of eager emigrants waiting for the opportunity to make the journey and imagined that Haiti would soon swell with vast numbers of African American migrants.[19] [. . .]

In many ways, American newspapers were correct about the numbers of African Americans who "availed" themselves of the emigration plan – at least initially. Boyer's plan was irresistible to many in the Black community and over the next few years, the Haitian government subsidized the transportation of over 6,000 free Blacks from the Northern US to Haiti. By the end of the 1820s, an estimated 13,000 African Americans had migrated to Haiti. Initial reports seemed favorable; statements sent back to the US spoke highly of the reception they received, and indicated that the settlers were thriving in their new surroundings. One report, for example, indicated that Secretary General Inginac had greeted new arrivals with excitement and a statement of Pan-African solidarity: "because the common blood of GREAT AFRICA makes unbreakable ties, all blacks are brothers regardless of language and religious distinctions."[20] However, transplanted African Americans soon found themselves confronting major problems. Despite Inginac's enthusiasm for racial solidarity, African Americans were culturally distinct from their Haitian brethren in a number of important ways, and they particularly struggled with language barriers and religious differences. The settlers also quickly became frustrated by the process of land distribution, and many suspected that they had been duped. Apprehensive that the government did not intend to deliver on their promise of land, settlers worried that they would be permanent laborers rather than independent landowners.[21]

In the face of these problems and obstacles, emigration to Haiti slowed and, in fact, there was a sizable "reverse migration" of African Americans returning to the United States. Black activist James McCune Smith reported, for example, that Peter Williams, Jr. had been compelled to return to Haiti and negotiate the release of their "disappointed, distressed, and dissatisfied brethren." In fact, in 1825, Haiti's secretary general stated that he believed nearly one-third of the original settlers had returned.[22] Amidst growing disillusionment, there was another blow to the Haitian project. Perhaps partly in response to this reverse migration, Secretary General Inginac announced in May of 1825 that the government would no longer subsidize the cost of bringing African Americans to the island.[23] The government insisted that their decision was prompted by the immigrants' poor attitude and performance, a belief that was echoed by a few Black migrants such as Benjamin Hughes. Hughes, the minister of Philadelphia's First African Presbyterian Church, had immigrated to Haiti in 1824 and maintained that many African Americans had overly romantic notions about what they would encounter upon their arrival in Haiti. In particular, he suggested migrants expected the Haitian government to provide for all of their needs, and were unprepared to perform agricultural labor.[24]

Clearly, the Haitian emigration movement was slowly unraveling. Even so, Haiti's political destiny still figured prominently in the minds of African Americans, particularly after the summer of 1825, when the French government finally agreed to recognize Haitian independence. Celebrations occurred in Black communities across the United States, as Black activists delighted in the vision of a free and fully autonomous Black republic.[25] [. . .] Yet over the next two years, Black leaders began to express serious reservations about the Haitian project.

In part, waning enthusiasm for Haitian emigration was due to Haiti's internal problems. Not only did the government revoke the inducement plan, but Boyer instituted rather controversial taxation plans, a decision which caused severe economic distress and political upheaval. As one emigrant noted, "Ruin stares every body in the face. . . . should this policy of the government be continued, we shall have to leave the Island." Perhaps most disappointing, however, was Boyer's decision to pay 150 million francs to France to secure Haitian independence, since his actions seemed to negate the armed struggle against slavery and caused major financial problems in the fledgling country. *Freedom's Journal* editor John Russwurm expressed his frustration with the "very questionable character of the late transaction with France" and maintained that Boyer's choice had dishonored the Haitian republic.[26]

In addition, there was ongoing concern about the US government's refusal to recognize Haiti's independence. In 1827, *Freedom's Journal* reprinted an article which lamented the fact that Haiti still "seems to hold its independence by a somewhat doubtful tenure." Perhaps in response to US policy toward Haiti, the Haitian government determined that they would no longer unreservedly welcome Americans into their country. *Freedom's Journal* reported in 1828 that Americans would thereafter be required to announce their presence in Haiti, or face considerable fines. [. . .][27]

As a result of tense relations between the US and Haiti, there was little agreement on how African Americans should relate to the Haitian republic in the post-independence era.

Thus, by the end of the 1820s, Haitian emigration was unreservedly deemed a failure. Reports in 1829 revealed that many of the remaining migrants were frustrated and disappointed. One traveler who visited extensively with a group of immigrants indicated that they were "generally, unpleasantly situated, and very much dissatisfied. They complained to me that the proprietors of the lands for whom they had laboured, for two years and a half, had entirely disappointed them . . . and said they had rather be slaves in North Carolina, than to remain there under the treatment they had received since their arrival." He also argued that given the cultural differences between Haitians and African Americans, no further consideration should be given to emigration schemes.[28] [. . .]

However, the decline in support for Haitian emigration was not simply due to Haiti's internal problems, or the United States' complicated policies toward the burgeoning republic – it also reflected larger trends among Northern Black activists who began to publicly distance themselves from emigrationist sentiment, especially after 1830. In an effort to bolster the movement for abolition and American citizenship, most Black activists turned away from emigration and Pan-Africanism and asserted their rights as Americans.[29] Yet despite their rejection of emigration, Black leaders remained in solidarity with the notion of Haiti as a free and autonomous island nation. In 1837, the *Colored American* newspaper printed a letter from an emigrant in Port-au-Prince that celebrated Haiti's progress and potential in order to inspire feelings of pride within the Black community. The article emphasized the growth of political and social institutions and reminded readers that even though Haiti was an independent country governed by Black people, it was recognized throughout Europe as a free country. [. . .] In the following year, the *Colored American* again rejoiced in Haiti's accomplishments noting, in particular, the republic's increasing success in building their infrastructure including commerce and agricultural development, as well as the creation of schools, roads, and other institutions. [. . .][30]

As the 1830s progressed, however, Black activists became increasingly frustrated with Haiti's position in the international political scene. In particular, they were enraged by the US government's obstinate refusal to recognize Haiti's existence [. . .]. Southerners worried that recognizing Haiti would be a tacit endorsement of slave rebellion and therefore ferociously opposed the idea of establishing formal diplomatic relations with the Black republic.[31] By the late 1830s, however, Black leaders' opposition to the government's stance was mounting.

In fact, Black activists' strong endorsement of Haitian independence remained consistent throughout the antebellum era. Theirs was a position deeply connected to the Black freedom struggle in the United States, since the US' denial of Haiti not only threatened the notion of Black autonomy, but it also bolstered the South's mission to strengthen slavery. As a result, in 1837, Charles Ray, editor of the *Colored American*, expressed his frustration about the government's policy toward Haiti in the pages of his own newspaper. "In most other countries we have ministers, or at least consuls, to watch over the interests of our merchants; but to send a minister or consul to St. Domingo, would be so revolting to the feelings of our Southern brethren, that they would probably threaten to dissolve the Union. . . ." In 1838, he issued another editorial emphasizing the importance of Haitian independence, and pleading with Black activists to pressure the US government to honor their status as a legitimate nation: "[. . .] Every patriotic and philanthropic citizen should petition Congress for the recognition of Haitien Independence. If it is important that we should have amicable relations and interchange national courtesies with any nation, it is so in regard to Haiti, a country that has won its freedom and independence and established them against the world."[32]

[. . .]

Beyond the issue of Southern racism, Ray also argued that the United States' position was completely unjustified since Haiti had been independent for more than thirty years, they had established themselves as a democratic republic, and the US profited tremendously from their trade relationship with Haiti. [. . .] Moreover, after the Haitian government imposed taxes on all commercial interactions with countries that refused to acknowledge them, the US position began to border on the absurd. "It is our *interest* to acknowledge Haitian independence, because . . . we actually pay *one hundred and one thousand dollars* per annum, rather than acknowledge her to be – what she is without our acknowledgment – an independent power."[33]

Significantly, the *Colored American* newspaper used a third strategy to highlight the contradiction of the United States' policy. Ray argued that the government was, in fact, obligated to honor Haitian independence because the US had won its own independence during the Revolutionary War only due to the participation of soldiers from Saint Domingue.

> But there is another and a stronger reason why we should be foremost in recognizing Haytian independence. [. . .] In our late war with Great Britain, it will be remembered that the most glorious event was the battle of New Orleans, on January 8th, 1815. . . . In that action, 200 men or nearly ONE-SEVENTH PART OF THE TROOPS ENGAGED, WERE VOLUNTEERS FROM ST. DOMINGO! And these men, in Gen. Jackson's own words— 'manifested great bravery' in the action.[34]

Despite the obvious logic in the Black leadership's argument, the US government [. . .] persisted in their nonsensical arrangement with Haiti;

they continued to participate in commercial endeavors, but turned a blind eye toward the republic in all diplomatic matters.

As a result, by the end of the 1830s, as Black activists and White abolitionists grew increasingly frustrated with governmental policy at home and abroad, they bombarded Congress with petitions demanding Haiti's recognition. In fact, between 1838 and 1839, Congress received more than 200 petitions in favor of Haitian independence.[35] While petitioning was a form of political activism that Black leaders had used since the colonial era, it was a particularly strategic method in this case because it simultaneously achieved two goals. Not only did it force Congress to address the issue of Haiti, it also placed the issue of slavery on the Congressional agenda at a time when there was a "gag rule" in effect against all anti-slavery petitions.[36] Southern politicians actually saw right through this attempted ruse, and responded angrily to this movement. [. . .][37]

Southern opposition to Haiti increased when Congressman (and former President) John Quincy Adams petitioned Congress to recognize Haiti. Although Adams had not extended diplomatic relations to Haiti during his reign as President, in 1839 he was finally willing to concede his earlier views. In so doing, however, Adams suffered severe attacks from his colleagues. [. . .] As the decade of the 1840s dawned, Jean Pierre Boyer and his fledgling republic remained diplomatically isolated from the United States.

Perhaps due to their frustrating defeat in the halls of Congress, abolitionists were comparatively silent about Haiti in the 1840s. Yet Black activists did their best to keep Haiti's interests in the public discourse. In 1841, for example, James McCune Smith – abolitionist, suffragist, and physician – delivered a compelling speech about Haiti, in which he presented his own historical timeline, documenting the events of the Haitian Revolution. [. . .] In his conclusion, Smith suggested that Americans had something to learn from the Haitian example: "far from being scenes of indiscriminate massacre from which we should turn our eyes in horror, these revolutions constitute an epoch worthy of the anxious study of every American citizen."[38] Unfortunately, Smith's argument became more difficult to make in the years that followed. Beginning in 1843, there were a series of military coups in Haiti. President Boyer was driven into exile, and over the next several years there were numerous short-lived presidencies culminating in the election of Faustin Élie Soulouque in 1847.

Once the political turmoil temporarily stabilized, Black activists began, again, to lodge their complaints about the US government's policy towards Haiti. As in previous years, critics clearly identified the link between Southern slaveholders' political power and the persistence of racism, both of which determined US relations with Haiti. In 1849, abolitionist and newspaper editor Samuel Ringgold Ward attacked the government for its blatantly racist policies: "Now one of the 'customs' of our Government is to refuse to acknowledge the independence of a Republic, the majority of whose citizens are black men, lest such an acknowledgement should offend negro haters in Washington by introducing a black minister into the society of the Capitol [. . .]."[39] Similarly, Frederick Douglass unabashedly blamed slaveholders, the system of slavery, and racism for the government's tenacious refusal to establish diplomatic relations with Haiti: "Our Government, under the influence of the violent slaveholders, has stubbornly refused to recognize Haiti, and thus severely injured the flourishing commerce we once carried on with that Republic . . . This is really too contemptible for a Government that has any pretensions to common intelligence. It is paying rather too much to gratify the *colorphobia* of a few fanatics." [. . .][40]

While Black activists continued to lambast the US government's non-recognition of Haiti, and contrasted free democratic Haiti with the tyrannical slaveocracy in the southern United States, this argument became more difficult to make, as Faustin Soulouque's rule became increasingly despotic. Late in 1849, President Soulouque was named Emperor Faustin I, and was officially crowned in 1852. This was not simply a change in name. The decision to embrace the title of emperor was a reflection of the fact that the Haitian government was moving away from its democratic republican values toward the vision of an empire. Faustin I emphasized class hierarchy, created a secret police and a personal army to destroy his opponents, and the government became more imperialistic in its foreign relations. Most notably, Faustin I launched a series of attacks against Santo Domingo, which had gained its independence in 1844. In the face of such disturbing political trends, Black activists found it difficult, although not impossible, to criticize American policy. In 1850, Frederick Douglass publicly blamed the US government for the political problems in Haiti. In his view, Faustin only turned to despotism because the US and other nations refused to acknowledge Haitian independence.

> What has our Government done in the Case of Haiti? It has scouted, with the most provoking contempt, any act, looking to welcome the Black Republic into the sisterhood of nations, until at length, that Republic, disgusted with the very name of Republicanism, abandoned all show of it; and put on the robes of Imperialism, finding as she has found, *far* more justice, honor, and magnanimity among European despots, than she has been able to find among American Democrats.[41]

In this clever reflection, Douglass not only distanced himself from Faustin's policies, but diverted attention away from Haiti's internal problems onto the failure of America's foreign policy.

Fortunately, Haiti's diplomatic case finally received some additional support in 1852. Despite Faustin I's controversial policies, a group of White Boston merchants petitioned Congress to recognize Haiti.[42]

Although the businessmen's actions were driven solely by their commercial interests and financial investments in Haiti, rather than anti-slavery principles, Black activists and their White abolitionist allies seized upon this development as an opportunity to advance their cause. [. . .] The petition was denied, and nearly a decade would pass before the United States finally recognized Haiti.

Regardless of such setbacks, anti-slavery advocates continued to press the issue of Haiti's diplomatic status. In 1855, both Frederick Douglass and Senator Charles Sumner delivered searing critiques of the US government's non-recognition policy, both blaming (as their predecessors had) the "Slave Power" and racial discrimination for Haiti's position as a diplomatic outcast. [. . .][43]

It was, perhaps, largely due to these very issues – the "Slave Power" and the tenacity of American racism – that by the 1850s some Black leaders demonstrated their support for Haiti, and their frustration with the United States by revisiting the emigration movement. [. . .] In 1853, Boston shipping tycoon Benjamin Cutler Clark advocated for emigration in a publication entitled "Plea for Haiti," and in the same year Black activist James Theodore Holly made a brief endorsement for emigration at a national convention. Holly continued to push the notion of Haitian emigration at the 1854 National Emigration Convention, which activist Martin Delany organized in Cleveland. [. . .] The Convention's National Board of Commissioners imbued Holly with the power to assess conditions in Haiti and determine the feasibility of a large-scale migration.[44]

Thus, in 1855, Holly departed for Haiti and during his visit was afforded the opportunity to meet with Faustin I. Holly presented the Haitian government with a detailed plan for emigration, including requests for land, citizenship, religious freedom, exemption from military service, and a series of other financial inducements. Unfortunately, however, the emperor was reluctant to agree to all of the terms, and instead provided a vague, obligatory statement in which he simply noted that the Haitian government would always be receptive to African American migrants. Despite Faustin I's less than enthusiastic response, Holly continued to champion the virtues of Haitian emigration upon his return to the United States.[45]

For the next two years, Holly attempted to seek support – both financial and political – for his endeavor. Yet it was not until 1857 that his movement began to garner support. In that year, he published a pamphlet about the Haitian Revolution and the benefits of emigration in which he argued that African Americans in the US should unite with the people of Haiti to create a powerful demonstration of Black Nationalism. [. . .][46]

By 1858, Holly was traveling extensively throughout the North promoting the movement. On at least one occasion, he reported that several thousand people were already preparing to depart. Moreover, his efforts apparently garnered the attention of Faustin I's government because the emperor sent a representative, Colonel Emile Desdunes, to encourage African American emigration from various locations including New Orleans and Missouri.[47]

Yet before Faustin I's plans were able to fully materialize, a monumental event occurred within the Haitian government. In January of 1859, Emperor Faustin I was deposed by a military coup d'état. Fabre Geffrard led a successful revolt against the Haitian leadership, ousted Faustin I, and re-established a republican government. Within days, Faustin I's removal was celebrated in the abolitionist newspaper *National Era*, and American newspapers watched the developments over the next several months with keen interest.[48] The *New York Times*, for example, initially expressed reservations about the viability of Geffrard's new government, implying in veiled language that Americans should not have high expectations about the potential of any Black-led government: "to look for a stable Republican government in that part of the Island, would be to anticipate more from its peculiar inhabitants than experience has taught us to expect from other republics of mixed white and African races, and certainly more than we are prepared to hope for from such a population as that of Hayti."[49]

Just a few months later, however, the *New York Times* was decidedly more supportive. The editor highlighted the Haitian population's widespread enthusiasm about Geffrard, and lauded the new government for its efforts to repair the damage that Faustin I's regime had done to Haiti's economy and infrastructure. Moreover, the article claimed that there had never been a "better commencement" to a new government and predicted that Haiti would "thrive under President Geffrard's rule." Perhaps the newspaper's change of heart was motivated by Geffrard's emigration program. In the spring of 1859, President Geffrard unveiled an incentive program that was nearly identical to President Boyer's plan nearly thirty years prior. [. . .] The *New York Times* marveled at the program, and repeatedly expressed bewilderment about why African Americans would choose to stay in the United States if Haiti was a viable option. Why, one article posed, would Black people remain "obstinately averse to emigration," when they are treated as an "inferior caste in the Free as well as the Slave States?" [. . .] Clearly, the editor argued, free Blacks should avail themselves of Geffrard's offer and escape to a country where they could find relief from the "prejudice which crushes him here."[50]

Throughout the summer of 1859, American newspapers such as the *Daily National Intelligencer* expressed enthusiasm for Geffrard's government and the prospect of Haitian emigration. [. . .] The *Times* also reprinted a lengthy document, which one of Geffrard's representatives had issued, entitled "Call for Emigration." The call highlighted the emigration plan's main stipulations, all of which addressed the main concerns that emanated from within the Black community. Geffrard emphasized Haiti's rich natural resources, and offered financial incentives (including free transportation and lodging), religious freedom, education, and exemption from military service. Perhaps most significantly, however, his message echoed the early Pan-African sentiment that Boyer had articulated in the 1820s. He stated his sincere desire to help African Americans escape the bonds of slavery and racism, and provide them with equality and citizenship.[51] [. . .]

By the end of 1861, approximately 3,000 African Americans had departed for Haiti from various regions throughout the United States. American newspapers closely monitored their exodus from city seaports, and regularly published appeals from James Redpath that celebrated the emigration movement and encouraged more African Americans to participate. [. . .] As a result, in October of 1861, the *Daily National Intelligencer* boldly declared: "The Haytien emigration movement is a success."[52]

However, many in the Black community vehemently disagreed. There was considerable hostility within the Black leadership toward the notion of emigration, particularly after the Civil War erupted. Early in 1861, Black activists began expressing their frustration with the Haitian emigration scheme. George Downing denounced the movement on the grounds that it was attempting to "create in the minds of the colored people the impression that they cannot be anything in this country." Likewise, James McCune Smith [. . .] pointed out that since a similar plan had failed in the 1820s, Black Americans should not be unceremoniously "dumped on the shores of Hayti," especially because, in his view, it was obvious that Black people wanted to remain in the United States and fight for abolition and citizenship. [. . .][53]

Perhaps the most powerful voice opposing Haitian emigration was Frederick Douglass, even though he briefly contemplated emigration. In the spring of 1861, Douglass toyed with the notion of Haitian emigration, despite his previously strong anti-emigrationist views. Apparently Douglass had grown despondent about political setbacks in the 1850s, particularly the Fugitive Slave Act and the Dred Scott decision, and had arrived at the painful conclusion that free Blacks might need to consider opportunities elsewhere. [. . .] As a result, in March of 1861, Frederick Douglass agreed to accompany Theodore Holly on a mission to investigate conditions in Haiti. Douglass sadly admitted, "We can raise no objection to the present movement towards Hayti. . . . We can no longer throw our little influence against a measure which may prove highly advantageous to many families, and of much service to the Haytian Republic."[54] [. . .]

Yet, in a powerful stroke of fate, Douglass never made the journey to Haiti; before they had a chance to embark, shots were fired at Fort Sumter and the Civil War commenced. The war prompted Douglass and many other Black leaders to relinquish their emigration schemes and refocus attention on the United States, in hopes that slavery might be vanquished. [. . .] As Douglass explained, "This is no time for us to leave the country

... We shall stay here and watch the current of events, and serve the cause of freedom and mankind." In July of 1861, Frederick Douglass declared bluntly [. . .], "I am not an Emigrationist."[55]

In many ways, Frederick Douglass' ideological shift reflects the predominant pattern among Black leaders; even those who initially endorsed Haitian emigration soon became consumed with the possible demise of slavery following the outbreak of the Civil War, and quickly shifted their attention back to the domestic scene. Moreover, anti-emigrationist sentiment was also bolstered by increasing reports about similar problems that had plagued the movement in the 1820s. Emigrants sent messages back to the United States about poor conditions, flawed land distribution programs, and conflict between Black settlers and Haitians – especially linguistic and religious differences. [. . .] As in previous decades, the enthusiasm for emigration eventually disappeared.[56]

Finally, more than a year after the Civil War commenced, the Haitian emigration movement reached a definitive end. Even staunch emigrationists had a change of heart.[57] [. . .] James Monroe Whitfield, the editor of the pro-emigration newspaper, the *Afric-American Repository*, recanted his earlier endorsement for emigration in 1862. Although he previously claimed that Black American patriots were "fools," Whitfield pleaded with free Black men to enlist in the military so the Union could have "the greatest and most valiant army the world ever saw."[58] Founding members of the Haytian Emigration Bureau, such as James Redpath and H. Ford Douglass, also severed their relationships with the movement; Douglass enlisted in the Union army, and Redpath became a military correspondent.[59] As a result, by the end of 1862, it was clear that most activists had abandoned the Haitian emigration project and were refocusing their energy on fighting slavery in the United States.

Ironically, however, the year 1862 also signaled the dawn of new hope for the Haitian people. At long last, the United States government finally agreed to recognize Haiti's independence and extend official diplomatic relations. Once the South seceded from the Union, there was no longer any compelling reason for the US to ignore Haiti's existence. Moreover, in late 1861, President Lincoln received communication from the government's commercial agent in Port-au-Prince that the American economy would suffer if the Union continued to deny Haiti's independence. As he explained, the government's non-recognition policy was "altogether disastrous to the interests of our commerce, and almost destroys the political influence of our government and its commercial agents." As a result, in December of 1861, Lincoln concluded that they should reconsider their position. In a statement to Congress he wrote, "If any good reason exists why we should persevere longer in withholding our recognition of the independence and sovereignty of Hayti . . . I am unable to discern it."[60]

Despite his initial support for the notion of recognizing Haitian independence, Lincoln and the Union government did not take immediate action. On the contrary, the issue dragged on for nearly a year until it finally came before Congress. Senator Charles Sumner, who had criticized the government's policy toward Haiti in 1855, strongly advocated on behalf of the measure, arguing that acknowledging Haiti would be an important step in destroying the vestiges of slavery.[61] Not surprisingly, there was significant opposition to the bill, but in June of 1862 President Lincoln finally enacted the law recognizing Haiti and appointed the first Haitian commissioner. The *Liberator* newspaper celebrated the decision, declaring, "It means that this Government henceforth recognizes Blacks as citizens, capable of a National life; not as chattels who have no rights which white men are bound to respect."[62]

However the *Liberator* might have been a bit too hasty in declaring victory. In the United States, of course, racism and the legacy of slavery proved more difficult to destroy than Black activists and their White supporters might have hoped. Moreover, the complex relationship between African Americans, Haiti, and the United States government persisted for more than a century. Even though the Civil War brought a legal end to slavery, African Americans still had to fight throughout the twentieth century to have their humanity and citizenship officially honored. Similarly, although the US finally recognized Haitian independence, most Americans remained unwilling to fully recognize the humanity and equality of Haiti and its people. In a poignant twist, these struggles were often intertwined and persist well into the twenty-first century.

NOTES

1 The author would like to thank Dr. Kevin Meehan, Director of the Haitian Studies Project at the University of Central Florida, for his extremely insightful comments. My research has benefited tremendously from his suggestions and feedback; I will be eternally grateful.

2 Haytian Emigration Society, *Address of the Board of Managers of the Haytian Emigration Society of Coloured People* . . . (New York, 1824), 3. Throughout this essay, the reader will notice that "Haiti" is spelled in various ways. In the 19th century, Americans used numerous different spellings, resulting in the appearance of terms such as "Hayti," "Haytien," "Haytian," and even "Haitien." In order to retain historical accuracy, the original spellings in these documents remain.

3 Sara C. Fanning, "The Roots of Early Black Nationalism: Northern African Americans' Invocations of Haiti in the Early Nineteenth Century" *Slavery & Abolition* 28, no. 1 (2007): 67–68.

4 James Oliver Horton and Lois E. Horton, *In Hope of Liberty: Culture, Community and Protest Among Northern Free Blacks, 1700–1860* (New York, 1998), 193.

5 Julie Winch, *A Gentleman of Color: The Life of James Forten* (New York, 2002), 211. [. . .]

6 Prince Saunders, *An address delivered at Bethel Church, Philadelphia; on the 30th of September, 1818* . . . (Philadelphia, 1818); Prince Saunders, *A Memoir Presented to The American Convention For Promoting the Abolition of Slavery, and Improving the Condition of the African Race* (Philadelphia, 1818); Horton, *In Hope of Liberty*, 192; Winch, *A Gentleman of Color*, 212.

7 Floyd J. Miller, *The Search for A Black Nationality: Black Emigration and Colonization, 1787–1863* (Urbana, 1975), 75; Winch, *A Gentleman of Color*, 213.

8 Miller, *The Search for A Black Nationality*, 77–78; Chris Dixon, *African America and Haiti: Emigration and Black Nationalism in the Nineteenth Century* (Westport, CT, 2000), 35; Leslie M. Alexander, *African or American?: Black Identity and Political Activism in New York City, 1784–1861* (Urbana, 2008), 40–41.

9 *Daily National Journal*, 25 December 1824; Don E. Fehrenbacher and Ward M. McAfee, ed., *The Slaveholding Republic: An Account of the United States Government's Relations to Slavery* (New York, 2002), 114.

10 Loring Daniel Dewey, *Correspondence Relative to the Emigration to Hayti of the Free People of Colour in the United States* ... (New York, 1824), 18, 7; Dixon, *African America and Haiti*, 35; Miller, *The Search for A Black Nationality*, 77–78; Alexander, *African or American*, 40–41.

11 Dewey, *Correspondence*, 7.

12 *Niles' Weekly Register*, 14 Aug 1824; Horton, *In Hope of Liberty*, 193; Winch, *A Gentleman of Color*, 214–216; Fanning, "The Roots of Early Black Nationalism," 75.

13 Haytien Emigration Society of Philadelphia, *Information for the Free People of Colour, Who Are Inclined to Emigrate to Hayti* (Philadelphia, 1825), 4; Winch, *A Gentleman of Color*, 217.

14 Dewey, *Correspondence*, 8, 9–10, 30; Haytien Emigration Society, *Address of the Board of Managers*, 3, 7; John Edward Baur, "Mulatto Machiavelli, Jean Pierre Boyer, and the Haiti of His Day," *Journal of Negro History* 32, no. 3 (1947): 325; Miller, *The Search for A Black Nationality*, 11; Dixon, *African America and Haiti*, 36; Alexander, *African or American*, 41–43.

15 Miller, *The Search for A Black Nationality*, 78.

16 *Daily National Intelligencer*, 24 July 1824. [. . .]

17 Benjamin Hunt, *Remarks on Hayti as a place of settlement for Afric-Americans* ... (Philadelphia, 1860), 11; Fanning, "The Roots of Early Black Nationalism," 75.

18 *National Advocate*, 28 July 1824.

19 *Maryland Gazette and State Register*, 26 August 1824.

20 Miller, *The Search for A Black Nationality*, 80. Emphasis is theirs.

21 Dixon, *African America and Haiti*, 34, 40; Alexander, *African or American*, 43–44.

22 Miller, *The Search for A Black Nationality*, 80–81; Baur, "Mulatto Machiavelli," 326–327; Alexander, *African or American*, 43. [. . .]

23 *Raleigh Register, and North Carolina State Gazette*, 27 May 1825.

24 *United States Gazette*, 18 April 1825; Julie Winch, *Philadelphia's Black Elite: Activism, Accommodation, and the Struggle for Autonomy, 1787–1848* (Philadelphia, 1993), 57; Horton, *In Hope of Liberty*, 194.

25 *Genius of Universal Emancipation*, August 1825; Dixon, *African America and Haiti*, 31.

26 *Freedom's Journal*, 12 October 1827, 13 July 1827.

27 Ibid., 13 July 1827, 31 October 1828.

28 *African Repository and Colonial Journal*, Vol. 5 (April 1829).

29 For more about the Black leadership's rejection of emigration and colonization, see chapters 3, 4, and 6 in Alexander, *African or American*.

30 *Colored American*, 11 March 1837; 22 March 1838.

31 Fehrenbacher and McAfee, *The Slaveholding Republic*, 112–116. [. . .]

32 *Colored American*, 1 July 1837, 10 November 1838, and 2 February 1839.

33 Ibid., 18 March 1837, 2 February 1839.

34 Ibid., 2 February 1839. Emphasis is theirs.

35 Fehrenbacher and McAfee, *The Slaveholding Republic*, 117.

36 Although it was deeply contentious, the "gag rule" was one of the stipulations in the Pinckney Resolutions, which were passed in the House of Representative in May of 1836. [. . .]

37 Fehrenbacher and McAfee, *The Slaveholding Republic*, 117.
38 James McCune Smith, *A Lecture on the Haytien Revolutions . . .* (New York, 1841), 27.
39 *Impartial Citizen*, 15 August 1849.
40 *North Star*, 5 January 1849.
41 Ibid., 13 June 1850.
42 *North American and United States Gazette*, 20 July 1852.
43 *Frederick Douglass Paper*, 16 March 1855, 23 November 1855.
44 *Minutes and Proceedings of the General Convention, for the Improvement of the Colored Inhabitants of Canada . . .* (Windsor, C.W., 1853), 2–3; C. Peter Ripley and Michael F. Hembree, eds., *The Black Abolitionist Papers* (Chapel Hill, 1992), 5: 302; Miller, *The Search For A Black Nationality*, 114, 161–2; Dixon, *African America and Haiti*, 90–94, 96. [. . .]
45 Dixon, *African America and Haiti*, 103–105.
46 James Theodore Holly, A *vindication of the capacity of the negro race for self-government, and civilized progress, as demonstrated by historical events of the Haytian revolution and the subsequent acts of that people since their national independence* (New Haven, 1857).
47 *New York Times*, 13 July 1858, 20 April 1859.
48 *The National Era*, 27 January 1859.
49 *New York Times*, 19 January 1859.
50 Ibid., 6 May 1859, 20 April 1859.
51 Ibid., 23 July 1859, 21 September 1859; *Daily National Intelligencer*, 2 July 1859.
52 *New York Times*, 26 January 1860, 4 January 1861; *Lowell Daily Citizen and News*, 14 November 1860; *The New York Herald*, 14 December 1860; *The Scioto Gazette*, 25 December 1860; *Bangor Daily Whig & Courier*, 27 March 1861; *Daily Cleveland Herald*, 2 December 1861; *Daily National Intelligencer*, 14 October 1861.
53 *Weekly Anglo-African*, 5 and 12 January 1861; Alexander, *African or American*, 150–151. [. . .]
54 *Douglass' Monthly*, March 1861; Alexander, *African or American*, 151.
55 *Douglass' Monthly*, May 1861, July 1861; Miller, *The Search For A Black Nationality*, 240; Rucker, *Unpopular Sovereignty*, 153; William Seraile, "Afro-American Emigration to Haiti during the American Civil War," *Americas* 35 (1978), 191.
56 Ripley, *Black Abolitionist Papers*, 4: 333–4; Dixon, *African America and Haiti*, 206.
57 Miller, *The Search for Black Nationality*, 262.
58 Dorothy Sterling, *The Making of an Afro-American: Martin Robinson Delany, 1812–1885* (Garden City, NY, 1971), 221–222; Rucker, *Unpopular Sovereignty*, 153.
59 Dixon, *African America and Haiti*, 207; Harris, "H. Ford Douglas," 229–230.
60 Rayford W. Logan, *The Diplomatic Relations of the United States with Haiti, 1776–1891* (Chapel Hill, 1941), 297–298.
61 *The Liberator*, 2 May 1862.
62 Ibid., 4 July 1862.

Section III

FROM THE OCCUPATION TO THE EARTHQUAKE
Haiti in the Twentieth and Twenty-First Centuries

To many foreigners, twentieth-century Haiti is synonymous with the brutal dictatorship of the Duvaliers: François "Papa Doc" Duvalier, whose rule lasted from 1957 to 1971, and his son Jean-Claude "Baby Doc" Duvalier, who controlled Haiti from 1971 to 1986. The viciousness of their reigns, with citizens tortured and their mutilated bodies dumped onto the streets, is widely acknowledged. Yet few foreigners are aware of how the Duvaliers came to power and what preceded their rise. The historical context of the first half of the twentieth century is essential for under-standing the Duvalier period and its aftermath.

This section includes essays on six of the most critical portions of twentieth-century and early twenty-first century Haitian history. The topics they cover include (1) the U.S. occupation of Haiti, (2) Haiti's "second independence" following the U.S. withdrawal and the Revolution of 1946, (3) the Duvalier years, (4) the Aristide years, (5) the damaging effects of foreign-aid "development" projects and (6) the 2010 earthquake. I also survey other major areas of scholarship on modern Haiti (including migration, gender and relations with other Caribbean countries) and reflect on how the historiography might develop in coming years.

At the dawn of the twentieth century, the situation in Haiti had changed little from the last decades of the previous century. Foreign economic control persisted, as did political turmoil. Though studies on this period are less numerous than for later in the century, some very valuable works exist on the period 1900–1915, in both French and English.[1]

Amidst the continuing instability in Haiti, and after decades of U.S. interest in Haitian resources, Woodrow Wilson's administration invaded the country in 1915 (as part of a larger strategy of intervention in the Caribbean

215

that also included occupations of the Dominican Republic, Nicaragua, Cuba and Honduras). The Marines installed a puppet president, Philippe Sudre Dartiguenave, and induced him to sign a treaty legalizing their presence. They also instituted martial law and press censorship, and changed the Haitian constitution to allow foreigners to own land in Haiti for the first time since 1804. Americans remained in control of Haiti for nearly twenty years. The details of their rule – and how Haitians reacted to it – have been the subject of a sizable scholarship, by both Haitians and Americans.[2]

The excerpt reprinted here on the occupation comes from Brenda Plummer's *Haiti and the United States: The Psychological Moment*. Plummer is the leading specialist on U.S. relations with Haiti. Her essay reminds us that current conditions in Haiti are not Haitians' fault alone; the U.S. occupation profoundly affected the course of Haitian history.

In considering *why did the United States invade Haiti, and what kinds of policies did it enact there?*, Plummer notes that the invasion "brought to fruition" U.S. efforts to control Haitian commerce and dislodge European interests. The United States justified its invasion by saying that anarchy reigned in Haiti and that foreign property needed protecting. Yet the nineteen-year occupation, Plummer explains, was "unprecedented in its duration, the racism that characterized U.S. behavior . . ., and the brutality associated with pacification efforts."

The occupation did not proceed unopposed. Frederick Douglass had warned in 1893 that any attempt to invade Haiti would not be received warmly: "Haiti will not surrender peacefully. . . . Haiti has no repugnance so deep-seated and unconquerable as the repugnance to losing control over a single inch of her territory."[3] U.S. policies that pressed Haitians into forced labor to build roads – and drained Haitian coffers to pay American bureaucrats – hardly convinced Haitians that the Marines were there to benefit them. *Caco* rebellions broke out, and an army officer named Charlemagne Péralte organized a campaign against U.S. forces. But by the early 1920s, U.S. counterinsurgency forces had crushed the Haitian resistance, at least temporarily.

The Marines' presence in Haiti also faced opposition from within the U.S. Protests came from pacifists such as Emily Balch, as well as from African-Americans who retained a keen interest in Haiti's fate (see Alexander's essay in Section II). In a 1920 report commissioned by the NAACP and published in *The Nation*, James Weldon Johnson protested that the United States had "sandbagg[ed]" a "friendly and inoffensive neighbor." Where the Wilson administration claimed to have entered Haiti on humanitarian grounds and to maintain order there, Weldon declared that economic motives drove the U.S. presence. Haitians had been slaughtered as a result:

> To understand why the United States landed and has for five
> years maintained military forces in that country, why some three

thousand Haitian men, women and children have been shot down by American rifles and machine guns, it is necessary to know . . . that the National City Bank of New York is very much interested in Haiti. It is necessary to know that the National City Bank of New York controls the National Bank of Haiti. . . . The overthrow of [President] Guillaume and its attending consequences did not constitute the cause of American intervention in Haiti, but merely furnished the awaited opportunity.[4]

Despite such complaints, anti-occupation activists had little effect on American policy, at least in the 1920s.

However, continuing resistance by Haitians – combined with the advent of both the Great Depression and the Good Neighbor Policy (which stressed cooperation with America's neighbors rather than coercion) – doomed the United States' remaining in Haiti for a third decade. The importation of Southern-style U.S. racial segregation angered Haitians; as J. Michael Dash has noted, "the crude, racist American officer" became a standard trope of Haitian literature.[5] In 1929, a student protest was followed by a nationwide general strike. When Marines fired on a crowd of protestors in the Aux Cayes area, the incident enraged Haitians and emboldened the occupation's opponents within the U.S.[6] In the early 1930s, President Herbert Hoover made plans to end the occupation; by the end of 1934, the last Marines departed. Unfortunately, as Plummer notes, "The United States had neither changed nor reformed Haitian politics but inadvertently strengthened and assured the survival of many of its worst features."

While the occupation has been studied in detail in recent works, what happened afterwards has received much less attention. Matthew J. Smith, a scholar at the University of the West Indies, Mona (Jamaica), who is one of the leading Anglophone historians of twentieth-century Haiti, has written seminal work on the period. His research helps us understand: *What happened to Haitian aspirations for democracy after the country's second independence? How did Haiti go from the U.S. withdrawal to the ascent of the Duvaliers?* Because the portion of Smith's work reproduced here focuses on the Haitian Revolution of 1946, it is useful to review what happened between the Marines' withdrawal and the events of that year.

The U.S. exit in 1934 left Haiti with what appeared to be a second independence, a chance to begin again. However, as in other modern decolonizations, even when the United States departed, it did not stop trying to intervene in Haitian affairs. Though ground forces disappeared, efforts to profit from Haiti continued. U.S. banks still controlled Haiti's financial system, and U.S. companies obtained monopoly rights for industries such as rubber and bananas, on land that had been cultivated by subsistence farmers. Haitian President Sténio Vincent, who had been a noted anti-occupation leader, transformed into a close ally of the U.S. He continued the transformation of the Haitian military that had begun under the Marines. Whereas in the nineteenth century, the army had been intended as a bulwark against foreign invasion, the newly professionalized Haitian army became a powerful institution designed to crush domestic opposition.[7]

Haitians who had dreamed that 1934 would give them a real chance for democracy were unwilling to abandon their hopes. The humiliating experience of the occupation had given rise to several different revolutionary movements and ideologies. One of these was Indigenism, propounded by Dr. Jean Price-Mars and other Haitian writers. Price-Mars argued that, reflecting the legacy of French colonialism, the Haitian elite had for too long sought to emulate European civilization. He argued that Haitians needed to reclaim and take pride in their African origins. Other Haitian intellectuals, who had forged ties during the occupation with African-Americans associated with the Harlem Renaissance, echoed Price-Mars. Marxism and trade unionism also took root in Haiti. President Vincent did his best to eliminate these movements; he banned the Haitian Communist party in 1936 and jailed or exiled suspected radicals.

In October 1937, building on longstanding Dominican antipathy toward Haiti, Dominican leader Rafael Trujillo massacred between 15,000 and 20,000 Haitians working in the Dominican Republic. President Vincent's muted reaction to the massacre sparked demonstrations in Port-au-Prince, which Vincent crushed brutally, leading to more discontent. Concern over the unrest led the U.S. Secretary of State, Cordell Hull, to consider renouncing the Good Neighbor Policy: "If we maintain a policy of 'hands off' internal politics [in Haiti] . . . we may well find the situation developing into a state of anarchy."[8] Vincent eventually agreed to step down; after a new round of elections, he was replaced in 1941 by Élie Lescot, a light-skinned Haitian who had been his ambassador in Washington. Lescot's administration enjoyed strong support from the U.S.; however, it became known in Haiti for its corruption and did little to satisfy Haitians yearning for a real independence. Meanwhile, the economic policies of the occupation and post-occupation years had led to considerable migration from rural Haiti to Port-au-Prince, giving rise to a discontented urban proletariat.

In 1946, Lescot's government was overthrown by a popular uprising that came to be known as the Haitian Revolution of 1946. The fall of Lescot offered Haiti a fresh start. Smith's essay "VIVE 1804! The Haitian Revolution and the Revolutionary Generation of 1946" explores the excitement of that year, as revolutionaries felt they could at long last "fulfill the historical promise of Toussaint and Dessalines."[9]

As in so many other revolutionary situations, however, the euphoria of January 1946 was short-lived. Where previously Haitian nationalists had been united in their opposition to the U.S. occupation and then to Lescot's neo-imperialist ties and corruption, the diversity of grievances soon became evident. The revolutionaries splintered into two main camps:

Marxists and *noiristes* (the latter of which was an early version of Black Power, emerging out of the Indigenist tradition). Smith explains that Marxists spoke in class terms: they defined "colonialism" and "bourgeois greed" as their enemies, regardless of whether capitalists were white, black or light-skinned. *Noiristes*, by contrast, also invoked social class, but they defined it in racial terms, as they denounced the "class of mulattoes" that had long exploited Haiti's "black masses." When elections were held later in 1946, Haiti's Marxists lost by a large margin. Given the racial tensions that had plagued Haiti since colonial times, the discourse of black nationalism turned out to resonate much more profoundly with voters. With the failure of a colorblind Marxism, Smith notes that "racial authenticity" became the new determinant of who should lead Haiti.[10]

One of the *noiriste* movement's young leaders, François Duvalier, was ultimately able to use this sentiment to rise to power in 1957 on a wave of popular and U.S. support. Duvalier was a medical doctor who had trained in Haiti and at the University of Michigan; one of his teachers had been Jean Price-Mars. Grassroots *noiristes* hoped that Duvalier's presidency would address longstanding social inequalities. However, Duvalier perverted *noirisme* into a brutal form of government that surpassed even his worst predecessors; it rewarded a small group of supporters while terrorizing ordinary citizens.

Patrick Bellegarde-Smith's essay, "Dynastic Dictatorship: The Duvalier Years, 1957–1986," drawn from his book *Haiti: The Breached Citadel*, is one of the many analyses of the Duvaliers' rule over Haiti. Bellegarde-Smith, who comes from an eminent Haitian family, is an emeritus professor of Africology at the University of Wisconsin-Milwaukee. He belongs to a generation of Haitian scholars who went into exile during the Duvalier years and who continued to write about their homeland from abroad. Because of censorship under the Duvalier regime and the survival of Duvalierist militia groups even after 1986, Haitian emigrés such as Bellegarde-Smith, Michel-Rolph Trouillot, Alex Dupuy, Robert Fatton Jr. and Claude Moïse have been on the leading edge of writing about the Duvaliers; they combine Haitian sensibilities and a deep knowledge of Haitian history with access to North American research libraries and the relative safety of North American universities.[11]

Bellegarde-Smith's essay addresses issues such as: *How did the Duvaliers stay in power, and what was the nature of their rule?* Bellegarde-Smith hardly absolves the Duvaliers of responsibility for their crimes while in office. However, he emphasizes that they could not have stayed in power without assistance from the United States. While scholars disagree about how much aid Papa Doc received from the U.S., Bellegarde-Smith notes that U.S. support for him rested on a core principle of the Cold War era: Duvalier was a reliable anti-Communist. Aside from a brief interval from 1963 to 1966, U.S. aid for the Duvaliers continued, even if sometimes through indirect channels.[12]

After François Duvalier became ill, he arranged for his nineteen-year old son Jean-Claude to succeed him in 1971. Baby Doc faced greater international pressure than his father had, as both Jimmy Carter's administration and that of François Mitterrand pressed him to respect human rights. However, Jean-Claude simply adopted cosmetic changes such as proclaiming a constitution that he never implemented. Meanwhile, he continued the core policies of his father's rule, and persecuted journalists who dared question his policies.[13] Jean-Claude also began what he called an "economic revolution" to complement his father's "political revolution." This included encouraging U.S. investment in Haiti, particularly in building low-wage garment factories (also called "sweatshops"). While his supporters enriched themselves, economic conditions for most Haitians worsened.

A number of factors contributed to Baby Doc's downfall. The lavish amount he spent on his 1980 wedding to a light-skinned Haitian disillusioned even his *noiriste* true believers. As poverty spread, more Haitians fled the country, risking their lives in flimsy vessels and revealing to the world the naked reality of life in Duvalierist Haiti. In 1983, Pope John Paul II visited the country, inspiring dissidents with his declaration that "Things must change here." In 1984–1985, Haitians who felt they no longer had anything to lose began demonstrating; after the government gunned down protesters, scores of Haitians took to the streets in solidarity. In January 1986, amidst a general strike, the Reagan Administration finally withdrew its support for Duvalier. Jean-Claude left the country on February 7, 1986; as Alex Dupuy has written, "The Duvalier regime, which had once seemed so powerful and unshakable, crumbled quicker than imagined."[14] However, as a parting gift to his fellow Haitians, Bellegarde-Smith notes that Jean-Claude "looted the national treasury." Haiti might be ejecting the Duvaliers, but Baby Doc would take their national capital with him to a luxurious exile on the French Riviera.

Even with the Duvaliers gone, Haiti's problems did not vanish. The country entered what scholars have called the "interminable transition to democracy," with Duvalierists and the army working to prevent civilians from taking power. The country also continued to deal with the consequences of the "development" projects that had begun under the post-occupation and Duvalier regimes, in concert with U.S. and international institutions.

Foreigners often look at the millions of dollars that have flowed into Haiti in recent decades and ask: *Is it useless to send aid to Haiti? How is it that we send money there, yet the country remains mired in poverty? Is Haiti simply unfixable?* A flurry of recent scholarship has addressed this question by focusing on how aid is conceived and who it really benefits. Scholars have noted that not only are so-called development programs often designed in ways that do not address the needs of Haiti's poor, but they sometimes exacerbate Haitians' plight.

The PEPPADEP project of 1981–1985 is an infamous example. The program involved replacing Haiti's native Creole Pig population with pigs imported from the U.S. After an outbreak of African swine fever among pigs in the Dominican Republic, the United States feared that the epidemic would spread to the American mainland via Haiti, devastating the American pork industry. The U.S. government, in conjunction with Canada, Mexico and the U.N., applied heavy pressure on Baby Doc in 1982 to slaughter Haiti's entire pig population preventatively; it promised to replace them with American pigs (bought from Iowa farmers at a cost of $23 million). Thinking that this would be an easy way to curry favor with the U.S., Baby Doc complied. Unfortunately, the Iowa pigs were not suited to Haiti's climate; they required expensive food and became sick easily.

The results of this fiasco have been devastating for Haitian peasants. As Bernard Diederich has written, "With no banking system available to him, the peasant relied on hog production as a bank account to meet his most pressing obligations: baptism, health care, schooling, funerals, religious ceremonies, and protection against urban-based loan sharks who would grab his land at the first opportunity." While economists have estimated the value of the lost pig population to be approximately $600 million, Diederich has noted that the "real loss to the peasant is incalculable."[15]

Paul Farmer, a Harvard-trained doctor and anthropologist who is also the founder of the NGO Partners in Health, has led the effort to uncover the tragedies behind programs such as PEPPADEP. One of the most significant aspects of Farmer's scholarship is his use of anthropological methods to capture the experiences of Haiti's poor. Even if some aspects of Michel-Rolph Trouillot's arguments about elites' control of history have been challenged (see Sections I and II), it remains incontrovertible that historical records generally record elites' perspectives, and historical narratives typically reflect these sources. Using written archives, historians have generally not been able to produce accounts of Haiti "from below" (with the exception of works such as Fick's in Section I). However, Farmer and other anthropologists who have built upon his work (such as Jennie M. Smith, M. Catherine Maternowska and Erica C. James) have lived among ordinary Haitians to understand and record their accounts of their historical experiences. These scholars remind us that historians cannot offer a complete description of the past without incorporating the lived experiences of all peoples. Based on their fieldwork, these anthropologists have identified myriad ways in which aid programs (from those seeking to lower Haitian fertility rates to those trying to improve peasants' lives) often do the reverse of what they intend.[16]

Farmer's essay "The Water Refugees" focuses on the human consequences of one infamous development program, the Péligre Dam. The dam was planned in the late 1940s by the U.S. Army Corps of Engineers in conjunction with the Haitian Organization for Development of the

Artibonite Valley; it aimed to produce hydroelectric power for industrial use in Port-au-Prince. Loans for the project, which eventually totaled $40 million, came from the U.S.-based Export-Import Bank; construction monies went to foreign firms such as Brown & Root in Texas. Farmer's article introduces us to the consequences of this project for Haitians who had previously lived in the Artibonite Valley (central Haiti). After completion in 1956, the dam permanently submerged their land, turning them into landless refugees. Most lost everything they owned, and were never compensated.

Farmer's work makes plain several truths about Haitian history. First, he emphasizes the importance of the physical environment and the material realities in which Haitians live. Second, he reminds us that environmental catastrophes are not all "natural" but are sometimes triggered by human actions. More importantly, Farmer's work and the other new studies of Haitian aid programs demonstrate that those who wish to help Haiti must work with Haitians themselves – not only elites – to understand what kinds of projects are most needed. Post-earthquake Haiti simply cannot afford "development" projects that worsen the plight of its most vulnerable citizens.[17]

The nefarious consequences of well-intentioned aid programs are not the only problem that Haitians have faced since Jean-Claude Duvalier's downfall. Authoritarianism has not disappeared after the 1986 *déchoukaj* (popular "uprooting") of Duvalier, vexing citizens and scholars alike. Aside from a four-month interlude in 1988 when historian Leslie Manigat served as President, Haiti's military continued to rule the country. Governing under the pretext that Haiti was not ready for democracy, Duvalierists such as General Prosper Avril unleashed state-supported terror against their opponents. After some truly horrific years, in which scores of refugees fled the country, a new *déchoukaj* in 1990 dislodged Avril from power. An interim government headed by Ertha Pascal-Trouillot (Haiti's first female Supreme Court Justice) was established, and the country again prepared for democracy and free elections.[18]

The victor in Haiti's first free election in 1990 was Jean-Bertrand Aristide, a priest who had been a leader of the anti-Duvalier movement in the mid-1980s. Aristide was a key figure in Haiti's liberation-theology-influenced Ti Légliz (Little Church) movement, and his advocacy of social justice made him wildly popular with ordinary Haitians. Aristide's party, Lavalas (Kreyòl for an avalanche, or cleansing flood), aimed to transform Haitian society. In sermons laced with Biblical passages, Aristide railed against social inequality and warned that change was coming:

> We are all living under a system so corrupt that to ask for a plate of rice and beans every day for every man, woman and child is to preach a revolution. . . . [W]hile the peasant eats his cornmeal mash with his fingers, men and women up on a hill high above

222

my dying Port-au-Prince are sitting at tables and eating steaks and pâté and veal flown in from across the water. . . . It is a violent situation, and one day the people . . . will rise up in righteousness, and knock the table of privilege over, and take what rightfully belongs to them . . . .

Haiti is a prison. In that prison, there are rules you must abide by, or suffer the pain of death. One rule is: Never ask for more than what the prison warden considers your share. Never ask for more than a cupful of rice and a drink of dirty water each day, or each week. . . . Another rule is: Remain in your cell. Though it is crowded and stinking and full of human refuse, remain there, and do not complain.

I say: Disobey the rules. Ask for more. . . . Organize with your brothers and sisters. . . . Keep hope alive.[19]

Such ideals, so contrary to the status quo, propelled Aristide to victory with 67.5 percent of the vote. Yet Aristide's term in office did not last long; less than eight months after he became president, a coup led by General Raoul Cédras sent him into exile. The coup leaders (who became known as the *de factos*) used terrifying measures to stamp out popular anger over their seizure of power.[20] Outside the country, friends of Haitian democracy (including the U.S. Congressional Black Caucus) pushed for an embargo against the *de factos* and for international forces to return Aristide to Haiti. From exile in Venezuela and then the United States, Aristide also conducted his own lobbying campaign.[21] His efforts gradually won supporters; in 1994, U.S. President Bill Clinton, after first trying to reach an accord with the *de factos*, sent the Marines to Haiti with Aristide in tow, though not without forcing Aristide to commit to some neo-liberal economic policies that were at odds with the economic reforms Aristide had long championed. Aristide completed his elected term from 1994 to 1996, then ceded power to his ally René Préval after elections in 1996. In 2001, Aristide returned to power after a vote that some accused of being rigged. As he continued to face entrenched opposition, critics (including intellectuals who had once supported him) began to charge that some features of his regime were veering dangerously toward Duvalierism, including state-sanctioned violence against opponents.

Aristide's actions – and his seeming contradictions – have produced an acrimonious scholarship. *Was Aristide a champion of the poor and a principled opponent of globalization, opposed only by elites fearful of losing power? Or was he a hypocritical demagogue and authoritarian, who came to be justly opposed even by many who had shared his goals?* The November 2009 issue of the journal *Small Axe* offers a window into the bitter debate on such questions. The issue included a forum on two 2007 books, *Damming the Flood: Haiti, Aristide, and the Politics of Containment* by the British philosopher Peter Hallward and *The Prophet and Power: Jean-Bertrand Aristide, the International Community, and Haiti* by the Haitian-born sociologist Alex Dupuy. Hallward, who has taken a more sympathetic attitude toward Aristide and emphasized elites' efforts to thwart his agenda, was lambasted by the Haitian writer Lyonel Trouillot (Michel-Rolph Trouillot's brother). In an essay entitled "Hallward, or The Hidden Face of Racism," Lyonel Trouillot accused Hallward of being naïve about Haitian realities and of acting as an apologist for Aristide. Hallward struck back with a response in which he depicted Trouillot as both disingenuous and anti-democratic. Dupuy, in turn, charged Hallward (and Nick Nesbitt, whose contribution to the forum echoed many of Hallward's points) with being unable to distinguish between legitimate and illegitimate violence. As Valerie Kaussen commented in the issue, the debate turned on a fundamental question: "Did Aristide organize a campaign of violence against his opponents or not? Did he arm gangs of supporters . . . and direct them to terrorize the opposition and the population at large? Dupuy says he did; Hallward says he did not."[22]

The essay reprinted here ("The Rise, Fall, and Second Coming of Jean-Bertrand Aristide") comes from Robert Fatton Jr., a Haitian-born political scientist who teaches at the University of Virginia. Fatton is one of the most respected authorities on modern Haiti, and his essay is one of the most nuanced analyses of Aristide's rise, fall and 1994 return to power. He helps us understand: *Who was Aristide, and what accounts for the opposition to his rule?* Fatton looks critically at both Aristide and at Haitian elites. He agrees with the notion that even if Aristide had been less confrontational in 1991, the dominant classes likely still would have sought to overthrow him because of the threat he posed to their status. Nevertheless, Fatton contends, over time Aristide's government began to show disturbing resemblances to the absolutism of leaders past. Indeed, Michel Hector argued in early 2004 that, because Aristide was squandering the historic opportunity he had to improve Haiti and was frustrating democratic hopes with authoritarian behavior, he was actually doing "more harm than Duvalier" to Haitian democracy.[23] The issue of continuities between different Haitian regimes – and the question of what accounts for authoritarianism's persistence – continues to be a hot spot of research and analysis.[24]

Fatton's story ends before 2004, when Aristide was escorted from Haiti by the U.S. Marines. The Bush Administration insisted that he voluntarily resigned for the good of Haiti; Aristide protested that he had been kidnapped in a new coup. An unelected council installed Gérard Latortue as prime minister (with Boniface Alexandre as a figurehead President); in 2006, new elections returned René Préval to the office of President.

Haiti faced several crises during Préval's presidency. The events of 2008 were especially devastating, with the global food crisis of that year cruelly compounded by four powerful hurricanes. Still, by mid-2009, there was cause for optimism in Haiti. Préval had chosen an energetic and capable prime minister, Michèle Pierre-Louis, who was working with the U.N. and other aid organizations to bring smart, sustainable development to Haiti.

New programs had begun to support women entrepreneurs and develop eco-friendly businesses. Bill Clinton became U.N. Special Envoy for Haiti and appointed Paul Farmer as his deputy; together they set to work with Pierre-Louis to improve public infrastructure so all could have basic health care and every child could go to school. The Obama Administration, conscious of the United States' troubled past with Haiti, made efforts to improve its relationship with the country. As Farmer later noted, "as 2009 drew to a close, there was a sense of progress" in Haiti: "macro-economic indicators suggested a boost in agricultural productivity and the beginning of a recovery from the storms of 2008."[25]

Then came January 12, 2010. At 4:53 pm, a massive earthquake struck Port-au-Prince, creating unimaginable scenes of destruction. Images of the horror were beamed around the world; billions of dollars were pledged to help Haiti rebuild. Foreign newscasters, struggling to explain both the earthquake's toll and Haiti's preexisting poverty, declared simply that Haitian leaders had always been corrupt and had never cared about their people. Even if scholars of Haiti have emphasized the dysfunctional aspects of the country's nation-state relationship, these remarks obscured much of Haiti's past; they linked Haiti's predicament entirely to internal factors while ignoring the long history of foreign interference in the country.

Trying to express the horrors unleashed by the earthquake in a few pages is a herculean task. The essay reprinted here, Évelyne Trouillot's "Eternity Lasted Less Than Sixty Seconds . . ." is one of the most insightful and moving set of reflections written after the earthquake. As a poet, novelist and French literature professor at the Université d'État d'Haïti, Trouillot is not technically a historian. At the same time, as a member of the Trouillot family, historical analysis is central to her worldview. Even while focusing on the human dimensions of the quake's monstrosity, she cannot help but raise the issue of whether historical factors worsened the tragedy's effects. Though many such factors have internal causes, Trouillot points out that for too long foreign institutions have pressured Haitian leaders into implementing globalization projects that do not benefit Haitians. Moreover, Trouillot laments that, as of May 2010, "reconstruction . . . is not taking into account the interests of the majority." Trouillot's ultimate focus is not on apportioning blame, however. Focusing on the future, she issues a clarion call for using the earthquake to reimagine Haiti, so that the deaths of the multitudes can contribute to "a new, fairer, more humane and transparent Haiti."[26]

* * *

Because of its unprecedented nature even in a country accustomed to tragedy, the earthquake will likely be the aspect of Haitian history that will receive the most scrutiny in coming decades. Scholars will consider questions such as: *What factors aggravated the earthquakes's effects? How did experiences vary among different portions of society? What exactly happened, and*

what was the precise death toll? What mistakes were made in the recovery effort?
How did foreign delegations, NGOs and the Haitian government interface, and
why was more not done quickly to save those who later died in tent camps? What
small signs of progress were still achieved? Initial answers are already being
proffered. One critique of the rescue effort's inadequacy has come from
scholars such as Bellegarde-Smith, Fatton, Farmer, François Pierre-Louis
and Nadève Ménard, who have criticized the "republic of NGOs" for
actually weakening the public sector. Felix Germain has also warned that
missionary efforts may aggravate the dislocation in Haiti by convincing
traumatized Haitians that their own cultural practices bear responsibility
for the disaster.[27] Further answers will emerge only as new information
becomes available and with the critical perspective of time.

Another area of research that will grow in importance is Haitian environmental history. Though some work on the topic had already appeared in
recent decades, the relationship between humans and nature in Haiti has
taken on new urgency since the earthquake. In the 1990s, the Swedish econ-
omist Mats Lundahl emphasized how government policies in Haiti had
worsened soil erosion and deforestation, which in turn contributed to
Haitian poverty. American medical historian Jared Diamond, building on
Lundahl in his 2005 book *Collapse*, compared Haiti with the Dominican
Republic, and argued that the former has been more vulnerable to natural
disasters because it has enacted more destructive land policies. Diamond
has attracted criticism for depicting Haitians as "choosing to fail" (for
instance, blaming the Haitian Revolution for destroying Haitian land rather
than the French colonial policies that cleared forests to make sugar plantations). However, new work by Crystal Felima and Jean-François Mouhot,
while more nuanced and historically sensitive than Diamond's, concurs
that human choices have worsened the impact of natural disasters in Haiti.[28]

Another growing area of research concerns the transfer of population
from rural areas to Port-au-Prince in the second half of the twentieth
century. Indeed, the earthquake would have caused substantially less
damage if not for the city's overpopulation and improvised living structures. The exponential growth of Port-au-Prince (from approximately
150,000 in the 1950s to 3 million in 2010) has been studied by Sabine
Manigat and others. There has also been greater acknowledgment recently
that foreign efforts to promote globalization in Haiti by shifting peasants
from self-sustaining agriculture to low-wage factory work contributed
greatly to this chaotic urbanization. After the earthquake, Bill Clinton
publicly apologized for his role in this shift:

> Since 1981, the United States has followed a policy . . . that we rich
> countries that produce a lot of food should sell it to poor countries
> and relieve them of the burden of producing their own food, so,
> thank goodness, they can leap directly into the industrial era. . . .
> It may have been good for some of my farmers in Arkansas, but it

has not worked. It was a mistake. It was a mistake that I was a party to. . . . I have to live every day with the consequences of the lost capacity to produce a rice crop in Haiti to feed those people.

Farmer and others have stressed the importance of rebuilding agricultural self-sufficiency in Haiti instead of seeking more industrial development.[29]

Another area of scholarship that is likely to expand concerns emigration from Haiti and the construction of the Haitian *dyaspora*. Although migrants have left the island for North America, France or other parts of the Caribbean since the 1790s, the increased exodus after 1957 has been the subject of numerous studies, paralleling the larger interest among world historians in migration. Recent scholarship has chronicled the experiences of Haitian migrants in the U.S. and Canada as well as those forcibly repatriated to Haiti; it has also examined the Haitian diaspora from the Caribbean to France. In addition, the experience of being a migrant has figured in works by Haitian-American writers such as the novelist Edwidge Danticat. Finally, new work has begun to appear on diasporic reactions to the earthquake.[30]

Haiti's relations with its Caribbean neighbors will likely also receive further attention. Twentieth-century Haitian relations with the Dominican Republic have already been the subject of much recent scrutiny. Where writers such as Michele Wucker have depicted Haitians and Dominicans as locked in longstanding hatreds, research by Samuel Martinez and Eugenio Matibag has offered a more complicated picture of Haitian-Dominican relations, noting that Haitians are often more indifferent than hostile toward Dominicans, and that even in the Dominican Republic feelings toward Haiti are not monolithic. Matibag has argued that, if the Haitian-Dominican relationship is reconceived, Dominicans can be important partners for Haitians in mutually beneficial development programs.[31] New historiography has also treated Haiti's relationship with other Caribbean islands. Matthew Smith, for instance, has argued that Haitian migration to Jamaica has been overlooked; he notes that several former Haitian presidents found refuge there. One urgent aim of work like Smith's has been to clear up misconceptions about Haitians and reveal the "multi-layered connections" Haiti has shared with its neighbors, in order to lessen distrust and increase the possibility of interregional cooperation.[32]

The history of Haitian women is another emerging subfield. An increasing number of scholars have taken a "history from below" approach to understand the particular challenges faced by Haitian women as well as to chart the rise of a women's movement in Haiti. Work in this area has been produced both by U.S.- and Haiti-based scholars; areas of study have ranged from sexual violence against women to women's role in development projects.[33]

Although scholarship on recent Haitian history might seem most imperative, the early twentieth century should also not be forgotten. Following the example of anthropologists who have written "from below" accounts of contemporary Haiti, historians of the earlier twentieth century should aim to discover how historical changes affected Haitian peasants. The first U.S. occupation is one area in need of such analysis. While noting peasants' opposition to the occupation, scholarship has not been very successful in tracing their lived experience under the Americans. Even studies that offer "Haitian" perspectives on the occupation have generally been based on the views of elite, literate Haitians.[34] While historians cannot interview those who experienced long-ago events as easily as anthropologists can for recent history, Carolyn Fick and Ada Ferrer have both demonstrated that archives can be used in creative ways to approximate the perspectives of those who did not write their own stories. One promising recent project by Alan McPherson (2010) uses U.S. archives to try to understand a wide range of Haitian women's responses to the occupation, from Charlemagne Péralte's mother to Haitian market women. The Haiti Group of the Oral History Project at Concordia University (Quebec) has also been using interviews with Haitian emigrés in Montreal to learn more about twentieth-century Haitian social history.[35]

The rise and fall of the mid-twentieth-century Haitian tourist industry also deserves further study. After the end of the U.S. occupation, and especially in the 1950s, Haiti sought to bolster its economy by marketing itself as a tropical paradise; it competed for tourist dollars with Caribbean destinations such as Cuba, Puerto Rico and Panama. In 1950, the Haitian government spent nearly $9 million on a "little world's fair," designed to highlight Haiti's natural beauty along with its distinctive art and culture. As Brenda Plummer has noted, though many U.S. tourists did vacation in Haiti (particularly African-Americans and liberal whites), this "golden age" of Haitian tourism lasted for only seven years; the rise of François Duvalier complicated the effort to brand Haiti as a vacationers' playground. While some work on the mid-century Haitian tourist industry exists, more could be done to reconstruct this aspect of Haiti's "lost moment" in the period from 1934 to 1957.[36]

Nevertheless, even the best new scholarship on Haiti will not contribute meaningfully to the country's future if it does not find an audience outside of a small circle of specialists. For too long, the existence of a fertile, lively and rigorous historiography on Haiti has been a well-kept secret. It is hoped that the essays gathered in this section – as well as in Sections I and II – will help draw a new set of readers to modern Haitian history, and help policymakers avoid proposing plans for Haiti that only repeat mistakes of the past. Haiti is hardly "unfixable," but its future can be improved only if its past is more widely understood.

NOTES

1 The most important studies on the period are volumes III–VI of R. Gaillard's *La république exterminatrice* series, covering 1902–1911, the first volume of his *Les*

blancs débarquent series covering 1914–1915 and the works by Gaillard, Gaillard-Pourchet, Turnier, Péan and Berloquin-Chassany cited in Section II. See also Plummer (1988).

2 The most detailed study of the occupation remains untranslated: R. Gaillard's six-volume series *Les blancs débarquent* (1974–1983). More recent French-language studies include those by Haitian scholars K. Millet (1978) and S. Castor (1988) and by the French scholar F. Blancpain (1999). Some key English-language works were authored during the occupation, such as Logan (1930) and Montague (1940, first written in the 1930s as a dissertation). Recent works in English include Schmidt (1971), the most in-depth Anglophone study of the topic; Castor (1974); Dash (1988); Shannon (1996); Renda (2001); Pamphile (2008); Ramsey (2011), ch. 3 and Dubois (2012), ch. 6. Other important works include Plummer (1982) and Polyné (2010) on African-American opposition to the occupation. On Charlemagne Péralte, the leader of the Haitian resistance, see Michel (1996) and Alexis (2011).

3 See Douglass, *Lecture on Haiti* (1893), reprinted in Jackson and Bacon (2010), p. 204.

4 Johnson (1920), p. 5, 7 and also Balch (1972).

5 Dash (1981), p. 49, 63n15.

6 See for instance "Marines Fighting in Haiti; Cruiser is Rushed There . . .," *New York Times*, December 8, 1929, p. 1.

7 M. Smith (2009b), p. 29, 14, 22; see also Laguerre (1993) and Verna (2005).

8 Cited in M. Smith (2009b), p. 37. On this period more generally, see M. Smith (2009b), ch. 2; M. Smith (2009a); and Dupuy (1989), ch. 6. On Haitian involvement in World War II, see Auguste (1998).

9 On this period, see also Lundahl (1988), Moïse (1988), M. Hector (1989), G. Gaillard (1991), Verna (2005), Auguste (2006), Bloncourt and Löwy (2007), Munro (2007), Kaussen (2008) and L. Manigat (2008).

10 M. Smith (2009a), p. 246. On the reception of Smith's arguments, see also forum on his work in the November 2011 issue of *Small Axe*, including Smith's essay "In the Presence of the Past: An Afterword on *Red and Black in Haiti*."

11 For more on the Duvaliers, see the works by these authors listed under For Further Reading, plus Diederich and Burt (1969), Hurbon (1979), Ferguson (1987), Abbott (1988), Laguerre (1993), Nicholls (1996), Danner (2009) and Diederich (2011a, 2011b).

12 On this point, see Dupuy (1989), pp. 166–167 and also Diederich (2011a): "being anti-Communist gave Duvalier a license to kill" (p. 3).

13 On the persecution of the journalist Jean Dominique, see *The Agronomist* (2005).

14 Dupuy (1989), p. 186.

15 Cited in Farmer (1992), p. 38.

16 See J. Smith (2001), Maternowska (2006), E. James (2010), and also Kovats-Bernat (2006) and Schwartz (2008).

17 On how development programs often benefit foreigners more than Haitians, see Ridgeway (1994), pp. 123–162; on the importance of NGOs engaging in needs-based activities, see also Zanotti (2010).

18 On 1986–1990, see M.-R. Trouillot (1989), C. Hector and Jadotte (1991), Barthélemy (1992), Barthélemy and Girault (1993) [esp. section V, pp. 153–232], Deibert (2005), Dupuy (2007), ch. 3 and Wilentz (2010). See also the films *Haiti, Dreams of Democracy* (1988), *Haiti, Killing the Dream* (1992) and *The Agronomist* (2005). On women in the 1980s democratic movement, see Charles (1995).

19 Aristide (1990), pp. 8–9 and 34. For a fuller picture of Aristide's agenda, see Aristide and Wargny (1993) and Aristide (1996 and 2000).

20 For a fuller analysis of the violence of these years, with particular attention to gender, see E. James (2010). On the refugee crisis of this period and reactions in

the United States, see Opitz (2004). For detailed chronology and analysis of 1991–1994, see also Ridgeway (1994).

21 See for example excerpts from Aristide's April 1994 speech at Stanford University, at http://news.stanford.edu/pr/94/940419Arc4323.html.

22 See forum in *Small Axe* 13, no. 3 30 (2009), pp. 128–175. For a fascinating analysis of the debate that leans toward Hallward's side, see Bongie (2010).

23 Comments made by Hector in the film *Haiti, Land of Tragedy: Haiti, Land of Hope* (2004). See also the remarks of Daniel Simidor (a pseudonym used by Haitian-American activist and librarian André Elizée) in 2004: "People spent so much energy and effort to get this guy back in power in 1994. . . . But when you speak to people now, . . . they feel personally humiliated and betrayed" (http://articles. nydailynews.com/2004–02-11/news/18258005_1_haitian-president-jean-bertrand-aristide-haitian-radio-station-supporters); and also Simidor, "Aristide's Last Great Disservice to Haiti," at www.haitipolicy.org/content/1943.htm? PHPSESSID =6321cf5e7fe78.

24 See Fatton (2004, 2007) and Hector and Hurbon (2009). Hector and Hurbon (pp. 14–17) provide an excellent overview of different models of the Haitian state's pathology: a "weak state" (A. Corten), a "state against the nation" even before Duvalier (M.-R. Trouillot), a "predatory state" acting as if citizens were there to serve it (M. Lundahl), a state against the peasants, who are constantly trying to escape its reach (G. Barthélemy) and a neo-patrimonial state (S.-P. Etienne). Other scholars who have joined this debate include Dupuy (who dissents from Trouillot's position in Dupuy [1989], p. 162); Fatton, who argues that there were more continuities between Duvalierism and earlier regimes than Trouillot suggested (Fatton [2007], pp. 193–194); Gros (2012) and the authors gathered in Heine and Thompson (2011). On the persistence of paramilitary forces in Haiti after 1986, see Carey (2005).

25 On the 2004 coup (as the scholarly consensus now calls it) and the period 2004–2007, see Chomsky, Farmer and Goodman (2004); Dupuy (2005); Shamsie and Thompson (2006); Dupuy (2007); Fatton (2007); Hallward (2007) and Robinson (2007). On the years preceding the quake, see Farmer (2011), ch. 2 (quote from pp. 50–51).

26 For other Haitian voices on the earthquake and on how to reconstruct Haiti, see the excellent collections edited by Munro (2010) and by Buteau, Saint-Éloi and L. Trouillot (2010). For more on E. Trouillot's historical consciousness, see Mehta (2009); E. Trouillot (2010); Marie Frémin, "Écrire la mémoire de l'esclavage en Haïti: Pour une réappropriation de l'Histoire par le peuple: Évelyne Trouillot et *Rosalie l'Infâme*," in Ménard (2011), pp. 21–37; Clerfeuille (2012); and the works by E. Trouillot listed in the Section I Introduction.

27 See the special issue of the *Journal of Black Studies* on the earthquake (March 2011), including articles by Bellegarde-Smith, Fatton, F. Pierre-Louis, J.-G. Gros and F. Germain; the many excellent articles (including Nadève Ménard's on NGOs) in Munro (2010); Farmer (2011); Gros (2012) and the forthcoming special issue of the *Revue de la société haïtienne d'histoire et de géographie*. Early attempts at capturing the earthquake in fiction include Dany Laferrière's *Tout bouge autour de moi* (2010) and Lionel-Édouard Martin's *Le Tremblement* (2010), along with the short stories by P. Sylvain, I. A. Zoboi and R. Saint-Éloi in Danticat (2010). For an older but more extended critique of the role of NGOs in Haiti, see Étienne (1997).

28 Lundahl (1992), Diamond (2005), Felima (2009) and Mouhut (2010). Mouhut is writing a full-scale environmental history of Haiti from 1492 to the present. For a critique of Diamond, see Louis Proyect, "Jared Diamond's *Collapse*, part 3," posting on Progressive Economics (Pen-L) Marxism listserv (April 12, 2005),

available at http://archives.econ.utah.edu/archives/marxism/2005w15/ msg00090.html.

29 See S. Manigat (1997) and Farmer (2011), pp. 55–56. A transcript of Clinton's remarks can be found at www.democracynow.org/2010/4/1/clinton_rice. On efforts to transform Haitians from farmers into factory workers as part of globalization, see Dupuy (1994) and Deshommes (2006). See also L. Dubois and D. Jenson, "Haiti Can Be Rich Again," *New York Times* (January 8, 2012), p. A19.

30 On migration, see Laguerre (1998), Catanese (1999), Schiller and Fouron (2001), Opitz (2004), Zéphir (2004), Pierre-Louis (2006), Bronfman (2007), Braziel (2010), Largey (2010), Zacaïr (2010), and Jackson (2011). See also Arthur and Dash (1999), pp. 176–208; Danticat (2001, 2007); Munro (2007) and Kaussen (2008). On the diaspora and the earthquake, see Lundy, "Transnationalism in the Aftermath of the Haiti Earthquake: Reinforcing Ties and Second-Generation Identity," in Lundy (2011).

31 See Wucker (1999), Martinez (2003) and Matibag (2003). On the history of Haitian-Dominican relations, see also Logan (1968), Castor (1987), Martinez (1999), Paulino (2001), Turits (2002), San Miguel (2005), Gates (2011) and the works on Haitian-Dominican relations cited in Section II introduction, note 31.

32 See articles by J. Dahomay, R. Silié and M. Duflo in Barthélemy and Girault (1993); M. Smith (2005); Casey (2011), expanded as "From Haiti to Cuba and Back: Haitians' Experiences of Migration, Labor, and Return, 1900–1940," Ph.D. diss., University of Pittsburgh, 2012; and articles in Jackson (2011) such as M. Smith's "From the Port of Princes to the City of Kings: Jamaica and the Roots of the Haitian Diaspora." The quote is from the latter article, p. 32.

33 See Bouchereau (1957), Pascal-Trouillot (1973), Nicholls (1985), Neptune Anglade (1986), Castor (1994), Charles (1995, 2003), *Haitian Women Between Repression and Democracy* (1995), Chancy (1997), S. Manigat (1997), Nérestant (1997), Racine (1999), Bell (2002), Hippolyte-Manigat (2002), Sanders (2009), E. James (2010), as well as the film *Poto Mitan: Haitian Women, Pillars of the Global Economy* (2009). Bellegarde-Smith (2004) has also emphasized the importance of women in Haitian history. Grace Sanders' forthcoming study traces Haitian women's struggle for political, social and economic rights from the end of the U.S. occupation through the fall of Jean-Claude Duvalier ("*La Voix des Femmes*: Haitian Women's Rights, National Politics and Black Activism in Port-au-Prince and Montréal, 1934–1986," Ph.D. diss., University of Michigan, expected 2012).

34 I owe this observation on the weakness of English-language historiography to Jake Lewis, who wrote a fascinating analysis of Anglophone literature on the occupation ("But Enough about *US*: A Historiographical Assessment of the 1915–1934 Occupation of Haiti") for my Fall 2010 graduate seminar at CSUSM on Haitian history. A similar critique can be made of Francophone historiography. R. Gaillard's studies of the occupation focus on Haitian political leaders and writers; Millet (1978) offers statistical information and excerpts from U.S. regulations but not much qualitative information on peasants' experiences.

35 The Concordia project (coordinated by Stéphane Martelly, with the participation of Carolyn Fick, Frantz Voltaire and others) focuses on the Duvalier years, especially on the violence that drove many Haitians to Quebec (see www. lifestoriesmontreal.ca/en/haiti-working-group). The interviews are also being used to understand other areas of Haitian social history, as in G. Sanders's work on Haitian women (see note 33).

36 See Plummer (1992), pp. 131–137; Yarrington (2010); Grace Sanders' forthcoming work on tourism to Haiti and also "Caribbean Carnival: 'Little World's

Fair' is Haiti's Big Bid for Tourists," *Life* (March 13, 1950), pp. 98–108 [available on Google Books].

FOR FURTHER READING

Abbott, Elizabeth. *Haiti: The Duvaliers and Their Legacy.* New York: McGraw-Hill, 1988 [revised edition published as *Haiti: A Shattered Nation* (2011)].

The Agronomist. Directed by Jonathan Demme. 91 min. ThinkFilm/HBO/Cinemax Documentary Films/Clinica Estetico, 2005. DVD.

Alexis, Yveline. "Nationalism and the Politics of Historical Memory: Charlemagne Peralte's Rebellion Against the U.S. Occupation of Haiti, 1915–1986." Ph.D. diss., University of Massachusetts-Amherst, 2011.

Aristide, Jean-Bertrand. *In the Parish of the Poor: Writings from Haiti.* Translated and edited by Amy Wilentz. Maryknoll, NY: Orbis Books, 1990.

Aristide, Jean-Bertrand. *Dignity.* Introduction by Christophe Wargny, translated and with an afterword by Carrol F. Coates. Charlottesville: University Press of Virginia, 1996.

Aristide, Jean-Bertrand. *Eyes of the Heart: Seeking a Path for the Poor in the Age of Globalization.* Edited by Laura Flynn. Monroe, ME: Common Courage Press, 2000.

Aristide, Jean-Bertrand, and Christophe Wargny. *Aristide: An Autobiography.* Translated by Linda M. Maloney. Maryknoll, NY: Orbis Books, 1993.

Arthur, Charles, and J. Michael Dash, eds. *Libète: A Haiti Anthology.* Princeton: Markus Wiener Publishers, 1999.

Arthus, Weibert. "Les Relations internationales d'Haïti 1957-1971: la politique étrangère de François Duvalier." Ph.D. diss., Université de Paris-I, 2011.

Auguste, Marcel Bonaparte. *La République d'Haïti et la Deuxième Guerre mondiale.* Cap-Saint-Ignace, Québec: AGMV Marquis, 1998.

Auguste, Marcel Bonaparte. *Élie Lescot, 1941-1946: Coup d'œil sur une administration.* Québec: Marcel Bonaparte Auguste, 2006.

Balch, Emily Greene, ed. *Occupied Haiti.* Originally published 1920; reprint edition, New York: Garland Pub., 1972.

Barthélemy, Gérard. *Les Duvaliéristes après Duvalier.* Paris: L'Harmattan, 1992.

Barthélemy, Gérard, and Christian A. Girault, eds. *La République haïtienne: état des lieux et perspectives.* Paris: Karthala, 1993.

Bell, Beverly. *Walking on Fire: Haitian Women's Stories of Survival and Resistance.* Ithaca: Cornell University Press, 2002.

Bellegarde-Smith, Patrick. *In the Shadow of Powers: Dantès Bellegarde in Haitian Social Thought.* Atlantic Highlands, NJ: Humanities Press, 1985.

Bellegard-Smith, Patrick. *Haiti: The Breached Citadel.* 2nd ed. Toronto: Canadian Scholars' Press, 2004.

Blancpain, François. *Haïti et les Etats-Unis: 1915–1934: histoire d'une occupation.* Paris: L'Harmattan, 1999.

Bloncourt, Gérald, and Michael Löwy. *Messagers de la tempête: André Breton et la révolution de janvier 1946 en Haïti.* Pantin: Temps des cérises, 2007.

Bongie, Chris. "Universal Envy: Taking Sides in the Trouillot-Hallward Debate." *Bulletin of Francophone Postcolonial Studies* 1, no. 1 (2010): 8–14.

Bouchereau, Madeleine G. *Haïti et ses femmes: une étude d'évolution culturelle.* Port-au-Prince: Les Presses Libres, 1957.

Braziel, Jana Evans. *Duvalier's Ghosts: Race, Diaspora, and U.S. Imperialism in Haitian Literatures*. Gainesville: University Press of Florida, 2010.

Bronfman, Alejandra. *On the Move: The Caribbean Since 1989*. New York: Palgrave Macmillan, 2007.

Buteau, Pierre, Rodney Saint-Éloi, and Lyonel Trouillot, eds. *Refonder Haïti*. Montreal: Mémoire d'encrier, 2010.

Cadet, Jean-Robert. *Restavec: From Haitian Slave Child to Middle-Class American*. Austin: University of Texas Press, 1998.

Carey, Henry F. "The Third U.S. Intervention and Haiti's Paramilitary Predicament." *Journal of Haitian Studies* 11, no. 1 (2005): 88–111.

Casey, Matthew. "Haitians' Labor and Leisure on Cuban Sugar Plantations: The Limits of Company Control," *New West Indian Guide* 85, no. 1–2 (2011): 5–30.

Castor, Suzy. "The American Occupation of Haiti (1915–34) and the Dominican Republic (1916–24)." Translated by Lynn Garafola. *Massachusetts Review* 15, nos. 1 and 2 (1974): 253–275.

Castor, Suzy. *Migraciones y relaciones internacionales: el caso haitiano-dominicano*. Revised ed. Santo Domingo: Editora Universitaria, UASD, 1987.

Castor, Suzy. *L'occupation américaine d'Haïti*. Port-au-Prince: Société haïtienne d'histoire, 1988.

Castor, Suzy. *Les femmes haïtiennes aux élections de 1990*. Port-au-Prince: Cresfed, 1994.

Catanese, Anthony V. *Haitians: Migration and Diaspora*. Boulder: Westview Press, 1999.

Chancy, Myriam J. A. *Framing Silence: Revolutionary Novels by Haitian Women*. New Brunswick, NJ: Rutgers University Press, 1997.

Charles, Carolle. "Gender and Politics in Contemporary Haiti: The Duvalierist State, Transnationalism, and the Emergence of a New Feminism (1980–1990)." *Feminist Studies*, 21, no. 1 (1995): 135–164.

Charles, Carolle. "Popular Imageries of Gender and Sexuality: Poor and Working-Class Haitian Women's Discourses on the Use of their Bodies." In *The Culture of Gender and Sexuality in the Caribbean*, edited by Linden Lewis, 169–189. Gainesville: University Press of Florida, 2003.

Chin, Pat, Greg Dunkel, Sara Flounders and Kim Ives, eds. *Haiti, A Slave Revolution: 200 Years After 1804*. New York: International Action Center, 2004.

Chomsky, Noam, Paul Farmer, and Amy Goodman, eds. *Getting Haiti Right This Time: The U.S. and the Coup*. Monroe, ME: Common Courage Press, 2004.

Clairefeuille, Laurence. "Marronage au féminin dans *Rosâlie l'Infame* d'Évelyne Trouillot." *Contemporary French and Francophone Studies*, 16, no. 1 (2012): 33–44.

Corten, André. *Haiti: misère, religion et politique – Diabolisation et mal politique*. Paris: Karthala, 2001.

Corten, André, and Marie-Blanche Tahon. *L'État faible: Haïti et République Dominicaine*. Montreal: CIDIHCA, 1989.

Corvington, Georges. *Port-au-Prince au cours des ans*. 3rd ed. 7 vols. Port-au-Prince: H. Deschamps, 1992–1994 [V: *La capitale d'Haïti sous l'occupation, 1915–1922*, VI: *La capitale d'Haïti sous l'occupation, 1922–1934*, VII: *La ville contemporaine, 1934–1950*].

Danner, Mark. *Stripping Bare the Body: Politics, Violence, War*. New York: Nation Books, 2009.

Danticat, Edwidge. *Brother, I'm Dying*. New York: Alfred A. Knopf, 2007.

Danticat, Edwidge, ed. *The Butterfly's Way: Voices from the Haitian Dyaspora in the United States*. New York: Soho Press, 2001.

Danticat, Edwidge, ed. *Haiti Noir*. New York: Akashic Books, 2010 [English-language anthology of short stories by É. Trouillot, E. Danticat, and other Haitian and Haitian-American writers].

Dash, J. Michael. *Literature and Ideology in Haiti, 1915–1961*. Totowa, NJ: Barnes & Noble Books, 1981.

Dash, J. Michael. *Haiti and the United States: National Stereotypes and the Literary Imagination*. New York: St. Martin's Press, 1988.

Deibert, Michael. *Notes from the Last Testament: The Struggle for Haiti*. New York: Seven Stories Press, 2005.

Delince, Kern. *Armée et politique en Haïti*. Paris: L'Harmattan, 1979.

Delince, Kern. *Les forces politiques en Haïti: manuel d'histoire contemporaine*. Paris: Karthala, 1993.

Deshommes, Fritz. *Haïti: la nation écartelée: entre "Plan Américain" et Project National*. [Port-au-Prince]: Editions Cahiers Universitaires, 2006.

Diamond, Jared M. *Collapse: How Societies Choose to Fail or Succeed*. New York: Viking, 2005 [ch. 11: "One Island, Two Peoples, Two Histories: The Dominican Republic and Haiti"].

Diederich, Bernard. *The Murderers Among Us: History of Repression and Rebellion in Haiti under Dr. François Duvalier, 1962–1971*. Princeton: Markus Wiener Publishers, 2011a.

Diederich, Bernard. *The Price of Blood: History of Repression and Rebellion in Haiti under Dr. François Duvalier, 1957–1961*. Princeton: Markus Wiener Publishers, 2011b.

Diederich, Bernard, and Al Burt. *Papa Doc: The Truth about Haiti Today*. New York: McGraw-Hill, 1969.

Dorsinville, Roger. *The Rule of François ("Papa Doc") Duvalier in Two Novels by Roger Dorsinville: Realism and Magic Realism in Haiti*. Edited and translated by Max Dorsinville. Lewiston, NY: E. Mellen Press, 2000.

Dubois, Laurent. *Haiti: The Aftershocks of History*. New York: Metropolitan Books, 2012.

Dupuy, Alex. *Haiti in the World Economy: Class, Race, and Underdevelopment Since 1700*. Boulder: Westview Press, 1989.

Dupuy, Alex. "Free Trade and Underdevelopment in Haiti: The World Bank/USAID Agenda for Social Change in the Post-Duvalier Era." In *The Caribbean in the Global Political Economy*, edited by Hilbourne A. Watson, 91–107. Boulder: Lynne Rienner, 1994.

Dupuy, Alex. *Haiti in the New World Order: The Limits of the Democratic Revolution*. Boulder: Westview Press, 1997.

Dupuy, Alex. "From Jean-Bertrand Aristide to Gerard Latortue: The Unending Crisis of Democratization in Haiti." *Journal of Latin American Anthropology* 10, no. 1 (2005): 186–205.

Dupuy, Alex. *The Prophet and Power: Jean-Bertrand Aristide, the International Community, and Haiti*. Lanham, MD: Rowman & Littlefield, 2007.

Duvalier, François. *Oeuvres essentielles*, 2nd ed. [Port-au-Prince: Presses Nationales], 1968 [rare English version published as *Essential Works*, 1969].

Étienne, Sauveur Pierre. *Haïti: l'invasion des ONG*. Montreal: CIDIHCA, 1997.

Étienne, Sauveur Pierre. *L'énigme haïtienne: échec de l'État moderne en Haïti*. Montreal: Presses de l'Université de Montréal, 2007.

Farmer, Paul. *AIDS and Accusation: Haiti and the Geography of Blame*. Berkeley: University of California Press, 1992.

Farmer, Paul. *The Uses of Haiti*, 3rd ed. Monroe, ME: Common Courage Press, 2006.

Farmer, Paul. *Haiti After the Earthquake*. Edited by Abbey Gardner and Cassia Van Der Hoof Holstein. New York: PublicAffairs, 2011.

Fatton Jr., Robert. *Haiti's Predatory Republic: The Unending Transition to Democracy*. Boulder: Lynne Rienner, 2002.

Fatton Jr., Robert. "The Haitian Authoritarian *Habitus* and the Contradictory Legacy of 1804." *Journal of Haitian Studies* 10, no. 1 (2004): 22–43.

Fatton Jr., Robert. *The Roots of Haitian Despotism*. Boulder: Lynne Rienner, 2007.

Felima, Crystal Andrea. "Haiti's Disproportionate Casualties after Environmental Disasters: Analyzing Human Vulnerabilities and the Impacts of Natural Hazards." *Journal of Haitian Studies* 15, nos. 1 and 2 (2009): 6–28.

Ferguson, James. *Papa Doc, Baby Doc: Haiti and the Duvaliers*. New York: B. Blackwell, 1987.

Foster, Charles Robert, and Albert Valdman, eds. *Haiti – Today and Tomorrow: An Interdisciplinary Study*. Lanham, MD: University Press of America, 1984 [esp. articles by Léon-François Hoffman, David Nicholls and Patrick Bellegarde-Smith].

Gaillard, Gusti-Klara. "Les Ressorts des intérêts français en Haïti dans l'entre-deux-guerres (1918–1941)." Doctoral thesis, Université Paris-VIII, 1991.

Gaillard-Pourchet, Gusti-Klara. *La corruption en Haïti: Esquisse historique, 1804–2004*. Port-au-Prince: Éditions Les Antilles/Programme des Nations Unies pour le Développement, 2005 [available at http://www.mpce.gouv.ht/corruption-haitiesquisse.pdf].

Gaillard, Roger. *Les blancs débarquent*. 6 vols. Port-au-Prince: R. Gaillard, 1974–1983. (*Les cent-jours de Rosalvo Bobo (1914–1915)* [1974]; *Premier écrasement du cacoïsme (1915)* [1981]; *La république autoritaire (1916–1917)* [1981]; *Hinche mise en croix (1917–1918)* [1982]; *Charlemagne Péralte le caco (1918–1919)* [1982]; *La guérilla de Batraville: 1919–1934* [1983]).

Gaillard, Roger. *La république exterminatrice*. 7 vols. Port-au-Prince: R. Gaillard, 1984–1998. (Vols. III: *La déroute de l'intelligence (mai-juillet 1902)* [1992], IV: *La guerre civile: une option dramatique (15 juillet-31 décembre 1902)* [1993], V: *Le Grand Fauve (1902–1908)* [1995], and VI: *Antoine Simon ou la modification (décembre 1908 – février 1911)* [1998]).

Gates, Henry Louis, Jr., writer/producer. *Black in Latin America: Haiti and the Dominican Republic: An Island Divided*. Directed by Ricardo Pollack. 51 min. PBS. 2011. DVD; available online at http://www.pbs.org/wnet/black-in-latin-america.

Girard, Philippe R. *Clinton in Haiti: The 1994 U.S. Invasion of Haiti*. New York: Palgrave Macmillan, 2004.

Greene, Anne. *The Catholic Church in Haiti: Political and Social Change*. East Lansing: Michigan State University Press, 1993.

Gros, Jean-Germain. *State Failure, Underdevelopment, and Foreign Intervention in Haiti*. New York: Routledge, 2012.

Haiti, Dreams of Democracy. Directed by Jonathan Demme and Jo Menell. 52 min. Clinica Estetico, 1988. DVD edition, 2005.

Haiti, Killing the Dream. Directed by Babeth, Katharine Kean, Hart Perry and Rudi Stern. 59 min. Crowing Rooster Productions, 1992. Videocassette.

Haiti, Land of Tragedy: Haiti, Land of Hope. Directed by Antoine Léonard-Maestrati. 55 min. RFO/Beau comme un image/Téléhaïti/CIDIHCA, 2004. DVD [on Haitian history from colonialism to the Aristide regime; includes vintage photos and newsreels, plus interviews with Jean-Bertrand Aristide, Duvalier supporters, and Haiti's leading historians and intellectuals, including M. Hector, L. Hurbon, G.-K. Gaillard-Pourchet, P. Buteau, L. Trouillot, M. Oriol and L. Manigat].

Haitian Women Between Repression and Democracy. Port-au-Prince: ENFOFANM Editions, 1995 [translated articles from *Ayiti Fanm*, a Kreyòl-language newspaper].

Hallward, Peter. *Damming the Flood: Haiti, Aristide, and the Politics of Containment.* New York: Verso, 2007.

Healy, David. *Gunboat Diplomacy in the Wilson Era: The U.S. Navy in Haiti, 1915–1916.* Madison: University of Wisconsin Press, 1976.

Hector, Cary, and Hérard Jadotte, eds. *Haïti et l'après-Duvalier: continuités et ruptures.* Montreal: CIDIHCA, 1991.

Hector, Michel. *Syndicalisme et socialisme en Haïti: 1932–1970.* Port-au-Prince: H. Deschamps, 1989.

Hector, Michel. *Crises et mouvements populaires en Haïti.* [Montreal]: CIDIHCA, 2000.

Hector, Michel and Laënnec Hurbon, eds. *Genèse de l'état haïtien (1804–1859).* Paris: Maison des sciences de l'homme, 2009.

Heine, Jorge, and Andrew S. Thompson, eds. *Fixing Haiti: MINUSTAH and Beyond.* Tokyo: United Nations University Press, 2011 [including articles by R. Fatton, R. Maguire, M. Manigat, P. Sylvain and others].

Hippolyte-Manigat, Mirlande. *Être femme en Haïti hier et aujourd'hui: le regard des constitutions, des lois et de la société.* Port-au-Prince: Université Quisqueya, 2002.

Hurbon, Laënnec. *Culture et dictature en Haïti: l'imaginaire sous contrôle.* Paris: L'Harmattan, 1979.

Hurbon, Laënnec. *Comprendre Haïti: essai sur l'état, la nation, la culture.* Paris: Karthala, 1987.

Hurbon, Laënnec. *Pour une sociologie d'Haïti au XXIe siècle: la démocratie introuvable.* Paris: Karthala, 2001.

Jackson, Maurice, and Jacqueline Bacon, eds. *African Americans and the Haitian Revolution: Selected Essays and Historical Documents.* New York: Routledge, 2010.

Jackson, Regine O., ed. *Geographies of the Haitian Diaspora.* New York: Routledge, 2011.

James, Erica Caple. *Democratic Insecurities: Violence, Trauma, and Intervention in Haiti.* Berkeley: University of California Press, 2010.

Johnson, James Weldon. *Self-Determining Haiti: four articles reprinted from* The Nation *embodying a report . . . made for the National Association for the Advancement of Colored People.* New York: The Nation, 1920 [available at http://www.archive.org/stream/selfdetermhaiti00johnrich ge/n0/mode/2up].

Kaussen, Valerie. *Migrant Revolutions: Haitian Literature, Globalization, and U.S. Imperialism.* Lanham, MD: Lexington Books, 2008.

Kidder, Tracy. *Mountains Beyond Mountains: The Quest of Dr. Paul Farmer, a Man Who Would Cure the World.* New York: Random House, 2003.

Kovats-Bernat, J. Christopher. *Sleeping Rough in Port-au-Prince: An Ethnography of Street Children and Violence in Haiti.* Gainesville: University Press of Florida, 2006.

Laguerre, Michel S. *The Military and Society in Haiti*. Knoxville: University of Tennessee Press, 1993.

Laguerre, Michel S. *Diasporic Citizenship: Haitian Americans in Transnational America*. New York: St. Martin's Press, 1998.

Largey, Michael D. *Haitians in Michigan*. East Lansing: Michigan State University Press, 2010.

Logan, Rayford W. "Education in Haiti." *Journal of Negro History* XV, no. 4 (1930): 401–460.

Logan, Rayford W. *Haiti and the Dominican Republic*. New York: Oxford University Press, 1968.

Logan, Rayford W. "James Weldon Johnson and Haiti." *Phylon* 32, no. 4 (1971): 396–402.

Lundahl, Mats. *Peasants and Poverty: A Study of Haiti*. London: Croom Helm, 1979.

Lundahl, Mats. *The Haitian Economy: Man, Land, and Markets*. London: Croom Helm, 1983.

Lundahl, Mats. "The Rise and Fall of the Haitian Labour Movement." In *Labour in the Caribbean: From Emancipation to Independence*, edited by Malcolm Cross and Gad J. Heuman, 88–119. London: Macmillan Caribbean, 1988.

Lundahl, Mats. *Politics or Markets? Essays on Haitian Underdevelopment*. New York: Routledge, 1992.

Lundahl, Mats. *Poverty in Haiti: Essays on Underdevelopment and Post Disaster Prospects*. New York: Palgrave Macmillan, 2011.

Lundy, Garvey, ed. *The Haiti Earthquake of 2010: The Politics of a Natural Disaster*. Special issue of the *Journal of Black Studies* 42, no. 2 (2011) [articles by G. Lundy, J.-G. Gros, R. Fatton Jr., F. Pierre-Louis, M. Orozco and E. Burgess, F. Germain, P. Bellegarde-Smith and M. K. Asante].

Manigat, Leslie F. "La substitution de la prépondérance américaine à la prépondérance française en Haïti au début du XXe siècle: La conjonction de 1910–1," *Revue d'histoire moderne et contemporaine* 14, no. 4 (1967): 321–355.

Manigat, Leslie F. *Eventail d'histoire vivante d'Haïti: des préludes à la Révolution de Saint Domingue jusqu'à nos jours, 1789–1999*. 3 vols. [vol. III: *La crise de dépérissement de la société traditionnelle haïtienne, 1896–2003*]. Port-au-Prince: CHUDAC, 2001–2003.

Manigat, Leslie F. *Les deux cents ans d'histoire du peuple haïtien, 1804–2004: réflexions à l'heure du bilan d'une évolution bi-centenaire*. Port-au-Prince: Éditions Lorquet, 2002.

Manigat, Leslie F. *"La Révolution de 1946": analyse d'une conjoncture de crise sortie des profondeurs*. Port-au-Prince: Centre Humanisme démocratique en action, 2008.

Manigat, Sabine. "Haiti: The Popular Sectors and the Crisis in Port-au-Prince." In *The Urban Caribbean: Transition to the New Global Economy*, edited by Alejandro Portes, Carlos Dore y Cabral, and Patricia Landolt, 87–124. Baltimore: Johns Hopkins University Press, 1997.

Martinez, Samuel. "From Hidden Hand to Heavy Hand: Sugar, the State, and Migrant Labor in Haiti and the Dominican Republic." *Latin American Research Review* 34, no. 1 (1999): 57–84.

Martinez, Samuel. "Not a Cockfight: Rethinking Haitian-Dominican Relations." *Latin American Perspectives* 30, no. 3 (2003): 80–101.

Maternowska, M. Catherine. *Reproducing Inequities: Poverty and the Politics of Population in Haiti*. New Brunswick, NJ: Rutgers University Press, 2006.

Matibag, Eugenio. *Haitian-Dominican Counterpoint: Nation, State, and Race on Hispaniola*. New York: Palgrave, 2003.

McPherson, Alan. "Personal Occupations: Women's Responses to U.S. Military Occupations in Latin America." *The Historian* 72, no. 3 (2010): 568–598.

Mehta, Brinda J. "Diasporic Fractures in Colonial Saint-Domingue: From Enslavement to Resistance in Évelyne Trouillot's *Rosalie l'Infâme*." In *Notions of Identity, Diaspora, and Gender in Carribean Women's Writing*. New York: Palgrave Macmillan, 2009.

Ménard, Nadève. *Ecrits d'Haïti: Perspectives sur la littérature haïtienne contemporaine (1986–2006)*. Paris: Karthala, 2011.

Michel, Georges. *Charlemagne Péralte and the First American Occupation of Haiti*. Translated by Douglas Henry Daniels from *Charlemagne Péralte: un centenaire, 1885–1985*. Dubuque, IA: Kendall/Hunt Pub., 1996.

Millet, Kethly. *Les paysans haïtiens et l'occupation américaine d'Haïti (1915–1930)*. LaSalle, Québec: Collectif paroles, 1978.

Moïse, Claude. *Constitutions et luttes de pouvoir en Haïti, 1804–1987*. 2 vols. Montreal: CIDIHCA, 1988 [vol. II, *De l'occupation étrangère à la dictature macoute, 1915–1987*].

Montague, Ludwell Lee. *Haiti and the United States, 1714–1938*. Durham, NC: Duke University Press, 1940.

Mouhot, Jean-François. "The Tragic Annals of Haiti," *History Today* 60, no. 4 (2010): 3–4.

Munro, Martin. *Exile and Post-1946 Haitian Literature: Alexis, Depestre, Ollivier, Laferrière, Danticat*. Liverpool: Liverpool University Press, 2007.

Munro, Martin, ed. *Haiti Rising: Haitian History, Culture and the Earthquake of 2010*. Liverpool: Liverpool University Press, 2010.

Neptune Anglade, Mireille. *L'autre moitié du développement: à propos du travail des femmes en Haïti*. Paris: Karthala, 1986.

Nérestant, Micial M. *La femme haïtienne devant la loi*. Paris: Karthala, 1997.

Nicholls, David. "Holding the Purse-Strings: Women in Haiti." In *Haiti in Caribbean Context: Ethnicity, Economy, and Revolt*. New York: St. Martin's Press, 1985, 121–129.

Nicholls, David. *From Dessalines to Duvalier: Race, Colour and National Independence in Haiti*. 2nd ed. New Brunswick, NJ: Rutgers University Press, 1996.

Opitz, Götz-Dietrich. *Haitian Refugees Forced to Return: Transnationalism and State Politics, 1991–1994*. Piscataway, NJ: Transaction Publishers, 2004.

Pamphile, Leon D. *Clash of Cultures: America's Educational Strategies in Occupied Haiti, 1915–1934*. Lanham, MD: University Press of America, 2008.

Paulino, Edward Ramon. "Birth of a Boundary: Blood, Cement, and Prejudice and the Making of the Dominican-Haitian Border, 1937—1961." Ph.D. diss., Michigan State University, 2001.

Pascal-Trouillot, Ertha. *Statut juridique de l'Haïtienne dans la legislation sociale*. Port-au-Prince: Impr. des Antilles, 1973.

Pascal-Trouillot, Ertha, and Ernst Trouillot, *Encyclopédie biographique d'Haïti*. Montreal: Éditions SEMIS, 2001.

Pauyo, Nicolas L. *Haiti: Re-foundation of a Nation*. Bloomington, IN: AuthorHouse, 2011 [translation of *Rebâtir l'État haïtien*. Paris: L'Harmattan, 2011].

Péan, Leslie J. R. *Haïti: économie politique de la corruption*. 4 vols. Paris: Maisonneuve et Larose, 2005 [vol. II: *L'état marron, 1870–1915*; vol. III: *Le saccage, 1915–1956*; vol. IV: *L'ensauvagement macoute et ses conséquences, 1957–1990*].

Pierre-Louis, François. *Haitians in New York City: Transnationalism and Hometown Associations*. Gainesville: University Press of Florida, 2006.

Plummer, Brenda Gayle. "Race, Nationality, and Trade in the Caribbean: The Syrians in Haiti, 1903–1934." *International History Review* 3, no. 4 (1981): 517–539.

Plummer, Brenda Gayle. "The Afro-American Response to the Occupation of Haiti, 1915–1934." *Phylon* 43 (1982): 125–43.

Plummer, Brenda Gayle. *Haiti and the Great Powers, 1902–1915*. Baton Rouge: Louisiana State University Press, 1988.

Plummer, Brenda Gayle. *Haiti and the United States: The Psychological Moment*. Athens: University of Georgia Press, 1992.

Plummer, Brenda Gayle. *Rising Wind: Black Americans and U.S. Foreign Affairs, 1935–1960*. Chapel Hill: University of North Carolina Press, 1996.

Polyné, Millery. *From Douglass to Duvalier: U.S. African Americans, Haiti, and Pan Americanism, 1870–1964*. Gainesville: University Press of Florida, 2010.

Poto Mitan: Haitian Women, Pillars of the Global Economy. Directed by Renée Bergan and Mark Schuller, narrated by Edwidge Danticat. 59 min. Tèt Ansanm Productions, 2009. DVD.

Price-Mars, Jean. *So Spoke the Uncle*. Translated by Magdaline W. Shannon from *Ainsi parla l'oncle*. Washington: Three Continents Press, 1983.

Racine, Marie M. B. *Like the Dew that Waters the Grass: Words from Haitian Women*. Washington: Epica, 1999.

Ramsey, Kate. *The Spirits and the Law: Vodou and Power in Haiti*. Chicago: University of Chicago Press, 2011.

Renda, Mary A. *Taking Haiti: Military Occupation and the Culture of U.S. Imperialism, 1915–1940*. Chapel Hill: University of North Carolina Press, 2001.

Ridgeway, James, ed. *The Haiti Files: Decoding the Crisis*. Washington: Essential Books, 1994 [including essays by N. Chomsky, B. Diederich and A. Burt, M. Laguerre, A. Wilentz, P. Farmer and others].

Robinson, Randall. *An Unbroken Agony: Haiti, From Revolution to the Kidnapping of a President*. New York: Basic Civitas Books, 2007.

Rotberg, Robert I., ed. *Haiti Renewed: Political and Economic Prospects*. Washington: Brookings Institution Press, 1997.

San Miguel, Pedro Luis. *The Imagined Island: History, Identity, and Utopia in Hispaniola*. Chapel Hill: University of North Carolina Press, 2005.

Sanders, Grace. "Women's Movement, Haiti." In *The International Encyclopedia of Revolution and Protest: 1500 to the Present*, edited by Immanuel Ness, VII: 3583–3586. Malden, MA: Wiley-Blackwell, 2009.

Schiller, Nina Glick, and Georges Eugene Fouron. *Georges Woke Up Laughing: Long-Distance Nationalism and the Search for Home*. Durham, NC: Duke University Press, 2001.

Schmidt, Hans. *The United States Occupation of Haiti, 1915–1934*. New Brunswick, NJ: Rutgers University Press, 1971.

Schuller, Mark, and Pablo Morales, eds. *Tectonic Shifts: Haiti Since the Earthquake*. Sterling, VA: Kumarian Press, 2012.

Schwartz, Timothy T. *Travesty in Haiti: A True Account of Christian Missions, Orphanages, Fraud, Food Aid and Drug Trafficking*. Charleston, SC: BookSurge Publishing, 2008.

Shamsie, Yasmine, and Andrew S. Thompson, eds. *Haiti: Hope for a Fragile State*. Waterloo, Ont.: Wilfrid Laurier University Press, 2006.

Shannon, Magdaline W. *Jean Price-Mars, the Haitian Elite and the American Occupation, 1915–1935.* New York: St. Martin's Press, 1996.

Small Axe: A Caribbean Journal of Criticism 13, no. 3/30 (2009), 128–175. Special forum on Aristide, focused on *The Prophet and Power* by Alex Dupuy and *Damming the Flood* by Peter Hallward [articles by L. Trouillot, N. Nesbitt, V. Kaussen, A. Dupuy and P. Hallward].

Smith, Jennie Marcelle. *When the Hands are Many: Community Organization and Social Change in Rural Haiti.* Ithaca: Cornell University Press, 2001.

Smith, Matthew J. "An Island Among Islands: Haiti's Strange Relationship with the Caribbean Community." *Social and Economic Studies* 54, no. 3 (2005): 176–195.

Smith, Matthew J. "Race, Color and the Marxist Left in Pre-Duvalier Haiti." In *Extending the Diaspora: New Histories of Black People*, edited by Dawne Y. Curry, Eric D. Duke, and Marshanda A. Smith, 245–269. Urbana: University of Illinois Press, 2009a.

Smith, Matthew J. *Red and Black in Haiti: Radicalism, Conflict, and Political Change, 1934–1957.* Chapel Hill: University of North Carolina Press, 2009b.

Suggs, Henry Louis. "The Response of the African American Press to the Occupation of Haiti, 1915–1934." *Journal of African-American History* 87 (Winter 2002): 70–82.

Tardieu-Dehoux, Charles. *L'éducation en Haïti de la période coloniale à nos jours, 1980.* Port-au-Prince: H. Deschamps, 1990.

Trouillot, Évelyne. *La mémoire aux abois: Roman.* Paris: Hoëbeke, 2010.

Trouillot, Michel-Rolph. *Haiti, State Against Nation: The Origins and Legacy of Duvalierism.* New York: Monthly Review Press, 1989.

Turits, Richard Lee. "A World Destroyed, A Nation Imposed: The 1937 Haitian Massacre in the Dominican Republic." *Hispanic American Historical Review* 82, no. 3 (2002): 589–635.

Turnier, Alain. *Quand la nation demande des comptes.* Port-au-Prince: Impr. Le Natal, 1989.

Verna, Chantalle. "Haiti's Second Independence and the Promise of Pan-American Cooperation, 1934–56." Ph.D. diss., Michigan State University, 2005.

Wilentz, Amy. *The Rainy Season: Then and Now.* New York: Simon and Schuster, 2010 [reedition of *The Rainy Season: Haiti since Duvalier*, with post-earthquake preface].

Wucker, Michele. *Why the Cocks Fight: Dominicans, Haitians, and the Struggle for Hispaniola.* New York: Hill and Wang, 1999.

Yarrington, Landon. "From Sight to Site to Website: Travel-writing, Tourism and the American Experience in Haiti, 1900–2008." M. A. thesis, College of William and Mary, Anthropology, 2010.

Zacaïr, Philippe, ed. *Haiti and the Haitian Diaspora in the Wider Caribbean.* Gainesville: University Press of Florida, 2010.

Zanotti, Laura. "Cacophonies of Aid, Failed State Building and NGOs in Haiti: Setting the Stage for Disaster, Envisioning the Future." *Third World Quarterly* 31, no. 5 (2010): 755–771.

Zéphir, Flore. *The Haitian Americans.* Westport, CT: Greenwood Press, 2004.

10

UNDER THE GUN

(Excerpt from *Haiti and The United States: The Psychological Moment*)

Brenda Gayle Plummer

In 1915 the United States began a military occupation of Haiti that lasted two decades. Citing widespread violence, anarchy, and imminent danger to foreigners' lives and property, the federal government ordered Marines landed at Port-au-Prince. The Haitian protectorate was unprecedented in its duration, the racism that characterized U.S. behavior in the black republic, and the brutality associated with pacification efforts. Political reorganization rapidly proceeded during the late summer of 1915, despite the uncertainty of President Woodrow Wilson and the State Department as to how to proceed. Many policies that lasted throughout the occupation took shape during these early months. These included the exclusion of European interference in Haitian internal affairs as well as the prohibition of any extrahemispheric exercise of naval power there.

The occupation brought to fruition a process begun years before. Long before the humiliating encounters between Marine officers and Haitian presidents, aliens dictated terms to Haitian leaders. Foreign battleships trained guns on Haitian shore installations before many Yankee veterans of the *caco* wars were born. The depression induced by the military regime's financial policies had its precedent in prior manipulations by expatriate financiers. Finally, the devaluation of Haitian culture by Protestant, positivist, and dogmatic North Americans recalled an age of imperialism that was rapidly becoming obsolete in other parts of the world.

After peace had been restored to Port-au-Prince following Sam's assassination, the U.S. Navy and State Department, through their field representative, Rear Admiral William B. Caperton, cast about for a suitable Haitian president to accept the terms they planned to dictate. Few volunteers could be found. Their choice finally settled on a willing candidate, Sudre Dartiguenave, president of the Haitian senate. The legislature duly held elections, this time under the duress, as Hans Schmidt points out, of the U.S. Marines rather than the *caco* armies of the past. Dartiguenave's election was soon followed by the promulgation of a Haitian-American treaty, passed without comment by the U.S. Senate in February 1916, which "legalized" the occupation. Its provisions included financial oversight by U.S. officials, the establishment of a native constabulary with Marine officers, federal supervision of public works, and the settlement of all foreign claims. Clearly the new government would boast scant local support.[1]

Haitian nationalists greeted the occupation with revulsion. Peasant insurgents mobilized in 1915 to repel the invaders. They were led by a handful of militant leaders, some of them educated, like Charlemagne Péralte, who as commander of Léogâne under the Sam government, had refused to surrender control of his district to the Marines. Outgunned, however, peasant guerrillas signed an armistice in September. Having ended armed resistance for the time being, occupation officials then went to work on the Haitian constitution. The traditional refusal to allow foreign ownership of land, embedded in the constitution of 1889, was then in effect. Foreign powers had long resented this clause, and development experts considered it a cause of the dearth of available investment capital. The Haitian legislature's refusal to approve a document drafted in the State Department in 1917 led to the twelve-year suspension of that body, effected dramatically by a U.S. Marine officer under President Dartiguenave's orders. A "popular" plebiscite in which less than 5 percent of the electorate participated approved the U.S.-endorsed constitution.[2]

Many other U.S. policies proved unpopular, such as the revival of the corvée, forced labor, which required peasants to work on road gangs away from their homes under armed supervision with nominal pay and inadequate food and lodging. Foreign guns also safeguarded a national bank that operated only for aliens' benefit. Handsome salaries for imported bureaucrats drained the Haitian treasury, while indigenous functionaries received less remuneration for the same work. Newly arrived U.S. personnel insisted on racial segregation and introduced it into hotels, restaurants, and clubs. Curfews, press censorship, and intensive surveillance made Haitian dissidence risky.[3]

These conditions and the failure to improve the local economy led to the resurgence of cacoism in 1919. Many of those who had deplored the guerrillas three years previously and assisted in routing them now saw them as heroes. Independent bands attacked foreign installations in the countryside, and especially targeted the properties of the Haitian-American Sugar Company and its clients. A thousand men massed in the frontier district of Hinche, under Péralte's command, and in Lascahobas. Raids on Port-au-Prince involved assassinations of selected prominent citizens, looting, and the capture of hostages for ransom. U.S. authorities realized that collusion between the cacos and urban residents facilitated these activities.[4]

The occupation forces responded by launching counterinsurgency strikes. Marines razed settlements and shot those believed to be rebels and bandits. Military officials acknowledged the deaths of over three thousand persons in these conflicts. Soldiers also assaulted and harassed urban residents. Abuse took on a particularly racial character. Marines tightened security in Port-au-Prince while initiating a new rural campaign. The *caco* war of 1919–20 was vicious and hard fought. Near Croix-de-Bouquets, just minutes by motor from Port-au-Prince, insurgents killed four Haitian civil engineers, whom they considered collaborators. In the North, Péralte's band seized a machine gun and ammunition drums from a downed U.S. reconnaissance plane and shot a crew member.[5]

Resistance centered in the departments of the North and the Artibonite, but numerous Haitians and foreigners in other parts of the country supplied financial and moral support for the movement. [. . .] In October 1917, Charlemagne Péralte, by now publicly associated with the spirit of revolt, led his brothers and sixty others in an attack on the U.S. commander of Hinche, his own hometown. Péralte was sentenced to five years at hard labor after the group's eventual capture. He escaped from prison and retreated to the mountains where he reunited with his comrades.[6]

The organization of a native constabulary to maintain a sadly lacking law and order had been one of the occupation's first projects in Haiti. The responsibility of confronting rebels would ultimately fall to the so-called Gendarmerie d'Haïti. U.S. military and civilian officials saw this unit primarily as a peacekeeping force, not an army. They recruited men who would have been *cacos* before 1915. The Marines planned to sell the old weapons that the guerrillas had surrendered to a stateside department store for retail as wall trophies, and they ordered new uniforms for the Gendarmerie.[7]

The Gendarmerie was not ready for a counterinsurgency campaign, however, and proved ineffective in the field. The U.S. military thus had to run the program directly, which it did with ruthless success. Marine Corps General Lewis B. "Chesty" Puller, a veteran of the Haiti campaign, pioneered the use of bombers and personally flew "dozens" of missions. The Marines used bush landing strips cut by prisoners of war for these early "search and destroy" missions. They could not accurately distinguish guerrillas from noncombatant peasants, and many Haitians suffered. [. . .]

After the pacification campaign of 1919–20, greater attention turned to "Haitianizing" the Gendarmerie and extending its powers, especially over public works, but it never overcame general opposition. It proved more successful in the intelligence realm. Until 1920 the organization relied on information from paid or intimidated informants. Thereafter, a small detective squad, consisting primarily of local leaders (*chefs de quartier*) supplied needed information. These men drew no salary but enjoyed favors. A criminal investigation and identification bureau, headed by a French civilian, organized the *chefs'* espionage activities. The regular constabulary fully incorporated the spy ring in 1927.[8]

Complaints persisted about Gendarmerie conduct, especially in rural areas, and the outfit's repressive responses to those witnessing brutalities or offering criticism of officers' behavior. As gendarmes were recruited from the same social groups as the former *cacos*, U.S. Consul Damon Woods suggested, greed and ignorance led them to expect support for breaches of good conduct. Thefts from and assaults upon peasants comprised the most frequent grievances. The Gendarmerie was also accused of favoritism in its operations and of using anti-Vodun campaigns to settle officers' personal grudges.[9]

The occupation regime had succeeded in creating a single military organization that controlled the entire country and yet subordinated itself to civilian control. For the moment, the Gendarmerie remained apart from national politics, but U.S. reforms did not alter the traditionally predatory relationship between the Haitian armed forces and the largely peasant community. The North American presence checked large-scale abuses of power during the 1920s. In spite of the violence that punctuated this decade, U.S. officials concerned themselves less with Gendarmerie abuses in Haiti than with political fallout abroad. They wished to keep Haiti out of the news.

The protectorate struck a critical blow against Haitian resistance when Marines finally located and killed Péralte in October 1919. A captain, supposedly in black face, stole into his camp and assassinated him. Péralte's chief lieutenant, Benoît Batraville, continued the struggle until May 1920, when he too was slain. When *caco* leaders died or surrendered, the event was heavily publicized in an effort to discourage further revolt. The Marines photographed Péralte's body on a litter of boards as if he had been crucified, and then buried him in concrete, allegedly to deter subsequent use of the corpse for superstitious purposes. The famous photograph of Péralte on the "cross" confirmed his pure martyrdom, and by the late twentieth century Haitians regarded this patriot as a major figure in their history.[10]

Military experts judged the "bandit suppression" work complete by mid-June 1920. Rumors about the war had drifted back to the United States, where they incited mounting criticism from Republican sources anxious to discredit the Democrats and from civil rights and peace advocates. Only after the most flagrant offenses had occurred, and the presidential election of 1920 had passed, did the U.S. Senate begin its investigation into the occupation. Subcommittee hearings chaired by Republican Senator Medill McCormick of Illinois also probed conditions in the Dominican Republic, similarly occupied from 1916 to 1924.[11] The Senate hearings provided the incentive for an improved administration of the protectorate and an end to the worst abuses. The senators called for continued occupation, but with control vested in a high commissioner. This functionary would possess diplomatic powers, answer to the State Department, and supervise an elaborate bureaucratic network.

The commission served Haiti as a shadow government that left the client state with little exclusive jurisdiction. The individual selected as high commissioner was John B. Russell of Georgia, a Marine officer and former judge advocate of the Navy. Russell had also served as brigade commander during the early years of the occupation. Russell's appointment demonstrated policymakers' belief that Haiti needed the discipline that a southern militarist could provide.

Bureaucratization was not only an end in itself, but a demonstration of the need to gain time to make permanent changes. Haiti required modernization if the occupation was to be justified and continuing peace ensured. Development questions could not be separated from strategic concerns. Military authorities, for example, attributed their counterinsurgency successes to the roads built under their auspices. Road-building policy clearly reflected the regime's priorities. Paved routes spanned areas without markets in a country that used animal, not motorized, transport. They gave rise to a new system of coast-bound trucking, but their continued upkeep required additional expenditure. The eventual deterioration of many of the roads indicated in part that Haiti could not afford them.[12] Other plans included clinic construction and agricultural and medical services. In most cases, these projects were undertaken without sufficient thought as to how Haitians could sustain them after the protectorate expired. They relied excessively on technical expertise from North Americans who gained their tropical experience in dependencies rather than sovereign states and who brought a determined moralism to their tasks. The missionary tone with which U.S. officials subsequently clothed the occupation surfaced less than a fortnight after the sailors and marines landed in 1915. William Jennings Bryan had assured Solon Ménos, the Haitian minister in Washington, that Haiti had nothing to fear from U.S. intervention. On the contrary, "The intelligent Haitians should feel gratified that it was the United States rather than some other power whose motives might not be as unselfish as ours."[13]

True to Bryan's words, official occupation rhetoric had a veneer of the same Progressivism that characterized domestic reform during the same era. The underlying philosophy in both instances pinpointed efficiency and competence as the elements necessary to ensure good government. During this period, many U.S. municipalities opted for city managers rather than mayors, believing that trained administrators would rise above the tawdry seductions of politics. [. . .] The realization of justice and social stability, Progressives felt, would stem from prudent management. Similar solutions to political problems, they believed, could aid foreign countries.[14]

[. . .]

This reasoning explains the technocratic character of the administration that the United States imposed on Haiti once it solved the problem of establishing military control. The regime could coexist with racist thinking, as the U.S. case had already demonstrated. The old civilizing mission of the nineteenth century, clad in Progressive trappings, remained intact. Paternalism was its most benign expression, and its most malevolent manifestation was the overt racism associated frequently with members of the military establishment.

Colonel Littleton W. T. Waller, who arrived shortly after the occupation began, exemplified the latter tendency. Though more flamboyant than others, Waller resembled them in his assumption that he "knew the nigger and how to handle him." He believed that cultural differences among blacks made little difference and, in any case, blacks had to yield to white domination. The Haitians "are niggers in spite of the thin varnish of education and refinement," he claimed. "Down in their hearts they are just the same happy, idle, irresponsible people we know of."[15]

The State Department expressed a more sophisticated variant of this prejudice. Certain officials, convinced that only vocational training suited blacks, consulted Thomas Jesse Jones, a noted purveyor of that philosophy, on Haitian prospects. Jones worked with the Phelps-Stokes Fund, a foundation that systematically undermined those independent educational institutions that refused to endorse its narrow definition of education for blacks.[16] The choice of Jones suggests that State Department officials tended to see Haiti primarily as a repository of cheap labor.

Technical advisers turned their attention to Haiti's chronic poverty, which Wilsonians believed made it vulnerable to revolution. Officials relied on the wisdom of select foreign bankers to analyze problems peculiar to the local economy. One of these, Domenick Scarpa, a National Bank of the Republic of Haiti (BNRH) vice-president, wrote a July 1916 report on the Haitian economy. Scarpa disingenuously suggested that real rehabilitation lay beyond the capacity of both the bank and occupation officialdom. His report is significant because of its breadth, his knowledge and authority, and the influential policy recommendations he made.

Scarpa pointed to the dual currency usage in Haiti. Foreign traders and members of the bourgeoisie were paid in dollars; gourdes were reserved for financial transactions with "the home trade." Gourdes slowly moved to the countryside during the harvest and returned to the cities during the "dead season," when peasants had no cash. This seasonal flow accounted for much of the fluctuation in the rate of exchange once the occupation regime curbed merchant-banker speculation.[17] Haiti's currency was a fiat money based on government decree rather than on a gold or silver standard. Exceeding the limits of its supply elasticity would prove disastrous. Haiti did not have industry or even a varied agricultural economy. Its one-crop dependency created urgent, short-term demands for cash. Interest rates could not be used to regulate the money supply because high risk-high rate conditions made lending impractical, as did the unstable rate of exchange.[18]

These conditions had long encouraged the development of speculative enterprises, Scarpa suggested, and discouraged the growth of businesses that would enhance the public welfare. A gold gourde or the exclusive use of U.S. currency could not help matters, for gold would simply drift back to the metropolitan centers as a result of Haiti's financial obligations and import dependency. Dollars would follow suit and raise the cost of real wages and production. Scarpa regarded this as an undesirable effect, for the conviction that Haiti's best hope resided in low wages had already become a truism by that time. Wages would naturally rise, according to conventional wisdom, once the Americans began to develop the country.[19]

The banker expressed enthusiasm about the anticipated progress. "*All is still to be made in Haiti. . . .* With cheap labor we may well hope to recoup the many, many years that have been wasted." Scarpa regarded the low standard of living and depressed income structure as Haiti's only asset in the struggle for development. "Put labor on the level of what it costs in Cuba or Porto Rico—and what will be the chances remaining for Haity [sic]?" Scarpa endorsed the maintenance of the gourde/dollar exchange rate at 5:1, a more liberal tariff convention, the abolition of export taxes, tax holidays for pioneering corporations, and port improvements.[20] His ideas helped create an enduring legacy. Fiscal austerity, permanently depressed living conditions, favored status for foreign investors, and low wages remained the cornerstones of financial policy to the present time.

On the face of it, occupation policies sought to maximize the possibility of foreign investment. In reality, a combination of opposition from U.S. critics, partiality and suspicion on the part of treaty officials, and internal resistance stymied industrial development plans. Many U.S. firms refused to invest in Haiti without strong guarantees. As a result, corporate interest in the black republic flickered. The Sinclair Oil Company could not agree with President Louis Borno on the government share of any oil it found. Borno sanctioned an exploratory concession, but Sinclair rejected his terms and left the country. The United States Geological Survey's research found Haitian mineral reserves commercially meager, and Texaco and Standard Oil of New Jersey, which had "prowled around," gave "it up as a bad job" by 1929.[21]

Rubber concerns also inspected Haiti in the 1920s. [. . .] [22] Liberia's success as a rubber colony and the onslaught of the Great Depression prevented the full-scale development of Haitian rubber cultivation during the epoch.

Despite these problems, U.S. officials did not lack a policy toward corporate enterprise. They simply played favorites. The activities of firms already in the field were just as questionable as new ventures that the State Department routinely rejected; the justification that the former were upheld because they predated the intervention and represented prior commitments does not explain why radical modification in their contracts could not have been made. On the contrary, the State Department backed these concessions, going so far as to block the development of other corporate initiatives in so doing.[23]

The record with regard to agriculture was similarly disappointing. Few of the expatriate technicians understood peasants' economic behavior, which they often dismissed as simply ignorant. Coffee, logwood, and sisal, all important exports, grew semiwild. Cultivators carelessly prepared these commodities for market because it did not pay them to handle them better. Speculators stood between the producers and the buyers, taking their percentage as well as the export tax out of the transaction. The resulting price did not warrant the expenditure of greater labor costs in processing the products.[24]

Few experts comprehended these economies. Most continued to pursue schemes to instruct Haitians in techniques and behaviors that were not necessarily appropriate to their circumstances. Occasionally, perceptive scientists made constructive suggestions but found their advice sometimes ignored. One botanist, for example, argued strongly for a program of afforestation. The high commissioner viewed his study as too pessimistic and had it suppressed. The man lost the job to a candidate who had more "tact."[25]

With a few exceptions, corporate plantations made little headway, but indigenous labor lost none of its appeal to entrepreneurs elsewhere. Cheap Haitian labor had long attracted sugar producers in Cuba and the Dominican Republic. Those workers who wanted more than the meager wages and one cupful of rice and bean hash per day provided by local companies had to emigrate. Labor joined coffee and other commodities as a significant export during the occupation years, and labor management provided a source of income for the Haitian bourgeoisie.[26] The major recruiter in Aux Cayes made enough money from what was popularly called the "slave trade" to invest in freight facilities, ice plants, and movie theaters. Consuls regarded Cuba as a sinecure and regularly cheated the Haitian government out of remittances due on each worker disembarked there. In 1919–20, of the $29,181 Port-au-Prince should have received, consuls sent it $1,984.30.[27]

Both Haitian and U.S. officials expressed concern over the exodus. They did not plan to give away what they considered Haiti's most valuable asset, its cheap labor, and remittances were then too small to significantly affect the economy. The high commissioner, himself a native of the Black Belt in the United States, approved of agricultural companies. He believed that the peasants needed to become habituated to wage labor and steady work, a striking contrast to their small-plot gardening experience. Russell wanted the United Fruit Company to set up plantations in Haiti but could not persuade the firm to locate there. United Fruit contented itself with recruiting Haitian workers for its operations elsewhere in the region.[28]

In the course of the 1920s, venture capitalists initiated schemes to grow cotton, pineapples, and other products. Most did not succeed. In some instances speculative companies never intended to plant. In other cases, they fell prey to poor management. Uncertainties related to land and water use hampered commercial agriculture. [. . .]

Historic legislation against alien real estate ownership had limited foreign plantation development, and peasant tenure continued to characterize national agriculture. [. . .]

The absence of sufficiently large individual estates further blocked the emergence of full-scale corporate agriculture on a contractual basis. [. . .] In 1928 officials launched a cadastral survey to help establish clear titles. This involved the aerial photography of land in the Artibonite and other parts of the country. They stored the negatives in a warehouse belonging to the Public Works Administration. Considerable fear existed in Haiti that the survey would lead to widespread evictions and the conversion of the peasantry into a landless proletariat. It is also probable that title registration would revive old feuds. That uneasiness temporarily abated when someone broke into the warehouse and set fire to the films.[29]

After the demise of the cadastral survey, Washington settled on prescriptive rights as the next best option. No one wanted to repeat the Dominican experience, where the expansion of sugar and lumber operations had dispossessed large numbers of rural people. Despite this apparent resolve, several plantation companies managed to acquire state lands for leasing during the 1920s. The Haytian-American Development Corporation held fourteen thousand acres in 1929, on which it planted sisal. The Haitian Agricultural Corporation had twenty-two hundred. HASCO, in addition to six hundred and thirty acres leased from the state, owned twenty-four thousand as a pre-1915 concessionaire.[30]

In 1930 the National Union, a Haitian organization that concerned itself with land questions, assailed the Haytian-American Development Corporation's sisal project. It accused the company of destroying houses and food supplies in various localities where sisal competed with provision crops and livestock for acreage. Petty government officials staffed company stores that kept peasants in debt peonage. Laborers' money went abroad in payment for imported food while locally owned shops lost custom. The Haytian-American Development Corporation had diverted a stream for its exclusive use in the Fort Liberté commune and had even taken its workers to the polls under military supervision so that each one could vote more than once for laws favorable to foreign interests.[31]

[. . .]

The occupation also sought to stifle foreign businesses that lay outside the U.S. orbit. Officials regarded Germany as their greatest challenger, but also acted quickly when they perceived Britain and France evincing growing independence. After World War I, for example, the British briefly attempted to regain their lost momentum in the Caribbean. The Royal Bank of Canada, headed by an energetic manager believed hostile to the occupation, was one of their agencies in Haiti.[32] Secretary of State Charles Evans Hughes endorsed a competitive policy aimed at curtailing the Canadian bank's ambitions. Fears that it would purchase French-held shares of the National Bank of the Republic of Haiti (BNRH) led the State Department to increase its vocal support of the National City Bank.[33]

Washington also fended off French complaints about arbitrary and bureaucratic mismanagement of the Haitian customs service. In drafts addressed to the French ambassador and German chargé in the U.S. capital, the State Department pointedly declared that no other nations would be invited to participate in reform of Haitian tariff regulations. The note for the French ambassador was not as curt as that addressed to Chargé von Haimhauser, but the message remained unambiguous. It also made clear that tariff policy in Haiti derived from Washington, and not from the high commissioner's office.[34]

Wartime restrictions on foreign businessmen mirrored the aggressiveness with which the United States supplanted European control in the Caribbean. The Webb-Pomerene Act of 1918 and the Edge Act of 1919 allowed corporations to form overseas trusts and cartels to facilitate trade.[35] Expatriates who endorsed the occupation usually prospered, for vocal support of the United States helped their businesses. The protectorate gradually loosened the foreign community's steadfast identification with European metropoles by using the carrot-and-stick method. The carrot represented law and order and the stable, if chronically depressed, economy that firm control ensured; the stick symbolized the threat of financial ruin and political reprisal against those who criticized or charted an independent course. If aliens accepted the discipline imposed on them, that is, the current reality of life in Haiti, they need not suffer unduly.[36] The new order transcended the old struggle between Haitians and foreigners for control of the export-import sector. The North American presence meant that both Haitians and foreigners had to accommodate themselves to the designs of new masters.

[. . .]

Europeans in Haiti formed part of Wilson's *comprador* class. Some, without strong allegiances to a fatherland, could be incorporated into New York or Chicago-centered business communities. Syrio-Lebanese already oriented themselves toward the United States. The task was now to assimilate the Europeans, many of whom would lose nothing in the process. The only losers (aside from Haitians) would be the continental metropoles.

The use of the European commercial community as manufacturers' representatives substantially assisted the growth of U.S. influence and the increased consumption of North American commodities. [. . .] Brand names became important. Haitians, British subjects, Syrians, and Danes sold Studebakers, Scott Tissue, and Gold Medal Flour. [. . .]

Plans to remake the black republic came undone on the reefs of the Great Depression. By the late 1920s most statesmen recognized that the Western Hemisphere's economic problems were structural. As a raw materials exporting region affected by the global slump in commodity prices and European financial failure, Latin America could not be altered through military intervention and the appointment of North American proxy officials. Neither could those expedients prevent the widespread defaults on government loans characteristic of the period. As Robert N. Seidel put it, "The depression proved to internationalist Progressives that their schemes for progress and development stood and fell, ultimately, according to the actions of economic laws which, unlike civil or corporate law, could not be easily amended."[37] Reformers could not fit Haitians into a framework made in the United States and wasted phenomenal sums of money in their attempts to do so. By the end of the decade, policymakers were uncertain that developing countries could absorb any "intelligent guidance," and Washington knew it lacked the capability to endow its less fortunate neighbors.[38]

The drive to normalize Haitian-American relations during the Hoover administration represented a repudiation of fifteen years of military rule. In 1930 the State Department raised the rank of its chief officer in Haiti to ambassador and sent the Latin Americanist scholar Dana G. Munro to fill that post. Munro did not blatantly exercise the dictatorial authority characteristic of General John Russell's High Commission, but his powers exceeded those of an ambassador. Late in 1931, for example, he ordered a moratorium on the payment of Haitian official salaries, including that of President Sténio Vincent, because he disapproved of certain appointments Vincent had made.[39]

An incident in 1929 at the agricultural training college at Damien precipitated an essential change in the direction and operation of the protectorate. Until 1929 the Haitian government had supplied scholarships totaling $10,000 to Damien students. Many recipients, members of the bourgeoisie, would not perform actual farm tasks, such as feeding livestock. These young men instead subcontracted such jobs to rural youths while they confined themselves to academic studies. In an attempt to halt this practice, the government began withholding 20 percent of the bursaries in order to support poorer students who had no qualms about dirtying their hands. The elite students objected strenuously and went on strike. They won the cooperation of law and medical students, who struck in sympathy with them and organized student demonstrations all over the country.[40]

Attempts to further enlarge the strike failed until 4 December, when the firing of an employee precipitated a walkout in the Port-au-Prince customs house. Other persons left their places of work and crowds gathered in the city. After a declaration of martial law, the Gendarmerie restored order. On 6 December, however, peasant sugar producers in the Aux Cayes area, already aggrieved by taxes, protested the competition levied against them by HASCO's nine-thousand-gallon-per-diem-capacity still. HASCO produced 40 percent of all the alcohol consumed in Haiti. Small distillers, unable to duplicate the corporation's economies, lowered the prices they paid to growers. Poor coffee prices also contributed to rural dissatisfaction. Coffee would become even more expensive to produce if occupation officials enforced the new standardization proposals currently under consideration.[41]

Fifteen hundred peasants went to Aux Cayes on 6 December to present their complaints to the authorities. They encountered a small detachment of twenty U.S. Marines who, unnerved by the size of the crowd confronting them, opened fire. They killed twenty-five persons and wounded seventy-five others. Despite the obvious economic root of popular discontent, U.S. officials persisted in attributing the agitation to the subversive activities of nationalists.[42]

Officials tried to suppress details of the Aux Cayes incident, but news reached the United States and banner headlines appeared. Opinion had changed dramatically since the *caco* war in 1919. The public had tired of U.S. policy in Haiti, and many now conceded that fifteen years of control had yielded too little significant change to warrant extension. Aux Cayes prompted President Hoover to appoint a commission of inquiry and a second commission assigned to review Haitian education. Black American educators, led by Robert R. Moton, president of Tuskegee Institute, staffed the education commission. They were expected to approve the system of "industrial education" in the Booker T. Washington mode that had led to the Damien conflict. They did not. During the 1920s, serious rebellions erupted on black American college campuses as students and faculty alike challenged the utilitarian Tuskegee philosophy and its concomitant focus on political acquiescence and abstention from protest. Washington's death in 1915 began a process that conservatives could not control. By 1919 Tuskegee Institute itself offered an education far more liberal than any had dreamed of earlier in the century. The Moton report on Haitian education contested the separation of agricultural and industrial training from the remaining curriculum and censured the Haitian government for failing to provide general public education. Its findings may also have been influenced by the racial discrimination that the group suffered at the hands of the U.S. Navy, which, intent on enforcing Jim Crow regulations, left it temporarily stranded.[43]

The commission of inquiry was a five-member, all-white group headed by former New Jersey Governor Cameron Forbes.[44] It did not call for the withdrawal of the Marines and showed little enthusiasm for the nationalist movement, whose ubiquitous, planned demonstrations, Forbes believed, lacked spontaneity, sincerity, and mass support. Most thoughtful Haitians wanted the United States to stay because they had no confidence in their own ability to govern. Forbes advocated a continued, if less visible, Marine presence.[45]

The commission of inquiry criticized Woodrow Wilson's original staffing of the treaty regime and noted its shortage of experienced colonialists. Forbes disliked the antidemocratic manner in which client presidents had been imposed on the country and "kept in by the bayonets of our own troops." He nevertheless sympathized with the current Haitian president, Louis Borno, and felt that he had a "right to feel sore" at the High Commission's undermining of his position. The Forbes Commission endorsed some important changes in the regime's structure. It called for the abolition of the High Commission, the resumption of presidential and legislative elections, and the restoration of normal diplomatic relations.[46]

The Hoover administration accepted these recommendations and began a phased disengagement and normalization. Hoover and Stimson planned a general revision of U.S. policy toward Latin America to end the expensive interventions thought particularly burdensome in a time of economic depression. The new approach substituted indigenous armed forces for U.S. troops. North American officers trained these national guards, perceived as police rather than an army, just as they did in the Dominican Republic and Nicaragua.[47] The Good Neighbor policy stressed cooperation rather than coercion, and in Haiti, it cleared Sténio Vincent's path to the presidency in 1930. Vincent had a reputation as a militant and outspoken critic of the treaty regime. Reinstatement of representative government resulted in the selection of a legislature some Americans considered radical and nationalist.

The Hoover administration reached an agreement to gradually terminate the occupation before Franklin D. Roosevelt became president of the United States in 1933. A new treaty abrogated all functions of the protectorate except those relating to financial administration, alienation of land, the avoidance of entangling alliances, and law and order. These exceptions were, of course, among the most essential aspects of government. By 31 December 1934, the constabulary, renamed in 1928 the Garde d'Haïti, would be completely Haitianized and the Marines withdrawn. Provisions were made for continuing fiscal oversight by Americans.[48] The United States had neither changed nor reformed Haitian politics but inadvertently strengthened and assured the survival of many of its worst features.

NOTES

1 Hans Schmidt, *The United States Occupation of Haiti, 1915–1934* (New Brunswick, N.J., 1971), 72–75.
2 Ibid., 97.
3 Admiral H. S. Knapp to the Secretary of the Navy, 2 Oct. 1920, State Department Decimal File (DF), 838.00/1704; Schmidt, *United States Occupation*, 101–7; Burke E. Davis, *Marine! The Life of Lt. Gen. Lewis B. (Chesty) Puller*, USMC *(Ret.)* (Boston, 1962), 41, 45; Georges Sylvain to James Weldon Johnson, 26 Nov. 1920, James Weldon Johnson Papers, Sterling Library, Yale University; J. Price-Mars to Walter White, 28 Mar. 1934, NAACP Papers, Library of Congress.
4 Gen. Catlin to the Maj. Gen. Commandant, 16 Mar. 1919, DF, 838.00/1572; Charles Moravia to the Secretary of State, 5 Apr. 1919, DF, 838.00/1578; C. Benoit to the Haitian Foreign Office, 9 Oct. 1919, in Russell to the American Minister, 20 Oct. 1919, DF, 838.00/1611; Russell to the Secretary of the Navy,

16 Jan. 1920, DF, 838.00/1612; Russell to Adm. T. Snowden, 10 Mar. 1920, DF, 838.00/1626.

5 Frederick M. Wise and Meigs O. Frost, *A Marine Tells It to You* (New York, 1919), 314, 315; Yvan M. Désinor, *Tragédies américaines* (Port-au-Prince, 1962), 132–33.

6 Suzy Castor, *La ocupación norteamericana de Haití y sus consecuencias (1915–1934)* (Mexico City, 1971), 120–23.

7 Davis, *Marine!*, 27; Alex S. Williams to Maj. Butler, 14 June 1916, Smedley Darlington Butler Papers, USMC Historical Museum, Washington, D.C.

8 Alex S. Williams to Maj. Butler, 14 June 1916; Butler to Gen. Lejeune, 23 June 1917, Butler Papers; *History of the Police Department of Port-au-Prince*, 15 May 1934, Haiti Collection, USMC Historical Museum, Washington, D.C.

9 Constantin Vieux to Littleton W. T. Waller, 10 June 1916, Kurt Fisher Collection, Schomburg Research Center, New York Public Library; Damon Woods, "Political Report for July and Aug. 1923," 1 Sept. 1923, DF, 838.00/1965; Winthrop R. Scott to the State Department, 4 Dec. 1924, DF, 838.00/2060.

10 Russell, Daily Diary Report, 1 Apr. 1920, DF 838.00/1634. See Roger Gaillard, *Hinche Mise en Croix* (Port-au-Prince, n.d.).

11 Schmidt, *United States Occupation*, 121–23.

12 Russell, Daily Diary Report, 20 June 1920, DF, 838.00/1647; Russell to Snowden, 10 Mar. 1920, DF, 838.00/1626; testimony of Richard E. Forrest in Senate, *Inquiry*.

13 Bryan to Wilson, 7 Aug. 1915, *Lansing Papers*.

14 Robert Neal Seidel, "Progressive Pan Americanism: Development and United States Policy Toward South America, 1906–1931" (Ph.D. diss., Cornell University, 1973), 11–13.

15 Waller to Lejeune, 11 June 1916; 13 Oct. 1915, John A. Lejeune Papers, Library of Congress.

16 Boaz Long's memorandum, 23 Nov. 1915, DF, 838.42/4; Jordan Stabler's memorandum, 11 Oct. 1918; Carter G. Woodson, *The Negro in Our History* (Washington, D.C., 1922).

17 Domenick Scarpa's report to J. Butler Wright, July 1916, 2–4, DF, 838.00/1404.

18 Ibid., 4–5, 6.

19 Ibid., 7; Louis Gation, *Aspects de l'économie et des finances d'Haïti* (Port-au-Prince, 1944), 7L.

20 Scarpa report, 7, 8.

21 Dunn to the Secretary of State, 1 Sept. 1923, DF, 838.00/1964; W.W. Cumberland in the *Herald Tribune*, 22 Dec. 1929; Millspaugh, 144; undated clipping in NAACP Papers, Library of Congress.

22 Russell to the Secretary of State, 21 Jan. 1929, DF, 838.52/Germans/2.

23 Blanchard to the Secretary of State, 15 Mar. 1921, DF, 838.516/166; Russell, Daily Diary Report, 24 Jan. 1921, DF, 838.00/1748; Hughes to the Secretary of the Treasury, 11 May 1921, DF, 838.516/167. Mayer to the Secretary of State, 11 Aug. 1917, DF, 838.00/1476; Scott to Munro, 12 July 1929, DF, 838.77/374; Grummon to the Secretary of State, 9 Oct. 1929, with enclosure. Mayer's memorandum, 28 Oct. 1918, DF, 838.61333/2. Dunn to the Secretary of State, 1 Sept. 1923, DF, 838.00/1964; *Herald Tribune*, 22 Dec. 1929, undated clipping, NAACP Papers, Millspaugh, 144.

24 Robert Dudley Longyear, "Haitian Coffee: Its Cultivation and Preparation for Shipment," 9 Sept. 1922, DF, 838.61333/40.

25 Munro to White, 9 Apr. 1923, DF, 838.61/26; author's interview with Dana G. Munro, 27 Apr. 1979.

26 Ferdinand Mayer, "United West Indies Company's Plans Regarding Haiti," 12 July 1918, DF, 838.52/12; Harry A. Franck, *Roaming through the West Indies* (New York, 1920), 153.

27 *Blue Book of Haiti/Livre bleu d'Haïti* (New York, 1920), 205; Senate, *Hearings before a Select Committee on Haiti and Santo Domingo* (Washington, 1922), 1354–1373.

28 Russell to the Secretary of State, 21 Jan. 1929, DF, 838.52/Germans; idem to idem, 28 Oct. 1927, DF, 838.504/5.

29 *New York Times*, 8 Apr. 1929, 3:1, 7; Russell to the Secretary of State, 18 Jan. 1928, DF, 838.00/2437.

30 Munro to the Solicitor, 3 June 1929, DF, 838.52/91; Arthur F. Millspaugh, *Haiti Under American Control* (Boston, 1931), 152, 153; Munro interview; Perceval Thoby, *Dépossessions* (Port-au-Prince, 1930), 11, 18, 19.

31 Thoby, *Dépossessions*, 21–23.

32 Charles Evans Hughes to the Secretary of the Treasury, 11 May 1921, 838.516/167; Shepherd to Simon, 2 Feb. 1933 and enclosure, Great Britain Foreign Office (FO) 371/16579.

33 Hughes to the Secretary of the Treasury, 11 May 1921; Dana G. Munro, *Intervention and Dollar Diplomacy in the Caribbean* (Princeton, 1964), 382. Special Report (NAACP) Notes, Haiti, Johnson Papers.

34 State Department to Haimhauser, 21 July 1924; State Department to the French Ambassador, DF, 838.51. French Legation file, Gendarmerie d'Haïti, United States Marine Corps Records, Record Group (RG), 127, National Archives, Washington, D.C.

35 Seidel, "Progressive Pan Americanism," 47–48.

36 Included in the extensive files of the Gendarmerie is a dossier on aliens thought especially dangerous. Gendarmerie Records, RG 127, National Archives.

37 Seidel, "Progressive Pan Americanism," 515.

38 Bryce Wood, *The Making of the Good Neighbor Policy* (New York, 1961), 123–35; Samuel Flagg Bemis, *The Latin American Policy of the United States* (New York, 1971), 221–23.

39 Bellegarde to Walter White, 28 June 1931; White to Ernest Gruening, 28 Oct. 1931, NAACP Papers.

40 Dana Munro, "Recent Events in Haiti," in Munro to Sen. Tasker Oddie, 9 Dec. 1929, DF, 9838.00/2639A.

41 Ludwell Lee Montague, *Haiti and the United States, 1714–1938* (Durham, N.C., 1940), 269, 269 n. 20.

42 Dana Munro, "Recent Events in Haiti"; Russell to the Secretary of State, 12 Dec. 1929, DF, 838.911/10.

43 Raymond Wolters, *The New Negro on Campus: Black College Rebellions of the 1920s* (Princeton, 1975); Kenneth James King, *Pan-Africanism and Education* (Oxford, 1971); Brenda Gayle Plummer, "The Afro-American Response to the Occupation of Haiti, 1915–1934," *Phylon* 43 (June 1982):125–43.

44 *Amsterdam News*, 11 Dec. 1929, 20; *The Crisis* 37 (August 1930): 275; (April 1930): 127; Schmidt, *United States Occupation*, 185; Plummer, "Afro-American Response," 141.

45 The Journal of Cameron Forbes, Library of Congress.

46 Ibid.; Forbes to William Allen White, 4 June 1930; Forbes to Elie Vezina, 19 May 1930; Forbes to White, 15 Apr. 1930, Journal.

47 Wood, *Making of the Good Neighbor Policy*, 392 n. 32.

48 Munro, *Intervention and Dollar Diplomacy*, 337–39; Smith to Little, 26 Sept. 1932, Louis McCarty Little Papers, USMC Historical Museum, Washington, D.C.

11

VIVE 1804!

The Haitian Revolution and the Revolutionary Generation of 1946

Matthew J. Smith

"1946 will be the year of freedom ... Long live Democracy in action ... Long live 1804!"[1]

"The victory of the proletariat is the victory of us all ... the hour is now for us to finally realize 1804."[2]

"Yes, this IS a revolution ... 1804 was a revolution ... and now 1946."[3]

"The Revolution of 7 January [1946] like that of 1804 was won by a large group ... to defend the interests of the working class and the masses we should rally together as true militants who believe firmly in TOUSSAINT."[4]

Introduction

On January 11, 1946, Élie Lescot, the thirtieth Head of State of Haiti, fled the black republic into exile.[5] Such events were nothing new in Haiti's troubled political history. Lescot's ouster had been the outcome of a five-day general strike precipitated by a left-wing student movement that drew inspiration from both communist and Black Nationalist ideologies. However, the revolutionary events of 1946 represented a first for Haiti and post World War II Latin America in the 1940s: a popular overthrow against a U.S.-supported dictatorship led by local radicals. In the months following the dramatic events in January, the black republic fell headlong into a fierce political debate that transformed the political history of the nation and introduced new ideologies into an already crowded political space. There were noteworthy developments: for the first time, a labor movement formed, the Haitian press gained unprecedented freedom with scores of radical newspapers sprouting up across the country, and Haitian Marxists, who were underground for over a decade, surfaced and presented a powerful challenge to the status quo.

Most significant of these developments was the rise of a new *classe politique*, consisting in the main of young black radicals, who relied heavily on distinctions of class, colour, and experience to legitimize their new position. One of the central ideas of the young revolutionaries of 1946 was their responsibility to fulfill the historical promise of Toussaint and Dessalines; now blacks with little foreign interference could finally rule Haiti. Most of these men subscribed to the black power ideology of *noirisme*, which advocated total control of the state apparatus by black representatives of the popular classes. Where their nineteenth-century forebears had failed, the young *noiristes* of the forties argued, was in their inability to retain political power, which had traditionally been controlled by the light-skinned oligarchy. 1946 presented an unprecedented context for real political change in Haiti, as the exploits of *mulâtre* rule were laid bare and the contenders for control of the state were mainly black. The conclusion to the months of intense political and ideological debate came on August 11 with the election of peasant-born black schoolteacher Dumarsais Estimé as president of the republic.

The idea of fulfilling the lost promise of 1804 figured heavily in the rhetoric of the leading radical groups in Haiti in 1946. What did 1804 mean to Haitian radicals in 1946? How did the *noiristes* and Marxists differ in their interpretations of the Haitian past at the intense moment of 1946? How did these differences contribute to the bitter divide in Haitian leftism and the breakdown of radical politics in Haiti by the 1950s?

This essay addresses these and other questions through a careful exploration of the emergence of various ideological strains of radical nationalism in Haiti during the 1946 movement and the role the Haitian Revolution played in the political rhetoric of various radicals. The essay draws heavily on the Haitian press of 1946, a large and under-exploited source. Special attention is given to the debates in the radical press and the relationships between these radical groups and the traditional power structure. Along the way, the essay offers several correctives to the complicated and often misunderstood narrative of this important period in modern Haitian history.

The Five Glorious Days: An Overview of the Haitian Revolution of 1946

The movement to topple Lescot emerged not from the disparate *noiriste* factions, but from the communist youth, a point underemphasized in most analyses of the period. The victory of the Allied forces in the war had invigorated young Haitians with a new sense of self-confidence, optimism, and the possibility to effect profound change in their society. For the minority who attended the Université de L'État, the desire for change was urgent.

On December 7, the first issue of the student weekly, *La Ruche*, appeared in Port-au-Prince. The editorial board was a group of fifteen students, the most important being Jacques Stephen Alexis, René Depestre, Gérald Chenet, Théodore Baker, Gérald Bloncourt, Gérald Montasse, George Beaufils, Raymond Pressoir, and Max Menard. The writers would often go into the popular areas of the city and translate the French articles into Kreyòl for their largely illiterate audience.[6] The articles in the paper were often bold, defiant, and idealistic, driven by a revolutionary zeal and naive optimism in Marxism. Unlike the *noiristes*, their resistance to Lescot did not derive from colour politics but from the repressive nature of the state, which they equated with fascist Italy. As Montasse remarked, "Our movement is not against the person of Élie Lescot. It is against colonialism and bourgeois greed. . . . that is the greatest sorrow of the Haitian people. We have given ourselves to a new politics. This new politics is national, anti-bourgeois, democratic, and socialist."[7]

The potent discourse of the *La Ruche* collective was fashioned not only from Marxism but also from French cultural theory. None proved more influential than surrealism. In early December André Breton, the doyen of the surrealist movement, visited Haiti for a series of lectures on surrealism and modern art.[8] The students were most fired by Breton's non-conformism, and staunch denigration of dictatorship of all kinds, given powerful emphasis by his refusal to greet Lescot after his third lecture on the 20th of December.[9] Emboldened by Breton's presence, the writers of the paper decided that the special edition they were planning to honor Haitian independence on January 1 would instead be a tribute to Breton. The paper brimmed with harsh critiques against all forms of oppression. The opening of Depestre's front-page article crystallized the exuberance of the youth: "The year 1946 will be a year of profound experiences. . . . January will no longer be called January but Justice, February, liberty, April will be called deliverance, May, union etc. A new future for man will begin."[10] It was, however, the scathing page-length tract they ran on the second page that proved most incendiary.

> 1946 will be the year of Freedom, when the voice of real democracy will Triumph over all forms of fascist oppression.
>
> Down with all the Francos!
> Long Live Democracy in Action!
> Long live the Youth!
> Long Live Social Justice!
> Long Live The World Proletariat!
> Long Live 1804[11]!

The appearance of that page, which was widely circulated in the city, was the straw that broke the camel's back. Two days after the paper appeared, police acting on Lescot's orders, stormed the Ruelle Roy headquarters of the newspaper and forced its immediate suspension. Depestre and two other members of the group were arrested and released the following morning. On the afternoon of January 4th Franck Magloire, the editor of *Le Matin*, whose printing press was used by *La Ruche*, was temporarily detained by the Garde and questioned about his involvement with the students.[12]

That night at Alexis's house Raymond Pressoir, Alexis, Depestre, Baker, Chenet, and Bloncourt met to strategize. They agreed that drastic action had to be taken against the government. Alexis and Pressoir suggested that the best way to demonstrate their anger would be to organize a student strike similar to the Damien revolt.[13] Damien's success owed much to the marines' reluctance to open fire on the students in the streets. A student strike, they averred, would precipitate a social revolution and the overthrow of the regime.

Shortly before ten o'clock on the morning of Monday January 7, the students alerted the press and the U.S. Embassy to the impending strike, which would culminate with a demonstration in the embassy's courtyard. The task of contacting the Embassy was given to Depestre who, fearing arrest, seized the opportunity to plead for U.S. asylum but was refused and immediately went into hiding.[14] That morning the strike began in earnest.

The members of *La Ruche*, along with their supporters from the law and agricultural faculties, filed out of their classes and met outside of the Medical School, shouting *"Vive La Révolution!"* No sooner had they gathered than they were met by the police who beat the students with batons. Alexis, who was badly beaten, urged Bloncourt to rally students from the nearby Lycée des Jeunes Filles where Bloncourt's mother taught. After convincing the female students that soldiers were beating university students, they entered the courtyard of the Medical school and formed a wall around the students, forcing the soldiers to desist from beating them. They marched toward the Champs de Mars, attracting a large crowd of secondary school students and workers along the way.

With clenched fists raised the students passed through the leading secondary schools, Lycée Pétion, St. Martial, St. Louis de Gonzague, and the all-girls St. Rose de Lima, singing the Haitian national anthem, La Dessalinienne.[15] The numbers of protestors grew remarkably as they marched throughout the central streets of the city. Using word of mouth, leaders of the strike rallied support by spreading false news that the purpose of the strike was the severe beating of two students by the soldiers. As the crowds moved through the heavily populated slum areas of Bel-Air, La Saline, and Croix des Bossales, nearby businesses closed down. The newspapers quickly issued appeals for order demanding the intervention of the parents of the rebellious students.[16] Once the protestors arrived at the embassy, members of the Garde were already on hand and temporarily detained several activists, most notably Max Menard, Bloncourt, Max Pennet, and the poet Jean Brierre. Several other students were severely beaten during the *mêlée*. Military intervention did little to dampen the resolve of the protestors.

Lescot, who had grossly underestimated the determination of the students, was shocked at the demonstration. Previously he ordered the head of the secret police, Lucien Marchand, not to keep the students under surveillance and to desist from harassing them, claiming that "the youth were not dangerous. They are only dialecticians."[17] Though he expected the strike to have subsided by Monday evening, he took no chances.

As soldiers packed into police jeeps patrolled the deserted streets of the city Tuesday morning, the students put into effect their new plan of attack.[18] Around midday in front of the Henri Deschamps bookstore on Grande Rue, Bloncourt, who had made his way downtown in disguise, attacked an unarmed soldier. Panicked storeowners closed their stores as bystanders began hitting pots on the telephone poles, sending signals of protest throughout the streets of Port-au-Prince.[19] Employees from the departments of labor, agriculture, and education, all of which were controlled by the unpopular Dartigue, joined the students.[20] Strong support also came from the Morne-a-Tuf region near the medical faculty, where a student from the community had died from beatings sustained during the protest the previous evening.

On Thursday the revolt intensified. In the morning, the Comité Démocratique Féminin, a women's movement headed by Jacques Roumain's wife Nicole, led a march to the cathedral to appeal for peace, freedom of the press, and the liberation of political prisoners.[21] When a few supporters shouted *À bas Lescot*, nearby officers fired into the crowd, killing two young men and wounding two women.[22] In retaliation, large mobs began to spread throughout the city; they stormed the police headquarters and hurled rocks at members of the Garde before dispersing in the streets. The houses and property of leading ministers and their henchmen were ransacked and destroyed and stores looted. In the hillside areas that surround the capital the sound of vodou drums and *rara vaksins* (hollow wooden instruments made from bamboo) reverberated throughout the city as the factories of government officials burned to the ground.

By that afternoon it was clear that the government was unable to deal with the crisis. Over two dozen people were killed and many more injured during the week of *dechoukaj* (uprooting). A wide range of workers including bus drivers, agricultural workers, bakers, and butchers went on strike for the first time in the city's history, and the U.S.-run companies of SHADA, Standard Fruit, and the Atlantic Refining Company were forced to close their operations. Led by Dr. Georges Rigaud, a coalition group of professionals, businesspeople, journalists, and opposition leaders formed the Front Démocratique Unifié (FDU) in Port-au-Prince, which openly supported the students and called for the right to form political parties. Similar groups formed among students and businesspeople in the southern department of the Grand'Anse.[23] The movement spread to the other departments by the end of the week. In Jacmel, where large numbers of students at the Lycée Jacmel had received and read *La Ruche*, student strikes on the 7th were augmented by the participation of workers and peasants the following two days by which time, according to one participant, "the Revolution had conquered Jacmel."[24]

In an effort to avoid overthrow, Lescot agreed to have the cabinet dissolved and met with George Rigaud and other political leaders intimating that he would resign on May 15, the anniversary of his installation. In a private audience with Col. Lavaud, the head of the Garde, a desperate Lescot ordered Lavaud to use all necessary force to breakup the mobs. Lavaud refused and Lescot ordered his immediate arrest. The second ranking officer of the Garde, Colonel Antoine Levelt, instead counseled with Lavaud and U.S. ambassador Wilson to decide the best course of action. In conjunction with the embassy they formed that evening a Conseil Exécutif Militaire (CEM) which demanded and successfully obtained Lescot's resignation once they had convinced him his life was in danger if he remained in Haiti a day longer. Petrified, the rest of the cabinet submitted their resignations that afternoon and fled the country. The three-man junta that headed the CEM, which included Paul Magloire, Levelt, and Lavaud, put Lescot under house arrest. At three o'clock, the morning of January 11, Élie Lescot and his family huddled in the back of a police car, drove to Bowen Field, then boarded a waiting plane to Miami, reviving a pattern of Haitian presidential exile.[25]

"The Spiritual Sons of Toussaint": Legend and Myth in 1946 Political Discourse

The immediate success of the radical movement in deposing Lescot was but the beginning of a wider movement for social change. Within days of Lescot's exit, the Haitian press was liberated and there was an unprecedented explosion in the numbers of political and social papers, with over a hundred appearing in Port-au-Prince alone.[26] This freedom was manifest in the widespread formation of political parties for the first time in the country's recent history. Nearly one hundred political parties formed across the island. On the day of Lescot's overthrow light-skinned conservatives resurrected the old Liberal Party renamed Parti Libéral Socialiste under the leadership of François Dalencour. Other conservative groups included Edouard Tardieu's Parti Populaire Social Chrétien and F. Burr Reynaud's Union Démocratique Haïtienne. It was readily apparent, however, that popular currents would not sustain these traditional groups. Radical groups figured more prominently on the political scene and none were more influential than those that derived from *noiriste* and communist political ideologies.

The *noiristes* formed the Parti Populaire National (PPN) in January with radical labour leader Daniel Fignolé as the vice president, and including

Lorimer Denis, François Duvalier, Love Léger, and Clovis Désinor. The party's organ, *Flambeau*, became the central organ for *noiriste* propaganda in 1946. For the PPN, 1946 was, after 1804 and 1930, the third national revolution in the country's history and the most important because it promised the total liberation of the black majority.[27] As Duvalier and Denis asserted, "Finally the Haitian bourgeoisie is no longer the master of power."[28] Duvalier and Denis, along with Emile St. Lôt, fast became the leading proponents of *noiriste* thought in 1946. For them, as with several other black intellectuals, 1946 was a new awakening. The black intelligentsia was the product of educational reforms dating to the late nineteenth century, and achieved a degree of social prominence by World War II. However, access to state power had been denied them largely through a well-entrenched system of light-skinned control of the means of production and the state.

The popular overthrow of Lescot from all sectors of Haitian society seemed to vindicate their ideas, nurtured in the 1930s, of the necessity for black rule in a black nation. Moreover, where the ideas of the *noiristes* of the thirties had up until then been the province of a few, in 1946 they found widespread support. This served to invigorate the chief ideologues, particularly Duvalier and Denis, who found in 1946 the fulfillment of a struggle for black democracy that began in 1804.

Duvalier and Denis, like other *noiriste* writers, reduced Haitian history to a fight between two opposing classes. However, colour became central to class and could not be divorced from it. In the early months of 1946, both men aligned themselves with Fignolé and his newly formed party, Mouvement Ouvriers et Paysans (MOP). MOP's central paper, *Chantiers*, became an organ where they could express their revised theories of colour, class, and history in Haiti. This was appropriate as *Chantiers'* editor, Fignolé, had long used the powerful imagery of the Haitian Revolution to incite class and colour consciousness. In 1942, for example, he wrote, "The lazy, ignorant, egotistical, and sectarian bourgeois way of life is an insult to the misery of the peasant ... who works for the pleasures of a class swollen with prejudices. These descendants of Toussaint and Dessalines are abandoned in filth and ignorance."[29] Sharing Fignolé's rabid *noirisme* and finding in him the leadership of the urban popular classes that they themselves could not provide, Duvalier and Denis put their support firmly behind him in 1946. In a lengthy series of articles in *Chantiers*, beginning in the middle of the year, Duvalier and Denis painstakingly retraced Haiti's history from the period of the slave revolt to 1946. They argued that since the revolution, the "class of mulâtres" have not played the proper role in maintaining a political system for the good of all Haitians.[30]

Two years later, Duvalier and Denis would complete this study and publish it as *Le problème des classes à travers l'histoire d'Haïti*.[31] Featuring the Dessalinienne flag of red and black on the cover, this work represents the most radical elaboration of *noirisme*. In the survey of Haitian history that opens the work, the authors argue that since the days of Salomon and Antoine Simon in the nineteenth century, blacks had enjoyed no access to political power until 1946.[32] The book's most distinctive feature, however, was its analysis of the social and colour divisions in the island. The superiority of black rule, once a scientific argument, was now axiomatic. The fundamental reasons for the domination of the black majority by the light-skinned minority was, they argued, a result of elite attempts to maintain "exclusivity" by dividing the black groups along class lines. As long as black groups remained complacent with minimal political and economic power, the problem in social relations was destined to persist. The only solution to this predicament was the creation of a powerful and unified "black class."[33] "If we are to rise as a strong class and be respected for achieving equilibrium in our Nation, we must meditate on these serious faults which have haunted us since the birth of our natural life."[34]

For Duvalier, as David Nicholls has pointed out, "equilibrium," the opposite of mulâtre "exclusivity," meant black power in all areas of political and social life.[35] "Since that famous night of August 1791 which prefigured the Revolution of 1804 . . . [the country] has fallen, over the past 144 years, into a night of opaque ignorance."[36] In this "era of the masses" Haiti had finally found equilibrium, which, according to Duvalier, was the final and perfect stage in the cycle of modern Haitian politics.[37] Only with a black head of state could the fundamental realignment of Haitian politics be realized.

Central to this discourse was the application of what Nicholls has called a "black legend" of Haiti's past.[38] Following in the footsteps of nineteenth century nationalists such as Louis Janvier, Duvalier and Denis argued that the country's most basic problem was created from Independence: the constant exploitation of the majority of the black inhabitants by a small minority. This thinking, in fact, can be found in Duvalier and Denis' earlier writings in the late thirties. In the journal Les Griots, Duvalier wrote in 1938 that 1804 was "more of an evolution than a REVOLUTION."[39] He had long maintained that there was a strong correlation between the colour of Haiti's leadership and its underdevelopment.

Although a powerful doctrine of black nationalism, noirisme was not the only political theory that captured the hearts of young Port-au-Prince radicals in the months following Lescot's ouster. During the first days of February a cadre of former supporters of Jacques Roumain and other Marxist sympathizers led by Edris St. Armand revived the PCH. The PCH, swept up by the enthusiasm of the moment, likened the events of January 7 not to the Haitian Revolution of 1804, but to the Russian Revolution of 1917.[40] In an editorial in the second issue of the party's organ Combat, St. Armand remarked that communism was the "only possible solution for the country to get out of the social stagnation and poverty."[41] The party's initial programme, which argued for the creation of a "Socialist Soviet Republic of Haiti," advocated inter alia, the socialization of all industries and land, Soviet-style organization of all political institutions, and the democratization of the Haitian Garde, which was to be renamed "the people's army."[42]

The PCH supported the Front Révolutionnaire Haïtien (FRH), a coalition of eleven radical groups including the PPN, which formed on February 8. The formation of the FRH indicated a certain level of unity among the radical groups during the first months of 1946. Perhaps the most important radical group to reform in these early months was the socialists. In late January, the Parti Socialiste Populaire (PSP) was officially formed, comprised in the main of contributors to the radical paper of the early forties, La Nation.[43] The party's leading members were Max Hudicourt, Anthony Lespès, Étienne Charlier, Jules Blanchet, Albert Mangonès, and Max D. Sam. The Marxist convictions among the members of the party differed somewhat as Hudicourt, though referring to himself as a socialist, retained a liberal nationalist outlook whereas Sam, Charlier, and Lespès were more fervently Marxist.[44] The party structure and ideology closely resembled both that of the Socialist Party in the Dominican Republic and the Cuban PSP (Partido Socialista Popular) with which it was aligned.

The philosophy of the PSP represented the starkest contrast to the noirisme of the other radical groups. The intellectuals in the PSP, most of whom hailed from the elite, privileged issues of class struggle over those of colour divisions as the most important threat to Haitian society. Like the PCH in the thirties, they argued that a reorientation of the polity based on colour would not bridge the country's fundamental economic cleavage. Noirisme, for them, was a political weapon used by the black petit bourgeoisie to attain control of the country but promised little for the welfare of the poor.

The Haitian Revolution cast a long shadow over Marxist analyses of the events of 1946. As we have seen, the young Marxists of the La Ruche clique, many of whom joined the PCH, employed the rhetoric of 1804 in their protest. This was both a political device used to incite wide-scale rebellion and a reflection of their idealization of a communist solution. The Socialist Party, however, had a more complex view of Haiti's revolutionary past.

Etienne Charlier, a principal member of the party and a leading thinker on Haitian politics, expressed most clearly in his writings the Socialist party's political position. His regular columns in the paper on the political problems in the country often included a Marxist interpretation of the country's past. Charlier held firm to Marxist doctrine, but did maintain that the colour question had been a central feature in Haitian conflicts since 1804. However, 1946 presented a unique opportunity for Haitians to rectify this and to unite, "independent of class and colour," to realize "true social democracy" in the country.[45] Much of his early writings in La Nation formed the foundation for his provocative Aperçu sur la formation historique de la nation haïtienne, published in 1954. In this work, Charlier criticized other

Haitian writers who, adopting the "black legend" of the revolution, argued that blacks were predisposed to revolutionary leadership of the nation, and *mulâtres* were by nature counter-revolutionary. This perspective was dangerous in Charlier's view, insofar as it presented a false image of Haiti's history as being determined by heroic black figures such as Toussaint and Dessalines, and it undermined the central role of the people. For him, the historical struggle for state domination was to be defined in terms of class and access to economic power. This position aroused harsh criticism from the communist party. The predominantly black and working-class PCH was markedly different in 1946 from its first incarnation twelve years earlier. It positioned itself against the PSP adopting the slogan of the *"Front Révolutionaire des Partis de Gauche Authentiques."*[46] In a departure from orthodox Marxism-Leninism which they claimed as their guiding doctrine, they emphatically declared the colour question as an "essential aspect of the present class struggle in Haiti," that, if ignored, would lead to the re-installation of a "bourgeois dictatorship."[47] The PSP, they argued, evaded the colour question because the party was largely *mulâtre* and consequently feared the threat that a black government might pose to their status.[48]

The PCH's strong emphasis on colour did not mean, however, that they agreed with the ideas of the *noiriste* politicians in the PPN. On the contrary, their exit from the FRH was in large part due to the disagreements they found with the "petit bourgeois" *noiristes*. Jacques Stephen Alexis, one of the most profound social critics in the party, argued that the *noiristes* were solely driven by a fight against the mulâtres but never attacked those "capitalists" he believed were most responsible for the exploitation of the country, the Syrians, Lebanese, Italians, and U.S. whites.[49] *Noiristes*, moreover, never advanced any meaningful political doctrine that sought to rebuild the country's damaged economy.

The contrasting perspectives on the question of ideology and the legacies of the Revolution held by the leading Marxist parties illustrate how divided radical forces were in Port-au-Prince in 1946. That the root of contention among Marxists was *la question de couleur* also highlights how successful the *noiristes* were in setting the terms of political debate. This situation would lead to a peculiar insistence on the part of some Marxists that colour should be the defining factor in Haiti's political future. Such was the approach of another Marxist party that formed during this period of which considerably less is known, the Parti Socialiste Haïtien (PSH) led by Dr. René Salomon, grandson of the celebrated president Lysius F. Salomon. Salomon had a notable presence among Haitian intellectuals of the mid-forties, having formed Cenacle des études, a political discussion group during the Lescot years. In 1946, however, he chose not to align himself with any of the dominant political groups, declaring himself a Marxist and choosing to form his own party, the PSH. What is most striking of the PSH was that it was a Marxist party that held a *noiriste* view of the country's revolutionary past. The party's April 7 manifesto was clear on this:

If the military battle of 1804 was won, it was principally because of the genius of one man: TOUSSAINT LOUVERTURE . . . Brilliant strategist, tactician, courageous, military genius, diplomat, unique negotiator, and celebrated leader, he had the first programme [of national development] . . . TOUSSAINT LOUVERTURE had a strong clear conscience and made it possible for Dessalines to realize national independence. It is the same situation in 1946. The spiritual sons of Toussaint Louverture are now leaders of a band of dissidents . . . the Masses are the victims of the counter-revolution against the spiritual sons of Toussaint. The Revolution of 7 January like that of 1804 will be won by a large group . . . We believe in Toussaint and work for a NEW HAITI, UNIFIED AND STRONG. FOR THE UNITY OF ALL AUTHENTICS OF TOUSSAINT LOUVERTURE WHO IS OUR SYMBOL AND GUIDE.[50]

It is evident then that the liberative principles of Toussaint and Dessalines inspired Haitian radicals of various persuasions to locate the January revolution in an historical context. At the same time, however, there was a conscious romanticization of the 1804 Revolution's objectives and outcomes. The treatment of the country's revolutionary forebears was naturally self-serving. *Noiristes* and black Marxists seldom addressed the early failures of the post-Revolutionary Haitian state, preferring instead to view the black leaders of the past as victims of *mulâtre* duplicity. Equally significant was the notable absence in *noiriste* analyses of any extended critique of foreign interference in Haitian affairs. The Lescot years were portrayed as the vulgar example of *mulâtrisme*, but not a legacy of nearly two decades of United States marine occupation. Although the socialists frequently drew reference to the postwar world and the reach of the United States in Caribbean politics, their counterparts in the communist, *noiriste*, and labour factions, realizing the necessity of U.S. support in the upcoming elections, chose to focus on the internal roots of the crisis.

Whatever their positions on colour or the Revolution, the political reality of post-Lescot Haiti would force the divided left into direct confrontation with the main powerbrokers in Haitian politics, the bourgeoisie and the military.

La Révolution en Marche: The 1946 Elections

The provisional military government upheld the constitutional provision that the successor of a deposed president had to be elected by a majority in the National Assembly. Over two hundred mainly black candidates presented themselves for election to the twenty-one senatorial seats and thirty-seven deputy seats.[51] After two successive dictatorships, the political field was open and the promise of a democratic Haiti finally seemed to be realized. For the first time in the country's history, leftist candidates had a large representation in the election campaign. Juste Constant from the PCH was running for president, mayor, and senator; PSP executives Max Hudicourt, Max Sam, Georges Rigaud, Étienne Charlier, and René Salomon all ran for seats in the Chamber of Deputies. Labor leaders Fignolé and the popular Henri Laraque also sought positions as Deputies for Port-au-Prince and Cap Haïtien respectively.

The results of the legislative election were staggering. With few exceptions the left candidates were defeated. Salomon, in an about turn, blamed the defeat on the disunity of the Marxist Left which should have buried their ideological conflicts and fought the "common peril."[52] Radicals were most aggravated by the reelection of several cabinet members closely associated with the Vincent and Lescot regimes, namely Charles Fombrun, H. Bourjolly, and Dumarsais Estimé. They charged that the election results were tampered with by the Ministry of Interior headed by Colonel Paul Magloire.

With their hopes of achieving success in the upcoming elections impeded, the leftists took to the press to object to the harsh new impositions. In *La Nation*, Max Sam wrote that five months after the fall of Lescot, the CEM had created a tragic situation and reintroduced totalitarianism, the "grave menace for the future of democracy in Haiti."[53] The PCH chose not to back any candidate in the presidential race since, according to St. Armand, all the candidates had the potential to "deceive the masses."[54]

Notwithstanding their hostility towards the *noiristes*, the PSP made a judicious evaluation of the political situation in the summer of 1946 and acknowledged that their candidate Georges Rigaud had little hope of success. They decided therefore to back Edgar Néré Numa, the conservative black deputy from Les Cayes. The decision to back Numa, according to Sam who was then General-Secretary of the party, was not taken because Numa was black but because he appeared most sympathetic to the goals of the socialist party even though he himself was not a socialist.[55] Still, the fact that a *mulâtre* candidate would never win in the heated political climate of 1946 was not lost on the socialists. They were well aware, as Sam concedes, that Haiti was not prepared for socialism and that a strong nationalistic president with no direct ties to *noiriste* factions would be the most realistic option. *Noiristes* like Roger Dorsinville, who thus far supported Numa, withdrew their support, claiming that they refused to "back an understudy," and put their efforts behind "the peasant" Estimé.[56] The PCH chose to temporarily side with its socialist rival. As the months wore on, the party leadership grew disillusioned with the electoral process, especially after their dismal showing at the polls in March. At a party meeting in mid June, Juste Constant argued that the party no longer supported the "dangerous" colour question created by French and U.S. forces to divide the nation and now used by the Fignolists and *noiristes* to gain power: "Proletarians have no colour line and the same hunger pinches all. The problem is international. The country is on the eve of great democratic currents. Do not surrender yourselves to barbarity under the pretext of the *noiristes*."[57] He also reorganized the political bureau of the party, withdrew his candidacy for presidency, and urged party members who supported *noiriste* ideas to resign.[58]

The Labour Party took a different approach to electoral defeat. The military's tampering with the election results denied Daniel Fignolé a seat, but it did not halt his determination. The necessity of having strong party support in electoral campaigns was made clear to Fignolé, who thus far had relied almost entirely on his personality. Along with a core group of supporters, including Duvalier, Denis, and some of his former students, Fignolé formed MOP as a party on May 13, with *Chantiers* as its official organ. Under his leadership, MOP became the most organized labor party in Haitian history and the largest mass organization in the pre-Duvalier era.

Once it became clear that the *noiristes* in the Senate and the military hierarchy would do everything in their power to prevent Fignolé from running in the presidential race, MOP decided to back a conservative candidate, Démosthènes Pétrus Calixte, the former head of the Garde who had recently returned to Port-au-Prince. The political bureau of MOP believed that Calixte had gained significant influence in the north and the south over the course of the past year. Popular support from the Fignolists in Port-au-Prince would provide him with the greatest chance to win the election. Although Fignolé seemed to prefer Duvalier's taciturn and unassuming demeanor to Calixte's strong personality, which often clashed with his own, he understood that a Calixte victory would provide him with the surest chance to enter the Palais.

The decision to back Calixte as the popular leader provoked considerable opposition among other radical groups. Radical Marxist students from the PDPJH who thus far had respected Fignolé were disappointed with MOP's decision.[59] In the pages of *La Nation*, prominent radical Georges Petit, who took sides with the socialists on several issues, launched a harsh critique against Calixte, pointing to his training under the U.S. marines, his close association with former president Sténio Vincent, his role in the assassination of several officers, and his decision as former chief of the Garde to seek haven in the Dominican Republic less than a year after the 1937 massacre of Haitians by Trujillo along the Dominican border.[60] Petit also took Fignolé to task, pointing to his contradictory endorsement of a military candidate following the harsh treatment he received by the CEM during the congressional elections. "Why," he asked, "should we take Démosthènes over Paul [Magloire] when Paul is already in place and also black!"[61]

Bickering among leftists in the Labour and Marxist parties could do little to prevent the CEM from pushing forward their chosen candidate. On the morning of August 16th as tanks and reinforced troops surrounded the cordoned off streets and the Palace Garde armed with submachine guns stood at strategic points around the Legislative Palace, the senators, dressed in white suits and carrying sidearms, took their seats and cast their votes for the republic's new president. Only two out of the customary four ballots were necessary. Estimé won the first with twenty-five votes. Six votes were counted for Calixte, and seven for Socialist Party candidate Edgar Numa. Following much discussion, the results of the second ballot were pulled from the urn and proved more decisive. Estimé again won the plurality with thirty-two votes. Elected to serve a six-year term, the deputy from Verettes became the first black president of the postoccupation republic.

Conclusion

The dominance of black nationalism in Haitian discourse after 1946 was the defining ideological development in the country's modern political history. The long and complicated course of events following the fall of Lescot and the election of Estimé, in which racial authenticity became the main criterion of political leadership, was evidence of the impact of *noirisme*. One participant in the movement of 1946 would later reflect: "I told you: I was a *noiriste*. And I will add that whoever in my social class in Haiti after Lescot, under Lescot, whoever was not a *noiriste* would have been scum . . . They ran the country as they would have a plantation. And me, living there, the fruits of a certain education, being conscious of my identity, I would not have been *noiriste*? Merde!"[62]

This comment, and the preceding discussion, forces us to consider several important points. First, the *noiriste* surge in the forties and the political project that evolved from it has to be explained by the increasing politicization of the Haitian popular classes. The fact that the Haitian laboring classes were more awakened to political and social issues made them identify with a political theory in which notions of authenticity were central. The weakened state of other opposition movements, particularly the Marxist movement, only gave greater strength to the appeal of *noirisme*.

Second, the *noiristes* used the rhetoric of 1804 to justify their claims to state control. But 1804, in the heated climate of 1946, became a political trope. It is clear that the euphoria that followed January 7 created a sense of fulfillment on the part of Haitian radicals. By equating the toppling of Lescot and the perceived fall of light-skinned domination of the state with the victory of Dessalines, they were able to legitimize the *noiriste* movement by creating a myth of a glorious revolution that had been derailed in the wake of Dessalines' assassination, and then re-ignited with Lescot's overthrow. The enemies of the revolution became an ever-changing mix of the bourgeoisie, the United States, the Marxists, the army, light-skinned Haitians, and non-authentiques. It was therefore the task of the 1946 "revolutionaries" to uphold this lost dream of 1804 by preserving black control of the state apparatus. This point emphasizes what Nicholls has called "the propensity of Haitians to discuss the past in terms of competing legends which have practical consequences for the present, rather than in terms of a disinterested and dispassionate attempt to understand the past for its own sake."[63]

Third, and related to this, was an underlying desire for political power. If ideological sympathies with Haiti's revolutionary beginnings served as early inspiration for the *noiriste* radicals of 1946, it fast lost prominence once the harshness of Haitian *realpolitik* set in during the long election campaign. On all sides, the central objective by July 1946 was not the establishment of a democratic system of governance in the country. Haiti had known nothing of democracy and the new political elite, in spite of their rhetoric, had no real intention of instituting it. Rather, the main intention was to consolidate a hold over the state. Indeed, the deep fractures in the *noiriste* movement, between those who supported Estimé and those who supported Fignolé, illustrate just how volatile this contest became and help explain why Estimé ultimately had to rely on corrupt alliances with army officials to secure his presidency. Estimé's victory, therefore, must be seen as part of a long power struggle in Haiti draped by an active mythologizing of the country's revolutionary past.

But in adhering to this myth, the revolutionary generation of 1946 created one of their own. Estimé, like other *noiristes*, would reference the revolution of 1946 frequently throughout his short-lived administration, as Haiti's most important modern turning point. A decade later 1946 would become a political myth itself, used by various factions in one of the fiercest battles in Haitian political history, the election of 1957. It would become the rallying cry for new generations of Haitian radicals and ultimately be absorbed under the dark cloud that was Duvalierism.

NOTES AND REFERENCES

1 *La Ruche*, January 1, 1946. Except where otherwise noted, all translations are mine.
2 *La Ruche*, January 19, 1946.
3 *Flambeau*, January 22, 1946.
4 *Classe Moyenne et Masse*, April 20, 1946.
5 Portions of this paper are taken from Matthew J. Smith, "Shades of Red in a Black Republic: Radicalism, Black Consciousness, and Social Conflict in Postoccupation Haiti, 1934–1957" (Ph.D. diss., University of Florida, 2002), Chapter 4.
6 René Depestre, *Bonjour et adieu à la négritude* (Paris: Éditions Robert Laffont), 213.
7 *La Ruche*, January 19, 1946.
8 Roger Gaillard, "André Breton et Nous," *Conjonction* (Decembre 1966): 67; see also Paul Laraque, "André Breton en Haïti," *Nouvelle Optique 26* (Mai 1971): 126–138.
9 Mark Polizzotti, *Revolution of the Mind: The Life of André Breton* (New York: Ferrer, Straus, and Giroux, 1995), 605.

10 *La Ruche*, January 1, 1946.

11 *Ibid.*

12 Orme Wilson to Secretary of State, January 4, 1946, Port-au-Prince, United States National Archives, College Park, MD [USNA] Record Group [RG] 84, 800/10–446.

13 Raymond Pressoir interview with author, Bethesda, Maryland, June 17, 2000. The student strike at the agricultural school of Damien was the catalyst for the launch of a popular movement against the U.S. occupation (1915–34) in 1930.

14 John C. Howley, "Memorandum to the ambassador," January 7, 1946, Port-au-Prince, USNA RG 84, 838.01/1-1946; Gérald Bloncourt interview with author, Paris, France, June 18, 2001 [hereafter Bloncourt interview].

15 *Le Matin*, January 8, 1946.

16 *Le Nouvelliste*, January 7, 1946.

17 Élie Lescot quoted in E. Séjour Laurent to Max L. Hudicourt, February 22, 1946, printed in *La Nation*, February 19, 1946.

18 *Le Matin*, January 9, 1946.

19 Bloncourt interview.

20 *Le Matin*, January 9, 1946.

21 It is interesting to note that several of the women in this group were wives of leading Marxists. Their manifesto appeared in *Le Matin*, January 8, 1946.

22 W. Abbott to Secretary of State, January 11, 1946, Port-au-Prince, USNA RG 84, 838.000/1-1146; *Le Matin*, January 10 and 12, 1946; *New York Times*, January 13, 1946.

23 *Le Matin*, January 11, 1946.

24 Bonnard Posy, "Jacmel 1946," *Conjonction*, no. 202 (Avril-Mai-Juin 1997): 60.

25 On Lescot's personal reaction to the events, see Élie Lescot to Maurice Dartigue, April 26, 1946, Québec, *Dartigue Papers*. Schomburg Research Center for Black Culture [SRCBC], New York.

26 Fitz Jean-Baptiste, "Étude thématique et bibliographique de la presse Haïtienne de 1946–1950," M.A. thesis, Université de L'État d'Haïti Ecole Normale Supérieure, 1999, 125.

27 *Flambeau*, January 19, 1946.

28 *Ibid*, January 22, 1946.

29 *Chantiers*, August 5, 1942. Not surprisingly, Fignolé's radical views won him the hatred of the Lescot administration and Chantiers was forced to close down in late 1942 only to reappear shortly after Lescot's ouster.

30 *Chantiers*, June 15, 1946.

31 François Duvalier and Lorimer Denis, *Le problème des classes à travers l'histoire d'Haïti* (Port-au-Prince: Imprimerie de L'État, 1948), reprinted in François Duvalier, *Œuvres essentielles*, Tome II (Port-au-Prince: Imprimerie de L'État, 1964).

32 *Ibid*, 357.

33 Nicholls, *From Dessalines to Duvalier*, 200.

34 Duvalier, *Œuvres essentielles*, 365.

35 Nicholls, 200.

36 Duvalier, *Œuvres essentielles*, 364.

37 *Ibid.*

38 Nicholls, *op. cit.*

39 *Les Griots*, Septembre-Novembre 1939, 3.

40 *Combat*, February 6, 1946.

41 *Ibid*, February 8, 1946.

42 *Ibid*, February 6, 1946.

43 *Le Nouvelliste*, January 23, 1946.

44 Max D. Sam [former General-Secretary of the PSP] interview with author, Port-au-Prince, Haiti, May 7, 2001.

45 *La Nation*, March 26, 1946.

46 *Combat*, February 28, 1946.

47 *Combat*, March 23, 1946.

48 The issues of the debate between the PCH and PSP are taken from Matthew J. Smith, "Race, Color and the Marxist Left in Pre-Duvalier Haiti," in *Extending the Diaspora: New Histories of Black People*, ed. Dawne Y. Curry, Eric D. Duke, and Marshanda A. Smith (Urbana: University of Illinois Press, 2009), 245–269.

49 *Combat*, April 16, 1946.

50 *Classe Moyenne et Masse*, April 24, 1946. Emphasis included.

51 *"Album de candidats à la Députation et candidats au Sénat,"* Bibliothèque Haïtienne F.I.C., Institut de Saint Louis de Gonzague, Port-au-Prince.

52 *Classe Moyenne et Masse*, May 26, 1946, 53.

53 *La Nation*, March 26, 1946.

54 Jack West to Ambassador, "Memorandum on Communist Meeting of July 16," July 16, 1946, Port-au-Prince, USNA RG 84, 838.00B/7-1646.

55 Sam interview.

56 *Demain*, June 12, 1946.

57 The meeting was reported in *La Nation*, June 18, 1946, and Jack West, "Memorandum to the Ambassador Re-Communist meeting," June 25, 1946, Port-au-Prince, USNA RG 84, 838.00B/6-2546.

58 *Ibid; La Nouvelle Ruche*, July 3, 1946. David Nicholls erroneously states that "by the beginning of August . . . radical black politicians were supporting Juste Constant" when in fact Juste Constant withdrew from the presidential race two months before. See Nicholls, *From Dessalines to Duvalier*, 189.

59 René Depestre, *"La révolution 46 est pour demain,"* 87.

60 *La Nation*, July 30, 1946.

61 *Ibid*.

62 Roger Dorsinville, quoted in Michel-Rolph Trouillot, *Haiti: State Against Nation* (New York: Monthly Review Press, 1990), 134.

63 Nicholls, *From Dessalines to Duvalier*, 203.

12

DYNASTIC DICTATORSHIP

The Duvalier Years, 1957–1986

(Excerpt from *Haiti: The Breached Citadel*)

Patrick Bellegarde-Smith

Historians will see the three decades of the Duvalier dictatorship as the worst in Haitian history and consider that dictatorship one of the harshest regimes in the Western Hemisphere. The Duvalier regime compares unfavorably with the dictatorships of Trujillo in the Dominican Republic (1930–1961), the Somozas in Nicaragua (1931–1979), and Alfredo Stroessner in Paraguay (1954–1989), but the Duvalier years also represented a form of stability that, when contrasted with uncertainty, always appealed to the region's paramount power, the United States. The United States played a significant role in the events that led to the establishment and the long duration of the dictatorship. [. . .]

François Duvalier (1907–1971), a mild-mannered physician whose father was said to be a French citizen from Martinique, was a middle-class black who had served as a cabinet minister under Estimé. Duvalier's association with the Estimé presidency, a very progressive government by Haitian standards, endeared him to many people. His scholarly defense of Haiti's African heritage also won him support among the Haitian intelligentsia. His middle-class background and mild manner won him the loyalty of middle- and low-ranking army officers, who chafed under slow promotions and a mulatto General Staff, and his intimate knowledge of popular culture and Vodou won him some powerful alliances in the countryside. There is evidence that he was "the U.S. candidate." He had studied briefly at the University of Michigan and had worked as a country doctor under U.S. auspices. Although he was a "black nationalist," Duvalier seemed less threatening than the Francophile Déjoie. Components of the U.S. embassy distributed charity in Duvalier's name, and Haitian anthropologist Rémy Bastien argued that "in 1957 it was the opinion of the United States Department of State that Haiti needed a middle-class, middle-of-the-road reformer. Of the four candidates for the presidency, only one met the requirements. . . . Dr. Duvalier seemed the perfect choice" (Courlander and Bastien, 1966: 55).

There is, however, disagreement about how much support Duvalier actually received from the United States, and Haitian political scientist Leslie F. Manigat—an early Duvalier supporter who was later exiled—argued much differently (Manigat, 1964: 43). What was important, however, was that Duvalier was widely perceived to be the U.S. candidate. Colonel Robert D. Heinl, Jr., head of a U.S. Marine training mission to the Duvalier government, wrote that U.S. Ambassador Gerald Drew "had serious reservations but was unable to keep an uncritical USAID (U.S. Agency for International Development) director from ostentatious support of the Duvalier bandwagon, a factor which very likely carried the election."[1] Although the U.S. government was to reveal in 1986 that it had had evidence of massive fraud in the 1957 election and that Déjoie had probably won (according to U.S government records obtained through the Freedom of Information Act), it did support the Duvalier dictatorship—for "lack of an alternative," in order "not to penalize the Haitian population," and because he "was consistent in his anti-Communism." U.S. policy thus seems to substantiate the belief that Duvalier was largely a U.S. creation and that he would never have survived without the United States.

[. . .]

The Duvalier dictatorship, in its two phases, *père* (1957–1971) and *fils* (1971–1986), was easily the most brutal experienced by Haiti in two centuries of national life. Between 20,000 and 50,000 Haitians are said to have been murdered by that government, and about one-fifth of the population now lives abroad in political or economic exile, the second-highest ratio in the Western Hemisphere—Puerto Rico has the highest ratio. By the mid-1960s, 80 percent of Haiti's professionals had already fled, by some estimates.

The efficiency in methods of repression was rendered more likely by the technological means made available through the modernizing efforts of the U.S. occupation and the centralization of power favoring Port-au-Prince at the expense of regional interests. Two specific instances were the road network built largely for pacification of the interior by the Marines and the modern army whose impact is felt from the *départements* (departments) to the small *sections rurales* (rural sections). The only other institution with a national scope was the Roman Catholic church, which was under foreign control and threatened by the decentralized national religion of Vodou. Decentralization is a key concept here.

History will not be kind to the Duvaliers, whose fortune is estimated to be between $400 million and $1 billion. The judgment of one U.S. scholar is not too harsh: "Haitians experienced tyranny, rapacity, and an all-encompassing, disfiguring dictatorship which surpassed all its Third World counterparts in single mindedness of purpose, tenacity and lack of redeeming social and economic features" (Rotberg, 1971:197–198).

François Duvalier came to power with the blessing of certain segments of the population. To many Haitians he seemed to be a non-threatening man of the people. As a middle-class politician, Duvalier had not enriched himself while serving in the Estimé cabinet and had defended the beliefs and value system of the peasantry. The harrowing brutality of his regime did not begin until six months after he had taken office and took most Haitians by surprise. The repression and terror of Duvalier's government continued unabated until his death by natural causes in April 1971. Duvalier's ability to hold power was largely the result of weak state institutions, his uncanny intelligence, and intimate knowledge of the Haitian culture, and the effectiveness and surprise tactics of his secret police and state apparatus.

Jean-Claude Duvalier succeeded his father as president of Haiti on April 22, 1971, at the age of nineteen. The succession was supported by U.S. Ambassador Clinton Knox and was accomplished within sight of U.S. naval units. This very smooth transition of power from father to son was unique in Haitian history and indicated both foreign and some domestic support for the Duvalier dynasty. Fourteen years of purges under the senior Duvalier had neutralized or decimated all political opposition and institutional resistance to the regime. The foundations of traditional elite rule had been destroyed and replaced by a rapacious group of political hacks and cohorts of diverse class backgrounds whose only unifying ideological feature was their unflagging allegiance to Duvalier and the status quo. Indeed, the duration, brutality, and economic plunder of the Duvalier dictatorship from 1957 until its collapse in 1986 may have permanently altered the norms of Haitian political culture. The eruption of the peasantry onto the national stage during the overthrow of the Duvalier regime signaled that changes are developing in the nation's political power structure. Time will tell whether the growing political participation of the peasantry will continue.

Duvalier's government had to withstand armed attacks soon after it came to power. Eleven different invasions, plots, mutinies, and palace intrigues were launched against "Papa Doc" during the years of his reign. Although political and economic conditions in Haiti worsened under Duvalier, none of these revolts succeeded in rallying the population against the regime. Throughout most of the Duvalier era the government's opponents were upper class elites; the rural population was indifferent to resisting the regime because most people believed that another elitist government would be as bad or worse than the Duvaliers. In contrast, the movement that finally overthrew the Duvalier government in 1986 originated in the peasantry and provincial centers with little visible support from other social groups or foreign governments.

Almost from the inception of his regime, Duvalier used prison, torture, murder, and exile to silence his opponents, and the armed forces were neutralized from the outset. In March 1958, Duvalier initiated frequent transfers and dismissals in the officer corps. The high officer turnover and politicized promotions destroyed the army's *esprit de corps* and solidified the president's control. The officers' candidate school, the Ecole Militaire, was closed, and the military chain of command was substantially altered to incorporate new crack units—a presidential guard, the Casernes Dessalines battalion; the infamous Tontons Macoutes (Volunteers for National Security), a secret police; and the Leopards, a U.S.-trained counterinsurgency unit that reported directly to the president. Armaments were stockpiled in the basement of the presidential palace, which also housed some of the regime's torture chambers. The only requirement for military promotion was loyalty to the president.

Political repression, martial law, dusk-to-dawn curfews, press censorship, and government by presidential decree became quasi-permanent features of the Duvalier rule and continued in various forms for nearly thirty years. In an interview in the late 1950s, François Duvalier claimed that under his leadership, Haiti had achieved political stability, and he boasted that he had the situation well in hand. To demonstrate U.S. support for his regime, Duvalier procured a seventy-man U.S. Marine Corps training mission in December 1958—which he expelled in 1963. These marines promptly became known as the "white Macoutes," and their presence was more than psychologically devastating to Duvalier's opposition, particularly when they were called upon to repel an invasion by anti-Duvalier Haitian exiles.

In May 1959, a U.S. Navy medical team was secretly flown into Haiti from the U.S. naval base in Guantanamo, Cuba, and remained at Duvalier's bedside for thirty days as he recovered from a nearly fatal heart attack complicated by diabetes. Duvalier succeeded in placating the United States until 1963, when he clashed with President John Kennedy regarding human rights in Haiti and Kennedy suspended economic assistance to Haiti until two years later, when Haiti delivered crucial votes at the Organization of American States and the United Nations in support of the U.S. 1965 invasion of the Dominican Republic.

Like all Haitian presidents since the first decade of the twentieth century, Duvalier assumed that his regime would not survive without the support or at least the benign neutrality of the United States. Based on the experience of the previous sixty years, most Haitians also believed that no regime in Haiti could maintain its power without U.S support. U.S. military missions had trained the Haitian army intermittently since 1939, and William Wieland of the U.S. State Department told the head of the U.S. Marines in Haiti that U.S. policy supported Duvalier and that the marines should strive to maintain the power of the Duvalier regime (Diederich and Burt, 1969: 133).

The United States provided $7 million in economic aid to the Duvalier government between February and September 1959 and another $11 million in 1960. U.S. aid amounted to $13.5 million, almost 50 percent of the Haitian national budget, in 1961 alone, and from 1957 to 1986, U.S. aid to the Duvalier regime may have amounted to as much as $900 million.[2] As late as 1983, 40 percent of the Haitian government's budget and 60 percent of its development funds came from foreign sources. In 1985, the government received $150 million from Western governments, including $54 million from the United States. Thus the Duvalier regime could ill afford to alienate its foreign benefactors in major areas affecting their economic interests.[3] Meanwhile, Haitians were becoming the most highly taxed people in the Western Hemisphere, and Duvalier initiated many schemes, including bond issues, payroll deductions from public employees, compulsory lotteries, special taxes, and tolls on major roads, to collect additional revenue. By the mid-1960s, more than 65 percent of the national budget was allocated to the many security forces (Weil et al., 1973: 117).

The United States may not have intended to support the Duvalier regime *per se*, but it did feel that it had no other options for establishing a base of influence in the Caribbean after the U.S. invasion of Cuba at the Bay of Pigs in 1961. François Duvalier's excesses and his fraudulent reelection in 1961 and as president for life in 1964 occurred at a time when the United States required Latin American support for its covert war against Cuba and its invasion of the Dominican Republic. Haitian support for U.S. policy in the Caribbean was crucial in these two instances, and Haitian political "stability" rather than social justice dictated U.S. policy toward Haiti. The policymakers failed to realize that the lack of social justice and economic development would be detrimental to political stability in Haiti in the long run.

In the final analysis, international considerations, economic and military aid, and "new contracts with commercial firms from the United States were . . . useful in the unremitting psychological wars between a Haitian head of state and those of his citizens who would make or break a regime" (Rotberg, 1971: 209). Although slow to materialize, U.S. private investments in Haiti increased dramatically after 1971, and that approach to economic development was systematized in the Caribbean Basin Initiative (CBI) launched in 1983. Foreign support aside, the dictatorship could not have survived without domestic support in key areas, particularly in the "new" military, the state bureaucracy, and the business sector. In this sense, a major difference in the two phases of the dictatorship, between father and son, revolved around the more personal power of the father being more or less institutionalized under the son. But despite cosmetic changes undertaken to satisfy the United States under the aegis of Haitian technocrats, domestic economic policies, international considerations, and extraordinary corruption remained similar throughout.

Controlled access to information is of critical importance to a dictatorship, and in the 1960s, no Haitian newspaper had a circulation of more than 5,000 copies, reflecting the country's literacy rate at that time of 10 percent. Yet, for 100 years, newspapers had been highly influential in elite politics, in the absence of popular participation. Within months, the printing shops of four major newspapers—*Haiti-Miroir, Le Matin, Le Patriote,* and *Indépendance*—were bombed or destroyed and their staffs tortured. The arch-conservative *La Phalange* proved more difficult—it was controlled by that other (foreign) elite, the Roman Catholic church—but it too, was finally closed in 1961. *La Phalange,* however, did become significant in the elder Duvalier's effort to control the church.

The press was muzzled, although the small amount of international news came from the *Agence France Presse* and the United States Information Service (USIS). Radio stations fared no better. For "hard news," most Haitians relied on the Voice of America, Radio Havana, the quite accurate *télédiol* ("ear-to-snout," word of mouth), and the New York-based paper, *Haiti-Observateur.*

The situation in Haiti remained essentially unchanged until 1972 when a period of "liberalization" was introduced under younger technocrats who had joined the government. President Jimmy Carter's human rights policy made the Haitian government's repression somewhat more restrained. Spearheaded by *Le Petit Samedi Soir,* Dieudonné Fardin's mimeographed newspaper that reached a circulation of 10,000, and the *Radio Haiti-Inter* led by Jean Dominique and Konpè Filo, Haitian journalists became bolder and more critical of the Duvalier regime, although they distinguished between the president for life and his hapless subordinates and blamed the latter, never the former. The "thaw" lasted the length of the Carter administration; President Ronald Reagan's election was marked by severe repression in Haiti, which most everyone in Haiti agreed was the dictator's gift to the new president. More than 100 leaders were arrested, and some of the most prominent of them were exiled in November 1980.

One difference between the 1958 and 1980 crackdowns was the more liberal use of exile and imprisonment in the latter period while torture and death had been the preferred solutions earlier. The *presse parlée* ("spoken press") acquired great importance in view of an overall illiteracy rate that remained constant, but the switch to Kreyol by journalists was also important. These journalists were turning to the Haitian people—a novel approach; nothing else had worked.

The Roman Catholic church has had a tattered record in Haiti. Declared the official religion by the 1860 concordat, it had become an ideological weapon in the hands of the elite and a force for Haiti's westernization. Intermittent church persecutions of Vodou had become an issue for progressive intellectuals and politicians, and for all people who spoke for Haiti's autonomous cultural development, by the mid-1940s. Inevitably, a clash would come, particularly since most clerics and the entire church hierarchy were foreign.

When the dictatorship was challenged by student groups aided by the church, Duvalier killed two *malfinis* (Haitian birds of prey) with one stone. He accused the arch-conservative Breton archbishop, François Poirier, of financially supporting Communist agitators. [. . .] Duvalier's persecution of the church lasted from 1959 until 1964 and culminated with the expulsion of the archbishop, two bishops (including Rémy Augustin, the only Haitian bishop at that time), and numerous priests. [. . .] The president and his entire cabinet were excommunicated but this censure was lifted in 1966 when formal diplomatic relations were renewed with the Vatican. The indigenization of the bishoprics had the blessing of both President Duvalier and Pope Paul VI. The former had weathered a strong challenge to his rule and by meeting that challenge, had ensured years of tranquillity in the process. Duvalier received enormous credit in Haiti for haitianizing the church, and he gave himself yet another title, that of "spiritual leader." The church had taken five years "to fall."

The student strikes were broken, their leaders killed or imprisoned. The church was neutralized. One critic wrote, "The cry of *Communism* had restrained the business community from providing greater help and barred any sympathy or tacit aid from the American Embassy" (Diederich and Burt, 1969: 167).

François Duvalier's accusations were without foundation, but they worked successfully on the United States. But the president had not anticipated that a Haitian church would later prove a mightier opponent because it *was* Haitian. The struggle was about differing conceptions and among various social classes. Despite a century in Haiti, and despite being the most efficient purveyor of education, the church was still alien and an interloper. It had defended the interests of France against those of Haiti, and it had sided unequivocally with the U.S. authorities during the occupation, supporting them in their "civilizing mission."

Throughout the Duvaliers' thirty-year tenure, they gave massive support to U.S. Protestant missions, which strongly backed the status quo while claiming to be apolitical, and active government support for some Vodou priests was a further element of control that also worked against the Roman Catholic church. One anthropologist reports that some fifty U.S. Pentecostal groups active in Haiti have encouraged "social and economic dependence" on the United States. He pursued this analysis in the following words: "Protestant missionaries teach Haitians that they are backward and poor because they are mired in sin. Thus Haiti's poverty vis-à-vis the United States is rationalized on spiritual grounds. A young Haitian convert echoed this when he said to me, 'The American people are the *real* people of God.' "[4]

The one-day visit of Pope John Paul II to Port-au-Prince in March 1983 crystallized opposition to the Duvalier regime that had been developing over several years. The pontiff appealed for social justice for Haiti's poor and declared, "I have come to encourage this awakening, this leap, this movement of the Church for the good of the whole country." Accused of aiding Communists in the early 1960s, the Catholic church now stood accused of being a Communist organization by Duvalier supporters. The

Roman Catholic archbishop, François Wolff-Ligondé, had been named by François Duvalier and was a relative of Madame Jean-Claude Duvalier. He was nonetheless obliged to heed the pope's warning that "something in this country must change."

More than 500 "base communities" were established by the Catholic church in the 1980s. This Ti Légliz (Little Church) movement sought to mobilize against the roots of Haitian poverty and provided an organizational framework in which peasants could challenge the system and demand change. The Ti Légliz movement was as concerned about the quality of life on earth as in the afterlife. A similar reassessment of Haitian society was also developing in other community organizations and in the Vodou community, and soon the Duvalier government could not control the flood of opposition. The Sunday mass and the Catholic Radio Soley also became popular sources of information after Duvalier muzzled the press in the 1980 wave of repression, and in July 1985, a seventy-one-year-old Belgian priest was murdered by government agents, and three foreign priests were deported.

The regime of Jean-Claude Duvalier ("Baby Doc") has claimed that it sought economic revolution in Haiti, whereas Papa Doc had claimed to seek political revolution. But François Duvalier had not pursued a nationalist policy or protected Haitian national interests; he had after all offered the United States the seaport of Môle Saint-Nicolas as a replacement for its base in Guantanamo, Cuba, in April 1961. Similarly, Jean-Claude Duvalier tried to lease historic Tortuga Island to the Dupont Caribbean Corporation in the 1970s. Both Papa Doc and Baby Doc plundered the nation's resources and relentlessly pursued the acquisition of wealth. For example, the World Bank reported that in 1977 about 40 percent of the Haitian government's revenues and expenditures were unaccounted for.[5]

Neither Jean-Claude nor François Duvalier undertook any significant national projects to develop the nation's economy. Although the son allowed some private foreign initiatives to operate as part of a new technocratic image, the plight of most Haitians actually worsened under Jean-Claude's economic policies. The massive emigration from Haiti that occurred after 1977 was largely the result of these new initiatives, and the worsening economic conditions, rather than demands for abstract political democracy, led to a simple but powerful equation in the minds of the Haitian people: *Aba lan mizè, aba Duvalier* ("Down with misery, down with Duvalier").

The Carter administration, the U.S. Congress, and the French Socialist government of President François Mitterrand pressured Jean-Claude Duvalier to create a more democratic "image" for his regime. The members of the congressional Black caucus were particularly active in criticizing the Duvalier government, and they alone appeared to have understood the aspirations of the Haitian people. Carter and Mitterrand, on the other hand, were more concerned that internal Haitian dynamics were destabilizing the Duvalier regime, which had served their countries' economic interests, and that worldwide conditions were not conducive to the maintenance of such a repressive government. Indeed, the Duvalier regime appeared to be a bubble about to burst.

To create a more suitable image, the regime conducted a series of mock elections and referenda between 1971 and 1985, and these were deemed "positive steps" by the U.S. State Department. In January 1971, a constitutional referendum to allow the nineteen-year-old Jean-Claude to succeed his ailing father was approved by a vote of 2,391,916 to 1! In July 1985, six months before the government was overthrown, another referendum conducted to reaffirm the principle of the life-presidency resulted in a 99.98 percent victory for the president. In the first instance, U.S. Ambassador Clinton Knox publicly called for increased U.S. aid to Haiti in response to the regime's seeming stability; in the second, U.S. Ambassador Clayton McManaway praised the referendum as a progressive step. U.S. Ambassador Branson McKinley told Haitian candidate Louis Déjoie II, that if disorders did not stop, both Haiti and the United States would be back to 1915. One State Department official declared that with all its flaws, the Haitian government was doing all it could.

The cynicism of these ambassadors reflected a long-standing problem in Haitian-U.S. relations. In a blatantly racist editorial that ignored the fact that François Duvalier could not remain in power without massive U.S. support, the *New York Times* on June 23, 1957, had blamed the Haitian people for their plight: "Haiti has been unfortunate in her political leadership in recent years. This was inevitable in a country with an illiteracy rate of over 90 percent. The highly emotional people, who have little but tribal rule and superstition to guide their thinking, have been notoriously susceptible to demagogic political appeal." This was not terribly different from what the *New York Times* had written on July 1, 1888: "The wealthy Haitians derive their revenues from ground rents in the cities and the spoils of office; consequently, they have little to lose by revolution, which is their occupation and amusement. By the black savages of the interior a revolution is always welcomed with fierce joy . . . ready at the first note of alarm to pour into the towns by thousands, and, maddened by rum, commit every imaginable excess." Not a trace of big power politics; no economic considerations. But plenty of racism. Simply, Haiti was inept at self-rule.

A far-reaching symbolic event was the marriage of Jean-Claude Duvalier to Michèle Bennett, the daughter of an elite family, in 1980. A latter-day Marie-Antoinette or Eva Perón, she and her husband spent $3 million on the wedding. In one sense, the marriage reunited old foes, the brown and the black elites. Duvalier's "black" supporters feared that this renewed alliance of black and brown would re-establish the mulatto-elite control that had existed in Haiti before 1946, and the founder of the Social Christian party, Grégoire Eugène, wrote in *Fraternité* (Brotherhood), "Are we not

281

handing back to the Right, on a silver platter, the political power we thought we had won in 1946?" (Prince, 1985: 33). This union did not presage a national alliance but a newly found unity between factions of an expanded ruling class. The middle class had lost its rhetorical position as the "vanguard" for urban and rural blacks, and the society was polarized further.

Traditional political parties, when they existed at all, were rarely more than an arrangement of convenience among a leader, his clients and followers. Deviating somewhat from the aforementioned pattern and following a Latin American trend, the late-nineteenth-century Liberal and National parties had represented variations on a theme of upper-class hegemony. Later, in the 1940s, Daniel Fignolé's Worker-Peasant movement (MOP) and the various Socialist and Communist parties were attempts to define political parties in more "institutional" terms.

Louis Déjoie's Haitian Democratic Alliance and, later, Duvalier's Sole Party of Revolutionary and Governmental Action were in the traditional Haitian mold, and so were the countless exile movements, parties, and groups that surrounded the candidacy of a presidential aspirant waiting for Duvalier to fall like a ripe mango. The most serious of these institutionalized parties was the fledgling Unified Party of Haitian Communists (PUCH), which merged many "tendencies" as it formed, or re-formed, in 1969.

In response to the political ferment of the late 1970s and early 1980s, the regime hastily organized a movement, the Conajec (National Committee of Jean-Claudist Action), in April 1978. The ferment had led to the creation of the Haitian League for Human Rights by Gérard Gourgue, Grégoire Eugène's Social Christian party, and the Christian Democratic party of Sylvio Claude, who was arrested and tortured eight times in five years.

The government seemed to lose its grip, and the last five years of the dictatorship saw an increase in political terrorism by the government. This increase was related to a further deterioration in the standard of living, which fueled political discontent. The government continually suspended constitutional guarantees, giving the president full power to rule by decree for periods of eight months when the rubber-stamp parliament, the Chamber, was not in session. Exile, prison, and torture increased during 1980–1985, and show trials, cabinet reshufflings, and the aforementioned referenda became common to assuage foreign sensibilities. But the constitution written for François Duvalier in 1957, another in 1964, another in 1971, and yet another in 1983—the last adopted by the legislature in one day—remained inoperative. In a 1982 report, the Inter-American Commission on Human Rights reached the following conclusion: "No progress has been made, . . . and there is no evidence that any government opening in the near future will re-establish [sic] free democratic life, ideological pluralism, or the free exercise of public freedom."[6]

The Duvalier government fell relatively swiftly, and its sudden collapse came as a surprise to most people, especially foreign observers. One factor had been the government crackdown of November 1980, which was precipitated by public unrest following the Cayo Lobos incident, in which 100 Haitian "boat people" were stranded on a desolate Bahamian cay, and government indifference to the emergency had inspired widespread protests.

Forty people were killed in food riots in May 1984, and riots broke out again in November 1985. In February 1985, 60,000 youths demonstrated in Port-au-Prince with the slogan, *Pito nou mouri kanpe pase nou viv a jenou* ("We would rather die on our feet than live on our knees"). Despite foreign aid to the regime and increased private foreign investments in the Haitian economy—or perhaps because of them—absolute poverty had increased. Military and economic aid from the United States, France, Canada, West Germany, Japan, Israel, Taiwan and South Korea kept Jean-Claude Duvalier in for a time but could not prevent his government from ultimately sinking in the sea of its own brutality, ineptitude, and corruption. Baby Doc was bungling his economic revolution just as Papa Doc had bungled his political revolution. An important difference between the two administrations, however, was that the xenophobic father had sought to control and restrict foreign influence in Haiti whereas the son welcomed foreign interests with open arms.

The Catholic church openly supported opposition to Duvalier, and the decentralized Vodou communities also organized significant resistance to the dictatorship. In response, anti-Vodou groups assassinated about 300 Vodou priests "in the name of Christ and civilization." Although the national movement to dispose of Duvalier soon spread throughout the nation, the rebellion first took root in provincial centers and avoided Duvalier's stronghold of Port-au-Prince. The cities of Gonaïves, where Haitian independence had been proclaimed 182 years earlier, and Petit-Goâve soon emerged as the centers of the revolt.

The leaders of the anti-Duvalier movement apparently decided to resist the government apparatus peaceably. Massive unarmed demonstrations led to military repression and countless deaths followed by more demonstrations. To mollify the army, the population demanded a military government to emerge from a Duvalierist officer corps. There were few other options: No *guerrilleros* ("armed rebels") were waiting in the wings to create a revolutionary government. The fall of Duvalier's comatose government was only a matter of time, and Duvalier toppled from power as soon as the United States "pulled the plug" on his regime by ordering him to leave Haiti and by prematurely naming his successors. The White House announced that Duvalier had left on February 1, but in fact he did not leave until February 7, 1986, after attending a lavish farewell party at the National Palace. Like the exiled Nicaraguan dictator Anastasio Somoza seven years earlier, Duvalier looted the national treasury before leaving the country.

NOTES

1 Robert D. Heinl, Jr., "Bailing Out Duvalier," *New Republic* 156 (January 14, 1967), p. 15.
2 See Allan Ebert, "The Days of 'Baby Doc' Are Numbered," *Newsday* (Long Island, NY), February 4, 1986.
3 "Haitian Dictator Heeds Washington's Aid Signals," *Washington Report on the Hemisphere* 4, no. 6 (December 13, 1983), p. 1.
4 Frederick J. Conway, "Pentecostalism in Haiti: Healing and Hierarchy" (Paper presented at the American Anthropological Association, November 30, 1977), pp. 5, 7.
5 World Bank, *Memorandum on the Haitian Economy* (Washington, DC, May 13, 1981), p. 6.
6 Organization of American States, OEA/Ser.L/V/II.57, 20, September 1982.

REFERENCES

Courlander, Harold, and Rémy Bastien. *Religion and Politics in Haiti*. Washington. DC: Institute for Cross-Cultural Research, 1966.
Diederich, Bernard, and Al Burt. *Papa Doc: The Truth about Haiti Today*. New York: McGraw-Hill, 1969.
Manigat, Leslie. *Haiti of the Sixties: Object of International Concern*. Washington, DC: Washington Center of Foreign Policy Research, 1964.
Prince, Rod. *Haiti: Family Business*. London: Latin America Bureau, 1985.
Rotberg, Robert I. *Haiti: The Politics of Squalor*. Boston: Houghton Mifflin, 1971.
Weil, Thomas E. et al. *Area Handbook for Haiti*. Washington: U.S. Government Printing Office, 1973.

13

THE WATER REFUGEES

(From *AIDS and Accusation: Haiti and the Geography of Blame*)

Paul Farmer

The best view of Do Kay is from atop one of the peculiarly steep and conical hills that nearly encircle the village. Two deep valleys lie between this perch and the road that cuts through the village. To the left is the Peligre Reservoir, or at least that part of it not obscured by other hills. Ba Kay, several hundred feet below, is invisible from this hilltop. Viewed from the sharp outcroppings of rock protruding from the grassy crest, Do Kay looks less like a "line town" stretching along the road than a collection of tiny tin-covered huts randomly scattered on the flanks of a single, large mountainside. Scanning from the left, one first notes a cluster of houses and trees. The trees have survived because they were planted near the second of four public fountains, the first of which is hidden behind one of the hills. Looking slightly more to the right, one can make out the road, and climbing the hill to meet it, the path leading to Vieux Fonds, the very path you have taken to reach this hilltop. High above the road, atop the almost treeless mountain, sits the house of Boss Yonèl. Next door is the empty house of his oldest son, Dieudonné, dead of AIDS in October 1988. Looking lower down and further to the right, the road disappears behind a small ridge, only to reappear near the third fountain, which again is surrounded by more than its share of trees. Now the road has curved into the line of vision; on the left is the home of Marie and Pierre. Also on the left side of the road is a corner of the rusty red roof under which Anita Joseph slowly died of AIDS. On the right, the top of the bakery is visible, as is the brand new house of Pierre's parents, M. and Mme. Sonson. The large, two-story school is almost completely hidden behind a stand of trees planted in the summer of 1983. There the road is also concealed by trees and by the hill upon which the school sits, but it soon swerves, cutting once again into the field of vision.

Turning further to the right, higher on the hill, one sees the dormitory and church built during the tenure of Père Jacques Alexis of the Église Épiscopale d'Haiti. With the school, these buildings form the heart of the "Complèxe Socio-éducatif de Kay," which serves the peasant families of over a dozen villages. There is even a thatched gazebo, encircled by sea pines and often full of people meeting for one reason or another. Further

285

to the right gleam the offices of Projè Veye Sante, the community-health project. Below that, obscured by more trees, are two long pigsties. The grunting of the pigs is quite audible, as are the sing-song voices of the invisible schoolchildren in the schoolyard.

Several other buildings make up the complex—a large clinic, a guest house, an artisans' workshop—but these are hidden by the hill, as is the house of Manno Surpris, formerly a teacher at the school. Manno was the first person on Do Kay to die of AIDS. Even further to the right, the road reappears, climbing over another of the stony, treeless shelves of lime. Plunging over the horizon, the road finally disappears into the upper portion of the central plateau.

A mere decade ago, Do Kay looked quite different from this vantage, and less than four decades ago, not a house was in sight. Writing a history of Kay poses special problems, many of which are not new to anthropology. The village is, upon cursory inspection, just another tiny settlement in the hills of Haiti. Most of its older inhabitants did not attend school; they do arithmetic with great facility, but neither read nor write. Most live in two-room houses, many with dirt floors, and cultivate plots of land that yield slowly diminishing returns. They have no tractors, electricity, or cars. Their hillside gardens are too steep for oxplows, even if they did have oxen. The people of Kay seem to be another "people without history." But the visitor who stays long enough and asks the right questions will soon discover the history lurking below the stereotype of the timeless peasant. Clues can be found in villagers' statements about themselves: "We are Kay people, but we are not from here," explained Nosant, a man in his fifties. "We are people of the valley." The apparent paradox is resolved when the speaker gestures out over the vast reservoir that lies at the base of the hills. The history of the Kay people is submerged below the still surface of this lake.

Before 1956, there was no Do Kay; the area was "a desert, a dry savanna with wind and birds and grass alone," as one of the area's first settlers described it. Most of the villagers who are now over thirty-five once lived in the valley. They were largely from an area called "Petit-Fond," a fertile and gently sloping area on either side of a stream known locally as Rivière Kay. Bursting forth from a cliff face, the largely subterranean stream joined the Artibonite River between the Rivière Thomonde and the Peligre Gorge, where the dam now stands. This small river still leaps from the bottom of the ravine, but now flows somewhat less briskly down to meet the Lac de Peligre, as the new reservoir was named. The area around the spring had long been settled, though sparsely, and it was called Kay. When the valley was flooded in 1956, much of Kay and all of Petit-Fond were submerged. Kay became divided into "Do" and "Ba." Petit-Fond became history.

Presenting a history of Petit-Fond is a legitimate, even necessary, undertaking for any anthropologist attempting to understand Kay as it is today. Even a history of the local AIDS epidemic cannot be fully understood without an appreciation of the effects the dam has had on the welfare of those who live behind it. "History" is not meant to suggest that there exists a true version of the story of the village, one that is ascertainable with careful use of accurate documents. For history varies, as has often been noted, according to winners and losers. The version presented here is that of the self-described losers. Though he was referring to an interclass struggle in a substantially different setting, Scott's (1984:205) observations are pertinent to the material gathered in Kay: "Having lived through this history, every villager is entitled, indeed required, to become something of a historian—a historian with an axe to grind. The whole point of such histories is not to produce a balanced neutral assessment of the decade but rather to advance a claim, to praise and blame, and to justify or condemn the existing state of affairs."

The substantive part of this account has been constructed from interviews: many of the older refugees were interviewed, as was Père Jacques Alexis, the catalyst for much of the recent change in Do Kay and the surrounding area. It is largely from these oral histories that I have reconstructed the history of one village's flight from the rising water and of the settlement of Kay.[1] Each narrative is profitably examined as "positioned rhetoric"—largely a rhetoric of complaint within a particular social and political context. The bounty and harmony of life in the *remembered* valley are the standard against which the present is assessed. More accurately, the remembered valley is the weapon with which the current state of affairs is attacked. And as political change has accelerated in Haiti, the critique has become more strident.

The villagers' story is usually recounted as beginning in the mid-1950s, but the irreversible steps leading to its decline were taken considerably earlier. The "Organisme de Développement de la Vallée de l'Artibonite" (ODVA) was born of an agreement, signed in Washington, D.C., in 1949, between the Haitian government and the Export-Import Bank. Although the loans for the construction of the dam were received in August 1951, the news that the residents of the valley would be forced to relocate seemed not to have traveled far up the valley. Most of those interviewed on Do Kay claim that they were apprised of the impending inundation only a month before it occurred. To cite Nosant, who was a young man when the dam was built: "It was during the month of January that we were informed. They would be filling the valley with water, they said, and we were to move right away. . . . I think it was only a month later, in February, that they stopped up the river." All those interviewed concur that little warning was given. Valley residents did not know, said Mme. Lamandier, "until the water was upon us. We heard only rumors, which we did not believe, until a couple of months before, when they sent someone to tell us to cooperate, that our land would be flooded. This also we did not believe." A few insist that no attempt was made to inform the valley dwellers of their impending losses. Most recall, however, that the community was alerted at a public assembly. Absalom Kola put it this way: "They called an assembly to say that they would be reimbursing everyone for their gardens and land. . . . They warned us, but we all said it can't be true, it couldn't be done. [. . .]."

That the residents of Petit-Fond claimed to know nothing of such an enormous project that would take years to build is striking. Construction went on only a few miles away, at Peligre Gorge, where hundreds of locals were employed at relatively high wages. Indeed, if the rural Haitian economy of the 1950s resembles the economy of today it is likely that some residents of Petit-Fond joined work crews in Peligre, although this is categorically denied by Mme. Gracia, one of the early settlers of Do Kay: "No, there wasn't anyone from Kay who went to work there. It was mostly people from Peligre or from the city [Port-au-Prince]. There were a lot of foreigners too. No one from Petit-Fond worked there."

The area residents' disbelief in the flooding of the valley was nearly unanimous. Many of those living around Petit-Fond did not move until the day the waters "chased us off our lands," as Nosant put it. When asked why they waited until the last moment, the response most often given involves, once again, their disbelief. Absalom Kola's comments are typical:

They warned us, but we all said it can't be true; it couldn't be done. We knew of nothing that could have stopped that great river. The Artibonite ran fast through the valley, and none of us believed it could be stopped. And so on the morning they stopped it up, I watched it rise. Towards two o'clock or so, everyone was rushing around, as the water took our homeland. Everyone ran and left their mills standing. The chickens were obliged to swim; we didn't have time to gather them.

Mme. Gracia underlines the counterintuitive nature of the project: "Everyone said 'water can't climb hills.' It made sense then!" Mme. Emmanuel invokes a more moral version of disbelief: "Of course they sent word. They even came and cut a few big trees. But there wasn't a soul who believed it was true, because we saw the beautiful things we had in our gardens, the gardens of our ancestors. We were sure that no one would do such a thing." She is echoed by Mme. Lamandier:

We just stayed put; we never moved because we believed it was untrue. We saw what sort of good land we had, and how we loved it, and how we had no other land to work, and we came to believe that it just couldn't be true. You have all this and someone tells you they will take it all away . . . you just cannot believe it. But when we saw the water upon us, when even the houses began taking in water, we ran to the hills. And our houses we left to the sea.

The valley residents' disbelief could not have been universal, however, as it seems that a few landowners heeded the government's warnings, and left for nearby towns, such as LasCahobas, Thomonde, or Mirebalais. Some were said to have been reimbursed "by the state" for their lands, but most of the former valley residents interviewed stated flatly, as did Absalom Kola, that they had not:

> They called an assembly to say that they would be reimbursing everyone for their gardens and land. My friend, that was a lie! They came to measure the lands, and indeed a few people did receive payment—only those who were well educated, those who had secured deeds. Our lands consisted of twenty-five *karo*.[2] This belonged to the Kola family; another twenty-five belonged to the Pasquet family. For these lands we received nothing. And there are many others who until this very day have received nothing.

A number of reasons were cited to explain the failure to reimburse the landholders. Mme. Dieugrand, who linked her lack of reimbursement to poverty, stated that "it was the rich peasants who were reimbursed. Truly, we were all doing well back then. But some of us didn't have much land. My mother was struggling. She had no husband and seven children. That's why she got nothing." The reason most commonly invoked, however, involved a different aspect of the political powerlessness of the rural population. Although more than one informant suggested that their powerlessness was a result of their "poverty," most who spoke of political powerlessness cited lack of education, not of lack of money: "Those who were literate and who had deeds were the only ones to get paid," explained M. Kola. "And there was the problem of splitting up [jointly held] lands. If you were uneducated, though, you got nothing. If it had happened nowadays, it would be different, because our children read and write."

All who mentioned the amount of money received for the lands spoke of the government offering insultingly small sums. Mme. Gracia, the one informant who stated that she had been reimbursed, attributed her recompense to the deed: "Yes, they gave me a little—$40 for twelve *karo* [over thirty-eight acres]! Those who had the papers got a little something. Truly, there were many who didn't. But $40 wasn't a fortune back then: we were planting a lot of rice." "To those who received money, they gave such little amounts that it would have been better to receive nothing at all," observed Mme. Nosant. "If it were now, and you owned that land," offered Mme. Lamandier, "there would be no one with enough money to buy it from you. Nor would you need to sell it, because the produce from the land would net you all the money you'd need."

Some mentioned that land tenure patterns were complicated and vested power in the hands of one person. As noted above, the relatively large holdings of the Kola and Pasquet families were jointly held by family elders:

PAUL FARMER

Our land was held communally (*an blok*), a land we called "eritye." Say for example your father had two *karo* that he received from his father (*sou dwa papal*), and his brother had two or three *karo*, but it was all one plot of land—that's called *eritye*. If you're the biggest holder, then the deed is likely to be in your keeping. When the time comes for the land to be paid for, you're the one they would turn to, you're the one who would receive the money. The other holders might get none of it. In this way, the dam turned brother against brother.

Corruption and graft also played an important part in who received reimbursement. A few "big shots" (*gran nèg*) did not fare poorly, it seems, and some of those interviewed note with bitterness that these same persons should have been advocates for the valley dwellers. The water refugees often note that "no one spoke up for us," or that "no one with power in their hands came to our defense." Some note with regret their "ignorance"—their illiteracy. "If we had had someone to speak for us," observed Sonson, "someone who could read and write, then at least we might have been reimbursed for our losses." One of the persons who might have come to the refugees' defense was Père Emmanuel Moreau, of the Église Épiscopale d'Haiti, the young priest who preceded Jacques Alexis as priest of the Mirebalais parish.[3] But Père Moreau answered the call of politics in a more fundamental way. In the year that the valley was flooded, he successfully ran for senator in his home district, and returned to the capital.[4] Alexis feels that a well-placed advocate might have altered the lot of the people of Petit-Fond:

I don't imagine that Moreau could have done anything about the dam; I don't imagine he would have wanted to. The logic was that the dam would help more people than it hurt. But what a pity that more voices were not raised against the abuse of the natives of the valley. . . . There was no [resettlement] plan and it was not long before some of those displaced by Peligre ran into new problems.

It was clear from interviews that, for many, the years following the inundation of their lands were bitter. For some refugees, reaching higher ground was not enough; their trials were not yet over: "It wasn't only the water that came after us," recalls Mme. Emmanuel, "it was also the dynamite." The department of public works, in conjunction with the ODVA and a team of U.S. engineers, had begun building a road along the hill that overlooked the reservoir. The ledge opened up by the completion of the road was known as "the terrace." The new road was to replace an older one, also drowned by the dam, that once ran from Las Cahobas to Hinch. The road crews, explained Mme. Emmanuel, used explosives:

290

As soon as you heard them shout 'Run!,' then rocks would fly everywhere. They crushed rocks up there endlessly. And they would do this without looking to see if someone might be below. We couldn't stay. We were all afraid we'd be crushed by the great rocks that came crashing down with no warning. We had to go. We were the ones who came here [Do Kay] first; everyone else followed and came to join us.

Others followed Mme. Emmanuel to the stony—but safer—hills above. When asked why she came to Do Kay, Mme. Gracia replied, "Well, we didn't have anywhere else to go; we got out to avoid being drowned. We didn't have time to save our belongings. We built little lean-tos on the hill, and resigned ourselves to our losses." Some informants report a dazed feeling, and an inability to act decisively: "For a year, I couldn't do anything. I just sat there. My children were always crying. I didn't plant a thing," said Louis, who has since managed to become a moderately successful peasant. Mme. Jolibois also reports "a heaviness, a difficulty in knowing where to go, what to feed the children. Now we're used to having nothing to offer them, but back then it was a shock." Mme. Gracia's remarks echo those of her neighbors. "We had no food and little money," she recalls; "it seems as if we couldn't act. We planted nothing. So I sold the cows, one at a time, in order to feed the children." Mme. Dieugrand recalls, "We were stunned. We didn't know where to turn. We waited for God's miracles, and nothing happened."[5]

Although the land in Do Kay was by unanimous acclamation "without value," it was safer than the land by the water's edge. More than dynamite rendered it hazardous. The reservoir level was altered several times, and those who planted near the shore lost their crops when the water level was raised.[6] Also disturbing to the refugees who settled Ba Kay was the state-sponsored planting of teak trees, locally termed bwa leta ("state trees"), near the high watermark. These were variably justified as protection against erosion and raw material for future utility poles, but many suspected that more land would be appropriated. For these and other reasons, Mme. Emmanuel's lead was followed by quite a few families. Père Alexis states that there were only "two or three" households when he first visited Do Kay, shortly after the basin had been filled. A 1962 mapping by photogrammetric methods from 1956 aerial photography suggests, however, that there were fifteen houses on Do Kay within a year of the inundation.

One thing that is striking, in even a cursory reading of the interviews, is the refugees' almost unanimous appreciation of a central irony to their story. Each interviewee has spoken of the unfairness of a project that destroys a way of life and offers benefits only to faraway Port-au-Prince. Mme. Gracia, in response to the question "Why did they build the dam?" offered the following observation: "Well, it was in order to light up Port-au-Prince with electricity, but I get nothing out of that. Port-au-Prince has light, but I'm in darkness—and I live right next door to Peligre! It's the big shots (*gran nèg*) in Port-au-Prince who are having fun now." She was seconded by Mme. Lamandier: "To have electricity for the city people and for the factories, that's why. The rich people, the city people bribe the bureaucrats so they can have electricity. Water makes electricity, but you need high water. So they flooded us out."

These analyses of the OVDA by former residents of Petit-Fond are scathing indeed. Mme. Emmanuel does not mince words: "I see not one speck of benefit in the water. What benefit there is goes only to the people living in the city. They all have light. Do I have things like that? It's the powerful man who gets it." A similarly dim view was offered by M. Kola, but his conclusions were tempered with a certain optimism:

> Look at me now; what do I have? Poverty has come after me. I'm resigned to it. But if they were to let loose these waters and say "Here's a little plot of your old land back," I'd build a little lean-to in which to sleep, and I can promise you that I'd soon be wealthy, I and all my family. But I won't find anything now. Still, since the terrace was built, we've found a light; we've found Père Alexis, who has come to give us a bit of knowledge. Yes, there has been that to offset our loss: the sole advantage we've found has been the Alexis advantage. He has helped us raise our children; he has worked hard so that our children might be educated.

Nineteen-fifty-six was thus a traumatic year for those who had come to love the land. Mme. Emmanuel speaks, as do others, of the profound depression that followed: "My friend, everyone saw their lives ending. There were those who died of grief. This is true. My father . . . well, it is grief that killed him." She is echoed by Mme. Gracia: "We were in a bad way. Our hearts were being torn out (*se kè nou ki t'ap rache*). But we couldn't speak. Some people just plain died from the shock. And from that day on, I've never felt right again."

NOTES

1 These narratives are complemented by other data, gathered during the last five years in an annual census conducted with the help of a small group of community health workers from Kay. In all households with members who were displaced by the reservoir, we conducted structured interviews using a rather crude questionnaire. Although these data are clearly of limited value, enough was learned from the questionnaires to discern a few modal patterns of relocation leading eventually to Do Kay. I am grateful to Ophelia Dahl for her insights to these patterns.

2 A *karo* (from the French, *carreaux*) is equal to 1.29 hectares or 3.19 acres.

3 The 1861 founding of this church by an African-American is recounted by Romain (1986) in his history of Haitian Protestantism. See also Hayden (1987) and Heinl and Heinl (1978).

4 There he met the same fate as many other politically active and independent-minded individuals. Moreau was arrested and never seen again. His successor as pastor of Mirebalais maintains that he was taken to the palace and shot in the head—while pleading on his knees to be spared. "His executioner," observes Père Alexis, "was rumored to have been none other than François Duvalier."

5 In an interview conducted in 1987, Melifèt Fardin recalled a movement to go and *dechouke*, or "uproot," the administrators of the ODVA, and make them release the waters of the Lac de Peligre. Other water refugees denied that any such movement was significant. "Just talk," said Absalom, laughing. "We didn't even know where the ODVA headquarters were." As for the "docility" of the displaced peasants, it is interesting to note the commentary of Kethly Millet in her study of peasant revolts during the U.S. occupation: "In his struggle to hang onto his little bit of land and win a measure of well-being, the peasant has always shown a deep respect for the sanctity of human life. Threats, the destruction of agricultural implements, and the 'sit-down' characterize the beginnings of revolt. Violence usually comes from the adversary. [Full revolt] is thus a reaction to repression from the governmental and [North] American authorities" (Millet 1978:137).

6 During the dry season, however, many peasants of the region still run the risk of planting corn, tobacco, beans, yams, and other crops below the high water-mark. They often lose bountiful harvests to early rains, which fill the reservoir just as the crops are ripening.

REFERENCES

Hayden, J. Carleton. "Afro-Anglican Linkages, 1701–1900: Ethiopia Shall Soon Stretch Out Her Hands Unto God." In *Journal of Religious Thought* 44, no. 1 (1986): 25–34.

Heinl, Robert Debs, Jr. and Nancy Heinl. *Written in Blood: The Story of the Haitian People, 1492–1971*. Boston: Houghton Mifflin, 1978.

Millet, Kethly. *Les paysans haïtiens et l'occupation américaine, 1915–1930*. La Salle, Quebec: Collectif Paroles, 1978.

Romain, Charles-Poisset. *Le protestantisme dans la société haïtienne*. Port-au-Prince: Imprimerie Henri Deschamps, 1986.

Scott, James. "History According to Winners and Losers." In *Senri Ethnological Studies* 13 (1986): 161–210.

14

THE RISE, FALL, AND SECOND COMING OF JEAN-BERTRAND ARISTIDE

(*excerpts*)

Robert Fatton Jr.

Lavalas in Power

In the period of the late 1980s, Haitian civil society comprised a multiplicity of private groups bent on curbing the predatory reach of the state. While it continued to encompass conservative, populist, and radical organizations, civil society soon came to be dominated by Lavalas, whose name symbolized the huge power of the nascent and loosely structured mass movement of the destitute. Lavalas carried Father Jean-Bertrand Aristide, the embodiment of the radical voices of Ti Légliz, to the presidency in the free elections of December 16, 1990, with close to 70 percent of the vote. Father Aristide had initially been opposed to the electoral process, which he described as an imperialist U.S. affair bent on emasculating popular forces and reempowering the "reactionary bourgeoisie." [...] He decried presidential candidates for suffering from *la présidentite*—the disease afflicting those who are interested in nothing but the exclusive promotion of their personal ambitions and interests. And yet, while Father Aristide declared his immunity from *la présidentite*, he was ultimately convinced to run for office.[1]

Aristide justified his candidacy as a historical necessity to stop reactionary forces from legitimizing their continued hold on privilege and to empower the marginalized poor majority. In short, he was left with no alternative; he had to lead Lavalas to the elections. As he put it in his autobiography: "The result of our electoral boycott would be a formal system that would eliminate all the lower classes. We would ultimately concede to the bourgeoisie a limited suffrage that they would not have dared to propose themselves?"[2]

Aristide announced his candidacy on October 18. It materialized at the last minute and generated Opération Lavalas, an uneasy coalition of the popular movement of the poor and progressive anti-Duvalierist parties.

The candidacy reflected on the one hand Aristide's partial acknowledgment that he could become the vehicle of an "electoral *déchoukaj*" and on the other hand the desire of reformist forces headed by the FNCD to replace their uninspiring candidate—Victor Benoît—by a more charismatic and popular leader.[3] Moreover, both Aristide and the FNCD were united in their opposition to Marc Bazin, who represented U.S.-supported conservative forces, and the Macoute Roger Lafontant.[4] In fact, the elections, as Claude Moïse and Émile Ollivier explained, became a confrontation between the "forces of evil" and the "forces of God."[5] In this confrontation, Aristide was the ideal candidate [. . .]; he was the messiah who would overcome all obstacles and triumph over the satanic forces of Duvalierism, privilege, and corruption. The vast majority of Haitians shared Ti Légliz's vision of him as the symbolic figure of the prophet who, inspired by God, would establish justice on earth and save the poor from the predations of the well-off.[6] [. . .]

Thus, in 1990, Aristide embodied the aspirations of the destitute; he was the personification of Lavalas. In turn, Aristide defined Lavalas as not just a "collection of a variety of movements and political parties"; it was "much, much more: a river with many sources, a flood that would sweep away all the dross, all the after-effects of a shameful past."[7] In Aristide's eyes, Lavalas was the united movement of the poor. As he put it in a message delivered in November 1988, "Alone, we are weak. Together, we are strong. Together, we are the flood."[8] Lavalas was the revolutionary flood that would sweep away all the vestiges of *duvalierisme* as well as the parasitic and exploitative bourgeoisie. [. . .]

Needless to say, all did not share Aristide's prophetic vision. He knew that old Macoutes, the military, and a segment of the bourgeoisie would oppose his call for social solidarity and for an equitable redistribution of wealth. Once in power, Aristide could not help but face these harsh realities.[9] In spite of his multiple condemnations of imperialist and capitalist exploitation, his economic policies remained extremely pragmatic; at most they entailed a commitment to social democracy and the World Bank vision of "basic needs." He was always appealing for the cooperation of what he called the "nationalist bourgeoisie," and he accepted the necessity of dealing with international financial organizations.

Aristide acquiesced to a program of structural adjustment designed by the World Bank and the International Monetary Fund—two institutions he had previously denounced as vile capitalist instruments sucking Haiti's blood.[10] He espoused strict fiscal austerity, an anticorruption drive, and the modernization of public enterprise. These economic reforms achieved significant success and gained massive international support. [. . .]

Thus, in spite of its radical socialistic rhetoric, Aristide's first administration committed itself to a very moderate economic program. It had few alternatives; moreover, given the utter predatory nature of the Duvalierist inheritance, the urban poor and the peasantry would hardly suffer from the imposition of fiscal restraints and the policy of privatization. The absence of a redistributive welfare state thus facilitated the imposition of a structural adjustment package. The Aristide regime attempted, however, to reform the package by introducing into it some of the policies associated with the "basic-needs" model that had gained a certain popularity in the 1970s. The effort sought to mitigate the most deleterious consequences of structural adjustment without alienating international financial institutions and donors.[11]

The Aristide administration was thus pursuing privatization with a "human face" while relying on a "social" market to minimize popular disenchantment and disaffection. In fact, only Duvalierist business people who pillaged the national treasury and public sector employees who had benefited from a paltry prebend could oppose such a variant of structural adjustment.[12] At any rate, Haiti's desperate material situation and profound dependence on external economic forces left Aristide with few choices. He was thus fully cognizant that his radical rhetoric had obdurate limits. As he put it, "I never ceased disputing the value of believing in miracles ... we cannot do everything or provide everything tomorrow; we will simply try to move from destitution to poverty."[13]

Such a modest project constituted, however, a revolutionary vision in a predatory society like Haiti. The vision encompassed three fundamental ideas: "dignity, transparent simplicity, and participation," which were symbolized in Lavalas's main electoral slogan: "*Chanjé Leta: ba li koulè revandikasyon pèp-la*" [we have to change the state: we will give it the colors of the people's demands].[14] The political implementation of that project was at odds with the constitutional constraints of liberal democracy that limited the executive power of the Lavalasian president and ultimately protected the privilege of the privileged.[15]

I do not wish to suggest that Aristide and the forces he represented were enemies of democracy; on the contrary, Aristide's brief first presidency marked the freest and most hopeful period of Haiti's modern political history. Rather, the Lavalasian conception of democracy departed from the liberal representative democracy that the constitution of 1987 sought to enshrine. Indeed, many in the Lavalas movement regarded the electoral process with ambiguity, if not disdain. It was not merely because of the tragic memory of the violence unleashed against the popular sectors in the aborted ballot of 1987; it was also because elections could be robbed and "bought" by the vast resources at the disposal of privileged groups. In addition, there was the distinct conviction that elections were both a machination engineered by U.S. imperialism and a form of "bourgeois" representation that would leave untouched existing alignments of wealth and power. Finally, radical Lavalasians believed that elections lacked the purity of a popular revolutionary uprising and would abort the desired *déchoukaj* of Duvalierism and its corrupt supporters.[16] Participation in the elections was a means to an end rather than a matter of principle. [. . .]

The reluctance with which Aristide opted for the electoral road generated, however, a series of contradictions and tensions once he seized and exercised power. He had little patience for the constitutional and parliamentary niceties that constrained his executive governance. [. . .] The compromises and gradualism entailed by constitutionalism coexisted uneasily with the Lavalasian desire for a messianic and prophetic transformation of society. [. . .]

Déchoukaj and parliamentarism remained in serious tension and ultimately proved incompatible. Such incompatibility was accentuated further by Aristide's failure to institutionalize a political society that may have helped mediate conflicts and minimize political deadlock.[17] Aristide's prophetic style of governance blinded him to the "princely" necessity of compromise and undermined his support for political society. In fact, his disdain for the entire political class caused inevitable and immediate divisions within the Lavalas movement. [. . .] He excluded the FNCD and other important components of his electoral coalition from his government.[18] [. . .]

Clearly, Aristide was bent on controlling the mass movement. He was not prepared to cede leadership of it to any independent party; his Lavalas Organization embodied the outward structure of a regime of friends who were totally devoted and loyal to his persona.[19] Aristide did not trust "professional politicians" who might quickly turn against him and abandon his transformative agenda. As Alex Dupuy put it,

> Aristide . . . entertained a jaundiced view of the existing political parties, even those on the Left like the FNCD that were close to his political views. He saw them basically as 'talk shops' that held congresses, engaged in legitimate but Byzantine discussions . . . and whose proliferation rendered them ineffective. . . . [Aristide's] allegiance was only to the people and to . . . *Opération Lavalas*— cleansing flood—movement, which he believed was more significant than the FNCD (or any other political organization then in place), and of which he was the self-proclaimed leader.[20]

His rejection of former allies, however, helped to undermine political consensus and exacerbated unnecessarily his relations with parliament. In fact, many observers have claimed that these divisions weakened Aristide's regime to such an extent that they were a major factor in the coup of September 1991.[21] From this perspective, it was Aristide's confrontational style symbolized in his toleration and indeed incitation of mob rule that was responsible for his own downfall. He never acquired the political skills required to seduce his opponents; he sought to silence them through intimidation rather than cooperation and compromise. Moreover, his loyalty to supporters was always tenuous and dependent on their blind subservience to his own changing agenda.[22] In short, Aristide had

neither the presidential stature nor the statecraft that would have empow-
ered him to accomplish his objectives. Robert Malval, who would become
Aristide's prime minister during his exile in Washington, summarizes
well this view:

> [Aristide] had only short-winded social rhetoric that he had taken
> from the doctrine of liberation theology and that he used on all
> occasions in order better to hide the absence of any real political,
> social, and particularly economic thinking. [. . .] If his discourse
> was consequently predictable, his action, on the other hand,
> disconcerted more than one observer. An idea may be as quickly
> approved as abandoned, thus giving to his political action a
> contradictory nature that will continue to prevent him from rising
> to the level of his incredible destiny.[23]

While it is true that Aristide's prophetic style and enigmatic policies
may have deepened the profound alienation existing between the popular
forces that he symbolized and the dominant classes, nothing suggests that
these classes would have responded positively to a more "princely"
demeanor. The dominant classes despised him, they engaged in plotting
maneuvers immediately after his election, and they never entertained the
idea of compromise.[24] Only surrender would have satisfied them. In
reality, whatever may have been Aristide's style of governance, his call for
social solidarity and for an equitable redistribution of wealth was bound
to incite the opposition of old Macoute leaders, the military, and a segment
of the bourgeoisie. Moreover, the dominant classes' hatred of Aristide
stemmed not from what he ultimately did, but rather from what he
symbolized. [. . .] As David Nicholls has pointed out, "Aristide's presence
in the presidential palace reflected and reinforced a new confidence among
the poor people of Haiti. Servants refused to do what they were told, and
were even heard to say that their master's luxurious house and cars would
soon be theirs. The rich became worried that their privileged position was
being threatened."[25]

The dominant classes' fears of a revolution and a world turned "upside
down" prompted their mobilization and support for the coup of September
1991. Moral appeals to share wealth and opportunities more equally, and
Aristide's hugely popular slogan that *tout moun se moun*, had very little
impact on the dominant classes' behavior. Clearly, the time for a Haitian
"deliberative" democracy had yet to arrive;[26] brute force would settle the
issue and Aristide could not help but face this harsh reality.

The failure of constitutionalism was largely caused by the unequal
balance of power between the contending political blocs. The counter-
vailing force of a popular civil society was still too weak, unorganized,
and defenseless to prevent the military coup; and while the Haitian
authoritarian habitus facilitated Aristide's overthrow, it was of very

secondary significance. In reality, a democratic consensus for a radical transformation of Haitian society was impossible given that the stark demarcation of class had historically generated a politics of ferocious struggles rather than civil compromises. The question really was, and still is, Would the Haitian dominant class be prepared to accept electoral defeat and relinquish its power to radical populist forces without resorting to a preemptive coup?

The overthrow of President Aristide on the night of September 29, 1991, clearly demonstrated that the ruling class contemplated nothing of the sort. It is clear that the military and the bourgeoisie felt increasingly threatened by Aristide's appeals for popular justice. [. . .] When Aristide made his famous "Père Lebrun" speech on September 27, the speech in which he rhetorically extolled in front of a huge crowd the virtues of necklacing his Macoute enemies, he had already lost the battle.[27] The speech was a desperate attempt to prevent the army and the bourgeoisie from striking down Lavalas.

Rather than articulating a clear strategy of revolutionary violence,[28] Aristide's wild rhetoric represented a last-ditch attempt to intimidate those who had been busy planning his overthrow. As he later explained, "I was using words to answer bullets."[29] His words, however, symbolized and underlined his preference for a radical discourse that masked Lavalas's inherent organizational and political weaknesses and incapacity to implement a revolutionary program. While such words electrified his mass followings, they betrayed impotence rather than strength and contributed to the inevitable fury of the dominant class and the military. [. . .]

While Lavalas's discourse was truly antagonistic and menacing to the privileged sectors of society, how could it have been otherwise? [. . .] Such attitudes were the logical response to the dominant class's utterly reactionary contempt for the masses. In their private as well as public utterances, members of the dominant class held *le peuple* in nothing but disdain, scorn, and ridicule. The intensity of their detestation expressed their conviction that the majority of their compatriots lacked the full attributes of the human species and embodied a gesticulating, savage, and animalistic mass, incapable of civilized and rational behavior. In the 1992 documentary film *Killing the Dream*, Aubelin Jolicoeur, a journalist and celebrity of Haiti's "higher circles," betrayed their fascist tendencies: "The people made a choice that is at the root of all our problems. Aristide was elected by 67 percent of the vote, maybe 70 percent. But that is an erroneous way of seeing democracy and perhaps a terrible error because people who cannot read cannot possibly make a valid choice."[30]

Simply put, the dominant class could not countenance the transformation of the *moun andeyo* into citizens;[31] it could not allow the world to "turn upside down." The new citizens, however, armed with the knowledge that *tout moun se moun*,[32] would no longer put up with being silent victims, they would no longer tolerate being ordered to *"pa fouré bouch ou nan afè moun"* [mind their own business]. Thus, the political discourse of the time betrayed the ugly realities of a naked political confrontation in a society deeply fissured between dominant and subordinate classes.

In fact, there was a new geography of class power that forced members of the dominant class into erecting walls of armed security to separate themselves from the *moun andeyo* who were increasingly "invading their territory."[33] Wealthy Haitians feared being overwhelmed by a vengeful, violent, and criminal mass of poor people who had trespassed the boundaries of private property to settle on land that had hitherto been the exclusive space of the rich. As Simon Fass explained, the collapse of the Duvalier dictatorship created a relative "breakdown of control permitting one significant act that for 30 years had proven impossible: land invasion and squatting."[34] Panic seized the dominant class; it dreaded living in close proximity to *la populace* and barricaded itself against Lavalas. As a wealthy Haitian told me in an alarming tone, "Ils sont partout, ils nous entourent, ils sont parmi nous!" [the masses are everywhere, they surround us, they are among us].[35]

Instead of bringing the classes together, the sense of social proximity generated a new impetus and energy to enlarge and consolidate the huge fissure dividing Haitians.[36] The fissure was indeed a chasm that conciliatory words could neither mask nor bridge. It is this chasm and not Lavalas's rhetoric that explains Aristide's overthrow. A decade later, Aristide himself reached the same conclusion:

> The human power in my country is the huge majority of the poor. The economic power is that 1% that controls 45% of the wealth.
>
> The *coup d'état* of 1991 showed how terribly afraid the 1% is of the mobilization of the poor. They are afraid of those under the table—afraid they will see what is on the table. Afraid of those in *Cité Soleil*, that they will become impatient with their own misery. Afraid of the peasants, that they will not be *'moun andeyo'* anymore. They are afraid that those who cannot read will learn how to read. They are afraid that those who speak Creole will learn French, and no longer feel inferior. They are afraid of the poor entering the palace, of the street children swimming in the pool. They are not afraid of me. They are afraid that what I say may help the poor to see.[37]

Thus, there was a structural inevitability to the tragedy of September 29, 1991.[38] Indeed, rumors of an impending coup, and the preparations for the coup itself, long preceded Aristide's "Père Lebrun" speech.[39]

Hence, while the speech came to haunt Aristide's three long years of exile, it had little to do with the coup itself. It provided the dominant classes, however, with a useful pretext for ushering in military rule and for the constitutionality of class privilege and abuse. The coup demonstrated beyond doubt that the old structures of power remained resilient: the army resisted civilian control, old Macoutes and Duvalierists were still influential, and the elites maintained their utter contempt for *le peuple*. What was striking about the post-Duvalier era even after Aristide was restored to the presidency and even after his chosen heir, René Préval, succeeded him peacefully was not the *déchoukaj* of the old state, but rather its persistence under new forms. The regime may have changed, but the ancient structures of class power have endured in spite of the emergence of new Lavalasian political rulers.

In fact, Lavalasian rulers have been increasingly accused of imposing a system of governance rooted in the despotism that had characterized Haiti's past. While there might well be an authoritarian momentum, it differs in significant ways from old dictatorial structures. Clearly, despite the Chimères and the wild rhetoric, the level of political repression is nowhere close to what it used to be under the military or Duvalier tyrannies. The press and the opposition, constrained as they may feel, operate freely. Civil society can still publicly challenge executive power and organize against the Lavalasian state. These realities should not mask, however, the emergence and consolidation of what I have called a predatory democracy—a form of democracy that shares the plebiscitary presidentialism of a "delegative democracy."[40] As Guillermo O'Donnell explains,

> Delegative democracies rest on the premise that whoever wins election to the presidency is thereby entitled to govern as he or she sees fit, constrained only by the hard facts of existing power relations and by a constitutionally limited term of office. [. . .] In this view, other institutions—courts and legislatures, for instance—are nuisances that come attached to the domestic and international advantages of being a democratically elected president. Accountability to such institutions appears as a mere impediment to the full authority that the president has been delegated to exercise.[41]

Both Aristide and his successor, Préval, have ruled with acute disdain for the legislative branch, emasculated the autonomy of the judiciary, and diluted the independence of the electoral council. Once elected, they governed as providential leaders, giving free rein to their executive powers. Their presidential monarchism has failed, however, to transform Haitian society. In fact, many of the old patterns of corruption, nepotism, and incompetence have resurfaced at all governmental levels. In addition, the emergence of a new Lavalasian political elite benefiting from unencumbered access to state resources has done precious little to shake the old balance of class power and the constellation of external forces that confines the country to utter dependence. The question, then, was and still is

301

whether, given entrenched class divisions and the constraints imposed by external sources of power, the promised Lavalasian transformation is at all realizable. Ironically, the conditions surrounding Aristide's U.S.-engineered return to the presidency in October 1994 have probably spelled the end of the Lavalasian illusion that had captured the hearts and minds of most Haitians.

Exile and Return

While the coup of September 1991 interrupted abruptly the "utopian moment," it failed miserably to gain domestic and international support. The United States and its key allies decided that the military had to return to the barracks and that Aristide's presidency had to be restored. These two objectives generated a frustrating and long series of international negotiations culminating in several ill-fated agreements. While the failure of diplomacy ultimately engendered the reluctant U.S. military intervention of October 1994, it debilitated Aristide's populist and nationalist credentials.

Aristide's gradual emasculation began with the vicissitudes of exile, intensified with the Governors Island Accord that was to have returned him to power on October 30, 1993, and truly crystallized with the Port-au-Prince agreement that did in fact result in his restoration a year later. It is readily apparent that these different pacts compromised significantly much of Lavalas's original program and vision. They eventually forced Aristide to accept the inclusion of old opponents in his new "enlarged" government of national reconciliation. At Governors Island, Aristide, rather than General Raoul Cédras and the other perpetrators of the coup, made the major concessions.[42] It is true that the Haitian junta signed the agreement on July 3, 1993, in response to growing international pressures and particularly the arms and oil embargo imposed by the UN Security Council a few days earlier.[43] However, as Mark Danner correctly pointed out, "[The accord] made no provision for justice: those responsible for the coup [would] simply retire . . . or be transferred to other posts. The Haitian army would not have to endure a 'housecleaning.' . . . In one way or another, under the . . . accord, Aristide would be expected to work with many of the same officers that had overthrown him and murdered his followers."[44]

Thus, as Ian Martin, former director for human rights of the Organization of American States (OAS)/UN International Mission in Haiti, put it, "Regrettably, the Governors Island Agreement made no reference to respect for human rights."[45] Moreover, the accord entailed the suspension of sanctions and the dilution of the Lavalasian component of Aristide's new government. The fact that in spite of these concessions Aristide's restoration failed to occur was ample proof that the military and the elites would not surrender easily.

The dramatis personae were locked in a dangerous equilibrium. Neither the populist democratizing bloc nor the neo-Duvalierist, authoritarian coalition was capable of imposing its respective agenda on the other. This impasse also reflected—until the shift in U.S. policy in May 1994—the military's conviction that the external forces advocating the reinstatement of Aristide had neither the will nor the power to impose his return.[46] Their conviction was further strengthened when the U.S. warship *Harlan County*, sent in accordance with the Governors Island Accord, failed to dock in Haiti in October 1993. Fearing a violent confrontation with army-backed thugs, the *Harlan County*, carrying nearly 200 U.S. troops on a non-combat mission to prepare the island for Aristide's return, pulled out of Haitian waters.[47]

Having successfully engineered the retreat of U.S. forces and thus the collapse of the Governors Island Accord, the Haitian military and elite believed that the international community and the United States in particular had grown tired of supporting Aristide and would eventually accept an "internal solution" that excluded Aristide and might lead to new elections.[48] Alternatively, the coup leaders were prepared to wait for new negotiations and more concessions, so that should Aristide return he would be totally *déplumé*—that is, totally fleeced.

The reading of the situation by the Haitian elites was reinforced by the collusion between the CIA and the Haitian military[49] as well as by the indecisive, confusing policies of the Clinton administration.[50] In fact, the United States had always been ambivalent about the power shift that Aristide's election symbolized and had traditionally supported the elite and the army.[51] Haitian politicians of very distinct ideological tendencies, and friends as well as foes of Aristide, have maintained that the United States had such a difficult time countenancing his 1990 victory that a delegation headed by Jimmy Carter asked him to desist in favor of Marc Bazin the very night of his electoral triumph.[52] The legacy of a strong U.S. undercurrent against Aristide inevitably impinged on the policies of the Clinton administration and paralyzed any decisive action.

Until May 1994, the United States had been unwilling to contemplate the use of military force and had been hesitant about imposing a total embargo. The U.S. objective at the time was to force Aristide into accepting the integration of an anti-Lavalasian front into his government. [. . .] Facing Aristide's rejection, the humiliation of the retreat of the *Harlan County*, intense domestic criticisms, and a growing number of boat people, President Clinton was forced into a major shift of policy.

By late April, the shift was formalized: William Gray, a former African-American congressman who had been very influential in the Congressional Black Caucus, replaced Ambassador Lawrence Pezzullo as special envoy to Haiti. The change in personnel symbolized a new determination to restore Aristide to the presidency. The Clinton administration then moved quickly to impose a total economic embargo on the island. It froze

U.S.-held assets of wealthy Haitians and banned U.S. commercial flights to Haiti. In addition, Washington indicated clearly that it was prepared to use force if sanctions failed to dislodge the coup leaders. At its urging, on July 31, 1994, the United Nations adopted Resolution 940, which authorized a multinational military force "to use all necessary means" to oust the military junta and restore Aristide to the presidency.[53]

While a U.S. invasion was becoming increasingly likely given the intransigence[54] of the Haitian military and growing waves of boat people,[55] it constituted an alternative that neither Clinton nor Aristide necessarily welcomed. Intervention was potentially costly for both men; it could become a quagmire for the United States and it could undermine Aristide's nationalistic credentials. The killing of eighteen U.S. Rangers in Mogadishu, Somalia, on October 3, 1993, had convinced many Washington policymakers that the loss of U.S. lives in the pursuit of vague international objectives in situations of minor strategic significance was intolerable. In this view, armed intervention was justified only when matters of vital "national interest" were at stake. Moreover, U.S. policymakers feared that in the absence of a clear timetable for an exit, any intervention might well degenerate into "mission creep." In other words, U.S. troops might find themselves shifting from the initial goals of peacekeeping, to peacemaking, and ultimately "nation building." In the eyes of many members of the U.S. foreign policy elite, this was a dangerous, counterproductive, and wasteful use of U.S. power. Haiti, with its extremely limited strategic value, was thus a very dubious place for U.S. military involvement.

On the other hand, intervention had the potential of becoming a very cheap triumph for President Clinton; it might well have enabled him to assert decisive leadership and eradicate the "Somalia syndrome" that had temporarily immobilized U.S. power.[56] [. . .]

Moreover, an intervention would inevitably deradicalize Aristide, transforming him from an anticapitalist prophet into a staunch U.S. ally committed to the virtues of the market. A U.S.-led restoration of Aristide's presidency was thus likely to dampen his populist appeal, erode his nationalist credentials, and emasculate whatever radical project he may have favored. It was the fear of such a fate that explained Aristide's ambivalence and ever changing attitude toward a U.S. military intervention. In the end, however, Aristide had no choice.[57] Indeed, his return was totally dependent on the exercise of U.S. power, over which he had no control.

The question, then, was whether after months of hesitation President Clinton would ultimately resort to military force. By September 1994, it became clear that diplomacy was exhausted and that U.S. credibility was at stake.[58] [. . .]

The ascendancy of Haiti in Clinton's agenda of priorities was not without some logic. Failure to intervene would have further diminished Clinton's already dwindling international prestige. At the domestic level, the African-American community—one of the president's most important constituencies—accused him of conducting a racist foreign policy. The well-publicized hunger strike of TransAfrica's director, Randall Robinson, and the Congressional Black Caucus's calls for military action clearly contributed to transform Haiti into a critical national security issue. Moreover, the political problems caused by the flood of Haitian refugees fleeing political persecution and material deprivation gave the United States added incentives to end the island's crisis promptly.

[. . .] Significant domestic considerations therefore contributed to the eventual decision to take military action against Haiti's ruling junta and launch Operation Uphold Democracy.

It is unlikely, however, that domestic interests represented a sufficiently powerful constellation of constituencies to force the issue. The Clinton administration had shown repeatedly that it could ignore and even alienate its allies in the African-American community at no real cost. Furthermore, while the Haitian refugees posed a political and moral dilemma for the president, they could be—and indeed were—rerouted to shores far away from Florida. Finally, with more than two-thirds of the U.S. public opposed to any military intervention, the Clinton administration had little to gain from invading Haiti and risking the loss of American lives. In fact, President Clinton himself thought a military strike against the "de factos" might well "ruin everything he had worked all his life to build."[59] He is reported to have confided to historian Taylor Branch,

> [that] his closest friends in the U.S. Senate advised him in person that his contemplated military intervention was worse than misguided or foolish—it was insane. As if it weren't bad enough to send Democratic candidates against the GOP Contract with America on weak political standing and a freshly failed health-reform crusade, now, they said, six weeks before the election, Clinton wanted to invade a country that nobody in America cared about. 'They were furious!' said Clinton.[60]

Why then the intervention? Laennec Hurbon, a prominent Haitian intellectual, has suggested that the intervention signaled a "new age" in international relations—an age in which the "Kantian idea of a human universal has begun to emerge as a concrete reality in the geopolitical sphere."[61] In Hurbon's view, this is the age when military force becomes the agent of democratic liberation rather than authoritarian repression. If this were not the case, asks Hurbon, how can we explain that American lives were put at risk "solely in order to assist a people in danger and to restore democracy to a country that has no such tradition [?]"[62]

While Operation Uphold Democracy cannot be fully accounted for without paying attention to the ideological power of a democratic aspiration, it would be exceedingly naive to fall into Hurbon's Kantian elation. The determining but not exclusive answer lies in the vicissitudes of U.S.

foreign policy toward Haiti. It is clear that, whatever may have been its role in the coup of September 1991, the U.S. government had very little sympathy for Aristide. In fact, Aristide's prophetic messianism and left-leaning tendencies made him an enemy of Washington's Cold Warriors. In the presidential elections of December 1990, the Bush administration opposed his candidacy and supported Marc Bazin, a former World Bank executive and minister of finance under Jean-Claude Duvalier. The CIA and the Pentagon, along with the Haitian elite, never accepted Aristide's victory—Raoul Cédras, Philippe Biamby, and many other key figures in the coup of 1991 were, after all, on the CIA payroll. In the *de factos* era, the CIA was involved in the creation of the violent paramilitary organization Front for the Advancement and Progress of Haiti (FRAPH), which was supposed to constitute a political force counterbalancing the Aristide movement.

It is not surprising that the support the *de factos* received from Washington convinced them that the external forces advocating the reinstatement of Aristide were prevaricated and had neither the will nor the power to impose his return. The *Harlan County* episode further reinforced this conviction. The U.S. retreat was emblematic of an incoherent foreign policy that vacillated between two contradictory goals: an accommodation with the de factos at Aristide's expense, and a determined commitment to return Aristide to the presidency. While this commitment crystallized in the massive military occupation of Haiti in October 1994, it responded more to the vagaries of U.S. domestic politics than to international norms of the UN or the OAS.

It is true that the "Santiago declaration" approved by the OAS in June 1991 guaranteed that the organization would respond decisively to any undemocratic transfer of power in any member state. Haiti was thereby catapulted onto the international agenda, which led to Security Council Resolution 940, the unprecedented UN endorsement of military intervention to remove power holders and replace them with the regime that they had previously overthrown. It is also true that the end of the Cold War generated a short-lived liberal euphoria about an "emerging right to democratic governance,"[63] superceding entrenched notions of national sovereignty. In short, while the international climate conspired against Haitian coup makers and facilitated Aristide's restoration, it cannot fully explain U.S. behavior.

Instead, I would argue that if we are to understand the U.S. decision to invade, we must analyze it in the context of the emerging new international order. With the end of the Cold War and in the aftermath of the Somalian fiasco, the United States was bent on reasserting its credibility as the only remaining superpower. To do so it had to engineer a triumphant display of strength. Haiti, with its brutal, small, ill-trained, undisciplined, and unpopular army, provided an irresistible opportunity. At little cost the United States could exhibit a renewed determination to use force when necessary in order to defend and protect human rights and democracy.

Haiti was the ideal place to demonstrate that armed intervention and high moral principles could be mutually supportive. [. . .]

Clinton wanted, however, to have his cake and eat it too. He wanted a forceful display of military power and resolve without the risk of U.S. casualties and the appearance of imperialism. Therefore, while he secretly set the invasion for the night of September 18, President Clinton sent a delegation to Haiti on September 17, headed by Jimmy Carter, in a last-ditch effort to stave off armed conflict. [. . .] After long hours of tense negotiations with the coup leaders, the delegation reached the so-called Port-au-Prince Agreement, which averted the U.S. invasion while allowing U.S. forces to enter Haiti peacefully. It is clear that this agreement was a consequence of the use of force rather than the outcome of a diplomatic triumph. The Haitian military rulers acquiesced to step down from power only when they learned during the last moments of their negotiations with the Carter mission that the invasion was under way, as U.S. warplanes were actually in the air. The junta leaders would never have signed on to the agreement had they only faced the rather gentle and understanding Carter. The agreement made possible the peaceful entry of U.S. troops in to Haiti, but it symbolized appeasement rather than justice.

The agreement mentioned neither President Aristide nor his government and provided no date for the reinstallment of either; it legitimized the military-imposed regime of Émile Jonassaint and promised to the coup leaders who were no longer required to leave the country an "early and honorable retirement" by October 15, 1994. [. . .] Not surprisingly, the Port-au-Prince Agreement stipulated that the "economic embargo and the economic sanctions" would be "lifted without delay" and that Haiti's "military and police forces [would] work in close cooperation with the US Military Mission." Suddenly, the men described by President Clinton as thugs and murderers became honorable people whom the United States would treat as partners.

[. . .]

While the fall of the military dictatorship and Aristide's "second coming" did away with the most vicious aspects of political repression, authoritarian tendencies persisted. In fact, Lavalas gradually began to establish the structures of a predatory democracy. Rooted in the Haitian habitus, the old patterns of messianic rule and presidential absolutism resurfaced and heralded times of dangerous uncertainties.

NOTES

1 Claude Moïse and Émile Ollivier, *Repenser Haïti* (Montreal: CIDIHCA, 1992), p. 142; see also Jean-Bertrand Aristide, *Aristide: An Autobiography* (New York: Orbis, 1993), p. 118.
2 Aristide, *Autobiography*, pp. 116–117.
3 Benoît condemned his party's choice of Aristide as "political adventurism," a dangerous descent into the unknown. See Marx V. Aristide and Laurie

Richardson, "Haiti's Popular Resistance," in James Ridgeway, ed., *The Haiti Files: Decoding the Crisis* (Washington, D.C.: Essential Books, 1994), pp. 67–68.

4 Ibid., pp. 145–150. Lafontant was ultimately banned from participating in the elections. The constitution of 1987 had provided for the exclusion of major Duvalierist figures from the electoral process for ten years.

5 Ibid., p. 148.

6 Ti Légliz's representatives put it in these words (as cited in Moïse and Ollivier, *Repenser Haïti*, p. 152): "The great prophet of the Haitian Church is Father Aristide. . . . Today, Father Aristide is a symbol of the struggling Haitian people and nobody has the right to steal this gift of the Spirit from all the poor and all the youth who have mobilized around him." (Translated by Carrol Coates)

7 Aristide, *Autobiography*, p. 126.

8 Ibid., p. 104.

9 See Moïse and Ollivier, *Repenser Haïti*, pp. 137–192.

10 Aristide used the French acronym FMI to call the IMF "Fonds des Malfaiteurs Internationaux" (Funds of International Criminals) and "Front de Misère Internationale" (Front for International Misery).

11 Alex Dupuy, *Haiti in the New World Order* (Boulder: Westview Press, 1997), pp. 93–113.

12 Alex Dupuy, "A Neo-Liberal Model for Post-Duvalier Haiti," unpublished manuscript, 1995, p. 21. See also Leslie Delatour, *Propositions pour le Progrès* (Port-au-Prince: Fondation des Industries d'Haïti, 1990).

13 Aristide, *Autobiography*, p. 128.

14 Ibid.

15 See Moïse and Ollivier, *Repenser Haïti*, pp. 149–174.

16 Amy Wilentz, *The Rainy Season* (New York: Touchstone, 1989), pp. 131–132, 330–331. [. . .]

17 See Jean-Claude Jean and Marc Maesschalck, *Transition Politique en Haïti* (Paris: L'Harmattan, 1999).

18 Greg Chamberlain, "Haiti's 'Second Independence': Aristide's Seven Months in Office," in NACLA, ed., *Haiti: Dangerous Crossroads* (Boston: South End Press, 1995); Delince, *Les Forces Politiques en Haïti*, pp. 299–300; Etzer Charles, *Le Pouvoir Politique en Haïti de 1957 à Nos Jours* (Paris: Karthala, 1994), p. 403; Robert Malval, *L'Année de Toutes les Duperies* (Port-au-Prince: Éditions Regain, 1996), pp. 43, 53–56.

19 Greg Chamberlain, "Le Héros et le Pouvoir," in Gérard Barthélémy and Christian Girault, eds., *La République Haïtienne* (Paris: Karthala, 1993), p. 227.

20 Alex Dupuy, "The Prophet Armed: Jean-Bertrand Aristide's Liberation-Theology and Politics," unpublished manuscript, p. 25. See also Aristide, *Autobiography*, p. 126.

21 Charles argues in his *Pouvoir Politique en Haïti* (p. 403): "Since the moment of the government's formation, a malaise has appeared at the heart of the Lavalas movement because there is no minister who comes from the FNCD. [. . .] In that climate of tension, the alliance is virtually broken apart; a climate weakening the seat of power and in which there are not lacking those who, in the shadows, are thinking of a coup d'état." (Translated by Carrol Coates). See also Delince, *Les Forces Politiques en Haïti*, p. 299; Moïse and Ollivier, *Repenser Haïti*, pp. 168–170.

22 Anthony Maingot, "Haiti and Aristide: The Legacy of History," *Current History*, February 1992, pp. 65–69 [. . .].

23 Malval, *L'Année de Toutes les Duperies*, p. 51. Translated from the original French by Carrol Coates.

24 In an attempt to prevent Aristide from becoming president, Roger Lafontant, a notorious Duvalierist and Macoute, launched a coup on January 6, 1991, against

the provisional government of Pascal-Trouillot. The coup failed when thousands of Aristide's supporters overwhelmed the streets of Port-au-Prince and forced the army to abort the coup. The mass mobilization of Lavalas supporters was not the only important factor contributing to the failure of the coup; Malval explains well that had it not been for the diplomatic intervention of the United States and France, such mass mobilization might well have failed to squash Lafontant's putsch (Malval, *L'Année de Toutes les Duperies*, p. 47). Aristide eventually became president on February 7, 1991.

25 David Nicholls, *From Dessalines to Duvalier*, rev. ed. (New Brunswick, N.J.: Rutgers University Press, 1996), p. xxx.

26 Irwin P. Stotzky, *Silencing the Guns in Haiti* (Chicago: University of Chicago Press, 1997).

27 The expression "Père Lebrun" originated from a tire commercial in which the salesman, Père Lebrun, would put his head through the tires. It became the Creole expression for the ghastly practice of "necklacing." Victims of "Père Lebrun" are forced into tires that are set afire with gas. Aristide's speech was at once surprisingly conciliatory and wildly threatening. Aristide began his address by imploring the bourgeoisie to "cooperate by using [its] money . . . to create work opportunities . . . so more people can get jobs. If you do not do so [he added], I feel sorry for you. Really I do. It will not be my fault because this money you have is not really yours. You acquired it through criminal activity. You made it by plundering, by embezzling. [. . .] Today, seven months after 7 February, on a day ending in seven, I give one last chance." [February 7 has a symbolic quality in Haitian politics. It marks the date of Jean-Claude Duvalier's departure in 1986 and of Aristide's installation as president in 1991.] Aristide then proceeded to make a plea to legislators to "work together with the people," and he reminded civil servants that "diverting state money is stealing, and thieves do not deserve to stay in public administration." Soon after, however, Aristide, encouraged by the loud cheers of the Lavalasian crowd, called metaphorically for the unleashing of "Père Lebrun" against all Macoutes. To tens of thousands of supporters he declared, "You are watching all Macoute activities throughout the country. We are watching and praying. If we catch one, do not fail to give him what he deserves. What a nice tool! [. . .] It is elegant, attractive, splendorous, graceful, and dazzling. [. . .] It is provided by the Constitution, which bans Macoutes from the political scene." The quotations are taken from Mark Danner, "The Fall of the Prophet," *New York Review of Books*, December 2, 1993, p. 52.

28 See Moïse and Ollivier, *Repenser Haïti*, pp. 157–160.

29 See Joel Attinger and Michael Kramer's interview of Aristide, "It's Not If I Go Back, but When," *Time*, November 1, 1993, p. 28.

30 Aristide, *Autobiography*, pp. 132–133.

31 Interview in the documentary film *Haiti: Killing the Dream*, Crowing Rooster Productions, 1992.

32 Gérard Barthélémy, *Le Pays en Dehors* (Port-au-Prince: Éditions Henry Deschamps, 1989).

33 The slogan *"tout moun se moun"* was the title of the French edition of Aristide's autobiography. It became a plea for equality and equity among Haitians.

34 Personal interview with an individual who asked not to be identified.

35 Simon Fass, *Political Economy in Haiti* (New Brunswick, N.J.: Transaction, 1990), p. xxix. [. . .]

36 These impressions derive from personal observation, conversations, and interviews with members of Haiti's dominant class.

37 In his book *Eyes of the Heart* (Monroe, Maine: Common Courage Press, 2000), Aristide defends the fact that his house in Tabarre has a large swimming pool

by pointing out that poor children use it on weekends. While this may be a convoluted justification, it does nonetheless illustrate the distressing reality of Haiti's social apartheid. Aristide writes (p. 44):

> The kids swim with us, with their teachers, with a group of agronomists who work with them on Saturdays, and with American friends and volunteers working at *Lafanmi Selavi*. A mix of races and social classes in the same water. Sometimes these images have appeared on television. Shortly after we began this experience we started hearing reports from friends among the upper classes of rumors that I was preparing these '*vagabon*,' these street children, to invade their swimming pools. Were it not tragic it would be comic. Perhaps the real root of the fear is this: If a maid in a wealthy home sees children from *Cité Soleil* swimming in a swimming pool on television, she may begin to ask why her child cannot swim in the pool of her boss.
> So it is a system of social apartheid that we are questioning.

38 Ibid., pp. 49–50.
39 Malval, in his *L'Année de Toutes les Duperies*, writes that he was convinced that Aristide would not last more than six months as president. In his view, Aristide's politics and style were bound to lead to his overthrow (p. 47).
40 Aristide, *Autobiography*, pp. 155–158; Malval, *L'Année de Toutes les Duperies*, pp. 61–75.
41 Guillermo O'Donnell, *Counterpoints* (Notre Dame: University of Notre Dame Press, 1999), pp. 159–173.
42 Ibid., p. 164.
43 Kate Doyle, "Hollow Diplomacy in Haiti," *World Policy Journal* 11, no. 1 (spring 1994): 53–55.
44 Danner, "The Fall of the Prophet," p. 53. See Kim Ives, "The Unmaking of a President," *NACLA* 27, no. 4 (January–February 1994): 16–29.
45 Ian Martin, "Haiti: Mangled Multilateralism," *Foreign Policy*, no. 95 (summer 1994): 80–85.
46 Martin, "Haiti," p. 81.
47 Malval, *L'Année de Toutes les Duperies*, p. 475.
48 Ibid., pp. 72–73. The incident represented a humiliation of U.S. power since the warship pulled out of Haitian waters because of a dozen agitated and threatening thugs of the Front for the Advancement and Progress of Haiti (FRAPH).
49 Emmanuel Constant, the leader of the paramilitary group FRAPH and main organizer of the *Harlan County* episode, declared, "My people kept wanting to run away. But I took the gamble and urged them to stay. Then the Americans pulled out! We were astonished. That was the day FRAPH was actually born. Before, everyone said we were crazy, suicidal, that we would all be burned if Aristide returned. But now we know he is never going to return." The quotation is cited from Martin, "Haiti," pp. 72–73. Constant's sentiment reflected the convictions of the Haitian elite. A member of the old mulatto bourgeoisie told me, "The U.S. would never send the marines to restore that little communist nigger [Aristide]."
50 A most obvious example of CIA support for the military, and opposition to Aristide, is Brian Latell's 1992 memorandum "Impressions of Haiti" to the agency's former director, Robert Gates. Declaring that "the Haitian regime barely resembles Latin American dictatorships I have known," Latell, the CIA's senior analyst for Latin America, went on to contend that he "saw no evidence of oppressive rule" during his July 1992 visit to Port-au-Prince. In fact, Latell

described the coup leader and army chief, Raoul Cédras, as "a conscientious military leader who genuinely wishes to minimize his role in politics, professionalize the armed services, and develop a separate and competent civilian police force." On the other hand, Latell portrayed Aristide as an erratic and even demented individual bent on fomenting mob violence against his opponents. Latell's view of the situation closely resembled that of the Haitian military and privileged classes who favored "an elite-dominated leadership to stabilize Haiti and begin a process of economic development." As cited in Doyle, "Hollow Diplomacy in Haiti," p. 52; see also *New York Times*, November 1, 1993, pp. A1–A8.

The CIA was also involved in the creation of the violent paramilitary organization FRAPH. [. . .] For a comprehensive report on the linkage between the CIA and FRAPH, see Alan Nairn, "Our Man in FRAPH," *The Nation*, October 24, 1994, pp. 458–461; and Nairn, "He's Our S.O.B.," *The Nation*, October 31, 1994, pp. 481–482.

The ambiguities of U.S. foreign policy toward Haiti are well summarized in Jane Regan, "A.I.D.ing U.S. Interests in Haiti," *Covert Action*, no. 51 (winter 1994–1995): 7–58. See also Nicolas Jallot and Laurent Lesage, *Haïti: Dix Ans d'Histoire Secrète* (Paris: Éditions du Félin, 1995).

51 Doyle, "Hollow Diplomacy in Haiti," pp. 52–57; Martin, "Haiti," p. 86.
52 Martin, "Haiti," p. 86.
53 Robert Malval, in his *L'Année de Toutes les Duperies*, confirms and describes the story (pp. 42–43).
54 See C-Reuters@clarinet, July 31, 1994.
55 The military's intransigence reached its climax when in May 1994 they illegally installed a new president, the octogenarian Émile Jonassaint.
56 Doyle, "Hollow Diplomacy in Haiti."
57 In a letter to Boutros Boutros-Ghali, UN secretary-general, Aristide ultimately acquiesced to a U.S.-led military intervention by calling for "swift and determined action" to restore him to power. The letter supported UN Resolution 940, which authorized "the use of all necessary means" to topple the military junta. See AP@clarinet, July 29, 1994.
58 As Martin put it ("Haiti," pp. 88–89), "It may indeed have been possible in 1993, had key errors not been made, to dislodge the Haitian military from power without the use of force. [. . .] But the international failure has rendered the military's peaceful removal from power in 1994 extremely unlikely."
59 Taylor Branch, "Clinton Without Apologies," *Esquire*, September 1996, p. 110. "De factos" is the term used to describe the military regime and its political allies.
60 Ibid.
61 Laennec Hurbon, "The Hope for Democracy," *New York Review of Books*, November 3, 1994, p. 38.
62 Ibid.
63 Thomas Franck, "The Emerging Right to Democratic Governance," *American Journal of International Law* 86 (1992): 46–91. [. . .]

15

ETERNITY LASTED LESS THAN SIXTY SECONDS . . .

Évelyne Trouillot

On Tuesday, January 12, 2010, eternity lasted less than sixty seconds. Less than sixty seconds of eternity to erase hundreds of thousands of lives, demolish thousands of homes and buildings, leave thousands of children orphaned, obliterate the educational infrastructure of the capital and of many provincial cities, and forever alter the landscape of a city, a country, and our memory.

It took less than sixty seconds to place us face to face with our weaknesses, our ugliness, to force us to bring forth an unbelievable amount of courage, to bring out our acts of solidarity. Less than sixty seconds to force us to look at ourselves unmasked.

It brought a destruction of the kind we've only seen in those films of planetary catastrophe where mutilated bodies, buildings, and infrastructure fall on all sides like insignificant little marbles confronted with the anger of an all-powerful giant. A destruction whose magnitude still makes one shudder four months later and that produces a feeling of distress that is exacerbated by the inactivity of the authorities.

Could so many deaths have been avoided? I leave that question to the experts. Some of the contributing factors appear quite obvious: the failings of urbanism, the concentration of the population, the degradation of the environment, the failure to raise awareness in and train the public – there would be so much to say about all these factors that no doubt contributed to making this catastrophe all the more cruel. This earthquake is still so vivid in our memories that a large part of the Haitian population hesitates to name it and speaks of it as "the incident" or "*goudougoudou*" or "*bagay la*" as if to mentally distance themselves from it as much as possible or to emphasize its monstrous, unnamable nature; neither case helps establish objective and rational thought vis-à-vis this natural phenomenon whose threat, according to expert opinion, is still present.

But who am I to tell anyone how to survive emotionally the horrors they experienced during those seconds that didn't even last a whole minute? What can one say to the former colleague whose two hands were

312

amputated? What can one say to the young woman who pulled her brother and her cousin from the rubble and, some hours later, dug her father's and her seven-year-old cousin's graves in her garden? What to say to the father who saw his house collapse on his wife and child? To the nine-year-old boy who, with trembling lips, relates his mother's dying words to his father? Who am I to even begin to touch the depths of their pain?

At the beginning of February, I went by my childhood neighborhood. It was the neighborhood where I was born, where I learned to love the sun and trample the earth. Pouplard Avenue's name carries with it my mother's sturdy and reassuring presence and the long speeches of my father, preparing his case for the next day. It was the neighborhood I came back to as an adult, after years of living outside the country, to live in my parents' house while I was waiting to move into my own home with my family. It was the neighborhood that I had left, then, a second time but that still lived on in me. Its contours, from the church bell tower to the familiar walls of the public school, had marked my memory more than any other place. It was the neighborhood that I had been avoiding in order to escape the nostalgia I felt when faced with its irreversible descent into the chaos of urban poverty. But when I saw its streets covered with debris, I realized that the transformation would be all the more painful for me this time. When I saw the site of the public school atop that hill that I had climbed so many times, when I saw the empty space cleanly stripped of its debris, with no trace of that structure which had been a part of my surroundings, I felt a savage and heavy gaping hole open up inside me. Elsewhere faced with the grotesque and terrifying shapes of collapsed buildings, I had already noted the extent of the damage, but suddenly I was asking myself if it wasn't worse to see the spaces cleaned out of all that had existed before, as if an invisible hand had forever removed all physical proof of human existence.

For all that it took less than sixty seconds to erase thousands of lives, the earthquake did not have the power to change the way our society functions. Immediately following the catastrophe, the international press arrived. Having come from Europe, North America, Latin America, and the Caribbean, the journalists surveyed the streets, questioned the local notables, flaunted cameras and microphones in the makeshift camps, and produced articles and news reports. With the lack of nuance they often show in unknown territory, some representatives of the western press denounced the inequalities that characterize Haitian society. Those inequalities have been perpetuated for so long that the minority benefiting from economic and social advantages seems to think it has a right to them, to the detriment of the great majority, and gets indignant whenever anybody talks about them. The schematic and reductionist quality of certain foreign news reports does not change the fact that even though all Haitians were effectively victims of the earthquake, the consequences

313

were entirely different depending on one's original economic status. If in some way we have all lost either a loved one, a roof, our confidence in the future, a school, a business, a workplace, a limb, a girlfriend, it remains nonetheless true that the horrors that we all lived through accentuate the already flagrant social divides. The country itself remains the biggest victim of this catastrophe in that the majority of its citizens finds itself in an even more difficult situation than before. Moreover, the number of mortalities and the extent of the material damage for the whole society were worsened by those social inequalities. Recognizing that fact would be only a first step, a very small one, toward the acknowledgement of an unacceptable situation.

After weeks of silence followed by clumsy directives, the national ministry of education at last set the date for the return to school, which took place under uncertain conditions. In the meantime, during that confusing interval when panic-stricken parents and distraught school principals were waiting for clear and direct instructions, the schools had already timidly begun to function. "Children have to go to school, after all," said some. Which children? Which school? Is it mere chance that certain private and religious schools were the first to be cleared from the rubble? Is it mere chance that certain private schools with an upper-class clientele were the first to open their doors, even before the ministry's announcement? Is it mere chance if the ministry seems only to pay lip service to the fate of thousands of children who attend hundreds of modest schools which have, for the most part, collapsed, and which are unable to function? It seems to me that we have missed an important opportunity here – the opportunity to make a decision that would put all children on the same level and would permit children of all social and economic back-grounds to see themselves as little Haitian boys and girls belonging to the same country and being entitled to the same privileges. Instead of starting school in uncertain conditions that only reinforce inequalities, it would have been better to have had the courage to delay the return to school for as long as it took to [ensure] a genuine and fair return to school. A return that didn't smack of favoritism and that would have distanced itself as much as possible from the usual practices of exclusion.

The earthquake can remind us that in death we are all equals, but it cannot erase the social, economic, and cultural injustice that has fed the structure of Haitian society for two centuries. The ability of some social groups to ignore the needs of the majority is proving to be more glaring than ever.

The state's inefficiency in helping the victims, its persistence in re-inforcing the supremacy of a minority over the majority, its abject capitu-lation before an "international community" that, more than ever, is concerned with the prerogatives of multinationals whose interests are tightly linked to those of powerful countries – all these elements reinforce the population's feeling that it has been forgotten. More resourceful than ever, it is a population that clings to life and refuses to give up. And in the streets of Port-au-Prince alongside the ruins, the piles of concrete block and sand, the small businesses are setting up shop, the neighborhood quarrels are being taken up again, laughter mixes with insults, life picks up where it left off. And though that fact pays homage to the population's resilience, it also raises concerns insofar as it illustrates that the old social practices of abandonment and exclusion can fall back into place with no difficulty.

Here we are more than four months later and the evidence is piling up, clearly highlighting the fact that this reconstruction we hear so much about is not taking into account the interests of the majority. There are prodigious sums, colossal donation promises, development plans that fall apart then come together only to break down again. There are NGOs that are created with the dollars collected, but we all know that this sum will be greatly reduced before arriving here, in the country itself. We also know that the sums that will arrive here will follow obscure routes, and we ask ourselves what percentage of the country will benefit from this so-called "aid."

It's nearly four months later, and for some, life goes on as if nothing had happened. The earthquake, that noisy and disturbing interlude, has gone and left only echoes of its trembling, which the body, if not the spirit, has gotten used to. Little habits are taken up again: the poorly compensated maid who has no right to paid leave, the worker who must accept a laughable salary that he already owes to the neighborhood businesses before he has even been paid, the supermarkets that raise their prices when they get visitors from big-spending foreign powers. There are some changes to note nonetheless: in preparation for the construction that is going on, the stores selling construction materials and hardware are seeing their revenues go up. On the other hand, the supermarkets are disappointed that the employees of international institutions sometimes get their supplies from their own sources and bypass the national market. Indeed, many of the experts called to help the Haitian population by mapping out training programs or by drafting development strategies live in luxurious spaces such as cruise ships or beachfront hotels that are relatively or even completely cut off from Haitian society. Are they being housed in these places to spare them the spectacle of misery and disarray of the population about which they are supposed to be experts?

It is four months later, and the image of those fateful seconds weighs heavily in my memory. Each time I speak of those seconds, it awakens the same feeling of unspeakable pain because it isn't just my pain; it belongs to a whole people. Every word is laden with fissures and stumblings that recall all those destroyed lives. And when I look upon a ravaged neighborhood, upon streets that now exist only in photographs and in our memories, I imagine them filled with those individuals who departed in less than a minute, quite simply, sometimes with no sounds other than those

315

of disintegrated walls and twisted metal. Thousands of people perished with no sound other than that of the crying of their relatives, sometimes with no sound other than that of the dust one clears away so that life can take its course. When I look upon my destroyed country, I want to salute the memory of all those who for the most part lived muted lives in the hopes that their deaths will not pass silently into history. May their deaths contribute to a reflection on our society, to a reorganization of things, and to a new, fairer, more humane and transparent Haiti.

May 2010
Translated by Robyn Cope

PERMISSIONS ACKNOWLEDGMENTS

1. Michel-Rolph Trouillot, "An Unthinkable History: The Haitian Revolution as a Non-event," in Michel-Rolph Trouillot, *Silencing the Past: Power and the Production of History*. Copyright © 1995 by Michel-Rolph Trouillot. Reprinted by permission of Beacon Press, Boston.

2. Carolyn E. Fick, "Slave Resistance," (ch. 2), from *The Making of Haiti: The Saint Domingue Revolution from Below* (Knoxville: University of Tennessee Press, 1990).

3. David Geggus, "Saint-Domingue on the Eve of the Haitian Revolution," in David Patrick Geggus and Norman Fiering, *The World of the Haitian Revolution*. Copyright ©2009, Indiana University Press. Reprinted with permission of Indiana University Press.

4. John K. Thornton, " 'I am the Subject of the King of Congo': African Political Ideology and the Haitian Revolution," *Journal of World History* 4, no. 2 (Fall 1993): pp. 181–214 (excerpts).

5. Ashli White, "The Politics of 'French Negroes' in the United States," *Historical Reflections/Réflexions historiques* 29, no. 1 (2003): 103–121 (excerpts). Reproduced by permission of Berghahn Books Inc.

6. Ada Ferrer, "Talk About Haiti: The Archive and the Atlantic's Haitian Revolution," in *Tree of Liberty: Cultural Legacies of the Haitian Revolution in the Atlantic World*, ed. Doris L. Garraway, 21–37. ©2008 by the Rector and Visitors of the University of Virginia. Reprinted by permission of the University of Virginia Press.

7. Mimi Sheller, "Sword-Bearing Citizens: Militarism and Manhood in Nineteenth-Century Haiti," *Plantation Society in the Americas* 4, nos. 2 and 3 (Fall 1997): 233–278 (excerpts). Reprinted with the permission of the author.

8. David Nicholls, "Rural Protest and Peasant Revolt, 1804–1869," from *Haiti in Caribbean Context: Ethnicity, Economy and Revolt*, published 1985, [St. Martin's Press]. Reproduced with permission of Palgrave Macmillan.

9. Leslie M. Alexander, " 'The Black Republic': The Influence of the Haitian Revolution on Northern Black Political Consciousness, 1816–1862," in Maurice Jackson and Jacqueline Bacon, eds., *African Americans and the Haitian Revolution: Selected Essays and Historical Documents* (New York: Routledge, 2010), 57–79.

10. Brenda Gayle Plummer, *Haiti and the United States: The Psychological Moment* (Athens: University of Georgia Press, 1992), excerpt from ch. 6 ("Under the Gun"), pp. 101–120, notes 258–263. Reprinted with permission of the University of Georgia Press.

11. Matthew J. Smith, "VIVE 1804! The Haitian Revolution and the Revolutionary Generation of 1946," *Caribbean Quarterly* 50, no. 4 (2004): 25–41. Reprinted with permission from Caribbean Quarterly, University of the West Indies.

12. Patrick Bellegarde-Smith, "Dynastic Dictatorship: The Duvalier Years, 1957–1986," from *Haiti: The Breached Citadel*, 2nd ed. (Toronto: Canadian Scholars' Press, 2004), pp. 123, 125–6, 128–143, notes on 275. Reprinted by permission of Canadian Scholars' Press.

13. Paul Farmer, "The Water Refugees," from *AIDS and Accusation: Haiti and the Geography of Blame* (Berkeley: University of California Press, 1992, 2006), pp. 19–27, 266–7.

14. Robert Fatton, Jr., "The Rise, Fall, and Second Coming of Jean-Bertrand Aristide," from *Haiti's Predatory Republic: The Unending Transition to Democracy* by Robert Fatton, Jr. Copyright © 2002 by Lynne Rienner Publishers, Inc. Used with permission by Lynne Rienner Publishers, Inc.

15. Évelyne Trouillot, "Eternity Lasted Less Than Sixty Seconds . . ." in *Haiti Rising: Haitian History, Culture and the Earthquake of 2010* (Jamaica: University of the West Indies Press, 2010; Liverpool: Liverpool University Press, 2010), ed. Martin Munro, 55–59. Reprinted with permission of Liverpool University Press.

INDEX

References to notes consist of the page number followed by the letter 'n' followed by the number of the note, e.g. 54n47 refers to footnote no.47 on page 54. References to tables are shown in **bold**.